Physical Education Sourcebook

Betty F. Hennessy, PhD
Los Angeles County Office of Education

Editor

Human Kinetics

Library of Congress Cataloging-in-Publication Data

Physical education sourcebook / Betty Hennessy, editor.
        p.   cm.
     Includes bibliographical references and index.
     ISBN 0-87322-863-4
        1. Physical education and training--United States.   2. Physical
     education and training--United States--Curricula.   I. Hennessy,
     Betty.
     GV223.P476   1996
     796'.07'0973--dc20   95-38833
                                                                  CIP

ISBN: 0-87322-863-4

All quotes from Griffin, 1989 in chapter 4 are from "Assessment of Equitable Instructional Practices in the Gym," by P. Griffin, 1989, *CAHPER Journal, 55,* pp. 19-22. Copyright 1989 by The Canadian Association for Health, Physical Education and Recreation. Adapted by permission.

The numbered list of questions on pp. 46-47 is adapted from "Guidelines for Appropriate Curriculum Content and Assessment in Programs Serving Children Ages 3 Through 8," by the National Association for the Education of Young Children and the National Association of Early Childhood Specialists in State Departments of Education, 1991, *Young Children, 46,* pp. 32-33. Copyright 1991 by the National Association for the Education of Young Children. Adapted by permission.

The information on materials from Educational Activities and Kimbo Educational in chapter 8 is courtesy of the manufacturers.

Acquisitions Editor: Scott Wikgren, PhD; **Developmental Editor:** Patricia Sammann; **Assistant Editor:** Henry Woolsey; **Editorial Assistants:** Jennifer Hemphill, Coree Schutter; **Copyeditor:** Sue Tyson; **Proofreader:** Pam Johnson; **Indexer:** Barbara E. Cohen; **Typesetting and Layout:** Julie Overholt; **Text Designer:** Robert Reuther; **Cover Designer:** Jack Davis; **Printer:** Versa Press

Printed in the United States of America

10   9   8   7   6   5   4   3   2   1

Human Kinetics
P.O. Box 5076, Champaign, IL 61825-5076
1-800-747-4457

Canada: Human Kinetics, Box 24040, Windsor, ON   N8Y 4Y9
1-800-465-7301 (in Canada only)

Europe: Human Kinetics, P.O. Box IW14, Leeds   LS16 6TR, United Kingdom
(44) 1132 781708

Australia: Human Kinetics, 2 Ingrid Street, Clapham 5062, South Australia
(08) 371 3755

New Zealand: Human Kinetics, P.O. Box 105-231, Auckland 1
(09) 523 3462

Contents

Chapter 7   Recommended Curriculum Materials to Enhance Student Learning   111
Bonnie S. Mohnsen
Orange County Department of Education, Costa Mesa, California

Chapter 8   Children's Books for Physical Education   133
Pat Bledsoe
Downey Unified School District, Downey, California

Chapter 9   Curriculum Material Producers and Equipment Suppliers   173

List of Contributors

Editor

Betty F. Hennessy has worked as a physical education consultant in the Los Angeles County Office of Education since 1979. As a specialist in the Division of Curriculum, Instruction and Assessment Services, Betty serves 94 school districts and is responsible for helping them find physical education resources related to curriculum and instruction. From 1986 to 1988, she also served as a visiting physical education consultant to the California State Department of Education. Prior to her consulting work, Betty spent seven years as a physical education teacher.

In 1984 Betty received a PhD in physical education from the University of Southern California, where she specialized in curriculum and administration. She is the coauthor of the *Essentials of Physical Education* textbook series, and she was a member of the writing committee for the 1986 *California Handbook for Physical Education*, which established a curriculum framework for California schools.

Betty is past chair of the National Council on Physical Education for Children and the National Council for City and County Directors. She is a recipient of the Honor Fellow Award, presented by the American Alliance for Health, Physical Education, Recreation and Dance, and the Honor Award, presented by the California Association for Health, Physical Education, Recreation and Dance.

Contributors

Pat Bledsoe is an elementary physical education specialist and an adapted physical education specialist for the Downey Unified School District. A teacher in Southern California for 20 years, she has also taught students with emotional disabilities and students with retardation and served as a resource specialist. Ms. Bledsoe received training in the Whole Language program, The UCLA Writing Process, and the State of California Mathematics Framework, and she was a mentor teacher in physical education for 7 years. In the process, she developed a fondness for literature about physical education, and with this background she created several lessons in physical education that complement the literature. Using these lessons, a teacher can instruct in multiple areas of the curriculum at a given time. The list of books that she has compiled can assist the users in teaching across the curriculum.

Louis Bowers is a professor of physical education and director of the School of Physical Education, Wellness, and Sport Studies of the University of South Florida. He received a master's degree from the University of Maryland and a PhD from Louisiana State University. He has taught for 28 years at the University of South Florida and previously for 7 years at the University of Southern Louisiana. Over the past 26 years, Dr. Bowers has written grant proposals, both alone and with his colleague, Dr. Stephen Klesius, that have brought in $2.6 million. These grants have funded research projects on the design of Developmental Play Centers for preschool children with disabilities, production of the I'M SPECIAL Videotape Instructional Modules, and development and evaluation of the I'M SPECIAL Interactive Videodisc Learning System. In addition, Dr. Bowers and Dr. Klesius have received funding for programmatic, research, and special projects from the U.S. Office of Special Education, national and state foundations, and local service clubs. Dr. Bowers has conducted workshops for university, elementary, and secondary faculty and has made numerous presentations in graduate classes on the art and science of identifying and securing grant funding.

Diane H. Craft is a professor in the Department of Physical Education at the State University of New York College at Cortland, where she teaches undergraduate and graduate courses in adapted physical education. She directed a federally funded master's program preparing physical educators to be resource specialists in adapted physical education. Prior to teaching at the college level, Dr. Craft taught secondary physical education in Johnstown, New York, and elementary physical education in Ridgewood, New Jersey. Her leadership in national organizations includes serving on the board and as vice president of the National Consortium of Physical Education and Recreation for Individuals with Disabilities (NCPERID) and being past editor of its newsletter, the

Advocate. She also has served as chair of the Adapted Physical Activities Council within AAHPERD. Dr. Craft's writing focuses on the issue of inclusion. She edited the JOPERD feature, "Inclusion: Physical Education for All," and has made local and national presentations on the topic.

Catherine D. Ennis is an associate professor in the Department of Kinesiology at the University of Maryland. She is on the editorial boards of *Quest* and *Journal of Teaching in Physical Education*, and she is conducting research on how diverse teaching contexts influence the selection and development of physical education curriculum goals. As a consultant she works with several school districts in the Washington and Baltimore areas on curriculum, and she assisted the Association for Curriculum and Supervision with its curriculum design for "Active, Healthy Living." Coauthor of the book *The Curriculum Process in Physical Education* and coeditor of *Enhancing Student Learning in Physical Education*, Dr. Ennis studied how teachers' values and beliefs influence their curricular decision making. She also was the section editor for pedagogy for the *Research Quarterly for Exercise and Sport*. Dr. Ennis was the chair of the Curriculum and Instruction Academy in 1990 and a curriculum keynote speaker at the 1991 NASPE conference Critical Crossroads in Middle and Secondary Physical Education. In 1993 she received the Celebration of Teaching Award from the University of Maryland's Center for Teaching Excellence.

Larry D. Hensley is a professor of physical education in the School of Health, Physical Education, and Leisure Services at the University of Northern Iowa. Following a brief tour in the Navy, he received a master's degree from Indiana University and a doctorate in physical education from the University of Georgia. A strong interest in applied measurement and evaluation in physical education and exercise science led to Dr. Hensley's work on developing sport skill tests including, more recently, a research focus on assessment practices in public school physical education. He has published extensively and is a frequent presenter at professional conferences. He recently served as president of the National Association for Sport and Physical Education (NASPE) and as a member of the task force that developed the national content standards for physical education and its accompanying assessment guidelines. He is a fellow in the Research Consortium of the American Alliance for Health, Physical Education, Recreation and Dance (AAHPERD) and a former chair of the Measurement and Evaluation Council of AAHPERD.

Bonnie S. Mohnsen is the physical education and integrated technology coordinator for the Orange County Department of Education in California. She also presents nationally on topics ranging from quality instruction to the use of technology. Dr. Mohnsen received a B.A. and an M.A. from California State University, Northridge, and a doctorate from the University of Southern California. She has taught physical education at the elementary, middle school, high school, and college levels. She was an administrator for physical education for district and county offices, and a consultant for numerous sites and districts. Dr. Mohnsen has written extensively on various aspects of physical education, especially on the use of instructional technology in physical education. Most recently she wrote the text *Using Technology in Physical Education.*

Judith R. Rink is a professor of physical education and chairperson of the Department of Physical Education at the University of South Carolina at Columbia. She has taught physical education at all levels in New York, North Carolina, and Ohio, and for most of her professional career she has been an advocate for quality physical education programs in the schools. Among her many publications is the textbook *Teaching Physical Education for Learning*, which is used extensively in U.S. teacher preparation programs. Dr. Rink has conducted extensive research on effective teaching and has been the editor of the *Journal for Teaching in Physical Education*. She also was chairperson of the Curriculum and Instruction Academy of the National Association for Sport and Physical Education and of the NASPE Task Force to develop national standards and assessment materials for K-12 programs.

Robert Ritson is currently the educational program specialist for physical education and fitness at the Oregon Department of Education. He works directly with school districts on curriculum development, staff development, and, more recently, reform legislation and implementation efforts in Oregon public schools. His background includes teaching elementary school and high school in Waverly and Des Moines, Iowa. Dr. Ritson was an assistant professor and coach at the University of Oregon and an associate professor at Boise State University before moving to his present position. He also served as a member of the NASPE Outcomes committee. An accomplished author, he has written a textbook, numerous articles, various grants, and other projects. Dr. Ritson has been a state president for physical education, vice-president in the Northwest District AAHPERD, and the national president of the Society of State Directors of Health, Physical Education and Recreation.

Judith C. Young is the executive director of the National Association for Sport and Physical Education.

She earned her masters and doctorate degrees in physical education from the University of Maryland, and she has conducted research and written numerous articles and presentations. Dr. Young was an assistant professor at George Washington University and the University of Maryland from 1980-1989, and she taught and coached K-12 levels at public and private schools from 1975-1980. A regional and national consultant with schools and service organizations, Dr. Young has presented workshops across the U.S., as well as in El Salvador and Europe. As a parent and youth sport coach, Dr. Young has participated in many physical activities, including running, tennis, bicycling, and badminton.

Preface

"Help! I need practical resources in physical education. Where can I go for assistance?" This is the plaintive cry heard over and over from teachers, curriculum directors, professional development leaders, and educational supervisors who have increasing responsibilities for, but limited expertise in, physical education. Where can these individuals turn for guiding principles to develop curricula? Where can they find sample curriculum guides; lists of appropriate textbooks, supplemental materials, software, or equipment manufacturers; or recommended literature for interdisciplinary connections?

These important professionals are caught in a dilemma of increasing magnitude. On the one hand, the critical role of physical education in the total education of the individual is becoming more apparent. Brain-based learning theories focusing on multiple intelligences and multimodal learning support the kinesthetic aspects of engaging the total student in the learning process. The personal and social development goals of physical education help students develop the support skills to participate in a diverse society, promote caring, and reduce violence. Health-related research underscores the role of physical education in promoting healthy lifestyles for all students. Healthy students are better able to learn. For these reasons, physical education is an important component of a Comprehensive School Health System and physical education is emphasized as an important objective in America's Goals 2000 (both of which are discussed in this volume).

On the other hand, personnel resources for physical education programs have declined. Many schools, districts, counties, regions, and even some states are without designated coordinators who have physical education expertise. The roles and responsibilities of teachers and administrators have increased dramatically, allowing them less time to devote to any one subject area. Physical education teacher preparation programs have been reduced at many institutions of higher education, contributing to a teacher shortage in physical education that is looming throughout the nation and reducing the availability of personnel in higher education to assist with public school programs.

Even for those in the field with physical education expertise, it is a time-consuming and daunting task to maintain current annotated resource lists given the plethora of resource materials that are becoming available at an accelerated rate. Furthermore, limited financial support for education underscores the need for resources that are cost-effective and aligned with the best learning practices. For this reason, a simple listing of resources is inadequate; rather, a *guide* to resources is necessary.

This particular guide to physical education resources will meet the needs of the teacher, whether beginning or experienced, and whether responsible for instructing students in multiple subjects or in the single subject of physical education. This guide will be particularly valuable for physical education curriculum leaders and committees as they design curriculum, preparing the "road map" for program implementation via instructional materials and professional development.

In their supportive roles to enhance programs, the educational administrator, physical education coordinator, and professional development coordinator will likewise find this resource guide to be a useful tool. Professors responsible for preservice programs at institutions of higher education may wish to share this resource guide with students embarking on teaching assignments in the field. Parent and community volunteers may also glean information from this guide that will assist in making site-based decisions regarding resources.

As the "Information Age" progresses, management of resources becomes an increasingly important issue. This resource guide is a significant addition to the literature because it is the first publication to provide a broad scope of resources with practical application to the classroom. Part I of the resource guide provides an overview of physical education in relation to curriculum, instruction, and assessment. The chapters in this part provide the reader with means with which to compare resource materials and determine their alignment with current literature. Part II provides annotated and recommended references to resources that support the ideas in Part I. Here the reader will find the information needed to order specific materials.

To assure adequate scope and depth in each part, chapter authors were selected based on their expertise in a particular resource area. All chapter authors are renowned in physical education at the state or national level.

Judy Young leads the way in Part I with the chapter "Current Trends and Issues in Physical Education."

As Executive Director for the National Association for Sport and Physical Education, Judy Young has had a finger on the pulse of the nation in relation to this subject area. Her chapter addresses the integral role of physical education in the total school program, as well as its importance as a component of a comprehensive school health system. She places physical education in the national context for curriculum, instruction, and assessment, and highlights trends, such as the focus on high school career pathways or "school to work" articulation.

In chapter 2, Cathy Ennis draws on her extensive research to provide direction for "Designing Curriculum for Quality Physical Education Programs." She discusses the various philosophical orientations that impact personal design of physical education curricula and provides a practical guide for articulating these curricula.

"Assessment in the School Physical Education Program" is co-authored by Judy Rink and Larry Hensley. Through the National Association for Sport and Physical Education, these authors have provided national leadership in developing outcomes and standards in physical education. In this third chapter, they share their expertise in developing curriculum-imbedded assessment of student progress.

Addressing the needs of students in an increasingly diverse society provides a challenge for teachers in the classroom. In chapter 4, "A Focus on Inclusion in Physical Education," Diane Craft shares legal aspects and effective strategies to achieve inclusion. Diane Craft is a well-known writer and presenter on the topic of inclusion, and her expertise is evident in this chapter.

A key resource for implementing effective programs is obviously funding. Based on his expertise as a successful grant writer, Lou Bowers was selected to share resources and strategies for chapter 5, "Securing Funding for Physical Education."

Part II contains annotations and recommendations for specific resources. In chapter 6, Bob Ritson leads the way by reviewing "State-Level Curriculum Guides and Contacts." As a past chairperson for the Society of State Directors for Health, Physical Education, and Recreation and as a leader in national projects related to curriculum, instruction, and assessment, Bob Ritson is particularly well qualified to bring a national perspective to this chapter. Many of these guides can provide practical models as curriculum development is begun at the state or local level. Important contact information is provided in the chapter's appendix.

Once the curriculum is in place, teachers need instructional materials to implement the curriculum. Chapter 7, "Recommended Curriculum Materials to Enhance Student Learning" written by Bonnie Mohnsen, reflects the author's successful instructional leadership as a teacher and administrator. Her expertise in the area of technology and software provides a unique contribution to the review of software and other curriculum resources.

Chapter 8 is particularly relevant for teachers striving to work with the whole child through curriculum connections. "Children's Books for Physical Education" provides annotations and recommended use of trade books and music that support the goals, outcomes, and themes of physical education curricula. The author, Pat Bledsoe, is a mentor teacher and statewide leader who has excelled in her efforts to connect literature to student learning in physical education.

Finally, chapter 9, "Curriculum Material Producers and Equipment Suppliers," provides a thorough listing of producers and equipment companies to facilitate acquisition of catalogs and detailed order information.

In conclusion, this guide is intended to provide teachers and school leaders with a road map to resources that assist with the process of developing curriculum, instruction, and assessment, leading to quality physical education for all students.

Betty Hennessy

Part I

Physical Education Today

In this part, we discuss the essential issues of physical education curriculum development and implementation. Both new and experienced teachers need to be aware of the latest trends and discoveries in physical education in order to improve their teaching. We have attempted to summarize what is happening in the field in several areas: curriculum design, student assessment, inclusion of all students, and funding.

The first two chapters cover curriculum, beginning with Judy Young's chapter on today's major trends and issues. She explains the relationship of physical education to the rest of the school curriculum and to extracurricular activities, shows the impact of physical activity research on physical education, and describes how national initiatives and new resources and materials have affected teaching. In addition, she briefly reviews six current areas of interest in physical education: inclusion, career education, integrated curriculum, lifestyle education, cooperative learning, and community collaboration.

The second curriculum chapter, by Cathy Ennis, goes into more depth about curriculum design. She begins by describing what an effective curriculum should be in terms of its characteristics, outcomes, and developmental appropriateness for students. Following this, she outlines six approaches to curriculum development: subject matter, learning process, student-centered, social responsibility, balance orientation, and profiles. These approaches accord with various curriculum models of

sport education, personal fitness, movement education, interdisciplinary approaches, self- and social responsibility, and personal meaning.

A key part of physical education is assessment, an area in which techniques have changed rapidly. In the third chapter, Judy Rink and Larry Hensley start by clarifying the terms and purposes of assessment and presenting an integrated model of instruction and assessment. They continue by defining the requirements for good assessment, including validity, reliability, objectivity, and practicality. After suggesting how to evaluate a program's assessment procedures, they list a number of informal assessment techniques that can be used in physical education. They end the chapter with examples of how assessment can be integrated into both elementary and secondary school settings.

Due in large part to legislation, students of all abilities are now being included in physical education classes. In chapter 4, Diane Craft gives us the history of that legislation as it relates to gender, limited proficiency in English, challenging physical conditions, and inclusion as a civil right. She then offers strategies for inclusion to promote acceptance, modify curricula, and encourage collaboration, and ends with suggestions for how to make caregivers partners and advocates in teaching.

Finally, in the last chapter of Part I, Lou Bowers provides guidance on how to obtain funding for physical education projects. He examines the whys and hows of writing a grant proposal and identifying and selecting funding agencies. He then continues with a broad outline of how the proposal should be organized, finishing the chapter with some reasons why proposals are not funded. An appendix at the end of the chapter lists a number of funding organizations and directories to help locate such organizations.

By the end of Part I, you should have the background you need to understand and use Part II, which offers practical information and sources for creating physical education curricula.

1

Current Trends and Issues in Physical Education

Judith C. Young
National Association for Sport and Physical Education

Physical education looks much different than it did at the beginning of the 20th century. It has changed from being a separate subject area to one more integrated with the rest of the school curriculum. Research, national initiatives, and improved resources have all helped upgrade the content and importance of physical education. A number of important issues have also become prominent considerations in curriculum design: inclusion, career education, integrated curriculum, lifestyle education, cooperative learning, and community collaboration. This chapter will give an overview of physical education as it looks today.

Status of Physical Education as a Component of Education: A Historical Perspective

The view that a full education had both physical and mental components led to the establishment of physical education as a part of education. In the mid to late 19th century, the physical component of one's education was seen as critical to health maintenance and physical vitality. It was believed that physical education classes could contribute to the emotional, social, mental, and physical development of children so that they might become well-rounded adults and contributing citizens. This perspective has defined physical education's role in education in the United States for over 100 years.

Towards the beginning of this period, the focus was somewhat more co-curricular than it is today: Physical education was often segregated from other parts of the curriculum and regarded as a ''special'' subject. It was generally thought that what went on in physical education had little direct relationship to other academic disciplines, and that the activities were fun, a form of physical

release that helped children focus on the academic learning tasks. In the elementary schools, classroom teachers organized active games on the playground (in contrast to today's formal physical education classes), and in secondary schools, the physical education curriculum focused specifically on calisthenics, rhythmic exercise, sport skills, and participation in competitive games and sports.

Professionals who chose to study and teach in physical education often were active sport participants who studied the scientific foundations of physical education, but did not always incorporate them into the programs they offered. Even though those who taught physical education learned about the relationships between physics, mathematics, chemistry, biomechanics, anatomy, physiology, and physical activity, these relationships were not well understood or recognized by other educators or by the public in general.

A columnist recently shared that she didn't use the algebra she learned in school, but could have endless uses for hand-eye coordination and a little more lung capacity. This statement, made in reference to the individual's lack of appreciation for her physical education experience, points to a need currently being addressed by new trends in physical education. Physical education programs have recently refocused on health-related fitness and development of physical competency in contrast to sport skills and athleticism.

Today, it is acknowledged that quality physical education programs provide preventive health benefits for a lifetime and options for the use of leisure time, as well as preparation for the physical demands of daily life. The new physical education combines the development of motor skills that allow one to complete daily chores safely and efficiently and to participate in a

3

variety of physical activity-based situations with active involvement in fitness-enhancing activity.

The shift to a health-related fitness focus occurred after several national studies suggested that the fitness status of children and youth was declining and that all citizens were not physically active enough (National Children and Youth Fitness Study, 1985, 1987; CDC, 1995b; U.S. Department of Health and Human Services—Public Health Service, 1990). For example, risk factors for heart disease are appearing at early ages in our children. The increase in obesity in children (which is an indicator of obesity in adults), high blood pressure, and sedentary lifestyles are factors that have been linked to cardiovascular and other diseases later in life.

Research indicates disproportionately low rates of participation in appropriate physical activity among certain groups, especially girls and women, people with physical and developmental disabilities, residents of cities, and people of low socio-economic status. Because a larger portion of our children's time has shifted from active chores and play to watching television, playing computer games, and other sedentary activities, the need for a focus on physical activity in education is especially important. However, this emphasis on developing fitness can be combined with instruction in skills and knowledge related to human movement to create a more complete form of physical education.

Physical education is no longer regarded as fulfilling a supportive but separate role in the school curriculum. Instead, it is regarded as an integral part of the education of the whole child. In today's school curricula, the physical education program contributes in an integral way to the entire school program, incorporating and relating information from other subject areas to the physical activities and the understanding of motor skills. In contemporary physical education, physical education specialists must participate in all aspects of the school program and help to design curricular, co-curricular, and extracurricular programs for the entire school.

Because healthy lifestyles and physical competence are basic to success in all areas of life, physical education can contribute in meaningful ways to preparing children for full participation in the real world of work and positive citizenship. It has a unique role in the education of children, enhancing physical fitness, well-being, and the development of physical competence and confidence as they learn a variety of motor skills.

Physical education also contributes in unique ways to the shared curricular goals of self-direction, enhanced self-esteem, positive social development, and cooperative behavior. In addition to improving the mental, emotional, and physical status of children and youth, studies (Seefeldt, 1986) show that children who are physically active and fit have higher grade point averages than those who are less fit.

Although awareness and interest concerning health and fitness have increased across the U.S., this has not resulted in significant increases in mandates for physical education across the country. Frequently, this has been due to financial pressures on local government. Still, in spite of dwindling funds, most states have not cut back on physical education mandates, and several states have even increased their physical education requirements for schools.

By surveying state departments of education on a regular basis, the National Association for Sport and Physical Education (NASPE) has tracked the requirements (by legislative mandate) relating to physical education across the United States. The number of states mandating physical education has increased from 42 to 46 since 1987. In 33 states, this mandate is implemented by local districts (NASPE, 1993).

Four states require daily physical education for elementary students, but because many states do not require a certified instructor for physical education in elementary school, often a classroom teacher is required to teach physical education. Four states (Arizona, Michigan, Missouri, and Wyoming) have no state mandate or recommendation relating to physical education. All states require a certification to teach at the middle and secondary school level (NASPE, 1993).

NASPE recommends that all students receive quality daily physical education in grades K-12 with a certified instructor planning and implementing the program (NASPE, 1992b,c, 1994b). Directors for physical education in state departments of education indicate that lack of physical education specialists at the elementary level, limited time in the curricula, and low public support for physical education are problems limiting program effectiveness and positive outcomes in terms of regular physical activity and healthy lifestyles.

The Comprehensive School Health Program Initiative

During the 1980s, there was expansion of and increased momentum for the idea of comprehensive school health as a way to coordinate and focus health instruction and health services. This expansion included the addition of physical education as a component along with other school programs and services relating to the total health status of students. A comprehensive school health program includes an organized set of policies, procedures, and activities designed to protect and promote the health and well-being of students and staff in school settings. Such a program is generally conceived of as including the following eight areas (Allensworth & Kolbe, 1987):

- Health education
- Physical education
- Health services
- Nutrition services
- Counseling, psychological, and social services
- Safe and healthy school environment
- Health promotion for staff
- Parent and community involvement

Because it addresses knowledge and skills that support a physically active lifestyle, the physical education instructional program is integral to the comprehensive school health program. Growth in critical thinking ability, problem-solving skills, social development, and fitness and skill development, all of which lead to lifelong healthy decisions, are the process and the product of quality physical education programs. The comprehensive school health initiative clearly defines the role of physical education in contributing to the overall health program of the school.

Relation of Physical Education to Extracurricular Physical Activity Programs

Physical education programs have unique and clearly defined instructional outcomes. The outcomes are defined in a content framework achieved through effective teaching strategies and assessed in relation to appropriate standards. The physical education program provides a foundation for all physical activity programs and should be part of every student's educational program. The skills and knowledge gained in an effective instructional program prepare the student who wishes to participate in extracurricular physical activity. The co-curricular and extracurricular activities provide reinforcement and practice for what is learned in physical education or other developmental experiences.

For those students who seek involvement in higher performance and competitive levels, opportunities for participation in an interscholastic athletic program should be provided with an appropriate educational focus. Extracurricular physical activity offerings in schools should be designed to include programs targeted to all levels of ability and personal interest (i.e., recreational, club, and competitive). Extracurricular programs should complement but do not and cannot replace a quality instructional program.

Although extracurricular and co-curricular programs have some goals and objectives in common with curricular physical education, it is not appropriate to substitute other activities in which the primary goals are distinctly different (e.g., athletic programs, marching band, pep

squad, drill team, or ROTC). Other activities may coincidentally involve physical activity, but such activity is not typically accompanied by an appropriate educational context for students to learn about exercise and motor skills, improve performance, or meet the typical objectives of a comprehensive physical education program.

Impact of Research Relating to Physical Activity and Exercise

Since 1953, a concerted effort has been made by the allied health and physical activity-related professions to inform the public of the importance of exercise and physical fitness for children, youth, and adults. At the same time, the discipline of kinesiology (study of the art and science of human movement) has developed and expanded the knowledge base pertaining to physical education. There is now a large body of scientific evidence that provides understanding about the effects of exercise, the development of health-related levels of physical fitness, and motor skill acquisition. The information provided by accumulating research findings has influenced teachers to revise priorities, add new objectives, set standards, and plan new student and program assessments.

We know that fit, healthy children will usually develop their physical potential through a dynamic process of participation in a range of appropriate movement experiences. Long-term studies have dramatically shown that active, healthy children tend to do well academically, have adequate energy and attention, show emotional stability, and have few behavioral problems (Seefeldt, 1986).

Statements by nationally respected and influential individuals and groups—those whose knowledge is based on the extensive volume of new research—have also influenced the direction and emphasis of instructional and extracurricular programs. For example, the President's Council on Physical Fitness and Sports (PCPFS), the American Medical Association (AMA), the American College of Sports Medicine (ACSM), and the American Alliance for Health, Physical Education, Recreation and Dance (AAHPERD) have all encouraged and supported physical education programs that include physical fitness and regular physical activity as priorities.

Another effect of the growth of the parent disciplines (biology, psychology, history) that support physical education is the development of subdisciplines relating to kinesiology/physical education. These subdisciplines include applications of psychology, sociology, history, physiology, and physics (biomechanics) to human movement. The development of each of the subdisciplines has promoted increased specialization in the scholarly efforts relating to our field, and this has in turn caused changes in the once quite homogeneous professional and scholarly community.

The rise of the new subdisciplines has been accompanied by a separation of research and applied interests and the development of many new employment categories (e.g., fitness directors and leaders, exercise specialists, sport managers, athletic trainers, cardiac rehabilitation personnel, and sports medicine specialists). Teacher preparation programs may now be located in separate units on college and university campuses. Departments of Kinesiology or Exercise and Sport Science have focused on developing the research basis in kinesiology and on creating curricula for the new applications of kinesiology. Though the number of college and university graduates in programs related to physical education may not have changed significantly over the last 10 years, the career goals of students have shifted, and fewer students are pursuing physical education teaching careers.

Research output relating to physical activity and sport and outlets for its dissemination have increased greatly. Annual conferences are now devoted to each of the subdiscipline specialties, and numerous journals have been founded in the past 20 years, in order to disseminate information in each of these specialties. Much of this research information has led to increased knowledge and awareness of the role of physical activity in health maintenance. Recently for example, the American Heart Association (Statement on Exercise, 1992) and the Centers for Disease Control (1995a) developed public statements emphasizing the importance of mild to moderate levels of physical activity in reducing morbidity.

Today's Curriculum and Instruction in Physical Education

NASPE, the nation's largest professional association of physical education teachers, believes that quality, daily physical education should be available to all children and that quality physical education is developmentally suitable for all children.

Appropriate physical education programs for children provide important first steps toward their becoming physically educated people. NASPE developed a conceptual framework for educational outcomes, *Outcomes of Quality Physical Education Programs* (1992d), identifying what students should know and be able to do as a result of K-12 physical education programs. This document defines a physically educated person as one who

- HAS learned the skills necessary to perform a variety of physical activities,
- DOES participate regularly in physical activity,

- IS physically fit,
- KNOWS the implications of and the benefits from involvement in physical activities, and
- VALUES physical activity and its contributions to a healthful lifestyle. (p. 11)

This work was then the basis for the development of the first National Standards for Physical Education. Together, these documents can help local education agencies develop appropriate curricula to help students achieve the skills and knowledge identified in the standards in ways that meet local students' needs. The standards are described and delineated with benchmarks for grades K, 2, 4, 6, 8, 10, and 12. The standards are these (NASPE , 1995b):

1. Demonstrates competency in many movement forms and proficiency in a few movement forms.
2. Applies movement concepts and principles to the learning and development of motor skills.
3. Exhibits a physically active life style.
4. Achieves and maintains a health-enhancing level of physical fitness.
5. Demonstrates responsible personal and social behavior in physical activity settings.
6. Demonstrates understanding and respect for differences among people in physical activity settings.
7. Understands that physical activity provides opportunities for enjoyment, challenge, self-expression, and social interaction.

The standards project also identified assessment strategies related to the standards and benchmarks. This document represents the first consensus in the physical education profession (supported by the public) of what a student should know and be able to do to meet the definition of a physically educated person.

As described in *Developmentally Appropriate Physical Education Practices for Children* (NASPE, 1992), *Appropriate Practices for Middle School Physical Education* (NASPE, 1995a), and *Developmentally Appropriate Practice in Movement Programs for Young Children Ages 3-5* (NASPE, 1994), developmentally appropriate practices in physical education are those that recognize students' changing capacities for skill acquisition in health-related fitness and increased physical competence. Such practices accommodate a variety of individual characteristics such as developmental status, previous motor skill experiences, fitness and skill levels, body size, and age. Developmentally appropriate physical education utilizes effective instructional practices that maximize opportunities for learning and success for all children.

No single method is appropriate for all learners, all learning outcomes, or all learning situations. Therefore, teachers need to develop a repertoire of knowledge, skills, and strategies to use in their instruction, and they must have the ability to select the most effective techniques at any given time.

For example, the philosophy that guides middle school education has implications for physical education at that level. Team participation with teachers from other disciplines and extensive club and co-curricular opportunities for physical activity-based programs are key parts of the middle school physical education program. These require teachers to have sound interaction skills that promote collaboration with other teachers. Contemporary high school physical education programs may have a lifetime fitness/wellness focus (as opposed to a competitive sport focus): This would require teachers to have skills to plan and implement a program that facilitates the development of personal fitness/physical activity goals and encourages all students to maintain lifetime participation in physical activity.

Physical education professionals continue to study and debate such instructional issues as the role of the teacher as a model (of physical activity and fitness), the infusion of concepts from the scientific foundations of physical education, the need for and use of resource materials (texts, videos, software, etc.) for students, physical education homework, and the viability of other instructional and content options.

The development of various technologies has also provided new instructional options and challenges for physical educators. These technologies include computer programs for record keeping, goal setting, assessment, and reporting; new fitness equipment; activity (heart rate) monitors; special photographic and video equipment and their application; programmed instruction; laser disc and CD-ROM applications, and more. Continuing technological developments require teachers to constantly seek new information and to consider how technology can improve their own effectiveness as well as enrich the physical education programs they provide. School systems must recognize that quality physical education programs will require availability of technological resources.

National Initiatives and Physical Education

The *Health Objectives for the Nation*, published in 1980 by the U.S. Public Health Service with a target date of 1990, included school physical education as a necessary program for all children. In support of this goal, Congress passed a resolution in 1987 calling on all jurisdictions to provide quality, daily physical education for K-12 students. However, a survey of the states at that time indicated that only one state had legislation to support

such programs. The 1990 baseline data indicate that the 1980 objective was far from met, with only 36% of students (K-12) participating in physical education (National Children and Youth Fitness Study, 1985, 1987; CDC, 1995b).

In 1990, the Department of Health and Human Services presented *Healthy People 2000*, a set of new national health promotion and disease prevention objectives that also included goals relating to physical activity and fitness. These objectives call for increased levels of activity for all citizens, including daily physical education for all children in grades K-12. Clearly, the objectives of quality physical education programs can complement and assist in meeting other *Healthy People 2000* objectives for physical activity levels, such as increasing the proportion of citizens who engage in light, moderate, and vigorous physical activity regularly or reducing the amount of obesity among youth and adults.

Quality programs help students make good decisions for developing and maintaining healthy lifestyles. In particular, physical education programs provide the knowledge and skills needed to include activity as one component of a healthy lifestyle. And, although the survey mentioned previously indicated that only one state has a K-12 mandate for physical education, some states and local jurisdictions have increased their support of physical education as an important part of the total educational program. Tennessee, through advocacy of AHPERD professionals, reduced class size for physical education. California, Kentucky, and New York have included physical education in the core learnings designed for all schools in the state. State AHPERD organizations in California, Illinois, Alabama, and Texas retained legislative consultants to assist in influencing legislation to support physical education.

Two additional actions have supported the *Healthy People 2000* objectives concerning physical activity. In 1992, the American Heart Association announced that epidemiological research indicated that physical activity was a significant factor in reducing risk of cardiovascular disease. In 1993, the Centers for Disease Control, in conjunction with ACSM, announced that even modest amounts (in terms of intensity and duration) of physical activity provide significant reduction in risk of heart disease. These research-based statements provide important support for assertions about the value of quality education about health-related fitness and the development of physical competence; this, in turn, provides support for broad physical activity options.

During the Bush administration, the governors of all the states convened in Charlottesville, VA, to establish an educational reform agenda (America 2000) for the United States. Although several important agreements were established, physical education was, notably, not addressed. In April 1993, President Clinton introduced to Congress his "Educate America Act: Goals 2000." The bill called for funding to help states initiate education reform by establishing standards and revising curricula. Unfortunately, however, physical education was not a part of President Clinton's proposal.

In a broad grass roots effort, physical educators and health educators called for amendments to the Goals 2000 Bill. Physical education leaders wrote the amendments and initiated strong advocacy efforts to generate support for them. Finally, Congress amended the bill to include Objective IV under Goal 3, provision of physical education and health education for all students, and President Clinton signed the bill into law on April 1, 1994.

Similar amendments have been called for in other education legislation. These legislative efforts have established increased standing for physical education in the total educational reform movement. The critical action is up to states and school districts who will be considering legislation that can direct and support educational reform for local schools across the country. Physical educators must be catalysts to initiate community support for quality physical education programs as a critical part of the total education of children.

The educational reform stimulated efforts to establish national voluntary standards for what students should know and be able to do in all the subject areas. NASPE published national physical education standards in June, 1995, that positioned physical education at the center of the standards-setting activities. The document provides 7 standards defined generally and specifically for grades K, 2, 4, 6, 8, 10, and 12 (see p. 6). The standards are further delineated through exemplary benchmarks and recommendations for appropriate assessment strategies for each of the standards and grades.

These NASPE materials establish new directions for physical education that focus on a comprehensive education about physical activity including health-related fitness for all children and the development of knowledge and physical competence that will enable students to participate safely and enjoyably in a wide range of physical activities, both work and leisure related, once they reach adulthood. The physical education programs based on the national standards will support the shift in focus from competitive performance in traditional sports to providing opportunity for and understanding of the motor skills used in all forms of physical activity. All educators need to consider the physical dimension of education and the basic nature of a healthy lifestyle for present and future success in all academic and work situations.

Central to the success of the education reform agenda is the issue of the opportunity to learn. As the new standards are considered at state and local levels, there will be more questions about how schools can help children meet the standards. National guidelines for elementary, middle, and secondary physical education programs can provide important recommendations for local school districts to consider in providing appropriate, high-quality physical education programs to all students (NASPE, 1992b,c, 1994b).

The guidelines, published by NASPE, include information about curriculum development, teacher qualifications, health and safety, scheduling, time allotments, class size, facilities and equipment, and evaluation. These areas impact the learning environment and the achievement of desired student outcomes. These national guidelines are continuously developed by national physical education leaders with broad input from across the country and revised to reflect changes in educational priorities and new directions for student learning (NASPE, 1992b,c, 1994b).

Resources and Materials in Physical Education

Generally, sport-related equipment has been considered the primary material for physical education, and there is no doubt that adequate facilities and equipment are critical to providing comprehensive physical education programs. Students should have access to equipment at levels that maximize opportunities to engage in physical activity and practice motor skills. This means, for example, that each student needs to have appropriate implements (such as balls, rackets, etc.) just as they need books or materials for other subject areas.

In recent years, however, additional resource materials (print materials, software, heart monitors, videos, etc.) have been developed for instructional use by students as well as teachers. In the future, more materials will become available as the scientific basis of physical activity is systematically incorporated into physical education curricula and new resource materials are developed.

There are many more materials available to teachers now than there were even 10 years ago. Major publishers have developed new publications to assist teachers in providing quality instruction in a wide range of specific skills as well as in health-related physical fitness, performance assessment, and knowledge about sport and physical activity. Resources include books, workbooks, videos, computer programs, lesson plans, music, and programmed instruction. Again, new technology will continually expand the options available for physical education programs and teaching. A variety of these resources are listed in this book and are described and exhibited widely in professional journals and at professional conferences.

Professional organizations, governmental agencies, trade associations, and corporate entities are other sources of useful resources for physical education teachers. These groups provide printed materials, hold meetings and conferences, and offer workshops to provide teachers with student materials or programmatic information.

The best-known and largest national organization targeted specifically for physical educators is the National Association for Sport and Physical Education (NASPE), an association of the American Alliance for Health, Physical Education, Recreation and Dance (AAHPERD). There are also related local, state, and district associations targeted at health, physical education, recreation, and dance professionals. These local and state organizations are valuable sources for networking information about state curricula, guidelines, and issues of interest to physical educators. At the national level, NASPE/AAHPERD provides Continuing Education Units (CEUs), professional books and journals, position statements, program and curricular guidelines, workshops and conferences, and consulting services relating to sport and physical activity in schools and other settings.

The associations in addition to NASPE that make up the American Alliance for Health, Physical Education, Recreation and Dance are these:

- American Association for Active Lifestyles and Fitness (AAALF)
- Association for the Advancement of Health Education (AAHE)
- National Dance Association (NDA)
- American Association for Leisure and Recreation (AALR)
- National Association for Girls and Women in Sports (NAGWS)

Other key organizations relating to physical activity include the following:

- American College of Sports Medicine (ACSM)
- National Recreation and Parks Association (NRPA)
- International Dance Exercise Association (IDEA)
- Various discipline-related organizations (e.g., North American Society for Psychology of Sport and Physical Activity [NASPSPA])
- National Strength and Conditioning Association (NSCA)
- Association for Worksite Health Promotion (AWHP)
- National Governing Body for each sport (NGBs)
- American Heart Association (AHA)
- National Association of Governor's Councils on Physical Fitness and Sports (NAGCPFS)

- American Lung Association (ALA)

Government agencies that may provide resources for physical educators include the following:

- The President's Council on Physical Fitness and Sports
- Governor's councils on physical fitness and sports (various states have different names)
- The Centers for Disease Control
- Local public health services
- State departments of education
- Local parks and recreation departments

Trade associations such as the National Dairy Council, the Sugar Association, the Beef Council, and the Sporting Goods Manufacturers Association or corporate programs such as Hershey's *Youth Program*, Nestle's *Fun & Fitness*, and McDonald's *Healthy Kids* also provide resource materials for physical education.

Current Issues in Physical Education

Some of the issues that concern physical educators today are continuations of movements and ideas that started some time ago, such as the concept of equity by race, color, creed, and gender for all individuals in programs of physical education and sport. Other issues that have special implications for physical education are continually developing nationally in the education field. This section will briefly address several issues that potentially have an impact on physical educators. They include inclusion and grouping, career education, integration of curricula, developing independent learners, cooperative learning and peer coaching, and community collaboration.

Inclusion

Legislation specifically states that inclusion is guaranteed to both genders, all races, and people with disabilities. Today, the concept of inclusion has broadened to include at-risk youth, children of all abilities, cultures, and races, and children with special needs. Children with disabilities must be fully serviced by appropriate programs of instructional, co-curricular, and extracurricular opportunities. Physical educators must decide on ways to provide meaningful educational experiences to all children in the least restrictive environment.

Physical education affords special opportunities to help at-risk youth develop positive skills for working with others and participate in community youth programs. Physical activity programs can provide attractive and positive alternatives to violence, drug abuse, and teen pregnancy. (See chapter 4 for more on inclusion.)

Career Education

Until the 1970s, career opportunities relating to physical activity were almost exclusively in the field of physical education teaching and coaching. Several roles were and are often still combined in school positions. Physical education teacher-coaches often have additional responsibilities relating to health education and other co-curricular programs.

Since the 1970s, when specialty areas relating to physical activity evolved in college and university settings, *physical education* has come to refer to a subspecialty focused on K-12 instruction. Whereas prior to 1975 career information offered to students focused on the teacher-coach option, now physical educators and college/university faculty need to make their students aware of the full range of career opportunities available for those interested in physical activity, sport, or both.

Individuals may specialize in exercise physiology, motor development, biomechanics, sport history, sport psychology, sport sociology, or measurement and evaluation. The body of knowledge for each of these fields has become highly specialized. Professional applications of these foundation areas include sports medicine, athletic training, sport management/business, fitness management, robotics, exercise testing, cardiac rehabilitation, physical therapy, sports journalism and photography, work as an equipment specialist, facility design, and more.

Integrated Curriculum

Certainly, one of the trends in education generated by concern for the crowded curriculum and growing indication that many students do not find school relevant to their interests or needs has been the concept of interdisciplinary curricula. Core knowledges are explored through a variety of disciplines and interrelated with various content areas in the school program. This can help students see the relevance of various subject areas to each other and to practical living.

Such an interdisciplinary curriculum demands the use of a greater variety of learning experiences. Teachers are viewed as facilitators of learning, not simply as information providers. The learner becomes an active decision maker instead of a passive recipient in the learning process, and decisions are made jointly between the teacher and the student. The teaching of isolated units gives way to an interdisciplinary program with programmatic outcomes that can be authentically assessed. (Authentic assessment involves collecting information on student application of skill and knowledge through some practical task, such as designing a personal fitness program.) The physical education curriculum not only fulfills the exclusive role of enhancing physical fitness and well-being and teaching a wide variety of motor skills, but also contributes to the shared educational goals of self-direction, self-esteem, and cooperative behavior.

Lifestyle Education

Clearly, current trends in physical education focus on the teaching of skills that contribute to a lifetime of good decisions promoting a healthy lifestyle. Some of the curricula refer to wellness, personal fitness, or fitness for a lifetime. The focus on active lifestyles, positive decision making, and balance is central to the lifestyle educational focus. Contemporary physical education must help students to establish positive lifestyles through development of skills and knowledge to facilitate decision making.

Cooperative Learning in Physical Education

Cooperative games and activities are not exclusive to physical education: One can see variations of these activities in community groups such as church groups, recreation centers, outdoor education programs, and counseling centers. However, the use of physical activities to facilitate the development of social skills and cooperative behaviors among students is an important facet of physical education curricula and is highly developed in some programs. Physical education has long been known for addressing competition, but it also offers rich opportunities for teaching cooperative behaviors along with physical activity skills. What constitutes the proper relative balance between cooperation and competition continues to be debated.

In addition to the wealth of literature available, professional development programs provide guidance on cooperative learning techniques and the facilitation of cooperative group activities. The learning of self-responsibility within the school setting is a focus within physical education as well as education in general.

Community Collaboration

An important part of all physical educators' responsibilities is being active and positive spokespersons for physical education. The critical need for advocacy for quality programs requires that busy teachers consider how to provide information to parents, community agencies, and organizations about the value of physical education, and that they work actively in the community to support and guide positive programs. Important groups with which to network include community leaders; physicians; other educators; parent groups such as the PTA; Chambers of Commerce; and youth sport providers such as YMCAs and YWCAs.

Conclusion

The current trends and issues in physical education result from physical education's long history of playing an integral role in the total education of children. Some amount of physical education is required in most states across the country. However, although research findings support the value of quality physical education for total functioning of the individual, many students still do not have access to quality physical education.

Contemporary physical education programs focus on health-related physical fitness and motor skill acquisition to support a high quality, physically active lifestyle. This focus clearly complements a comprehensive school health perspective while expanding the students' knowledge of and abilities in all forms of physical activity. Recent research findings have supported the importance of physical activity to the maintenance of maximal health. Therefore, students need to establish the skills to sustain physically active lives in a variety of satisfying and safe ways.

Quality physical education is implemented through developmentally appropriate instruction provided by specially prepared teachers who design learning experiences that enable students to achieve appropriate outcomes. As in other areas of education, instructional strategies for physical education have developed over the past 20 years. Physical education teachers now provide coeducational instruction, maximize active participation, monitor fitness, and provide current information about exercise and motor skills.

The national agendas relating to health and education include objectives that support quality physical education instruction for all students. The profession has initiated the development of high but realistic standards for achievement in the physical domain that will support and complement achievement in all areas. All physical education professionals must assume responsibility for educating the public about the ''new'' physical education and its potential for addressing important educational goals.

References

Allensworth, D.D. & Kolbe, L.J. (1987). The comprehensive school health program: Exploring an ex-

panded concept. *Journal of School Health*, **57**(10), 409-412.

American Heart Association. (1992). Statement on exercise benefits and recommendations for physical activity programs for all Americans. *Circulation*, **86**(1), 340-344.

Centers for Disease Control (CDC). (1995a). *Guidelines for promotion of physical activity and reduction of sedentary lifestyles in school age youth*. Atlanta: Author.

CDC. (1995b). Youth risk behavior study. *Morbidity and Mortality Weekly Report*, **44**(SS-1), 4+.

National Association for Sport and Physical Education (NASPE). (1992). *Developmentally appropriate physical education practices for children*. Reston, VA: Council on Physical Education for Children.

NASPE. (1992b). *Guidelines for secondary school physical education*. Reston, VA: Middle and Secondary School Physical Education Council.

NASPE. (1992c). *Guidelines for middle school physical education*. Reston, VA: Middle and Secondary School Physical Education Council.

NASPE. (1992d). *Outcomes of quality physical education programs*. Reston, VA: NASPE Outcomes Committee.

NASPE. (1993). *Shape of the nation*. Reston, VA: NASPE Public Relations Committee.

NASPE. (1994). *Developmentally appropriate practice in movement programs for young children ages 3-5*. Reston, VA: Council on Physical Education for Children.

NASPE. (1994b) *Guidelines for elementary school physical education*. Reston, VA: Council on Physical Education for Children.

NASPE. (1995a). *Appropriate practices for middle school physical education*. Reston, VA: Middle and Secondary School Physical Education Council.

NASPE. (1995b). *Moving into the future: National standards for physical education, a guide to content and assessment*. St. Louis: Mosby.

National Children and Youth Fitness Study. (1985). *Journal of Physical Education, Recreation and Dance*, **56**(1), 44-91.

National Children and Youth Fitness Study II. (1987). *Journal of Physical Education, Recreation and Dance*, **58**(9), 50-97.

Seefeldt, V. (Ed.) (1986). *Physical activity and well being*. Reston, VA: AAHPERD.

United States Department of Health and Human Services. (1990). *National health promotion and disease prevention objectives: Healthy people 2000*. Washington, DC: Author.

2

Designing Curriculum for Quality Physical Education Programs

Catherine D. Ennis
University of Maryland

Physical education has the potential to make a significant contribution to the health, educational achievement, and well-being of students across the United States. Programs focus on teaching students how to participate in sport, dance, and fitness activities. They also provide a way to teach cognitive, personal, and social concepts such as problem-solving, self-efficacy, and cooperation.

Curriculum decisions focus on the question ''What content is most important for students to learn at this time in their lives?'' The answer to this question depends on a blend of teacher values, student characteristics, and the limitations and opportunities present in the school setting. Teaching physical education today presents opportunities and challenges that were not evident in the past. We now have excellent opportunities to link our physical education curriculum with other subject areas to emphasize the relationships that make knowledge meaningful and useful. This increases the relevance of educational information to students. It motivates them to want to engage in physical activity and to become a viable class and group member.

Perhaps the biggest change and the greatest challenge in physical education is responding to the needs and interests of very diverse students in our classes. Some students come to us ready and eager to listen, follow directions, and participate in activity. Others need help to make responsible decisions about their own health and physical activity and to learn to work positively with others in stressful situations.

This chapter describes the teacher's role as the primary decision maker in quality physical education programs, and explores the educational beliefs that teachers use to select goals and implement lessons. A variety of factors, such as students' prior knowledge and skills and their own beliefs about physical education, are factors in this decision-making process. Several curriculum models are described for consideration. Each model provides a curriculum plan that is feasible within school programs.

Overview of Curriculum in Physical Education

Curriculum is the planned sequence of formal instruction presented by teachers to enhance student learning. Curriculum decisions address questions such as ''What are the intended student outcomes?'' and ''Why is this content important for students to learn?'' Decisions based on answers to ''what'' and ''why'' questions help teachers focus on the overall plan for the curriculum.

Curriculum decisions about the content to be taught are often called decisions about the scope or range of content included in the program. For example, middle school physical educators often decide which activities to include in their program. They may choose to teach many different activities, but spend only a few weeks on each. A program such as this has a broad scope but very little depth. On the other hand, other teachers may want students to master the skills and strategies of a few activities at an intermediate level. This program has a narrower scope and would probably devote long units (30-50 lessons) to each activity.

Curriculum decisions about how to organize, or *sequence*, content are among the most critical for student achievement of skills, knowledge, and fitness goals. Because we know that students do not learn effectively when tasks and activities do not follow proven educational sequences, we sequence tasks and activities to take advantage of the students' prior knowledge about the activity. These sequences or progressions should closely follow children's cognitive and motor development.

For example, ninth-grade students who have not learned an effective overhand throwing motion will have difficulty serving in tennis or volleyball (Clark, 1994). In this case, the high school physical educator must go back and teach the overhand pattern despite the belief that students should have learned it in elementary or middle school physical education. Students must learn to perform an overhand throw effectively before they will be successful in sports requiring throwing movements.

Effective physical education curricula are sensitive to the students and the settings in which we teach. We must do more than make a list of activities and place them in a logical order. Curriculum development today is an interactive process, and information gathering is an important part of this process. In order to refine our programs to meet the changing needs of our students, we need to periodically examine our rationale for selecting program goals and teaching methods.

Grundy (1987) suggests that "curriculum is not simply a set of plans to be implemented, but rather is constituted through an active process in which planning, acting and evaluating are all reciprocally related and integrated into the process" (p. 115). We need to be willing to create or learn new tasks or ideas from others. We should think reflectively about an idea's potential for success in our programs, and then actually test the idea with students. Talking, reflecting, and acting occur in a circular or spiral progression. We can start with any of these three and move among them as needed to plan and implement a quality physical education program.

Curriculum Change

Many people, including professionals, school board members, administrators, lead teachers, students, and parents, influence the curriculum process at one time or another. Changes can originate at the central or district office level, at the site level, within the community, or in the class itself. Programs designed for physical education, such as fitness or movement education, are most effective when the goals and expectations match those of the administrators, teachers, students, and community members who will be involved in the program.

Administrators may attempt to improve programs by purchasing curriculum packages or adopting a curriculum developed outside the school district (e.g., fitness education). This change process, known as "top-down" change, relies on outside experts to design the curriculum (Cuban, 1992). Other top-down initiatives developed with teacher input recognize the opportunities and limitations in the physical education setting. These initiatives usually include funds for release time for teacher training and for the purchase of new materials and equipment (Sparkes, 1991a, 1991b). When teachers believe that the change will be an improvement, they are quite willing to test the idea with their students and make changes in their curriculum plan (Darling-Hammond, 1990).

Other types of curriculum changes are developed by the teacher in response to a particular problem or opportunity (Fullan, 1991). Often one or two teachers can develop and test a new task or lesson with their students. Unfortunately, these changes rarely influence decisions in other classrooms. There are simply too few opportunities for teachers to interact (Locke, 1992). These curriculum initiatives, known as "bottom-up" changes, have only a limited impact outside the particular classes.

The most effective form of curricular change combines top-down and bottom-up change (Fullan, Bennett, & Rolheiser-Bennett, 1990). Widespread change in physical education requires good ideas from teachers. In these instances, teachers work with administrators to create, reflect upon, and test ideas that are of value throughout the school district. Effective lessons and programs become the focus of district-wide inservice sessions to inform and train teachers. Ideas can be packaged and presented by teachers to teachers as effective solutions to common problems (Deal, 1990).

School districts often contract with their teachers to design a new curriculum. Teachers may be selected based on their interest in the innovation or because they have already been experimenting with new ideas. They usually begin by establishing student outcomes and by identifying ideas or tasks that assist students to learn and that students find particularly meaningful and interesting. Over a period of days or weeks, teachers, with the help of a curriculum facilitator, identify and organize the main topics and goals for the new program. Together, they create specific objectives, tasks, and lesson plans that make the document more useful to teachers.

There is no instant gratification in curriculum development: When expectations for a quality product are high, the process can take several months or years. Curriculum development requires group process skills and a willingness on everyone's part to discuss ideas openly and think reflectively about the rationale and consequences of each suggestion. Reasonable expectations must be set for each phase of the project. Usually the individuals involved are busy people and have limited time to focus on the process. By keeping the task manageable at each stage, curriculum designers can see the tangible products of their work in the changes that result gradually as the program is implemented.

Characteristics of Effective Curricula

Effective curricula match the content to students' needs and interests. Kirk (1995) points out that most physical education programs probably have not changed very much in the last 40 years. However, anyone who has taught or even visited a school recently is probably well aware of the tremendous changes that have occurred in the student population during the same period. Students represent many different ethnic groups each with their own customs and preferred forms of physical activity. For example, Hispanic boys often want to play soccer at the exclusion of others sports, while African American boys want to play basketball. Many girls from Middle Eastern countries may not feel that sport is an appropriate movement form for them. They may prefer to dance or participate in fitness or wellness activities. We must continue to increase our own knowledge by talking, reading, reflecting, and acting in an effort to design curriculum for all students in our classes.

Students vary in the way they think about the role of physical activity in their lives. Some, for instance, participate in many after-school sport activities and clubs. They experience movement as a meaningful part of their lives. In some households, family members may model active lifestyles and support and encourage students' interests in physical activity. In other households, leisure time may be spent in a sedentary fashion, such as watching television. Community recreational opportunities may be limited. Such factors may make it more difficult for students to learn to appreciate a healthy, active lifestyle.

Parents', administrators', and teachers' concerns for the well being of students often extend beyond a narrow focus on academic goals. Wentzel (1991) reports that all of the national educational reports in the last 100 years have included goals associated with social responsibility. Families, community members, and school personnel believe that the ability to work cooperatively with others is critical to the daily lives of youth and realize that the ability to solve problems through discussion and collaboration is a critical skill for future employment. Some argue that the development of caring and concern for others is as important as the development of academic skills (Ford, Wentzel, Wood, Stevens, & Siesfeld, 1989).

There are many opportunities in physical education for students to learn self- and social responsibility. For example, teachers can include students in management and content decisions such as those concerning where and with whom they will work and which tasks they will perform and in what order they will participate. There are also more formal curriculum models which have been designed to provide an effective structure for teaching self- and social responsibility. One of these, the "Self- and Social Responsibility Model," will be described later in this chapter.

Outcomes of a Quality Physical Education Program

Conceptual frameworks help teachers and students identify and organize the key content elements in a curriculum and focus on the relationships among them. Understanding the elements and their relationships helps teachers to sequence content effectively and encourages students to remember the content and use it advantageously in skill, sport, and fitness activities. Frameworks often become the basis for elaborate programs or curriculum models that help teachers organize and sequence content to enhance student learning.

In 1992, the National Association for Sport and Physical Education (NASPE) published guidelines, entitled *Outcomes of Quality Physical Education Programs*, to help physical education teachers answer the question "What should students in physical education know and be able to do?" The excerpt from this document shown in Figure 2.1 outlines 20 outcomes for quality programs within five categories. The physically educated person "HAS learned skills necessary to perform a variety of physical activities"; "IS physically fit"; "DOES participate regularly in physical activity"; "KNOWS the implications of and the benefits from involvement in physical activities"; and "VALUES physical activity and its contributions to a healthful lifestyle" (NASPE, 1992, p. 5).

This NASPE document provided the basis for another historic document that expands the conceptual framework for physical education. *Moving Into the Future: National Standards for Physical Education* was published in 1995 and uses the Outcomes Project as the basis for establishing seven national standards describing content for physical education (see list on p. 6).

Both the Outcomes Project and the National Standards include benchmarks (see Figure 2.2) to further define the physical education content and provide direction for assessment of student progress. The standards and benchmarks are further delineated for grades K, 2, 4, 6, 8, 10, and 12.

Developmentally Appropriate Physical Education

The Council on Physical Education for Children (COPEC) and the Middle and Secondary School Physical Education Council (MASSPEC), substructures within

A Physically Educated Person:

- **HAS learned skills necessary to perform a variety of physical activities**

  1. ...moves using concepts of body awareness, space awareness, effort, and relationships.
  2. ...demonstrates competence in a variety of manipulative, locomotor, and nonlocomotor skills.
  3. ...demonstrates competence in combinations of manipulative, locomotor, and nonlocomotor skills performed individually and with others.
  4. ...demonstrates competence in many different forms of physical activity.
  5. ...demonstrates proficiency in a few forms of physical activity.
  6. ...has learned how to learn new skills.

- **IS physically fit**

  7. ...assesses, achieves, and maintains physical fitness.
  8. ...designs safe, personal fitness programs in accordance with principles of training and conditioning.

- **DOES participate regularly in physical activity**

  9. ...participates in health enhancing physical activity at least three times a week.
  10. ...selects and regularly participates in lifetime physical activities.

- **KNOWS the implications of and the benefits from involvement in physical activities**

  11. ...identifies the benefits, costs, and obligations associated with regular participation in physical activity.
  12. ...recognizes the risk and safety factors associated with regular participation in physical activity.
  13. ...applies concepts and principles to the development of motor skills.
  14. ...understands that wellness involves more than being physically fit.
  15. ...knows the rules, strategies, and appropriate behaviors for selected physical activities.
  16. ...recognizes that participation in physical activity can lead to multicultural and international understanding.
  17. ...understands that physical activity provides the opportunity for enjoyment, self-expression, and communication.

- **VALUES physical activity and its contributions to a healthful lifestyle**

  18. ...appreciates the relationships with others that result from participation in physical activity.
  19. ...respects the role that regular physical activity plays in the pursuit of life-long health and well-being.
  20. ...cherishes the feelings that result from regular participation in physical activity.

Figure 2.1. Definition and outcomes of the physically educated person.
Note. From *The Physically Educated Person* (pp. 11-13), by the National Association for Sport and Physical Education, 1992, Reston, VA: American Alliance for Health, Physical Education, Recreation and Dance. Copyright 1992 by the American Alliance for Health, Physical Education, Recreation and Dance. Reprinted with permission.

NASPE, have recently developed statements further outlining effective curriculum and teaching practices necessary to support and achieve the NASPE standards. COPEC's (1992) statement, *Developmentally Appropriate Physical Education Practices for Children,* and MASSPEC's (1995) *Appropriate Practices for Middle School Physical Education* synthesize the research on effective programs in physical education. Both papers emphasize specific beliefs about physical education at their respective levels. First, there is the belief that "physical education and athletic programs have different purposes" (COPEC, p. 4). Whereas athletic programs tend to be designed for physically gifted children who want to focus on one particular sport, tasks and activities in physical education help all children develop the skills, knowledge, and attitudes necessary for healthy, active lifestyles. Physical education is for every

child, including both the physically gifted and the physically challenged.

The second premise, "Children are not miniature adults" (COPEC, 1992, p. 4), and "early adolescents have special needs" (MASSPEC, 1995, p. 2) indicates that children and youth have very special developmental needs consistent with patterns of physical growth and cognitive and emotional development. Simplifying adult games does not address these needs. Games designed and taught specifically for the developmental level of the learner enhance the learning of all students.

A third premise states "Children in school today will not be adults in today's world" (COPEC, 1992, p. 4; MASSPEC, 1995, p. 4). These children must learn to live in a changing world as they prepare for the future. Games, sports, and fitness activities may change rapidly over the next decade. Students need the opportunity to

Examples of Benchmarks—Sixth Grade

As a result of participating in a quality physical education program it is reasonable to expect that the student will be able to:

HAS	6	1. Throw a variety of objects demonstrating both accuracy and distance (e.g., Frisbees, deck tennis rings, footballs).
HAS	6	2. Continuously strike a ball to a wall, or to a partner, with a paddle using forehand and backhand strokes.
HAS	6	3. Consistently strike a ball, using a golf club or a hockey stick, so that it travels in an intended direction and height.
HAS	6	4. Design and perform gymnastics and dance sequences that combine traveling, rolling, balancing, and weight transfer into smooth, flowing sequences with intentional changes in direction, speed, and flow.
HAS	6	5. Hand dribble and foot dribble while preventing an opponent from stealing the ball.
HAS	6	6. Keep an object continuously in the air without catching it (e.g., ball, foot bag) while in a small group.
HAS	6	7. Consistently throw and catch a ball while guarded by opponents.
HAS	6	8. Design and play small group games that involve cooperating with others to keep an object away from opponents (basic offensive and defensive strategy) (e.g., by throwing, kicking, or dribbling a ball).
HAS	6	9. Design and refine a routine, combining various jump rope movements to music, so that it can be repeated without error.
HAS	6	10. Leap, roll, balance, transfer weight, bat, volley, hand and foot dribble, and strike a ball with a paddle, using mature motor patterns.
HAS	6	11. Demonstrate proficiency in front, back, and side swimming strokes.
HAS	6	12. Participate in vigorous activity for a sustained period of time while maintaining a target heart rate.
IS	6	13. Recover from vigorous physical activity in an appropriate length of time.
IS	6	14. Monitor heart rate before, during, and after activity.
IS	6	15. Correctly demonstrate activities designed to improve and maintain muscular strength and endurance, flexibility, and cardiorespiratory functioning.
DOES	6	16. Participate in games, sports, dance, and outdoor pursuits, both in and outside of school, based on individual interests and capabilities.
KNOWS	6	17. Recognize that idealized images of the human body and performance, as presented by the media, may not be appropriate to imitate.
KNOWS	6	18. Recognize that time and effort are prerequisites for skill improvement and fitness benefits.
KNOWS	6	19. Recognize the role of games, sports, and dance in getting to know and understand others of like and different cultures.
KNOWS	6	20. Identify opportunities in the school and community for regular participation in physical activity.
KNOWS	6	21. Identify principles of training and conditioning for physical activity.
KNOWS	6	22. Identify proper warm-up, conditioning, and cool-down techniques and the reasons for using them.
KNOWS	6	23. Identify benefits resulting from participation in different forms of physical activities.
KNOWS	6	24. Detect, analyze, and correct errors in personal movement patterns.
KNOWS	6	25. Describe ways to use the body and movement activities to communicate ideas and feelings.
VALUES	6	26. Accept and respect the decisions made by game officials, whether they are students, teachers, or officials outside of school.
VALUES	6	27. Seek out, participate with, and show respect for persons of like and different skill levels.
VALUES	6	28. Choose to exercise at home for personal enjoyment and benefit.

Figure 2.2. Examples of NASPE benchmarks for grade six.

Note. From *The Physically Educated Person* (pp. 11-13), by the National Association for Sport and Physical Education, 1992, Reston, VA: American Alliance for Health, Physical Education, Recreation and Dance. Copyright 1992 by the American Alliance for Health, Physical Education, Recreation and Dance. Reprinted with permission.

learn fundamental motor patterns so they can apply them to games and activities not yet invented! Children must learn how to learn movement skills so they can teach themselves and others to perform based on a solid foundation of skills and understandings.

The COPEC and MASSPEC documents list appropriate and inappropriate practices for various components of physical education programs. These range from fitness instruction to games and rhythmic activities. Principals and parents can use the document to develop a vision of quality in physical education and define areas in need of change, and school personnel can compare their programs and teaching practices to these standards. Figure 2.3 shows an example of a COPEC component. Figure 2.4 shows an example of a MASS-PEC component.

Values and Beliefs That Influence Physical Education Curriculum

Our values and beliefs influence the decisions we make in the gym. If we believe that students should be fit, we structure our program to emphasize the fitness components. On the other hand, if we believe students should use sport and activity to develop a positive self-concept, our programs might include a variety of activities that are challenging, but well within the range of student ability. The extent to which we teach skills and sport, and choose to link physical education to other subject areas, depends on our educational beliefs.

If we had an unlimited amount of time to teach physical education, we could teach all of the content that we believed to be important. Unfortunately, this is not true in most programs. Because of limited contact time with students, we have to make choices. We must decide "What content is most important for students to learn in our program?"

Much of the reflective thinking necessary to design effective programs occurs as teachers talk and work with colleagues and students. We reflect carefully about the match between content and student needs and interests. Some teachers believe that traditional sport, skill, and fitness content is most appropriate. Others use the content to help students achieve other goals such as self-esteem, teamwork, and leadership. It is easy to say we believe in all of these and want to do them all well. Unfortunately, we probably don't have time. Quality physical education depends on student achievement within the limitations of time, facilities, staff, and equipment.

When we examine curriculum guides or textbooks, it is relatively easy to ascertain which goals or beliefs are of most worth to the curriculum developers. It is more difficult, however, to untangle the complex beliefs that drive our own curriculum decision making in the gym. The following sections describe five different beliefs or value orientations that can be used to organize physical education curriculum. These are beliefs in the importance of (a) subject matter, (b) learning process, (c) a student-centered approach, (d) social responsibility, and (e) balance. Each value orientation described here can be used to design an effective, quality physical

Appropriate Practice	Inappropriate Practice
All children are involved in activities that allow them to remain continuously active.	Activity time is limited because children are waiting in lines for a turn in relay races, to be chosen for a team, or because of limited equipment or playing games such as Duck, Duck, Goose.
Classes are designed to meet a child's need for active participation in all learning experiences.	Children are organized into large groups where getting a turn is based on individual competitiveness or aggressive behavior.
	Children are eliminated with no chance to re-enter the activity, or they must sit for long periods of time. For example, activities such as musical chairs, dodgeball, and elimination tag provide limited opportunities for many children, especially the slower, less agile ones who actually need activity the most.

Figure 2.3. COPEC component: Active participation for every child.

Note. From *The Physically Educated Person* (pp. 11-13), by the National Association for Sport and Physical Education, 1992, Reston, VA: American Alliance for Health, Physical Education, Recreation and Dance. Copyright 1992 by the American Alliance for Health, Physical Education, Recreation and Dance. Reprinted with permission.

Appropriate Practice	Inappropriate Practice
Depending on the school and community resources available, a wide range of activities is provided from the following areas: team and individual activities, gymnastics, rhythms and dance, outdoor and challenge pursuits, aquatics, and cooperative activities.	All school, community, and natural resources are not fully utilized to provide a variety of curricula offerings.
The students receive sequential instruction in a variety of activities based on their needs and interests. The types of activities are team and individual activities, rhythms and dance, cooperative activities, aquatics, gymnastics, and outdoor and challenge pursuits. The need to provide variety is balanced with ample opportunities to achieve the skill, fitness, knowledge, and social/emotional goals of the program.	There is an overabundance of one type of activity, with little consideration given to the wide range of developmental needs and interests of the early adolescent. Or, so many different activities are offered that sufficient time is not provided for the development of competence.

Figure 2.4. MASSPEC component: Variety of activities.
Note. From *Appropriate Practices for Middle School Physical Education* (p. 9), by the Middle and Secondary School Physical Education Council, 1995, Reston, VA: American Alliance for Health, Physical Education, Recreation and Dance. Copyright 1995 by the American Alliance for Health, Physical Education, Recreation and Dance. Reprinted with permission

education program. Some teachers have clear priorities for one over the others. Most teachers, however, seem to support some blend of the five (Ennis, 1992). The diversity in teacher value orientations is one reason that physical education programs vary from school to school.

Subject Matter

Teachers who place a high priority on the *subject matter* value orientation believe their students should develop skills and knowledge from the physical education disciplinary knowledge base. Disciplinary knowledge includes knowledge and performance of movement skills, sport, and fitness as well as foundational knowledge from the subdisciplinary areas, such as biomechanics, exercise physiology, sociology, and psychology. Unfortunately, as previously mentioned, the limited time available in most physical education programs means that often teachers must limit their curricular goals to the development of one major aspect of the knowledge base.

For example, some subject matter teachers may believe that all students should learn the sport skills and strategies necessary to be skilled performers. If they exposed their students to many different sports with little opportunity to practice and compete, students would not master the skills. Instead, these teachers choose to limit the number of sports and increase the amount of time to learn and practice. Other teachers with a high priority for the subject matter orientation believe that students should be fit and learn to monitor and adjust their own fitness programs.

Despite different emphases, both skill and fitness content reflect a subject matter orientation: The content originates within the traditional sport, movement, and exercise knowledge that provides the foundation for physical education subject matter in the United States. Teachers with this orientation strive for high student involvement and mastery of appropriate skill and fitness tasks in every lesson.

Subject matter orientation teachers believe that students should achieve skills to a predetermined level of mastery. They believe that students should develop physical skills, cognitive understanding, and an appreciation for the activity. We know that individuals who become expert performers must understand the complex aspects of the sport or activity. They have to enjoy practicing to develop the high levels of skill necessary for mastery. Subject matter teachers believe that self-esteem, cooperation, problem-solving, and teamwork are a necessary part of the process of learning sport, movement, and exercise. However, they consider these concepts as means to achieving the end goal of skill and fitness.

Physical education supervisors often use criteria from the subject matter orientation to judge the effectiveness of quality programs. They evaluate teachers based on continuous student involvement at appropriate levels of difficulty. Supervisors expect teachers to present information clearly and to provide specific, corrective feedback to enhance student performance. They encourage teachers to provide opportunities for as many students as possible to participate throughout the lesson and expect teachers to evaluate students on their ability to meet clearly stated objectives.

Unfortunately, some teachers seem unable to overcome barriers in the school setting that limit program effectiveness. They argue that students get bored easily in long units needed to master skills. They may not have an adequate budget to buy equipment or adequate time allotted to physical education practice.

In our research, however, we have found that most teachers with a high priority for the physical education subject matter find a way to help students become skilled and fit (Ennis, Ross, & Chen, 1992). They have the same barriers in their programs that most of us have. Yet, they gradually teach themselves how to overcome these barriers and make content meaningful and interesting, finding ways to motivate even the most difficult students. They make, beg, and borrow equipment needed to teach skills and fitness. This takes a lot of time and energy. Nevertheless, these teachers find the time and are willing to expend the energy because they believe that skills and fitness are the knowledge of most worth to their students.

Learning Process

The skill, sport, and fitness subject matter of physical education is also important to teachers who place a high priority on the *learning process* orientation. Knowledge and skill performance outcomes, however, are not the primary goals of their program. Instead, they use the subject matter as a means to the goal of teaching students how to solve movement problems and think critically about performance.

These physical educators believe that students need to *learn how to learn* movement, sport, and exercise. They realize that sport and fitness opportunities change dramatically depending on the region of the country, season of the year, and age of the participant, and that it is therefore important for students to decide about activities that are right for them. If students are to learn to adjust to many different situations, they must have knowledge of a variety of skills and fitness activities. Students must also learn how to select or match the information available to the problem to be solved. Within a learning process curriculum, students use knowledge and performance skills to solve movement problems. For example, in sport units, teachers may challenge students to design a basketball play to score in the final 15 seconds of the game. In a subject-matter-oriented curriculum, the teacher would design and teach the play and the students would execute it; in the learning process orientation, students use the knowledge and skills they have learned in class to design and test their play.

Similarly, if the learning process orientation were applied to a fitness curriculum, fifth-grade students might solve problems associated with exercising within their target heart range. The lesson would then focus on activities selected by students to keep their hearts in the target range throughout the class. To offer another example, young children in a movement education curriculum stressing learning process would select different skills to make a sequence that includes flying, stepping, and rolling movements.

Although the knowledge base is important in the learning process orientation, the curricular focus is on the students' ability to apply the knowledge to tasks they find meaningful and useful. For instance, to solve sport problems involving throwing for distance, they must remember content taught in other units. They may need to synthesize information about angle of projection, sequential joint action, and line of force in order to perform an accurate and powerful throw.

Of course, many students can throw effectively without understanding what they are doing and why it works. Nevertheless, learning process teachers believe that students should understand effective performance *and* be able to perform effectively. Such teachers encourage students to analyze movement using biomechanical principles and test their knowledge in crucial situations. For instance, in soccer they may use knowledge about angle of incident and angle of rebound to score on a corner kick. The critical thinking skills of analysis, synthesis, inference, and prediction discussed in class become the basis for problem solution. Strategic reasoning and logic are central to the problem-solving process.

School districts can use learning process curricula in physical education to teach critical thinking skills (e.g., Howard County Public School System, MD, 1988). Students solve problems related to a range of movement, sport, and fitness activities. When supervisors use learning process criteria to evaluate effective teaching, they focus on the physical educator's ability to design interesting and relevant problems for students to solve. They expect teachers and students to spend more time discussing, explaining, and answering questions than they would in a subject matter curriculum. Academic learning time or time on task becomes time spent working on the problem. This can be time devoted to movement, group discussion, or individual reflection. Students solve the problem alone or work with partners or small groups to design a solution. Teachers may present a problem with only one correct answer or pose one that has many correct responses. In the second option, teachers encourage students to be creative, designing unique solutions to interesting situations.

Learning process teachers believe that *all* students can solve problems. They are as likely to use problem-solving formats with children who have limited movement backgrounds as with those who have had many experiences. It is taken as a given that both girls and boys can solve complex problems and are likely to work well together when working to find a solution.

Some teachers say they support these curricula, but point out that their students just cannot pay attention or solve the problems. Nevertheless, our research (Ennis, 1992) suggests that teachers with a high priority for learning process goals teach their students *how* to solve problems. They teach them to learn how to learn and to remember information by storing and retrieving it effectively. They also analyze their task progressions to make sure they include small steps that lead all students to acceptable answers. When students cannot solve the problem, teachers examine their own task sequences and their teaching styles before blaming the students for a poor performance. They argue that anyone can learn process skills. Learning process teachers spend large amounts of time planning and fine tuning their lessons, because they are convinced that process skills are the knowledge of most worth in physical education.

Student-Centered

Teachers who center the curriculum around the students' needs and interests believe that content decisions should be meaningful and relevant to students. These teachers favoring the *student-centered* value orientation help students develop strong self-concepts. They assist them in learning strategies for how to work alone and take pride in their personal accomplishments. Students select activities that they find interesting and useful and become more responsible for their own actions. This responsibility includes simple tasks such as remembering to bring their homework or in more difficult challenges such as showing self-control when angry. Students try a wide range of activities early in the program to discover those that they like or those in which they have ability. Students identify goals they think are important and work individually or in small groups with the teacher to develop a program that is meaningful and interesting to them.

Although the curriculum is sensitive to student preferences, teachers also consider student needs. At times, teachers may insist that students try new activities that will be useful later in life. Otherwise, some students would choose only to play basketball or to engage in other favorite activities. Student-centered teachers realize that students need skills in other activities. Students often become interested in new tasks when teachers help them connect the activity to their personal or job-related goals.

Effective teachers within a student-centered orientation focus on student growth. They develop a positive rapport with students and talk with them about important problems. The traditional knowledge base of sport and fitness becomes a means to encourage the development of self-concept and self-efficacy. Skillfulness and fitness are often essential ingredients for success and feelings of accomplishment. Therefore, student-oriented teachers often teach sport and fitness tasks to give students the skills and knowledge they need to be successful.

It takes physical and emotional energy to be a student-centered teacher. Student-centered teachers must be knowledgeable in a wide variety of skill, sport, and fitness activities to match their students' needs and interests. These teachers are often the first to teach new activities such as in-line skating, cycling, or skateboarding. They are usually available to chat with students before and after school and in the hall between classes. Curriculum that contributes to the growth and maturity of students is the content of most worth to these teachers.

Social Responsibility

Teachers who place a high priority on social responsibility focus on developing students' abilities to work well with others. They select tasks that provide opportunities for students to work together in cooperative and team activities. Teachers who design a *social responsibility* curriculum help students control themselves when they are angry or frustrated with themselves and with others. They encourage students to become involved in class activities and contribute to the success of their team (Ennis, 1994).

The ultimate goal of many social responsibility teachers is to encourage students to help and care for others. As students develop self-responsibility skills, they learn to help others carry equipment, practice skills, and become team members. Students become less self-centered and less preoccupied with their own welfare. They also become more self-directed in their selection of safe and healthy activities. Effective programs gradually help students learn skills needed for caring and social responsibility.

Hellison (1985) reminds us that individuals must have most of their own needs met before they can reach out to others. Some students do not have support and love at home and must take care of themselves and other family members. At times it is difficult for these students to help and care for other students when many of their own needs for love and attention are not being met.

Extensive interviews with physical educators with a high priority for social responsibility indicate that they do more than manage the class and maintain order (Ennis et al., 1992). They use skills, dance, and fitness content to teach students to cooperate, show respect for others, and become involved positively in group activity. Teachers are careful to mix teams not only by culture and gender, but by various skill levels. Teachers within this value orientation teach problem resolution skills and take class time to help groups or individual students solve arguments through discussion. They teach students to recognize the power of appropriate group processes to set rules, develop strategies, and settle disputes.

Valued skills of effective teachers who have a high priority for social responsibility include the ability to plan tasks and activities that encourage students to work together toward a common goal. Students motivate each other to participate and contribute to the group. Teachers provide recognition and extrinsic rewards for students and teams who show positive self-control, involvement, and self-direction. Rewards might include certificates for participation, appropriate behavior, or leadership. Students might be rewarded by being permitted to participate with friends or in favorite activities. Teachers use effective group dynamics skills to place students in squads or teams based on their level of social interaction skills. For example, they might spend class time at the beginning of the year to encourage students to learn about each other and develop trusting relationships within their group. Students would be encouraged to take ownership for their team's activities and affiliate with the goals and purposes of the class.

Critics complain that social responsibility curricula emphasize affective content such as cooperation and teamwork at the expense of skill, sport, and fitness goals. Social responsibility advocates reply that many students do not come to class able to focus on content: They must first learn to control themselves and work with others before they can participate positively in team play. In schools and classes where many students have not learned these skills, it is extremely difficult to teach sport or fitness using a traditional activity approach to physical education. Teachers with a priority for social responsibility spend time and effort finding ways to use movement and fitness as a means to teach students to behave more responsibly. They believe that helping students learn to become self-directed, caring, and effective group members provides them with the skills of most value in physical education.

Balance Orientation

Teachers with a *balance* orientation attempt to balance goals associated with the subject matter, the student, and the social setting. They believe that students should apply the knowledge about movement and physical activity to situations that are personally meaningful. They acknowledge that students use sport, dance, and fitness skills in social situations, and think that students should learn to use knowledge gained in class to work effectively in group and team situations.

Such teachers acknowledge that outside events influence classroom events: When students have an argument in the hall before class, for instance, this influences student interactions during class. These teachers also help students make connections among subject areas and between school and community. For example, content learned in language arts, mathematics, and science classes can positively influence student interest and understanding in physical education.

A student's self-concept and ability to work with others influences the student's ability to practice skills and learn to perform. Although skills and fitness are important, so too are the student's needs and interests within a group or social setting.

Teachers encourage students to look beyond their present interests and concerns to prepare for a positive future. They discuss how students can use physical education content after graduation to maintain a healthy, active lifestyle (Association for Supervision and Curriculum Development, 1993). Students create a vision or a future scenario of their ideal sport, fitness, or leisure activities (Jewett, Bain, & Ennis, 1995). Teachers structure the curriculum to help students learn skills needed to realize their future goals.

Effective balance orientation teachers acknowledge, plan for, and focus on the interactions between the subject matter, individual students, and the social or group settings in their classes. For instance, on days when students need more individual attention, the subject matter and the group focus must wait; on other days, when activities are running smoothly, teachers can focus primarily on the subject matter. Over the course of the unit or the year, teachers work to achieve a balance among these elements, building connections for students between their personal needs and those of the group. They help students use the knowledge learned in class to make better personal decisions and to work positively with other group members.

Effective teachers within a balanced curriculum attempt to give equal weight to the emphasis on the subject matter, the needs and interests of the learner, and the responsibility to the social group. Many interactions occur naturally such as when students use their knowledge of performance (subject matter) to help the team achieve success. This also helps individuals to feel good about themselves and pleased with their performance. Teachers also plan activities to promote positive student interactions. Students learn to value physical education subject matter when they comprehend the meaningful connections with their lives. For example, they often connect the concept of pacing in fitness to the ability to continue to perform on a team for extended periods of time, thus helping themselves or their teammates achieve success.

Balance-oriented teachers may prefer to write objectives that cross two or three domains (e.g., motor, cognitive, and affective). Instead of writing a knowledge objective for a skills test, for example, they might write the objective to emphasize using a skill appropriately to help the team score points. In this way they connect the skill to something meaningful to students. There is an immediate, concrete reward for learning. The test score might be the team's score. If everyone has participated and contributed, then the score itself has a valid connection to the goals of the curriculum.

Teachers with a high priority for balance assist students to use the physical education knowledge base to make positive personal decisions in social settings. They believe that this content is of most worth to students in physical education.

Value Orientation Profiles

As you read the preceding section, you probably found many of your professional goals and values embedded in more than one value orientation. Because this is true for most teachers, we describe teachers' combination of value orientations as their value *profile*. Profiles can be determined by using the Value Orientation Inventory. A profile, like the one shown in Figure 2.5, describes the influence that each orientation has on the teacher's overall perspective.

Ennis and Chen (1993) revised the Value Orientation Inventory (VOI) to help teachers and supervisors describe their own value profiles. The VOI permits teachers to rank their curriculum priorities. Designed with

the understanding that there is rarely enough time to teach using all value orientations effectively, the rank order format asks teachers to select the knowledge that is of most worth to them. Teachers who consistently rank items high that focus on mastery of skills and fitness have a high priority for the subject matter orientation. Those that consistently rank items low that reflect social responsibility have a low priority for this orientation. The major characteristics of each value orientation are summarized in Table 2.1.

The results of studies utilizing VOI scores indicate that physical education teachers' high priorities distribute almost equally across each orientation. In other words, there are as many teachers with a high priority for balance, a student-centered approach, and social responsibility as there are for subject matter and learning process. Supervisors and department heads should be alert to this when attempting to convince teachers to implement a curriculum with a strong focus in one particular orientation. It is likely that some teachers will support the innovation as very consistent with their value orientation profile while others will reject or ignore it as inconsistent with their value perspective. We must acknowledge and respect teacher diversity just as we do student diversity. There are many ways to create effective physical education programs. By acknowledging and supporting several alternative goals within the

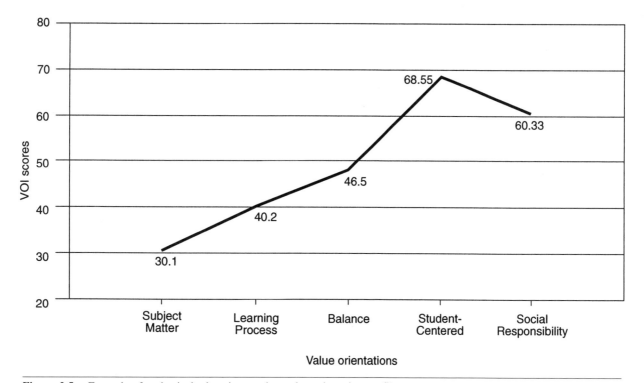

Figure 2.5. Example of a physical education teacher value orientation profile.
Note. From Ann E. Jewett, Linda Bain, and Catherine D. Ennis, *The Curriculum Process in Physical Education,* 2nd ed. Copyright © 1995 Wm. C. Brown Communications, Inc. Reprinted by permission of Times Mirror Higher Education Group, Inc., Dubuque, Iowa. All Rights Reserved.

Table 2.1 Assumptions of Value Orientations

Subject matter	Learning process	Student-centered	Social responsibility	Balance
Students learn physical skills and activities	Students learn how to learn	Students learn to be self-directed and take responsibility for their own actions	Students are encouraged to develop positive social interactions	Students apply knowledge to personal and socially meaningful situations
Students develop cognitive understandings	Students apply knowledge to solve movement, sport, and exericse problems		Students learn to work cooperatively in groups and teams	Students can explore new activities to identify those in which they would like to participate in the future
Students learn to value and appreciate physical activity	Students develop an understanding of content relationships	Students learn to work independently	Students learn to participate in activities to benefit the group	Students learn to balance their needs with those of their group or team
Students develop proficiency	Students connect content in different subject areas to that taught in physical education	Students develop a strong self-concept	Students develop respect for others	Students develop a balance between social expectations, personal needs, and the demands of the subject matter
		Students participate in tasks related to their needs and interests		

curriculum, diverse curricula can be provided to meet the varied needs of a diverse student population.

Curriculum Models

Curricula published or created for use within a school district often blend two or more value orientations to form a coherent focus. This section will provide a discussion of six curriculum models. Examples of each model are published and available for

- Sport education
- Personal fitness
- Movement education
- Interdisciplinary approaches
- Self- and social responsibility
- Personal meaning

As you think reflectively about the curriculum models described in this section, try to identify the educational perspectives that influence curriculum choices. You can then compare the author's emphasis with your own beliefs to determine the curriculum's value to you.

Each of the models represents a prototype or generic example of curriculum design and implementation. Administrators and teachers are encouraged to modify the model to particular teaching situations.

The discussion will begin with an overview of each model followed by a brief section describing the value orientations and how they influence the assumptions and conceptual framework. Remember that the conceptual framework reflects the content organization or the scope of the model. The discussion will then continue with a description of the origins of the model and the role of the teacher in each model. Each section will conclude with a scenario providing an example of how the model might look in practice.

Sport Education

Sport education programs structure secondary physical education classes to reflect many of the characteristics of an educational sport setting (Siedentop, 1994). The conceptual framework or scope of the model describes skills, strategies, rituals, and customs associated with each sport taught in the curriculum. This model is consistent with some aspects of the COPEC and MASSPEC guidelines for developmentally appropriate physical education practices because it gives *every* student (not just the most talented) an opportunity to compete on a sport team. It encourages the teacher to modify the game to accommodate diverse skill levels.

The sport education model uses a subject matter value orientation to focus the curriculum on learning the skills and knowledge to perform effectively in sporting events.

Designers of the model assume that individuals enjoy playing activities and want to be engaged in progressively more skillful play. Teachers design curriculum to teach the basic skills and strategies necessary to compete successfully and become better sport participants.

Sport education is different from traditional multiactivity physical education because the sport units reflect a sport season. Seasons are usually 8 to 12 weeks long and involve several subunits such as preseason, competitive play, and tournament play. The preseason begins with each student's placement on a team. The teacher or a sport board composed of student representatives or captains makes the team selections. Teams balanced by ability, gender, race, and neighborhood improve the chances that every team member will find success.

Preseason in a sport education unit focuses on the development of sport skills essential for success. This 2- to 4-week period provides opportunities for students to learn skills, get to know team members, and develop a team affiliation. Teams may earn preseason bonus points by hard work and skill accomplishments. As the preseason continues, there are fewer drills and more coached games to help students develop playing ability within their team.

The competitive season may consist of a round robin tournament that allows each team to be involved in team play. Schedules posted early in the preseason encourage teams to anticipate and prepare for particular opponents. Off-days, or days without a competitive event, permit teams to regroup, plan, and practice more complex strategies for future opponents. Team members rotate as players, score keepers, referees, and line judges to learn every phase of the game. As tournament time arrives, team members have bonded together as a competitive unit. Teachers assign teams to a league based on their round robin results. Winning teams can compete against the winners of other classes in after-school or weekend competitions.

Teachers can serve as coaches or officials to reinforce skillful and fair competition. Their primary job is to teach students to move skillfully. They help students to understand the sport's rules, strategies, rituals, and customs. They provide expert instruction, effective practice organization, and drill selection.

Teachers also make a special effort to help players affiliate with their team. They might provide tangible rewards for teams that have successfully included each player in team activities. They can change the game to provide an appropriate level of difficulty for their students. For example, they might change the size of the field or court, the number of players, the length of the game, or the rules for play. They match the game's structure to the students' physical, cognitive, and emotional abilities.

The sport education approach provides all students with the opportunity to participate in a positive team setting. It is especially enjoyable for low-skill students because they are given instruction and an opportunity to play as a legitimate member of a team. It is different from varsity sport because it follows a ''Sport for All'' model that is used extensively in physical education in Europe, Australia, and New Zealand. This model is based on modified games that allow all students to participate. It retains and teaches the most positive aspects of sport to each new generation of students.

Scenario

The physical education program at Fairland High School provides a scenario to demonstrate how the sport education model might be implemented. At this school, the teaching staff uses the model for all of their sport units. In the soccer unit, each of the four physical educators takes on specific responsibilities to organize and administer the practices. They team teach and combine their classes for the period to run the soccer unit.

Each physical education teacher is assigned a specific responsibility. For example, Jim Geoffrey is the Sport Council leader. He helps the student captains select players for their teams, explaining that each team should have a balance of skill level, gender, and neighborhood representation. Jill Apple is in charge of scheduling. She posts the round-robin schedule and assigns fields for each game. She records the scores at the end of each period and develops the league assignments and schedules for the final tournament. Bill Rogers lines the fields and makes sure the equipment and fields are safe. Jane Phillips plans the preseason practices and assigns each teacher to coach specific skills. During the preseason, students rotate to each teacher for expert training in specific soccer skills and strategies. At the conclusion of the preseason, each team has a game plan and an understanding of the rules and strategies for effective competition.

During the competitive season, each team plays two shortened games each day. Scores from each game are used to create leagues or handicaps for use in seeding the final tournament. Awards are given for the most improved individual on each team as well as the most improved team. Additional awards are given for the best team cheer, the best team name and mascot, and the team with the best display of fair play and etiquette. Players develop a strong team affiliation and are often sorry when the season is over.

Personal Fitness

Fitness curricula evolved over the years from a militaristic form of calisthenics to a personalized approach to healthy, active living. *Personal fitness* curricula are most successful when they blend an emphasis on the fitness knowledge base with an emphasis on the individual's concerns for an enjoyable, interesting program. The personal fitness model reflects both the subject matter and the student-centered value orientations. Students integrate knowledge about fitness within their personal lifestyle.

Corbin and Lindsey (1991) suggest that students must first acknowledge the need for fitness. They must answer the question ''Why should I exercise?'' The answer to this question combines many factors about their lives and their interests. The threat of illness or death is not meaningful to most students. Initially, they may be motivated by other reasons to exercise, such as weight management and physical prowess.

After acknowledging the need for fitness, students are encouraged to try a number of different activities to find those most interesting to them. They should develop skills necessary to participate successfully in activities with aerobic value. Students learn to test themselves and to set realistic personal goals. They interpret the scores and use the test results to develop a fitness program that is right for them within realistic frequency, intensity, duration, and activity guidelines. Of course, creating a program is easy compared with exercising regularly to meet the goals. Students begin to develop the self-discipline necessary to follow their program over the semester or year.

The teacher's primary role is to provide knowledge about fitness and help students relate this information to their lives. Effective teachers create a pleasant atmosphere where students feel comfortable asking questions about fitness. Students are encouraged to try a variety of fitness activities and learn to analyze their own fitness needs. Although teachers accept a variety of student goals, they continue to advise students on programs that are too intense for long-term maintenance and on those that are not adequate to develop aerobic capacity.

Fitness programs can be developed for elementary school students as well as secondary students. Elementary programs often focus on cognitive understanding of the components of fitness and of the immediate effects of exercise on the heart and body. Implementation can be aided by the use of creative task structures: For example, elementary school students may flow through a circulatory system obstacle course in the same way that oxygen and blood flow through the lungs, heart, and circulatory system. They begin to learn the names of muscles and joints that are important in developing muscular strength, endurance, and flexibility, and learn to find their pulse and calculate their resting and target heart rates. Students also begin to learn how to monitor their response to exercise and to select activities to keep their heart rate in the target zone.

The Florida Department of Education has taken a leadership role in designing a personal fitness curriculum for students in grades 9 through 12. As stated in *Florida's High School Education Program*, "The intent is to provide all high school students with a basic fitness concepts course that will contribute to the compelling state and national interest of having a physically-fit citizenry" (Florida Department of Education, 1992, p. 3). Students can develop an individual optimal level of physical fitness. They learn physical fitness concepts and understand the significance of exercise on fitness and health.

The scope of the course includes knowledge and assessment of physical fitness components, goal setting, stress management, nutrition, and consumer issues related to physical fitness. Figure 2.6 lists the specific subcomponents of Standard 9.

The Florida program provides a detailed outline of the scope and sequence requirements for a comprehensive high school personal fitness program. Many school districts and teachers throughout the country have adopted this kind of curriculum and are making it the core of their high school physical education program.

After successfully completing this course, the student will:

Standard 9: Select from a variety of activities which will improve health-related physical fitness.

The student will:

    9.01 identify a variety of static and dynamic stretching exercises which promote flexibility.

    9.02 identify a variety of aerobic activities wihch promote cardiovascular fitness.

    9.03 identify a variety of activities which promote muscular strength and muscular endurance.

    9.04 identify a variety of activities which promote ideal body weight.

    9.05 identify a variety of activities which promote stress diversion.

Figure 2.6. Florida Department of Education personal fitness curriculum: Subcomponents of Standard 9.

Note. From *Florida's High School Physical Education Program* by the Florida Department of Education, 1992, Tallahassee, FL: Florida Department of Education.

Scenario

The following scenario provides an example to demonstrate how the model might be implemented: Carol Carneal teaches ninth-graders at Thurgood Marshall High School using the personal fitness model. They begin by examining the skills and fitness levels necessary to engage in vigorous physical activity. They watch films of Olympic and professional athletes and learn skills to increase their performance efficiency. As the unit progresses, Carol begins discussing the health benefits that regular participants gain from exercise. They also discuss the chance of injury from intense levels of participation, and examine the effects of exercise on the body using a variety of problem-solving tasks.

Tenth-graders review principles of target heart rate learned in ninth grade and explore the concept of pacing. They participate in a variety of sport and repetitive activities attempting to maintain a predetermined pace. They examine in detail the five fitness components: muscular strength, muscular endurance, body composition, cardiovascular efficiency, and flexibility. They think reflectively about appropriate pacing in weight lifting and when stretching out before and after activity.

Eleventh- and twelfth-graders use the knowledge they have gained to develop an effective personal fitness program. They review the principles of fitness and test themselves to determine their current fitness levels. They then determine time and distance requirements for running and walking based on simple formulas that Carol posts in the gym.

These students also design tasks to enhance flexibility before and after their weight training workout. Throughout each unit, they test themselves and analyze progress toward their personal goals. They discuss their programs with Carol who gives them information to assist them in program revisions. Students graduate with a clear understanding of the fitness knowledge base and its application to a healthy, active lifestyle.

Movement Education

Movement education models focus on the development of fundamental movement patterns and skills that form the basis of all sport and fitness activities. A movement framework developed by Rudolph Laban provides the conceptual framework for most movement education programs. This framework identifies the primary aspects of movement as they relate to the concepts of "body," "space," "effort," and "relationships." Content is taught within the framework of educational games, dance, and gymnastics. The movement framework as adapted by Logsdon and her colleagues (Logsdon et al., 1984) is presented in Figure 2.7. The definitions of each aspect and element help teachers write and teach movement objectives.

The subject matter value orientation has strongly influenced the development of movement education curricula. However, some authors blend this perspective with a focus on the learning process and the student (e.g., Logsdon et al., 1984). The focus on solving problems and exploring various dimensions of movement reflects the learning process orientation. Students may explore different ways to perform a movement or to combine different movements in sequences. Student-centered orientations encourage teachers to focus on the student's developmental level and to plan tasks consistent with each student's abilities. Effective teachers emphasize a steady progression toward movement that is efficient and effective. Students learn to gain control of their bodies and to coordinate movement to perform complex tasks.

The teacher's role in this model is to teach the body of knowledge about fundamental movement. Teachers create tasks to encourage students to apply this knowledge to other subject areas and to their lives. Effective teachers make cross-curricular connections with many other subject areas. For instance, students can use their bodies to test mechanical and physiological concepts taught in science and to write about moving in language arts. Teachers plan appropriate tasks that challenge each student to progress toward the next level of development. These tasks may involve developmental sequences in which there is more than one level of difficulty embedded in the activity. Students learn to assess their own skill level and select the next level of difficulty in which to practice.

Scenario

John Abel teaches a movement education curriculum at Parkdale Elementary School. He is teaching his fifth-grade students to enhance their jumping performance. Students begin by exploring various kinds of jumps using vertical and horizontal flight patterns. John encourages them to focus on joint actions needed and on how adding or involving more joints in the jump can increase its power (height or distance). He then encourages students to adapt their jumping pattern to situations in which they must jump from a medium height box to the floor or jump from the floor up onto a medium height box. After each task, students discuss with their partner how they refined their takeoff pattern to create power and how they absorbed force when they landed. Students also

design short routines to demonstrate their ability to perform a variety of jumps and landings.

Interdisciplinary Approaches

Interdisciplinary approaches to physical education use the large and complex body of knowledge that serves as the basis for physical education, drawing from many disciplines to study the way the body moves in dance, sport, and exercise. For example, effective performance requires an understanding of physics to optimize the mechanical functions of the body. Biology and physiology contribute information for a focus on fitness and exercise. Team activities depend on a knowledge of group dynamics from psychology and sociology. Students can communicate feelings about moving and competition through writing, painting, speaking, dancing, or singing.

They find that it is easy to find natural connections between physical education and other subject areas. Connections between physical education and the life sciences occur as their bodies become laboratories for movement experiments. They see first hand how intense activities increase their heart rates and cause their bodies to respond with increased respiration and perspiration. Students can use their arms, legs, hockey sticks, and baseball bats as levers to project objects much farther than with hands or feet alone. Lacrosse sticks provide an excellent example of centrifugal force, while Bernoulli's Principle of fluid dynamics explains the efficiency of movements when swimming and sailing. Many students and teachers relate experiences with team competition as they discuss the effects of stress on the ability to interact positively with others. The skills needed to act responsibly in language arts and mathematics are similar to those needed to work independently on a personal fitness plan.

Curriculum models such as those developed by Lawson and Placek (1981) and *Basic Stuff: Series II* (Carr, 1987) make interdisciplinary connections an important curricular focus. Lawson and Placek's approach uses a problem-solving format to encourage students to use knowledge or information acquired in one subject area to solve problems in a different subject area. This can mean using physical education knowledge in science, or using science content in physical education. The artificial boundaries between subject areas become fuzzy and begin to disappear. Advocates of these models insist that new information, to be meaningful, must be connected with knowledge that has already been learned. Physical educators reinforce learning that has occurred in other subjects, and they use that knowledge as the base for more complex understanding in physical education (Placek, 1992).

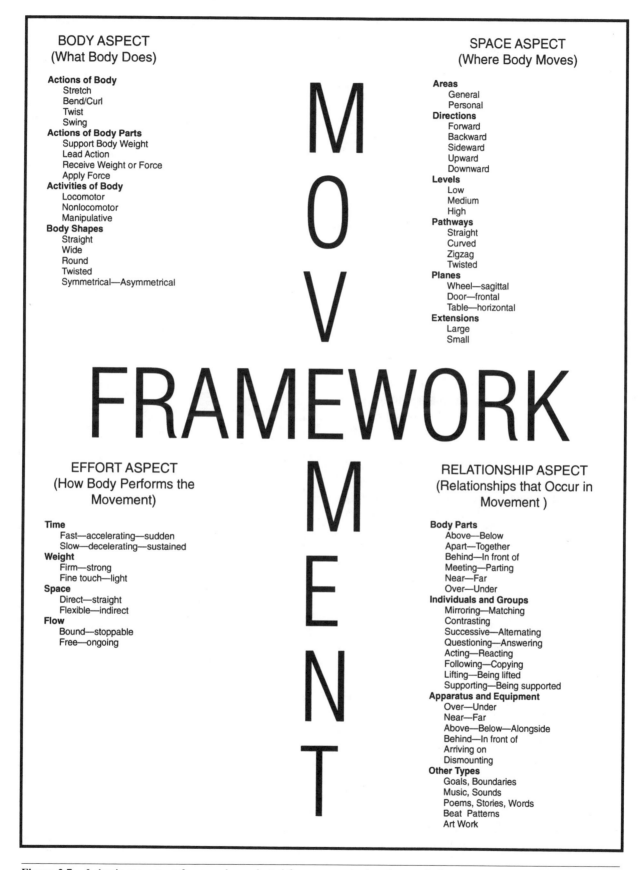

BODY ASPECT
(What Body Does)

Actions of Body
  Stretch
  Bend/Curl
  Twist
  Swing
Actions of Body Parts
  Support Body Weight
  Lead Action
  Receive Weight or Force
  Apply Force
Activities of Body
  Locomotor
  Nonlocomotor
  Manipulative
Body Shapes
  Straight
  Wide
  Round
  Twisted
  Symmetrical—Asymmetrical

SPACE ASPECT
(Where Body Moves)

Areas
  General
  Personal
Directions
  Forward
  Backward
  Sideward
  Upward
  Downward
Levels
  Low
  Medium
  High
Pathways
  Straight
  Curved
  Zigzag
  Twisted
Planes
  Wheel—sagittal
  Door—frontal
  Table—horizontal
Extensions
  Large
  Small

EFFORT ASPECT
(How Body Performs the Movement)

Time
  Fast—accelerating—sudden
  Slow—decelerating—sustained
Weight
  Firm—strong
  Fine touch—light
Space
  Direct—straight
  Flexible—indirect
Flow
  Bound—stoppable
  Free—ongoing

RELATIONSHIP ASPECT
(Relationships that Occur in Movement)

Body Parts
  Above—Below
  Apart—Together
  Behind—In front of
  Meeting—Parting
  Near—Far
  Over—Under
Individuals and Groups
  Mirroring—Matching
  Contrasting
  Successive—Alternating
  Questioning—Answering
  Acting—Reacting
  Following—Copying
  Lifting—Being lifted
  Supporting—Being supported
Apparatus and Equipment
  Over—Under
  Near—Far
  Above—Below—Alongside
  Behind—In front of
  Arriving on
  Dismounting
Other Types
  Goals, Boundaries
  Music, Sounds
  Poems, Stories, Words
  Beat Patterns
  Art Work

MOVEMENT FRAMEWORK

Figure 2.7.   Laban's movement framework as adapted for movement education curriculum.
Note. From *Physical Education for Children* (p. 140) by B. Logsdon, et al., 1984, Philadelphia: Lea & Febiger. Copyright 1984 by Lea & Febiger. Reprinted with permission.

The teacher's role in interdisciplinary curricula is to search for natural connections across subjects. Effective teachers have a clear, up-to-date understanding of the physical education knowledge base and are familiar with informational resources in biology, physiology, physics, language arts, and mathematics. They discuss content connections with the teachers in other subject areas. They can plan theme units in which the team of teachers presents the same concepts at the same time in different subject areas.

Scenario

The Howard County, Maryland, Public Schools system's (1988) primary educational goal is to enhance student thinking skills in a cross-curricular or interdisciplinary format. Teachers work with their colleagues in other subject areas to identify natural connections that cross traditional curriculum areas. Scenarios for elementary and high school programs emphasize relationships across the disciplines. One elementary physical educator, Teresa Shelton (1992), worked with the science teacher at her school to develop several lessons to teach and reinforce the concepts of rotating and revolving. Students learn simultaneously about the concepts in their science and physical education classes. In science, the teacher discusses the concepts as they relate to the planets' movements. Teresa then applies the concepts in her unit on ball control. Students discuss how balls can rotate or spin and explore the effects of rotation on flight and speed. Students discover that balls also can revolve around other objects, such as the body on "round-the-back" dribbles. She uses the basic concept to connect the movements to those of all spheres. Students have the opportunity to participate in knowledge and movement experiences to develop a more in-depth understanding of the concepts.

In another example, Marty McDonald uses an interdisciplinary curriculum at James Madison High School. Her ninth-grade students are taking a statistics class and apply concepts learned there to keep game statistics in softball. Each person keeps personal stats for hitting and fielding. The team captain then compiles the team stats and reports them to Marty. Dick Lofton, the mathematics teacher, collects the sheets and provides student feedback. Homework assignments include listening to a baseball game on the radio and calculating the stats for four batters during the game. Students use their knowledge of frequency and descriptive statistics to calculate team and class averages for activities they find fun and exciting.

Self- and Social Responsibility

The *self- and social responsibility* model, founded on the social responsibility and the student-centered value orientations, helps students resolve conflicts between commitment to self and responsibility to others (Hellison & Templin, 1991). The model's conceptual framework presents a progression of goals toward which students should strive. Each level represents values as well as behaviors important in becoming more self- and socially responsible.

A summary of the self- and social responsibility levels can be found in Figure 2.8. Level I, Self-Control, focuses on the student's ability to maintain self-control and to respect the rights and feelings of others. Level II, Participation and Effort, emphasizes participating in class activities and making an effort to learn and contribute to the group or team. Level III, Self-Direction, emphasizes goal setting and self-improvement in activities that the student finds interesting and useful. Level IV, Caring and Helping, requires students to think about others instead of themselves.

The teacher's role is to help the student become aware of the expectations for responsible behavior as described

---

Hellison and Templin (1991)

I. Self-control and respect for the rights and feelings of others
   A. Self-control
   B. Inclusion
   C. Negotiating conflicts
   D. Internalizing respect

II. Participation and effort
   A. Going through the motions
   B. Exploring effort
   C. Redefining success

III. Self-direction
   A. Independence
   B. Goal-setting
   C. Knowledge base
   D. Plan and evaluate

IV. Caring and helping
   A. Supporting others
   B. Helping others
   C. Group welfare

Figure 2.8. Levels of the self- and social responsibility model.

Note. From *A Reflective Approach to Teaching Physical Education* (p. 104) by Donald R. Hellison and Thomas J. Templin, 1991, Champaign, IL: Human Kinetics. Copyright 1991 by Donald R. Hellison and Thomas J. Templin. Reprinted with permission.

in the four levels. Students make choices to determine their personal levels of participation. Teachers use problem-solving strategies to assess various behaviors. For example, students may be assigned to teams and asked to design a soccer strategy to score on a penalty kick. Students working at the self-direction or caring level might find this task interesting and stimulating. Conversely, students working at the self-control level might have difficulty permitting others to speak, accepting others' suggestions, and participating fully in the experience. From this task, teachers can determine students' self- and social responsibility level and plan future activities to help students develop behaviors to increase their level of responsibility. It is important to note that students' levels may change based on the activity and their comfort level with other students on their team. The teacher must work to assess students' progress in each activity and to present tasks that are appropriate to students' ability. Students engaged in responsible problem-solving tasks can share their observations with others in class or small group discussions and learn to think reflectively about their actions and behaviors while participating. Teachers also spend time listening and providing feedback to students individually and in small groups. Students express both negative and positive feelings and learn to work with the teacher and other students to improve behaviors.

Scenario

The following example describes how the self- and social responsibility model might be implemented at a junior high school. At Martin Luther King, Jr. High School, Bill Williams uses a self- and social responsibility model with his students in weight training class. Students work in pairs to test themselves and to spot each other. Bill closely monitors the students working at the self-control level (I). He gives them a specific workout each day and monitors each lift until the students demonstrate they can work safely and act responsibly. Students at the participation and effort level (II) work independently and in pairs to follow a posted workout. Bill circulates periodically around the weight room to ensure that students are involved in the workout and are performing the lifts correctly. Students who are working at the self-direction level (III) design their own programs with Bill's help. They begin by testing themselves and setting goals for muscular strength, endurance, and flexibility. They select weight, repetition, and set specifications and then self-test and adjust their workout as their bodies adapt to exercise. Bill checks with each student during the class and reviews his or her personal workout card. Students work in pairs throughout the class offering each other

supportive and helping comments whenever appropriate (IV).

All students are aware of the self- and social responsibility levels. They assess various behaviors at each level to determine those that are acceptable and lead to enhanced performance. Bill encourages his students to help each other in spotting the lifts and adapting personal workouts. He realizes that some students can work independently, while others require additional support and guidance. Students think reflectively about the levels and talk with other students and the teacher about their progress. Self- and social responsibility is the primary theme of the class.

Personal Meaning

Personal meaning curricula reflect many physical education goals described by Eleanor Metheny in her speech, "Moving and Knowing" (1961). Metheny suggested that individuals will not enjoy participation in movement and exercise unless it is meaningful to them. For example, one of the reasons that individuals may have difficulty participating in regular physical activity is because the monotonous, repetitive movement required for jogging, cycling, or swimming may not be meaningful. Other individuals, however, may enjoy the experience and look forward to the opportunity to focus on efficient movements as they exercise.

Personal meaning curricula are constructivist in nature (Brooks & Brooks, 1993), meaning that they encourage students to have a voice in shaping the learning process. Students develop a sense of agency in that they are the "agents" through which decisions are made. Of course, students often come to physical education not having had these experiences before. In these curricula, students learn how to become proactive, creating a physical education program that has value for them.

Ann Jewett and her colleagues developed a personal meaning curriculum that encourages students and teachers to search for meaningful ways to engage in physical activity. The model is based on the Purpose Process Curriculum Framework (PPCF), which includes both the scope and a recommended sequence for the development of tasks and activities (Jewett & Mullan, 1977). The PPCF can be found in Figure 2.9

The *purpose* component of the PPCF includes 23 purposes for engaging in physical activity that individuals find meaningful. Purposes are grouped into three categories: Individual Development, Environmental Coping, and Social Interaction. The framework reflects a balance value orientation because relatively equal emphasis is placed on these three framework components.

Teachers assist students to learn the content from the knowledge base that contributes to the development of

Key Purpose Concepts

I. Individual Development: I move to fulfill my human developmental potential.

    A. Physiological Efficiency: I move to improve or maintain my functional capabilities.

        1. Circulorespiratory efficiency. I move to develop and maintain circulatory and respiratory functioning.
        2. Biomechanical efficiency. I move to develop and maintain range and effectiveness of motion.
        3. Neuromuscular effiency. I move to develop and maintain motor functioning.

    B. Psychological Well-being: I move to achieve personal integration.

        4. Joy of movement. I move to derive pleasure from sensory experience or environmental sensitivity.
        5. Self-understanding. I move to gain self-knowledge.
        6. Self-perception. I move to enhance my self-image and self-efficacy.
        7. Catharsis. I move to release tension and frustration.
        8. Challenge. I move to test my prowess and courage.

II. Environmental Coping: I move to adapt to and control my physical environment.

    C. Spatial Orientation: I move to relate myself in three-dimensional space.

        9. Awareness. I move to clarify my conception of my body and my position in space.
      10. Relocation. I move in a variety of ways to propel or project myself.
      11. Relationships. I move to regulate my body position in relation to the objects or persons in my environment.

    D. Object Manipulation: I move to give impetus to and to absorb the force of objects.

      12. Maneuvering weight. I move to support, resist, or transport mass.
      13. Object projection. I move to impart momentum and direction to a variety of objects.
      14. Object reception. I move to intercept a variety of objects by reducing or arresting their momentum.

III. Social Interaction: I move to relate to others.

    E. Communication: I move to share my ideas and feelings with others.

      15. Expression. I move to convey my ideas and feelings.
      16. Clarification. I move to enhance the meaning of other communication forms.
      17. Simulation. I move to gain a strategic advantage.

    F. Group Interaction: I move to function in harmony with others.

      18. Teamwork. I move to cooperate in pursuit of common goals.
      19. Competition. I move to test my competence in interaction with other performers.
      20. Leadership. I move to motivate and influence group members to achieve common goals.

    G. Cultural Involvement: I move to take part in movement activities which constitute an important part of my society.

      21. Participation. I move to develop my capabilities for taking part in movement activities of my society.
      22. Movement appreciation. I move to become knowledgeable and appreciative of sports and expressive movement forms.
      23. Multicultural sensitivity. I move to understand, respect, and appreciate cultural diversity.

Movement Process Categories

    A. **Generic movement.** Those movement operations or processes which facilitate the development of characteristic and effective motor patterns. They are typically exploratory operations in which the learner receives or "takes in" data as he or she moves.

(continued)

1. *Perceiving:* Awareness of total body relationships and of self in motion. These awarenesses may be evidenced by body positions or motoric acts; they may be sensory in that the mover feels the equilibrium of body weight and the movement of limbs; or they may be evidenced cognitively through identification, recognition, or distinction.

2. *Patterning:* Arrangement and use of body parts in successive and harmonious ways to achieve a movement pattern or skill. This process is dependent on recall and performance of a movement previously demonstrated or experienced.

B. **Ordinative movement:** The processes of organizing, refining, and performing skillful movement. The processes involved are directed toward the organization of perceptual-motor abilities with a view to solving particular movement tasks or requirements.

3. *Adapting:* Modification of a patterned movement to meet externally imposed task demands. This would include modification of a particular movement to perform it under different conditions.

4. *Refining:* Acquisition of smooth, efficient control in performing a movement pattern or skill by mastery of spatial and temporal relations. This process deals with the achievement of precision in motor performance and habituation of performance under more complex conditions.

C. **Creative movement:** Those motor performances which include the processes of inventing or creating movement that will serve the personal (individual) purposes of the learner. The processes employed are directed toward discovery, integration, abstraction, idealization, emotional objectification, and composition.

5. *Varying:* Invention or construction of personally unique options in motor performance. These options are limited to different ways of performing specific movement; they are of an immediate situational nature and lack any predetermined movement behavior which has been externally imposed on the mover.

6. *Improvising:* Extemporaneous origination or initiation of personally novel movement or combination of movement. The processes involved may be stimulated by a situation externally structured, although conscious planning on the part of the performer is not usually required.

7. *Composing:* Combination of learned movement in personally unique motor designs or the invention of movement patterns new to the performer. The performer creates a motor response in terms of a personal interpretation of the movement situation.

Figure 2.9. Purpose Process Curriculum Framework.
Note. From *Curriculum Design: Purposes and Processes in Physical Education Teaching-Learning* (pp. 4-5, 9-10) by A. E. Jewett and M. R. Mullan, 1977, Washington, DC: American Association for Physical Education and Recreation. Copyright 1977 by the American Association for Physical Education and Recreation. Reprinted with permission of the American Alliance for Health, Physical Education, Recreation and Dance.

self-esteem and positive social interactions. Students learn new skills and ways to participate in activities that they may never have attempted before. They also learn to create positive future scenarios that describe the role of movement and exercise in a healthy, active lifestyle. Students learn physical, cognitive, and emotional skills necessary to make their scenario a reality. In this curriculum, students share many decisions with the teacher. These decisions can include what activities they will learn, with whom they will work, and in what order they will complete the assigned tasks.

The California Department of Education Physical Education Framework (1994) provides an excellent example of a personal meaning model articulated with an interdisciplinary focus. California recently adopted a balanced, interdisciplinary approach in a K-12 framework. The framework is structured around three goals that emphasize the knowledge base, the student's personal development, and social interaction goals such as cooperation and teamwork.

Each goal area is clearly connected to its foundational knowledge base. For example, Goal 1, movement skills and knowledge, draws directly from the knowledge in motor learning, biomechanics, exercise physiology, and health-related fitness. Goal 2, self-image and personal development focuses on the disciplinary knowledge found in human growth and development, psychology, and aesthetics. Goal 3, social

Table 2.2 Characteristics of Curriculum Models

	Curriculum model					
	Sport education	**Personal fitness**	**Movement education**	**Interdisciplinary**	**Self- and social responsibility**	**Personal meaning**
Value orientation	Subject matter value orientation	Subject matter, student-centered value orientations	Subject matter, learning process, student-centered value orientations	Learning process, subject matter value orientations	Social responsibility, student-centered value orientations	Balance value orientation
Emphasis	Units designed to reflect a positive educational sport/games setting	Role of fitness and exercise in healthy, active living	Development of fundamental movements and skills	Emphasizes natural knowledge connections	Based on four progressions or levels of social development	Participation in movement and exercise must be meaningful
Goals	Students learn rules, strategies, rituals, and customs associated with sports/games	Responds to students' questions about fitness	Students learn to perform skillfully and to value and appreciate movement	Students learn to apply knowledge learned in physical education to other classes	Students resolve conflicts between personal needs and group interests	Students learn that they are the primary decision makers about their own movement
Role of teachers	Teachers modify sports/games to accommodate diverse skill levels	Teachers provide knowledge about fitness and assist students to design a program to meet their needs	Teachers use refining, extending, and applying tasks to enhance skillfulness	Teachers design curriculum to emphasize concepts that cross traditional units and bodies of knowledge	Teachers help students become aware of expectations for responsible behavior	Teachers help students to become skillful/knowledgeable and to apply this to personal and social goals
Special considerations	Extended instructional units to promote skill development, team affiliation	Testing is used to provide knowledge about personal performance necessary to set realistic goals	Content is taught within the framework of educational games, dance, and gymnastics	Physical educators interact with teachers from other subject areas to design cross-curricular content themes	Students learn to think reflectively about their behaviors while participating in physical activity	Purpose Process Curriculum Framework is the basis for curriculum decision making

34

development, reflects the knowledge found in sociology and historical perspectives in physical education. Each discipline is connected to physical education and provides a bridge between subject areas. Goals are organized into themes appropriate for each grade level, with examples for each grade taken from across the eight disciplines.

Scenario

Ann Jenkins uses the PPCF to structure her physical education program at Greenwood High School. The ninth-grade curriculum focuses on developing student awareness of a range of movement purposes that can be satisfied through physical activity. Students participate in a variety of movement, dance, sport, and fitness activities to identify those that they enjoy and would like to learn more about. Ann helps students connect the purposes of physiological efficiency with jump rope activities, and biomechanical efficiency with skill development. Students focus on the spatial orientation and communication purposes of awareness, relocation, and relationships in their sport and dance units.

The curricula for 10th through 12th grade focus on developing students' skills and fitness levels to pursue activities and movement purposes that they find most meaningful. Students might engage in units designed to apply object projection and reception concepts in a variety of sports and games. They focus on the joy of movement, self-understanding, and catharsis purposes to develop intrinsic motivation to engage in a healthy, active lifestyle in all facets of their lives. Students graduate from the program with enhanced ability to perform, an increased knowledge of factors that contribute to performance, and an appreciation of the intrinsic value of movement in their lives.

Overview of Curriculum Models

Curriculum models discussed in this chapter articulate alternative approaches to quality physical education. An overview of model characteristics is presented in Table 2.2. Curriculum designers and teachers may find programs described in these models to be helpful in their own curriculum planning.

Conclusion

Physical education teachers make curriculum decisions based on an in-depth understanding of the role and importance of the subject matter, the needs and interests of the individual, and the educational and social setting in which students are learning. They must understand the knowledge base of physical education in order to select and sequence goals and activities. They acknowledge student personal and social characteristics that influence student movement and exercise needs and interests. Teachers realize that the physical education setting in which they work contains inherent opportunities and limitations that shape the program. Curriculum decisions focus on what content is most important and how the content should be sequenced to enhance student learning.

Curriculum change can occur formally in top-down efforts by administrators, or informally in bottom-up efforts by teachers to design and implement unique innovations. With administrative support, teacher-designed lessons and tasks can be disseminated throughout the school district and the state. Teachers make program and lesson changes to respond to changes in their teaching situation. They respond to opportunities and barriers by designing programs that use knowledge to help students solve problems in their lives.

Teachers' educational value orientations influence the diversity of goals and objectives they consider most important for student learning. The influence of the subject matter, learning process, student-centered, social responsibility, and the balance value orientations influence the content that students practice and the extent to which they become skilled, confident performers and team members. There are a number of published curriculum models that can serve as prototypes for curriculum development: sport education, personal fitness, movement education, interdisciplinary approaches, self- and social responsibility, and personal meaning. Teachers and administrators should think carefully about the educational values and the characteristics of their students and setting before attempting to modify and implement a model. Physical education programs that match the curricular goals with those of the student, community, and school district provide the most effective plans to enhance student learning.

References

Association for Supervision and Curriculum Development. (1993). The healthy, active living curriculum. In The Curriculum Technology Resource Center (Ed.), *The curriculum handbook* (pp. 9.1-9.76). Alexandria, VA: Author.

Brooks, J.G., and Brooks, M.G. (1993). *The case for constructivist classrooms*. Alexandria, VA: Association for Supervision and Curriculum Development.

California Department of Education. (1994). *Physical education framework for California public schools: Kindergarten through grade twelve*. Sacramento: Author.

Carr, N. (1987). *Basic stuff: Series II.* Reston, VA: American Alliance for Health, Physical Education, Recreation and Dance.

Clark, J.E. (1994). Motor development. In V.S. Ramachandran (Ed.), *Encyclopedia of human behavior* (Vol. 3). San Diego: Academic Press.

Corbin, C.B., & Lindsey, R. (1991). *Concepts of physical fitness with laboratories.* Dubuque, IA: Wm. C. Brown.

Council on Physical Education for Children (COPEC). (1992). *Developmentally appropriate physical education for children.* Reston, VA: American Alliance for Health, Physical Education, Recreation, and Dance.

Cuban, L. (1992). Curriculum stability and change. In P.W. Jackson (Ed.), *Handbook of research on curriculum* (pp. 216-247). New York: Macmillan.

Darling-Hammond, L. (1990). Instructional policy into practice: ''The power of the bottom over the top.'' *Educational Evaluation and Policy Analysis,* **12**(2), 233-241.

Deal, T.E. (1990). Reframing reform. *Educational Leadership,* **47**(8), 6-12.

Ennis, C.D. (1992). The influence of value orientations in curriculum decision making. *Quest,* **44**(3), 317-329.

Ennis, C.D. (1994). Urban secondary teachers' value orientations: Social goals for teaching. *Teaching and Teacher Education,* **10**, 109-120.

Ennis, C.D., & Chen, A. (1993). Domain specifications and content representativeness of the revised value orientation inventory. *Research Quarterly for Exercise and Sport,* **64**, 436-446.

Ennis, C.D., Ross, J., & Chen, A. (1992). The role of value orientations in curricular decision making: A rationale for teachers' goals and expectations. *Research Quarterly for Exercise and Sport,* **63**(1), 38-47.

Florida Department of Education. (1992). *Florida's high school physical education program.* Tallahassee, FL: Author.

Ford, M.E., Wentzel, K.R., Wood, D., Stevens, E., & Siesfeld, G.A. (1989). Processes associated with integrative social competence: Emotional and contextual influences on adolescent social responsibility. *Journal of Adolescent Research,* **4**(1), 405-425.

Fullan, M.G. (1991). *The new meaning of educational change* (2nd ed.). New York: Teachers College Press.

Fullan, M.G., Bennett, B., & Rolheiser-Bennett, C. (1990). Linking classroom and school improvement. *Educational Leadership,* **47**(8), 13-19.

Grundy, S. (1987). *Curriculum: Product or practice.* New York: Falmer Press.

Hellison, D.R. (1985). *Goals and strategies for teaching physical education.* Champaign, IL: Human Kinetics.

Hellison D.R., & Templin, T.J. (1991). *A reflective approach to teaching physical education.* Champaign, IL: Human Kinetics.

Howard County Public School System. (1988). *Action for critical and creative thinking: A plan for the improvement of thinking.* Ellicott City, MD: Author.

Jewett, A.E., Bain, L.L., & Ennis, C.D. (1995). *The curriculum process in physical education.* Madison, WI: Brown and Benchmark.

Jewett, A.E., & Mullan, M.R. (1977). *Curriculum design: Purposes and processes in physical education teaching-learning.* Washington, D.C.: American Association for Health, Physical Education, and Recreation.

Kirk, D. (1995). Physical education and cultural relevance: A personal statement. In A.E. Jewett, L.L. Bain, & C.D. Ennis, *The curriculum process in physical education.* Madison, WI: Brown and Benchmark.

Lawson, H.A., & Placek, J.H. (1981). *Physical education in secondary schools: Curricular alternatives.* Boston: Allyn & Bacon.

Locke, L.F. (1992). Changing secondary school physical education. *Quest,* **44**(3), 361-372.

Logsdon, B., Barrett, K.R., Ammons, M., Broer, M.R., Halverson, L.E., McGee, R., & Roberton, M.A. (1984). *Physical education for children.* Philadelphia: Lea & Febiger.

Metheny, E. (1961). The unique meanings inherent in human movement. *The Physical Educator,* **18**(1), 3-7.

Middle and Secondary School Physical Education Council (MASSPEC). (1995). *Appropriate practices for middle school physical education.* Reston, VA: American Alliance for Health, Physical Education, Recreation and Dance.

National Association for Sport and Physical Education (NASPE). (1992). *The physically educated person.* Reston, VA: American Alliance for Health, Physical Education, Recreation and Dance.

Placek, J.H. (1992). Rethinking middle school physical education curriculum: An integrated, thematic approach. *Quest,* **44**, 330-341.

Shelton, T. (1992, April). *Cross-curricular connections in elementary physical education.* Paper presented at the Howard County, MD, Public School supervisor's meeting. Ellicott City, MD.

Siedentop, D. (1994). *Sport education: Teaching sport in physical education.* Champaign, IL: Human Kinetics.

Sparkes, A.C. (1991a). Curriculum change: On gaining a sense of perspective. In N. Armstrong and A.C. Sparkes (Eds.), *Issues in physical education* (pp. 1-19). London: Cassell.

Sparkes, A.C. (1991b). Exploring the subjective dimension of curriculum change. In N. Armstrong and A.C. Sparkes (Eds.), *Issues in physical education* (pp. 20-35). London: Cassell.

Wentzel, K. (1991). Social competence at school: Relation between social responsibility and academic achievement. *Review of Educational Research,* **61**(1), 1-24.

3

Assessment in the School Physical Education Program

Judith R. Rink and Larry D. Hensley
University of South Carolina and University of Northern Iowa

Greater demands are placed on assessment today than at any time in the history of American education. Widespread concern about the effectiveness of American schools has led to an increase in calls for accountability and for educational reform, with assessment linked to high priority standards as a cornerstone in the systemic educational reform movement. However, if one mentions the word ''assessment'' or ''evaluation'' to most any teacher, including those in the field of physical education, the response is generally negative. Even seasoned veterans and those who are recognized as good teachers often cringe at the mere thought of assessment. Although the professional preparation of most physical education teachers usually includes at least one course on assessment practices, often titled ''Tests and Measurements'' or ''Measurement and Evaluation,'' the value of and respect for assessment quickly diminishes in the eyes of the practicing physical educator.

Perhaps no other element of the instructional process is so often maligned or abused as the assessment process. Why is this so? Although many physical education teachers use a variety of tests, and there are hundreds of tests to choose from, they frequently feel dissatisfied with what these tests reflect. They know that students are learning, yet the use of these tests seems neither to facilitate learning nor to provide a very good indicator of what has been learned. Furthermore, many of the available techniques and tests are impractical to use in the typical physical education class setting and are hardly conducive to enhancing instruction.

Whereas there may be many reasons contributing to the sad state of affairs surrounding assessment practices in physical education, we would suggest that a limited perspective regarding the role and the means of assessment may be the most important barrier to overcome

in making assessment an integral part of the teaching and learning process. Retooling the educational system includes changing the nature of assessment from a separate entity to a program that becomes more fully integrated with the overall teaching effort and that provides more meaningful information about student learning and achievement. The purpose of this chapter is to explore issues and concerns related to assessment, provide a framework to give physical education teachers a clear understanding of its meaning, role, and implications, and discuss the current trends in assessment practices.

New Trends in Assessment Practices

Will our children be ready for the demands of the 21st century? What do children need to know and be able to do now in order to prepare for their futures? These and other questions are being asked by parents, teachers, educational leaders, business executives, and politicians as part of the school reform movement that has been growing over the past 10 years. Assessment is the cornerstone of education reform, enabling educators to create high-level goals, set standards, develop instructional pathways, motivate students, provide diagnostic feedback, monitor progress, communicate progress to others, and make appropriate decisions about students and programs.

Yet the demands for greater accountability and higher standards, as well as this heightened emphasis on assessment, come at a time of growing dissatisfaction with the traditional forms of assessment, whether this be the use of multiple-choice, machine-scored tests or the use of standardized sport skill or physical fitness tests. A transformation of the current accountability and assessment systems used in most classrooms to outcome and performance-based assessment is taking place across the country today, and physical education reflects this movement.

The whole area of assessment, especially day-to-day teacher-initiated assessment, is being carefully scrutinized and is evolving into processes focusing on significant outcomes for students and the definition of important goals of formal instruction. Terms such as performance-based assessment, authentic assessment, and alternative assessment are used in discussing these alternatives to conventional assessment, and although there are no universally accepted definitions, these terms generally indicate types of assessment that require students to generate rather than choose a response.

Performance-based assessment usually refers to assessment tasks in which the student demonstrates specific skills and competencies rather than selecting one of several predetermined answers to an exercise. *Authentic assessment* usually refers to the context or setting in which student performance is assessed: It is designed to take place in a ''real-life'' setting, one less contrived and artificial than those in which traditional forms of testing take place. For instance, using a standard tennis skills test which may require the student to hit a tossed ball into a target area on the other side of the net represents an artificial setting, whereas subjectively judging the student's ability to hit the ball while actually playing a game of tennis is much more authentic. Although authentic assessment should be performance based, performance-based assessment is not always authentic.

Moreover, authenticity should not be seen as a dichotomous characteristic, as if authenticity were either wholly present or wholly absent; rather, authenticity is a multidimensional characteristic that exists in varying degrees. In other words, some assessments are more authentic than others. *Alternative assessment*, meanwhile, generally refers to any form of assessment other than traditional paper and pencil, machine-scored, or multiple-choice tests. Journals, portfolios, demonstrations, teacher observations, logs, oral or written reports, and exhibitions are examples of alternative assessment and are described later in this chapter.

Although some types of authentic assessment are being heralded as innovative, many of these assessment techniques have actually been used by teachers for years. This is particularly true in physical education, where the very nature of the content frequently manifests itself in directly observable behavior. As a result, physical education teachers often employ observational analysis and subjective (qualitative) methods of assessment. The current interest in authentic assessment seems to legitimate these methods. It is important, however, that the physical education teacher strive to refine the criteria

used in the authentic assessment process and to clearly articulate the desired behaviors (standards) expected of students.

Although we present a case for the use of authentic assessment, we neither say that all assessments need to be of this type nor do we reject the use of standardized performance tests that have been popularized in the literature in physical education. In reality, there is no one right way to assess students. All assessments, even the very best, are imperfect and fallible. We would propose that a balanced approach to assessment is the prudent path to follow—one that uses authentic assessment methods in concert with the more systematic, standardized testing.

Clarifying the Terms

Before examining the variety of purposes for which assessment may be used, it is important to have an understanding of the basic terminology associated with this area. Simply stated, *assessment* may be thought of as the process of gathering information and interpreting what that information means. Inherent to assessment, *measurement* is often defined as the process of collecting information, whereas *evaluation* refers to the interpretation process in which some judgment is made of the value or worth of the collected information. For instance, once a skinfold measure has been taken, say 15 mm for a triceps skinfold on an 18-year-old girl, what does that information mean? *Testing*, meanwhile, refers to the use of an instrument or procedure to facilitate the collection of information. Assessment, then, becomes a term that describes a multifaceted process that blends together several related yet distinct components to collect information and give meaning to that information. Formative assessment is the day-to-day assessment which occurs during the instructional unit, whereas summative assessment takes place at the end of the unit, often for the purpose of evaluating achievement to give a grade.

As an integral part of the overall assessment process, evaluation warrants additional discussion. First of all, it is important to note that the success of the evaluation depends on the quality of the data or information collected. If the measurement process results in data that are not consistent and truthful, accurate evaluation is impossible. Evaluation, meanwhile, involves judging the value of these data according to some standard. The two most widely used types of standards are criterion- and norm-referenced.

Criterion-referenced standards are used to judge whether a student has attained a specified behavior or level of skill. This approach to evaluation underscores the recommendation of the National Council on Education Standards and Testing (Selden, 1992), which proposes that "there should be absolute, substantive standards in core academic subject areas in the elementary/secondary years" (p. 1). Similarly, measurement experts and curriculum specialists in physical education have recommended the use of a criterion-referenced approach to evaluation. Whereas there is considerable merit in using a criterion-referenced approach to evaluation, its main limitation lies in the specification of an appropriate criterion behavior. There does not presently exist a body of knowledge we can turn to that tells us precisely what behavior we should expect for the multitude of outcomes normally prescribed in a physical education class. In the absence of this definitive body of knowledge, criteria are commonly based on individual teacher opinion, or in some cases the recommendations of recognized authorities or experts in the area.

A *norm-referenced standard* is used to compare a student's performance to that of other members of a well-defined group. This group could be composed simply of students in a single classroom, or it may include students throughout the district, state, or nation. This approach to evaluation may be most useful when gauging the performance of individuals against widely accepted norms or when judging the effectiveness of a school's program compared to that of others.

In effect, norm-referenced standards are used to compare the performance of one student to another, whereas criterion-referenced evaluation is used to judge the performance of a student against the standard or desired level of performance, not to compare it to the performance of other individuals. Historically, the use of norm-referenced standards for evaluation has been the method of choice for physical education teachers, although that trend has abated over the last 10 to 12 years as more and more teachers are moving to the use of criterion-referenced standards. This shift toward the use of criterion-referenced standards reflects the contemporary recommendations of many curriculum and measurement experts as well as the fact that physical education teachers have become more dissatisfied with the usefulness of norm-referenced standards. The question is not whether one approach is better than the other; rather, it is a question of when is it more appropriate to use norm-referenced or criterion-referenced evaluation. Both have value in the educational system.

Purposes of Assessment

Assessment is an integral part of good teaching, and not merely an appendage to the process for the purpose of determining a student grade. Unfortunately, assessment and the administration of tests occur too often without a definite purpose in mind, or with the singular purpose of deriving a grade. It is important that teachers recognize from the outset that assessment is more than merely grading. In our opinion, the narrow identification of assessment with grading is a significant factor contributing to inappropriate assessment practices as well as to the negative attitude associated with the assessment process.

Although the specific uses of information gathered through the assessment process may vary from one situation to another, depending upon the perspective of the user, we propose that assessment serve two basic purposes in a school setting:

- Teaching and learning facilitation
- Program evaluation

Whereas teachers and other school officials may use assessment for discrete tasks such as providing feedback to learners for motivation and self-realization purposes, placement, grouping of students, diagnosis of learning needs, evaluation of achievement, adjustment of instruction and curriculum, grading, selection of students for special services, and so forth, the essence of all these tasks is to facilitate teaching and student learning. Program evaluation, meanwhile, provides summative information to appropriate officials to guide them in making decisions about curriculum needs, program effectiveness, resource allocation, and policy development, among other things.

Table 3.1 illustrates the similarities and differences between assessment for instruction and assessment for program evaluation. Although these two purposes overlap to some degree, it is important that the physical education teacher understand the context in which assessment is being used and design an assessment program appropriately. Therefore, in order to provide the most help to teachers with their day-to-day classroom responsibilities, the remainder of this chapter is directed towards assessment with a primary purpose of facilitating instruction and learning.

Integrated Model of Instruction and Assessment

Assessment is a powerful tool. It has great potential for shaping instruction and for affecting how students feel about school and themselves, yet a reform of assessment practices is not a panacea for completely reforming the educational system, as some imply. Rather, good assessment is an integral part of good instruction. Assessment procedures are used during all phases of instruction: first, to determine the needs of students and

Table 3.1 Comparison of Assessment for Instruction versus Program Evaluation

Type of assessment	Purpose of assessment	Primary & secondary audiences	Formality	Who is assessed	What is assessed
Assessment for instruction	Formative information to guide instruction, provide feedback to students, and facilitate grading	Teachers Students Parents Others	Informal; less rigorous in terms of validity and reliability; practical and expedient; teacher-mandated	All students	All content prescribed by course objectives
Assessment for program evaluation	Summative information for documenting effectiveness, making policy, developing curriculum, and program accountability	Teachers Administration Public State & federal governments Accrediting groups	Formal; more rigorous validity and reliability; system-mandated	Samples of students: classes; schools; districts; states; nation	Samples of content linked to standards and high priority objectives

aid in the shaping of course goals and objectives; next, to systematically monitor, diagnose, and remediate student performance; and finally, to evaluate student achievement and communicate progress to students, their parents, school officials, and others. All of these major roles of assessment facilitate teaching and enhance student learning.

Figure 3.1 provides an illustration of an instructional model that shows how assessment is intertwined with the overall teaching process. Whereas most models of instruction provide a linear framework, starting with course goals that are followed in turn by instruction and assessment, the integrated model shown here attempts to weave assessment throughout the pre-instruction, instruction, and postinstruction phases of teaching. The challenge we face is changing people's perspective on the role of assessment in the instructional process.

We would propose that collecting information on student performance and making a judgment about it is at the heart of good teaching and should be an ongoing part of instruction. Formative assessment and the accompanying feedback should positively influence the learning and teaching that takes place in the class by empowering both the teacher and student to take greater responsibility in the learning process.

As the model presented above illustrates, assessment is not an appendage to the instructional process, nor is it an end in itself. Good assessment enables us to accurately characterize students' behavior and performance and to make sound decisions that will improve education. It is critical, however, that teachers and others understand and value highly the role of assessment in the instructional process.

Without valuing assessment and the information provided through assessment activities, it is unlikely that teachers will seek to improve their assessment techniques and strategies. In addition, it is equally unlikely that they will embrace the notion that assessment is an integral part of good instruction. Assessment ultimately supports instructional improvement and thus student learning.

Requirements for Good Assessment

Unlike most other subject areas, physical education content typically includes learning objectives from three domains—cognitive, affective, and psychomotor. As such, a variety of techniques and standardized tests are required to measure student achievement in these diverse areas. Although the measurement techniques and the types of tests available to the physical education teacher may vary considerably, each possesses certain characteristics that enable teachers to judge the appropriateness of a specific technique or test for the use intended. It is important to remember that teachers do not always use a formal, standardized measurement tool for assessment: Informal techniques such as casual observation of student performance play a significant role in the day-to-day assessment of student performance in the classroom.

The selection of an appropriate assessment technique or standardized test for use in a school setting should be based upon specific psychometric criteria such as validity and reliability as well as upon a variety of

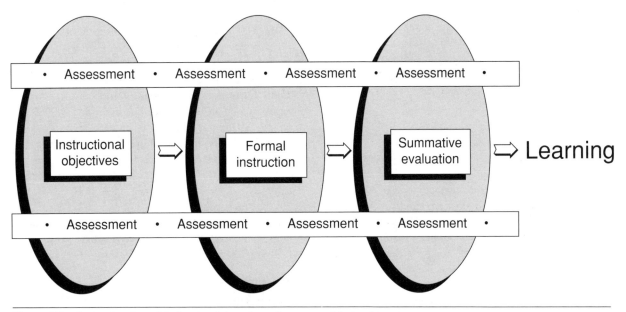

Figure 3.1.   Instructional model showing integration of assessment in teaching process.

practical issues (e.g., time required to conduct assessment, equipment needed, availability of norms or standards). Regardless of the specific technique used and whether it is collected formally or informally, teachers need to have confidence that the information about the student's performance is credible. Furthermore, it is important to recognize that there is no such thing as an ideal assessment tool: Appropriateness varies depending upon the purpose of the assessment as well as upon factors such as age, gender, ability, and a variety of ecological factors such as the availability of needed facilities and equipment. We will begin by defining and briefly describing three basic characteristics of effective assessment—validity, reliability, and objectivity — plus practical issues of test usage.

Validity

The first and, arguably, most important characteristic of an assessment tool is its *validity*. A test is said to possess validity if it accurately measures the attribute that it is designed to measure. A good assessment tool, whether it is a standardized sports skill test or an authentic event task, should measure what it is supposed to measure. According to Safrit (1990), for the assessment process to be valid there must be agreement between what is actually measured and the behavior it is intended to measure. Obviously, an integral part of this concept is defining the attribute to be assessed. If this is not articulated, the whole process is misguided and should probably be aborted.

There is no one way to evaluate validity. In fact, it is possible for an assessment instrument to have many validities. For instance, an assessment instrument may have different validities for different populations. The 1-mile walk test has been shown to have relatively high validity when used with an adult population, but only modest validity when used with children. There also are three common types of validity: content, criterion-related, and construct. A brief description of each type follows.

Content Validity

The American Psychological Association, or APA (1985), has defined *content validity* as "the degree by which the sample of items, tasks or questions on a test are representative of some defined universe or 'domain' of content" (p. 10). This type of validity is usually associated with paper and pencil instruments. If a match exists between the content of an examination and the table of specifications or test blueprint developed for the instrument, content validity is claimed.

In terms of assessing psychomotor performance, content validity can be claimed if it can be logically determined that the test measures the attributes associated

with the particular performance of interest. This then represents the test blueprint for examining content validity of our assessment. Furthermore, although the determination of content validity is necessary for judging a measuring instrument or assessment procedure, it is generally recommended that additional evidence of validity be provided (criterion-related validity or perhaps construct validity).

Criterion-Related Validity

To determine *criterion-related validity*, test scores or obtained information must be compared with another variable or variables that are considered direct measures of the characteristics or behavior in question. This direct measure is known as the criterion. There are two types of criterion-related validity: *concurrent* and *predictive*. Concurrent validity is the most widely used procedure for validating tests in physical education and represents the degree of relationship between the test and the selected criterion. This relationship is determined by calculating the correlation coefficient between scores on a test and the criterion measure, resulting in what we commonly call a validity coefficient. For example, the use of a distance run test to estimate cardiorespiratory endurance ($\dot{V}O_2$max) illustrates concurrent validity. Predictive validity, like concurrent validity, involves comparing a test score with a criterion measure, but this criterion measure represents future behavior or performance. For example, students graduating from high school often take the A.C.T. or S.A.T. for entrance into college because scores on these tests have been shown to be predictive of future success in college. Since the criterion measure for validating these tests, generally undergraduate grade-point average, is not known until sometime in the future, this illustrates predictive validity.

The APA has not addressed what constitutes acceptable concurrent or predictive validity coefficients. However, there appear to be guidelines to help in the selection of appropriate measuring instruments. Safrit (1990) suggests that concurrent validity coefficients of .90 or higher are desirable, but adds that values exceeding .80 are acceptable. Furthermore, we would expect that assessment techniques that rely heavily on subjective judgment and observations by the teacher would have lower validity coefficients. For predictive reliability, lower values are regarded as being acceptable, but they usually must be above .50. There are a variety of factors associated with these validity coefficients. The reader is referred to textbooks by Safrit (1990) and Baumgartner and Jackson (1991).

Construct Validity

According to Mehrens and Lehman (1984), *construct validity* is the degree to which one can infer certain constructs in a psychological theory—such as motivation, assertiveness, and intelligence—from test scores. Construct validity is important for tests measuring these and other such constructs, and has been discussed extensively in psychological literature. There has been less use of this type of validity in the assessment of motor behavior.

Reliability

Reliability is defined as the consistency with which a test or procedure measures whatever it measures. If scores on a test are reliable they are dependable, and relatively free of error. Reliability is related to validity. Specifically, in order for an assessment to be valid, it must first be reliable. However, reliability does not guarantee validity. For instance, grip strength can be reliably determined for different age groups. However, a grip strength score is not regarded as an appropriate or valid overall measure of an individual's strength.

Although several different forms of reliability are reported in the literature, *test-retest reliability* is the most common form used in physical education. Test-retest reliability provides a measure of stability from one test administration to another. At least two testing sessions are required to determine this measure. The results of the two sessions are correlated to determine their consistency. This technique has been widely used with many types of physical performance measures and is generally applicable to the newer forms of assessment that are being recommended.

A variety of factors should be considered when interpreting reliability estimates. Such factors as ability level of the group being tested, the range of ability of the group, the length of the test, and type of assessment all need to be understood when examining reliability estimates. Because of the variety of factors involved, no standards have been addressed for what is a minimally acceptable reliability coefficient. However, according to Safrit (1990), reliability estimates below .70 are rarely acceptable.

Objectivity or Rater Reliability

Objectivity is defined as the degree of agreement between scores assigned by two or more judges: If the same test is administered by two different individuals, or if two different individuals subjectively rate a student's performance, each pair of raters should obtain similar results. Objectivity depends upon two factors. The first is related to the scoring system used. Where there is a clearly defined method of scoring such as in using a stopwatch to measure the time for someone to cover 100 meters, minimal error is likely. Conversely, a teacher judging exercise intensity of subjects using weak, non-specific criteria would have difficulty in claiming objectivity.

A second factor affecting objectivity is the degree to which a person using a defined scoring rubric can do so accurately. For different individuals to obtain similar scores, the need exists not only for well-defined criteria but for scorers to be properly trained as well. During competitive events in gymnastics, diving, and ice skating, groups of judges are responsible for observing performers and assigning scores based on clearly described scales. Observational techniques similar in nature to this judging are widely used in the assessment of psychomotor, affective, and cognitive abilities in physical education classes. In order to increase the objectivity of this type of observational procedure, it is important that the scoring system be well defined and that the observer be qualified and clearly understand how the scoring rubric should be used.

Practical Test Characteristics

The most important characteristics associated with the assessment process are validity and reliability. If the process is lacking one or more of these characteristics, this essentially negates the usefulness of the information collected, and alternative types of assessment should be investigated. However, adequate reliability and validity guarantee neither the suitability of a measuring instrument nor that the assessment is satisfactory. Methods selected to measure the high priority outcomes in physical education classes, regardless of the domain of behavior, should possess additional, and important, attributes. Below are examples of some of these attributes.

1. Effective assessment should discriminate among different levels of ability. The scoring system should permit a range of scores, making it possible to differentiate individuals with a high level of what is being measured versus others who are at the lower level. For example, when used with young children, the traditional pull-up test does not discriminate among ability levels very well. This is because a substantial percentage of those tested are unable to complete even one pull-up. The same criticism would apply to a rating scale in which virtually all students in a heterogeneous class would receive the same rating on the performance being assessed. When used with a criterion, the assessment should determine accurately students who have met that criterion and students who have not.

2. Assessment should be appropriate for the age, gender, ethnicity, and ability level of the subjects. Some types of assessment may be reliable and valid with high school students, for instance, but not with children in lower elementary school. Although common sense will

often suffice in determining the appropriateness of assessments, teachers should carefully consider the intended purpose and target population for published tests and instruments.

3. Consideration should be given to any special equipment required for obtaining the assessment and also to special training required for personnel who will administer the assessment. If expensive equipment is needed or if special training is required, this may negate the selection of this procedure or instrument, regardless of acceptable psychometric properties.

4. Does the method of assessment affect the behavior or interest of the subject (e.g., having an observer present, requiring the participant to perform in an unnatural setting, allowing another student's behavior to influence performance)? Many sport skill tests have been criticized because of the unnatural environment in which the testing is being conducted. Ideally, one would like the most accurate and meaningful assessment without altering the normal activity of the participant during the measurement process.

5. How much time and effort (sometimes called "participatory burden") is required on the part of both the student and the teacher to satisfactorily complete the assessment? The compilation of journals, log books, and perhaps portfolios is particularly time-consuming for the participant, but direct observations and interviews create high demands on the teacher. Such practical considerations warrant primary consideration when determining the assessment technique to be used in physical education classes.

Evaluating a Program's Assessment Procedures

The development of an appropriate and relevant assessment program is a challenge all teachers face, yet it is at the heart of good teaching. Just as there is not a national curriculum in physical education, there is not a single assessment program that adequately meets the needs of all teachers or students. Assessment has emerged as a trend in itself over the past few years; however, if it is to effectively facilitate teaching and learning in physical education, teachers must recognize assessment's importance in everyday classroom activities and embrace the concept that assessment is inextricably intertwined with the teaching process. Prior to beginning a discussion of specific assessment techniques, strategies, and tools, the presentation of a series of questions designed to facilitate the shaping of one's assessment program is warranted. The following questions, adapted from "Guidelines for Appropriate Curriculum Content and Assessment in Programs Serving Children Ages 3 Through 8" (NAEYC & NAECS/SDE, 1991), should provide a framework for designing and evaluating a contemporary assessment program in physical education:

1. Is the assessment procedure based on the goals and objectives of the specific curriculum used in the program?
2. Are the results of the assessment used to benefit children, that is, are they used to plan for individual children, improve instruction, identify children's interests and needs, and individualize instruction? Does the assessment provide useful information that is relevant and meaningful to the students? Do the results help motivate students to establish and achieve reasonable goals?
3. Does the assessment procedure address all domains of learning and development—affective and cognitive as well as psychomotor?
4. Does assessment provide useful information to teachers to help them do a better job?
5. Does the assessment procedure rely on teachers' regular and periodic observations of children's everyday activities and performance so that results reflect children's behavior over time and not simply at one instance in time?
6. Does the assessment procedure occur as part of the ongoing teaching process in class rather than in an artificial, contrived context?
7. Is the assessment procedure performance-based rather than only testing skills in isolation?
8. Does the assessment rely on multiple sources of information about children, such as observations using rating scales or checklists, anecdotal records, student journals, standardized performance tests, and portfolios of student work in physical education?
9. Does the assessment procedure reflect individual, cultural, and ethnic diversity? Is it free of cultural, language, and gender biases?
10. Do children appear comfortable and relaxed during assessment rather than tense or anxious? Do they find the assessment enjoyable and meaningful?
11. Does the assessment examine children's strengths and capabilities rather than just their weaknesses or what they do not know or cannot do?
12. Is the teacher adequately trained to perform the recommended assessment?
13. Do children have an opportunity to reflect on and evaluate their own learning and performance?
14. Is there a systematic procedure for collecting assessment data that facilitates its use in planning instruction and communicating with parents?

15. Is the assessment procedure founded upon acceptable levels of validity, reliability, and objectivity?

16. Is there a regular procedure for communicating the results of assessment to students and family members or guardians that reports children's individual progress in meaningful language, rather than in letter or number grades?

Assessment Techniques, Strategies, and Tools

The content of physical education has always presented the physical education teacher with some unique problems and opportunities in regard to assessment techniques, strategies, and tools. Physical education teachers have almost always described their programs in terms not only of psychomotor outcomes, including fitness outcomes, but also in terms of affective and cognitive outcomes.

Assessment of the program should focus on all three domains; however, the psychomotor domain is unique in that it is both an advantage and a disadvantage when it comes to assessment. Unlike much classroom work, the psychomotor content results in directly observable behavior that can be assessed in a variety of ways. On the other hand, unless technology such as a video camera is used, no permanent products are produced and assessment of psychomotor abilities takes place at the time of performance. Without using technology, the record of the actual performance is lost and not recoverable: Teachers cannot take student work home to assess it later.

Although many of the assessment techniques, strategies, and tools advocated in the past for physical education have been discussed primarily in the context of assessment for the formulation of objectives and the summative evaluation of instruction (see Figure 3.1), more recent trends in performance-based assessment and formative evaluation have stressed the use of assessment to guide the process of instruction. Teachers are encouraged to design assessment materials that are meaningful and can be responsive to the particular setting and curriculum of a school. The sections that follow offer examples of strategies and techniques teachers can use to develop their own materials and list recently developed resources for physical education.

Anecdotal Records of Student Behavior and Performance

One of the more recent trends in assessment is the notion that assessment should be used primarily to collect information in order to guide instruction. Whether a teacher keeps a formal record of each student's performance or reflects informally on students' progress, the use of an anecdotal record of student performance can aid teachers in developing lesson plans appropriate to the specific needs of individual classes and students. An anecdotal record is a short description of information collected through observation; most often it describes student behavior in relation to an objective. Teachers who can describe where each student is in relation to an objective have a firm foundation on which to make decisions about instruction.

Usually anecdotal records are not evaluative: The teacher describes the behavior without adding evaluative words like "poorly" or "very good." The evaluative judgment is made after the observation. A teacher who engages in this process of description for each student, or sample of students, brings observations to an awareness level where they can be acted upon. In addition, the process of writing an anecdotal record may change the teacher's focus in additional observations.

Examples

Jessica can move to receive a pass and can pass to a moving player if the experience is at a slow pace. She loses control if the action gets too fast.

Jose works productively about half the time. He is often distracted by others. He wants to work with others but usually finds himself a loner because of his lack of maturity.

Tamika often does not participate—particularly if it involves very vigorous activity. She is quite skilled in spite of her weight problem, and if you do not make a big deal of her nonparticipation she will find herself participating.

Checklists and Rating Scales

Checklists are observational tools that record whether or not a phenomenon exists, and rating scales generally divide phenomena being observed into qualitative or quantitative dimensions. Both are very useful techniques for quantifying observations for assessment. Although it is difficult to compare anecdotal records of student performance, data that are quantified through checklists or rating scales can be compared. For both techniques, teachers must identify what is important to look for in an observation.

Teachers must also define what they think is important in order to determine when to give credit for seeing it (whatever this may be) and when not. This is the difficult part of both rating scales and checklists. They are both deceptively simple, in that they are easy to design but difficult to learn how to use with a great deal of reliability in observation. The more that teachers are willing to take time to define categories accurately and the more willing to practice using the categories, the more reliable and valid will be the information collected.

Because it is difficult for observers to focus on more than a few ideas at a time, most rating scales and checklists have tended to be narrow in their scope (only a few criteria are listed for a psychomotor skill, for example). A more recent trend has been to not break down everything observed into finite components, but rather to deal with performance in a more holistic way. When teachers observe more holistically, they must still know what constitutes each level of performance, but they do not have to analyze each component of each level separately.

The basketball dribbling and passing example that follows represents a simple rating scale that looks at an entire skill and rates the level of performance on that skill. In this instance, the teacher might establish a criterion for a particular objective and class and use this scale to rate performance. The more levels of discrimination required in this type of assessment, the more difficult it becomes to discriminate those levels. Generally three or four levels are the maximum levels of discrimination a teacher can use and still have an adequate degree of reliability.

Examples

Observational checklist: volleyball forearm pass

_____ *1. Gets into a low "get set" position*

_____ *2. Makes an appropriate platform for the ball*

_____ *3. Shrugs shoulders at contact*

_____ *4. Uses leg/hip extension to drive the shot*

_____ *5. Follows through in line of direction of target*

Rating scale: receiving a tennis serve

_____ *1. Rarely contacts the serve*

_____ *2. Sometimes receives the serve in control but most of the time the ball is out of control or does not make contact with the ball*

_____ *3. Receives the serve under control almost every time**

*In this example, the teacher would need a clear notion of what constitutes "control" and "almost every time."

Rating scale: basketball dribbling and passing

Students who achieve the dribbling and passing objective for the class and go beyond the objective receive a score of 5. Students who have not met the objective to any degree receive a score of 1. All other students receive a score somewhere in between, reflecting proximity to the objective.

Self-Assessment

Because there are no permanent products of student performance in the motor area in particular, testing students usually takes a great deal of class time. This valuable class time can be saved with the use of self-assessment techniques. Newer directions in assessment encourage teachers to make the learning experience and assessment the same thing: Providing opportunities for self-testing activities or for students to apply evaluative criteria to their own work is a valuable learning experience that helps students to develop a full understanding of that criteria. This is particularly true in motor skills, where a cognitive understanding of the skill is a first step to good performance.

Valid and reliable data can be collected by students through self-assessment techniques if students are trained and held accountable for accurate information and good management. The ability to self-assess is a critical program goal having implications for life-long learning. In what follows, several examples of self-assessment options are provided; teachers should recognize that there are limitless possibilities for self-assessment, from the application of formal to informal criteria.

Examples

Self-testing: Count how many continuous sets you can do in the next few minutes of practice and record your score in your notebook.

Application of limited criteria: On the sheet in front of you (or on the poster on the wall) are several pictures of people doing a set shot. Indicate which picture best describes your performance.

Application of more specific criteria: Check off the following characteristics after you have achieved them for your sequence.

_____ *My sequence begins with a still stop and a clear body shape.*

_____ *My sequence includes a controlled jump, balance, and roll in any order.*

_____ *The moves of my sequence are connected smoothly.*

_____ *My sequence ends with a still position.*

Use of videotape: When you think you have mastered the skill, take your video cassette over to the camera and record your performance. Use the check list to evaluate the strengths and weaknesses of your performance, and put everything back in your folder.

Peer Assessment

Using peers to help with assessment is one of the most efficient ways in which teachers can collect a great deal of reliable information on student performance in a short amount of time. Peer assessment tends to be more reliable than self-assessment techniques. The process of evaluating the work of others is a valuable learning experience for the student who is doing the assessment as well.

The value of peer assessment is contingent upon the degree to which peers are knowledgeable about the criteria for assessment and their willingness to take seriously their responsibility to apply the criteria objectively. It is the responsibility of the teacher to impart this knowledge and sense of responsibility to the students. The ability of the peer to provide useful data is increased if teachers start with a limited role for the peer (e.g., counting, filling out a yes/no checklist, observing limited criteria, etc.) and a high degree of structure (e.g., "The next time your partner jumps, see if your partner's toes reach for the floor to land softly.") Increase the responsibility given peer assessors as they feel more comfortable.

Peers can use any of the means used in self-assessment, including rating scales, checklists, and self-testing activities. In addition, peers can also score the more formal tests described in the next section.

Video Analysis

The widespread use of camcorders and computer technology has made the use of video access for the collection of observational data very practical. Students and teachers can use videos and computers to record and later analyze performance. Video technology can be set up in the gym for students to record their performance when they are ready to be assessed, or the teacher can choose a student to record other students doing skills.

Video access is also useful for teachers who are working on affective goals in a class, such as student independent work skills or objectives related to student inclusion in activity. It is much easier to analyze what is going on in a class from the relative tranquillity of one's home than in the midst of an active class. Video technology provides an opportunity to view and study everything that is visually occurring in a class. Teachers can use video access to determine the degree to which affective goals for class behavior are being met. They can also share this opportunity with students by having students view the video to look at the degree to which particular objectives are being met.

Event Tasks

One of the products of the recent emphasis on authentic assessment is the emergence of the *event task* as a structured learning experience for evaluation of performance. Event tasks are culminating, relevant activities that require the student to demonstrate skills and abilities in real settings rather than contrived settings. In physical education, an event task could be a dance, gymnastics routine, the game, lifetime recreation activity, personal fitness program, or outdoor education field trip. The notion is that, rather than testing an ability in a setting that is "unnatural," educators should be testing the ability to use knowledge, skills, and abilities displayed in a more natural setting. In developing assessment materials, the teacher designs an event task and a scoring rubric (holistic rating scale) intended specifically for that event task. Utilizing a holistic approach combined with the notion of authenticity, a teacher in physical education might develop the following event task and assessment strategies:

> **Activity:** *Tennis*
> **Assessment Objective:** *Game rules, etiquette, strategy, and basic skills*
> **Scoring rubric:** *(See Figure 3.2)*

In this example the teacher is looking at knowledge of tennis rules, affective behavior, and motor skills in an actual game situation.

Student Portfolios

Much as they are used in other content areas, *student portfolios* collect the best examples of a student's work in a content area as evidence of performance. These examples of student work are then evaluated to determine whether they meet established criteria. Although portfolios of student work in physical education may include written work, journals, or records of participation, portfolios would also have to include video examples of student performance and improvement over time. This performance could be more authentic in nature, such as that seen in event tasks (participation in a game or in a self-designed routine or dance), or it could be a skill test performance.

Students can be required to bring in a blank videotape or other media, in much the same way that they are required to bring in a notebook. Storage of and access to video information is becoming more convenient with the increased availability and use of video computer disks.

Student Questionnaires and Interest Inventories

A very quick way to get information from learners on their perceptions, interests, and so forth is the written questionnaire. Teachers can use the questionnaire to

Level Four

- Makes no observable errors in scoring or in interpreting the rules of the game
- Returns to home base after each play
- Varies the type of stroke used appropriately
- Forces the opponent to move on the court for each potential offensive stroke
- Can serve or return a normally playable ball with good form using the forehand, backhand, volley, smash, and lob
- Calls out-of-bounds balls honestly
- Recognizes a good play by an opponent and acknowledges such to opponent
- Does not show undue disappointment at his or her own performance

Level Three

- Knows how to play by and how to interpret the rules most of the time
- Returns to home base appropriately more often than not
- Most of the time uses an offensive strategy to return the ball, with occasional lapses
- Most of the time can serve or return a normally returnable ball using a forehand and backhand
- Most of the time calls out of bounds rules honestly
- Only occasionally acknowledges a good play by an opponent
- Only occasionally shows undue disappointment at his or her own performance

Level Two

- Does not demonstrate knowledge of the rules of the game on a regular and consistent basis; relies mostly on others for this information
- Occasionally returns to home base after making a play
- Only occasionally uses an offensive strategy
- Uses most basic strokes most of the time, but ineffectively
- Rarely calls out-of-bounds balls honestly
- Never responds positively to a good play by an opponent
- Occasionally shows undue disappointment in his or her own play in a manner that is disruptive to the game

Level One

- Demonstrates a lack of understanding of rules, scoring, and procedures for tennis on a regular basis
- Never returns to home base after a play
- Rarely returns a ball with any intent to demonstrate a strategy
- Has a limited level of effectiveness in a few basic strokes
- Argues over out-of-bounds balls on a regular basis
- Calls attention to opponents' errors rather than to good performance
- Disrupts the game on a regular basis after a disappointing play

Figure 3.2.   Scoring rubric for tennis game play.

obtain information from students on any topic. Physical educators are often interested in the effect of their programs on students outside of the school setting. Questionnaires give teachers the opportunity to collect information from many different students in a short amount of time.

Examples

Sample questions:
- *Do you play basketball outside of school? Where? How long have you played?*
- *What are your favorite and least favorite activities?*
- *What can the teacher do to help you learn?*
- *How do you feel about working in small groups chosen by the teacher?*
- *Would you be interested in an after-school program?*
- *Do you participate in any sport activities outside of school?*

- *What do you usually do when you come home from school?*
- *How do you spend your weekends?*

Questionnaires should be as brief as possible. If you are going to give them to a lot of students, it is always wise to ask a few students to answer the questionnaire first so that you can check any misperceptions in questions as well as reading level. Questionnaires are more useful when followed up by interviewing a sample of students to get information not usually communicated in writing by students, such as why students choose a response and their feelings and attitudes regarding responses.

Student Journals, Diaries, and Logs

Student journals, diaries, and logs are useful ways for teachers to gather information from students about their perceptions, feelings, and attitudes. Journals permit students to write down their thoughts and feelings on their class experiences in very unstructured ways. They are also useful learning experiences because they provide students with the opportunity to reflect on their own progress, behavior, or feelings about physical education content. Journals and logs can be part of a student's notebook in physical education. Some teachers begin or end each physical education lesson with written notes and written work related to a lesson, and some bring out a journal once a week.

Examples

Student perceptions of ability, improvement, and participation: How good are you at the following skills? Why do you think you are good or not good? Describe one thing you did today that contributed to another person learning or feeling good about themselves. Describe one thing you did today that contributed to another person feeling badly about themselves.

Student feelings: Of all the activities we did today, what did you like the best? Why? Describe one thing that happened in physical education today that made you feel good. Describe one thing that happened today that made you feel bad.

Student participation: Record your daily activity, including walking, vigorous activity, sedentary activity, and so forth, for a 2-week period. Based on these data, estimate the amount of time spent each week in light activity, moderate activity, and vigorous activity.

Student Interviews

All students have important messages to share with teachers about the content and the learning experiences in physical education. However, the verbal responses of the most vocal in class are not necessarily representative of the feelings and attitudes of the membership of a class. In physical education, the aggressive student is most often heard but views of nonaggressive students often go unheard.

Teachers need to take time to periodically interview students in a more formal way in order to rectify imbalances in who is being heard. Students often have great insight into experiences that can be a great help to teachers in understanding their classes. A teacher should choose a representative sample of students to interview periodically. The interviews can yield valuable information to determine whether experiences are appropriate for all students within a class. Interviews can be conducted on a one on one or small group basis before or after school, at lunch, or at other prearranged times. It is important that students understand that teachers want open answers and will not hold what they say against them.

Integrating Assessment Into a Program

Once teachers have chosen assessment methods, they must then decide how to implement them within the structure of a program. The following are two examples, one for elementary and one for secondary school.

Elementary School Assessment Example

Here are the steps taken before, during, and after instruction to integrate assessment into a sample elementary program.

Pre-Instruction Phase

Willie is an experienced teacher who just took a new job at an elementary school in a new community. She moved in several weeks before the school year started and began to collect information on the physical activity and sport programs sponsored by the school and other community organizations. Willie found out that a very large percentage of the students she will be teaching play soccer, basketball, and softball in community leagues that start children at young ages. She talked to the teachers at the middle school and the high school and asked them to share their curriculum with her.

During the first weeks of school Willie interviewed the principal and other teachers in the school to get their perceptions on what the curriculum at the school had been and what they thought it should be. Several student representatives from the upper grades were interviewed to describe the program that had been in place before Willie came to the school. Willie also asked these students what they most liked and did not like about the way physical education was conducted in the past. She wanted to know what the expectations of these client groups were before implementing her program.

In the 1st week of school, Willie conducted several lessons that were videotaped including locomotor work with the younger children and ball handling, gymnastics, and dance lessons with several classes across the grade levels. She then looked at these lessons to get a general idea of students' basic skill levels in these areas. Willie observed the videotapes from several perspectives, at times observing specific students who represented different skill levels and at times scanning the group quickly to get an idea of how many students were able to do what she asked them to do. Observing the tapes allowed her to determine levels of student independence in following directions. From a management perspective, Willie was then able to make a decision about the degree of structure that lessons would initially require.

Willie's pre-assessment data enabled her to better prepare the curriculum for the year. She knew that adjustments would have to be made but felt better about her instructional plans to begin the year.

Instruction Phase

Willie's first units were locomotion in the younger grades; ball handling skills with the middle grades; and soccer with the upper elementary students. She used various assessment techniques throughout her units. For example, during the locomotion lessons, Willie decided to focus on six students in each class period, making sure to observe these students sometime during the lesson. After the lesson, she checked off where each student was in the development of basic locomotor skills as shown in Figure 3.3.

Willie knew that these ratings were rough estimates of performance, but she felt good about being able to identify where most students were in their ability to perform these skills.

In her ball handling unit, Willie did several self-testing activities with the students. Activities included keeping track of how many successful catches were made from a partner toss, how far a student could throw, and successful catches from a ball rolled on the ground

20 feet away. Students marked their scores on a personal task card on the 1st day and used a peer assessment model toward the end of the unit. On the 1st day of the soccer unit, Willie videotaped student performance in a four-on-four game with modified fields. She analyzed student performance in terms of their motor skills and their use of basic offensive and defensive strategies. Her observations became the basis for determining the content of the lessons of the units.

The older students ended each class period by listing at least one idea that was learned each day about soccer. Sometimes the teacher helped with this, and sometimes students were free to list whatever occurred to them at the time. Students were also asked to draw a rating scale from 1 to 10 and to identify where on this scale they would put their effort for the day (E), their success for the day (S), and the degree to which they enjoyed the class (J). Figure 3.4 shows this scale.

Via their journals, students were free to write a message to the teacher on any given day. Messages were often positive and occasionally insightful, such as:

I can't do any of this.
Make those other students stop fooling around.
Why don't you ever tell me I'm doing good.
When are we going to play a game.
The grass is too wet in the morning.
I had fun today.

Willie often reviewed the notebooks and used the information students had given her to try to adjust classes to make the experience more appropriate for different students. She would often talk to individual students, acknowledge their responses, and thank them for sharing their ideas with her.

Willie frequently used self-testing activities with her classes. Students recorded their scores for the day in

Figure 3.4. Sample rating scale.

Debbie B.		run	jump	hop	skip	leap	combinations
		3	2	2	1	1	0

	Where	0 = Not mature pattern
		1 = Good mature pattern in simple conditions
		2 = Can vary speed smoothly
		3 = Can use all directions smoothly

Figure 3.3. Sample assessment sheet for instruction phase.

their notebooks and then noted improvement based on previous scores.

Postinstruction

Willie believed that instruction should be provided in units of adequate length so that learning could occur and students could recognize progress. She always set time aside at the end of the unit to assess student learning. Willie sent home an assessment of each student in terms of basic motor skills, physical fitness, group interaction skills, and personal responsibility. Accompanying this information were some suggestions for what parents could do to help their children in these areas.

Willie had all students in the soccer unit identify a question from their notebooks for a written test. The test was comprised of questions the students had written. The psychomotor test on soccer skills utilized peer assessment. Students were given a set of criteria to look for in a situation such as a two-versus-one game that involved dribbling and shooting against a defender. Peers used a simple check sheet to identify when criteria were observed and when they were not observed. Because Willie had helped students become knowledgeable about these criteria during instruction, the students felt competent to use the criteria for assessment.

Secondary School Assessment Example

Wade was a very experienced teacher and coach and was head of the physical education department in a large urban high school catering to a diverse student body. School personnel had worked hard to develop policies of inclusion and create a positive social environment. Wade was very instrumental in promoting collaboration and positive relationships among students and teachers.

While students were still in middle school, basic tests in ball handling skills, fitness, and rhythms, as well as a questionnaire regarding interest and experience in different physical activities, were administered. Student portfolios were also developed. The high school and middle school physical education faculty of the district had worked together on creating the assessment instruments and the portfolio format. The questionnaire asked students for information regarding their experiences with different activities. The interest inventory was a checklist in which each student rated personal interest and experience with sports and activities within the physical education program as well as those outside the school setting.

The skills tests, questionnaire, and portfolios were used at the high school to modify curricular and instructional plans and design program objectives to better meet the needs of students. Each of the units were carefully designed with clear criteria for performance

and knowledge. Pretests were conducted to assess where students began.

During Instruction

Extensive assessment activities were standard in each unit. Course materials included information accessed on multimedia computers. Written material included information on how to do and how to practice skills. Written tests were often taken on student time outside of class using the computer in the media center and an assigned student ID number. Students were also encouraged to check out videotapes that would provide some self-help for each activity.

Assessment activities were built into class instruction. Self-assessment activities that would provide students with the skills to learn how to learn movement skills were a high priority. Videotape was used extensively by all teachers. Often the camera was set up and students put their cassettes in the camera to tape their own performance. They could request analysis by peers or teacher assistant, or they could leave the video for the teacher with a note to provide some feedback.

After Instruction

In the fitness unit, students were required to determine appropriate personal objectives with their instructor for their own development and maintenance of fitness. Students then had to plan and conduct a program based on those needs, and were assessed frequently on their progress in attaining the objectives. Parents and community members volunteered a few hours a day to help students with the assessment process.

Assessment of students in other physical education units included evaluations of appropriate event tasks for each activity. Most of these evaluations were based on videotapes of game play, a match, or a final performance, all of which were thought to demand an adequate level of ability to make participation enjoyable. Students could choose the performance they wanted to submit for evaluation, and also determined the evaluation criteria in many activities.

Conclusion

Newer perspectives on assessment have the potential to change the role of assessment from being a part of teaching generally avoided by most practicing teachers to its being a central part of their work. When teachers use assessment as a tool to collect information on student progress on a regular basis, assessment becomes part of the teaching and learning process rather than something apart from it. Time once considered wasted on collecting information becomes time well spent when the instructional process is guided by an informed decision maker.

References

American Psychological Association (1985). *Joint standards for education and psychological tests.* Washington, DC: Author.

Baumgartner, T.A., & Jackson, A.S. (1991). Measurement for evaluation in physical education and exercise science (4th ed.). Dubuque, IA: Wm. C. Brown.

Mehrens, W.A., & Lehman, I.J. (1984). Measurement and evaluation in education and psychology (3rd ed.). New York: Holt, Rinehart, and Winston.

National Association for the Education of Young Children & the National Association of Early Childhood Specialists in State Departments of Education (NAEYC & NAECS/SDE). (1991). Guidelines for appropriate curriculum content and assessment in programs serving children ages 3 through 8. *Young Children,* **46**(3), 21-38.

Safrit, M.J. (1990). Introduction to measurement in physical education and exercise science (2nd ed.). St. Louis: Times Mirror/Mosby.

Selden, R. (1992). National standards and testing. *The State Board Connection: Issues in Brief,* **12**(4), 1-12.

Appendix

Commercially Produced Materials for Assessment in Physical Education

The following sources are commercially available for teachers to use and modify in their assessment activities. Although assessment materials representing some of the newer ideas expressed in this chapter are not yet available, the reader will find these sources helpful for many traditional forms of assessment.

> *AAHPERD skills test manuals*
> AAHPERD
> 1900 Association Drive
> Reston, VA 22091
> 703-476-3400

Archery (1967)
    Brace, David (test consultant)
Basketball for Boys and Girls (1984)
    Hopkins, D.R., Shick, J., & Plack, J. (Eds.)
Football (1965)
    Brace, David (test consultant)
Softball for Boys (1966)
    Brace, David (test consultant)
Softball for Girls (1966)
    Brace, David (test consultant)
Volleyball (1969)
    Clayton, Shay (test consultant)

• • •

ASCD - Redesigning assessment series
ASCD Marketing
1250 N. Pitt St.
Alexandria, VA 22314-1453
703-549-9110

Complete series of videotapes and facilitator guides to redesign the way teachers look at how to assess student learning.

• • •

Johnson, B., & Nelson, J. (1986). *Practical measurements for evaluation in physical education* (4th ed.). Edina, MN: Macmillan.

Specific tools to measure fitness components, motor ability items, rhythm and dance, kinesthetic perception, basic sports skills, social qualities and attitudes, posture, and so forth. Generic principles are provided as well as tools that are practical to use. Good references are provided for a broad range of physical education content and objectives.

• • •

McGee, R., & Farrow, A. (1987). *Test questions for physical education activities.* Champaign, IL: Human Kinetics.

Between 250 and 400 multiple-choice questions drawn from many sources for 15 different activities covering history, terminology, equipment, principles, techniques, strategies, and rules of competition; suggested reading.

• • •

Physical best: A physical fitness education and assessment support program (1988)
    AAHPERD
    1900 Association Drive
    Reston, VA 22091
    703-476-3400

Comprehensive physical fitness education program including assessment materials as well as curriculum materials for school settings by grade level.

• • •

The Prudential Fitnessgram (1993)
    Cooper Institute for Aerobics Research
    12330 Preston Road
    Dallas, TX 75230

Health-related physical fitness test, computer program, and materials for reporting and analyzing fitness data from school settings.

• • •

The reader is also encouraged to refer to *Moving Into the Future: National Standards for Physical Education, a Guide to Content and Assessment* developed by the National Association for Sport and Physical Education (1995). This source provides standards and examples of how those standards can be assessed using a variety of newer and traditional assessment strategies and is available from the following:

National Association for Sport and Physical Education
1900 Association Drive
Reston, VA 22091
703-476-3400

4

A Focus on Inclusion in Physical Education

Diane H. Craft

State University of New York College at Cortland

What is inclusion? In physical education, inclusion is a set of attitudes, actions, and activities that together provide a welcoming and supportive educational environment, one that is respectful and appreciative of individual differences, and in which all students participate fully regardless of gender, race, motor ability, or challenging condition (disability).

Why is inclusion necessary? "We . . . live in a culture where sexism, racism, and motor elitism are persistent social problems" (Griffin, 1989, p. 19). As physical education programs are not exempt from reflecting societal mores, we must think about the ways in which these programs are constructed and conducted, for they will serve either to perpetuate or to help eliminate these problems. This chapter provides information on the inclusion of all students in physical education instruction. Pertinent legislation, strategies for promoting acceptance, important curricular considerations, and the role of collaborating with others are presented, followed by a listing of resources.

Let us begin by discussing the inclusion of students with challenging conditions. In physical education, mention of the word *inclusion* often evokes strong, emotional responses from teachers who have had or will have to deal with the realities of designing and implementing an inclusive program. Some teachers view inclusion as a burden, but others see it as an opportunity. What is clear from the comments from physical educators is that today the word inclusion means many things to many different people.

For perhaps a decade, inclusion has been an issue in special education, where three critical phrases have helped define and clarify the concept: In special education, inclusion is the practice of educating a student with a disability, *even a severe disability,* in regular classes with typical peers *in the neighborhood school,* not as an occasional visitor, but *as a full member of the class.* An examination of the concept of inclusion as used in the context of special education might give more focus to the issue for physical educators.

1. The placement of a student with a disability, *even a severe disability*, into regular classes marks a sharp departure from earlier special education practices. The label *severe disability* refers to students who are among the lowest intellectual functioning 1% of the school-age population. In the past, many people suggested that students with mild and perhaps moderate challenges could occasionally be placed in regular classes. The needs of students with severe challenges were so extensive that placement in regular classes was not seriously considered. Recently, a group of pioneering educators and parents have demonstrated that, given appropriate support systems, even students with severe challenges can learn in regular classes. Experience is showing that such placements are not penalizing and they often benefit the education of classmates (Stainback & Stainback, 1990). Examples of appropriate support systems are team teaching with an adapted physical educator, utilizing the assistance of a paraprofessional, conducting in-service education in inclusion, planning time for collaboration, or a combination of these.

2. Placing students with challenges in their *neighborhood schools* marks another departure from earlier practices. Neighborhood schools are the ones their next door neighbors and siblings attend and the ones they would attend if there were no disability. By implication, then, inclusion means the end of full-time placement in special education classes, whether in a special education cooperative or in the neighborhood school.

3. The placement of students with challenges in regular classes, not as visitors, but as *full members,* reflects natural proportions throughout the population. So, with inclusion, how many students with challenges can a physical educator expect in a typical class? Teachers can anticipate approximately 1 student with a severe challenge among every 100 students. The phenomenon in which all students with challenges from a self-contained special education class travel as a group to attend an already large physical education class is counterproductive. Inclusion does not, however, preclude students with challenges from going out of their classes for special instruction, just as other students go out of the classroom for enrichment or supplemental instruction in such subjects as instrumental music, mathematics, reading, and the like.

How did we get to the point of discussing inclusion? Karen DePauw's perspective (1986) helps explain the gradual changes over the past half century in special education placement. She describes educational philosophy and practice as a continuum, represented by a pendulum that swings left and right between exclusion and inclusion, slowly spiraling upward toward a position of inclusion and acceptance. A simplified overview of the history of inclusion follows (Brown et al., 1983).

Before 1940, there were few educational opportunities for people with challenges. Some thought that students with severe challenges could not or should not learn. During the 1940s and 1950s, many segregated, private schools developed and demonstrated again and again that students with challenges were quite capable of learning if given proper instruction. During the 1960s through 1980, educational opportunities for students with challenges became a public education responsibility. Many segregated public schools, such as special education cooperatives, came into existence in response to Public Law 94-142 of 1975.

During the 1980s, the pendulum swung toward inclusion as increasing numbers of students with challenges were placed in regular classes in public schools. These students, however, were often placed in age-inappropriate settings: For instance, an older child with special needs was placed with younger children working on similar goals. In the 1990s, the pendulum continues to swing toward inclusion as increasing numbers of professionals and parents advocate total inclusion. They seek to have all children, even those with severe challenges, educated in regular, age-appropriate classes in neighborhood schools.

At this point, it should be mentioned that the movement toward total inclusion is somewhat different from *mainstreaming,* a popular phrase from 1975 through the 1980s. In the past, students with disabilities were mainstreamed into regular classes when they had the skills needed to participate in the *traditional curriculum.* With inclusion, the diverse needs of students in the regular class may require that *expanded curricula* be taught. "Inclusion does not mean that all students necessarily work toward or are expected to achieve the same educational goals using the same instructional methods" (Block, 1994). (A later section of this chapter, entitled "Modify Curricula," provides further ideas on expanding the curriculum.)

Is inclusion "dumping"? No, *inclusion does not mean dumping.* Can dumping be masked in the name of inclusion? Yes. To place students with challenges into regular physical education classes without the necessary support systems for their proper education is dumping. Dumping is unfair to the student, the classmates, and the teacher. A single teacher, especially one with large classes, cannot teach successfully alone. (A later section in this chapter, entitled "Collaborate," provides further ideas for collaborating with other professionals and parents.)

Is there a law requiring inclusion? No. *Inclusion is an educational philosophy, not a law.* The rationale for inclusion is the philosophical position that it is a *right* of children with challenges to be educated in society and to participate fully with everyone else. Although inclusion is not a law, legal mandates for the equitable treatment of all students in physical education have been important influences in the development of the philosophy of inclusion. The following section will highlight some of these laws.

Legislation Regarding Inclusive Physical Education

The history of educational opportunities for people with disabilities in this country parallels the development of opportunities for females and people of color in the United States. Originally, public education in the United States was primarily for European-American boys and men. European-American girls and women only gradually gained educational opportunities well after their male counterparts. In 1954, people of color gained the legal right to an integrated education for the first time. Today, students with challenges seek this same right, but as history indicates, change comes slowly.

An important precedent leading to inclusion was set in the Supreme Court school desegregation case, *Brown v. Board of Education,* in 1954. This landmark case for the integration of schools in the U.S. presented a rationale that continues to influence the issues of inclusion. The court explained that where a state seeks to provide the opportunity for an education, the education must be equal for all.

Many subsequent pieces of legislation have their roots in this 1954 decision that a separate education is inherently unequal. In 1972, Title IX of the Education Amendment of 1972 legislated gender equity in education. Title VI of the Civil Rights Act of 1964 legislates equal educational opportunities for students with limited English proficiency (LEP). The Rehabilitation Act of 1973, the Education of All Handicapped Children Act of 1975 (EHA; Pub. L. No. 94-142), the Education of All Handicapped Children Act Amendments of 1986 (EAHCA; Pub. L. No. 99-457), and the newer Education of the Handicapped Act Amendments of 1990 (IDEA; Pub. L. No. 101-476), along with the Americans with Disabilities Act (ADA) of the same year (Pub. L. No. 101-336), have become cornerstones of educational and civil rights for individuals with disabilities. Together, these pieces of legislation form the legal mandate for the inclusion and equitable treatment of all students in physical education. An overview of some of these laws is presented in Figure 4.1.

In what follows, gender equity will be discussed first, followed by equal educational opportunity for students with limited English proficiency. The chapter will conclude with an examination of the educational rights of students with challenges.

Gender

Title IX of the Educational Amendments of 1972 is considered to be the mainstay of gender equity in education. It states, "No person shall, on the basis of sex, be excluded from participation in, be denied the benefits of, or be subjected to discrimination under any . . . education program or activity that . . . benefits from Federal financial assistance" (Education Amendments of 1972, p. 444). Title IX seeks to ensure that all students, regardless of gender, have opportunities to benefit from instruction in physical education. This means that all students, grades K through 12, must have *access* to physical education and have *equal opportunities* within physical education. All physical education instruction must be *coeducational*, with the lone exception of units in human sexuality. Requirements for participation of both sexes must be the same, with evaluation based on objective standards that do not adversely impact students of one sex.

It is illegal to establish separate male and female physical education departments. It is also illegal to discriminate on the basis of sex in hiring physical education teachers. And, all students must have access to instructional facilities (Project SEE, 1986). Covertly managing roll lists and offering program choices in which students are allowed to choose between aerobics and touch football results in sex-divided groups. Locating the weight training room where the only access is through the boys'

locker room effectively denies girls access to the weight training facility.

Limited English Proficiency

The language counterpart of Title IX, Title VI of the Civil Rights Act of 1964, was interpreted to extend equal educational opportunities to students with limited English proficiency. Ten years later another law was passed that specifically addressed bilingual education. The Equal Educational Opportunities Act (Education Amendments of 1974) states, "No State shall deny equal educational opportunity to an individual on account of his or her race, color, sex, or national origin, by . . . (f) the failure by an educational agency to take appropriate action to overcome language barriers that impede equal participation by its students in its instructional programs" (p. 484).

Challenging Conditions

Title IX and Title VI are important laws on gender and language equity. IDEA, which stands for the Individuals with Disabilities Education Act (as previously mentioned, the Education of the Handicapped Act Amendments of 1990), and its precursor, EHA (the Education of All Handicapped Children Act of 1975), are the most significant laws regarding the education of persons with disabilities. IDEA guarantees the right of every child with a challenging condition to a *free and appropriate public education*. Five major provisions of these laws follow.

1. Physical education is required under IDEA. Special education is specifically defined to include instruction in physical education. *The term special education means specifically designed instruction, at no cost to the parent, to meet the unique needs of a handicapped child including . . . instruction in physical education* (IDEA, 1990, p. 1103). Every child with a challenge is required to receive instruction in physical education—even if all other students in the same school do not receive such instruction.

2. Physical education is defined as "(i) . . . the development of: (A) physical and motor fitness; (B) fundamental motor skills and patterns; and (C) skills in aquatics, dance, individual and group games, and sports (including intramural and lifetime sports). (ii) The term includes special physical education, adapted physical education, movement education, and motor development" (Education of All Handicapped Children Act of 1975, 1977, p. 42480). Therefore, keeping score, serving as a human marker, handing out towels, or going to the library does not constitute instruction or participation in physical education.

Name of Law:	Title VI of the Civil Rights Act of of 1964
Number and Date:	PL 88-352
Population Addressed:	Students with limited English proficiency (LEP)
Major Focus of Law:	Provides for equal educational opportunities for students with LEP
Name of Law:	Title IX of the Education Amendments of 1972
Number and Date:	PL 92-318
Population Addressed:	Girls and women
Major Focus of Law:	Provides for equal opportunities in education for girls and women
Name of Law:	Education of All Handicapped Children Act of 1975 (EHA)
Number and Date:	PL 94-142
Population Addressed:	Children with disabilities, 3-21 years of age
Major Focus of Law:	Provides for free, appropriate, public education to students with disabilities
Name of Law:	Education of All Handicapped Children Act Amendments of 1986 (EAHCA)
Number and Date:	PL 99-457
Population Addressed:	Children with disabilities, 0-5 years of age
Major Focus of Law:	Extends the educational rights of EHA to infants and toddlers with disabilities
Name of Law:	Education of the Handicapped Act Amendments of 1990 (IDEA)
Number and Date:	PL 101-476
Population Addressed:	Children with disabilities, 0-21 years of age
Major Focus of Law:	Replaces and extends provisions of EHA to guarantee educational rights of students with disabilities
Name of Law:	Americans with Disabilities Act of 1990 (ADA)
Number and Date:	PL 101-336
Population Addressed:	Individuals of all ages with disabilities
Major Focus of Law:	Provides for equal opportunity in employment, community living, and education for individuals with disabilities

Figure 4.1. Legislation regarding inclusive physical education.

Note. From ''Guidelines for Appropriate Curriculum Content and Assessment in Programs Serving Children Ages 3 Through 8,'' by the National Association for the Education of Young Children and the National Association of Early Childhood Specialists in State Departments of Education, 1991, *Young Children*, **46**, pp. 32-33. Copyright 1991 by the National Association for the Education of Young Children. Adapted by permission.

3. The individualized educational program (IEP) is the mechanism provided by IDEA for tailoring an educational program to the specific needs of each student with a challenge. An IEP is developed annually for each student by a group of people that includes the child's parent or legal guardian, teacher(s), school administrator, and the child, if appropriate. The IEP must contain five components: (a) the student's present level of performance, (b) annual goals and short-term instructional objectives, (c) educational services to be provided for the child, (d) starting and ending dates of services, and (e) evaluation criteria and procedures for determining whether the program objectives have been achieved. IDEA requires that writing the IEP be a joint effort

between parents or legal guardians and professionals.

4. Another hallmark of IDEA is parent or legal guardian participation in the major educational decisions regarding the child. Should the parent(s) and school personnel be unable to agree on the best educational approach for the child, with the right of due process, an impartial judge can make the decision regarding the child's educational program.

5. Inclusion is consistent with the spirit and practices of IDEA and EHA. Both laws promote placing students with their typical peers wherever possible and educating children with challenges in the least restrictive environment. The least restrictive environment is defined as the following:

(1) That to the maximum extent appropriate, handicapped children, including children in public or private institutions, are educated with children who are not handicapped, and

(2) That special classes, separate schooling or other removal of handicapped children from the regular educational environment occurs only when the nature or severity of the handicap is such that education in regular classes with the use of supplementary aids and services cannot be achieved satisfactorily (Education for All Handicapped Children Act Amendments of 1986, Sec.121a.550).

When EHA was passed, it only covered individuals who were 3 to 21 years of age. Later, the Education of All Handicapped Children Act Amendments (EAHCA) of 1986 (Public Law 99-457) was added to the foundation of EHA. These amendments renewed the provisions of EHA and extended the services to infants and toddlers between birth and 3 years of age who need early intervention services. The Individualized Family Service Plan (IFSP) was introduced with the amendments. The IFSP, similar to an IEP, is a mechanism for working directly with families in providing early intervention services.

EHA, IDEA, and EAHCA all address *educational rights*. Their legislative counterpart in the arena of civil rights of individuals with disabilities is the Americans with Disabilities Act (ADA) of 1990 (Public Law 101-336), which replaces and includes all important aspects of its precursor, Section 504 of the Rehabilitation Act of 1973. ADA requires that persons with disabilities be provided equal opportunities in all aspects of life—at work, school, play, and home. Facilities must be made readily accessible. Otherwise qualified individuals may not be denied access to physical education and athletic programs just because they are not able to perform all of the activities (Eichstaedt & Kalakian, 1992). Sanctions for noncompliance include the loss of all federal and state moneys.

Inclusion as a Civil Right

In summary, Title IX mandates an equal opportunity in physical education for girls and boys. Title VI mandates an equal educational opportunity for students with limited English proficiency. IDEA, EAHCA, and EHA form the framework for providing physical education to students with challenges. And the rationale that a "separate education is inherently unequal," found in *Brown v. Board of Education* in 1954, is the basis for inclusion as a civil right. Although the educational philosophy of inclusion is not specifically mandated in any of these laws, it is very consistent with the requirement in IDEA that a child be educated in the least restrictive environment with typical peers to the maximum extent

appropriate. This sentiment is reflected in the following quote about inclusion, referred to as integration herein:

Is integration a good idea? . . . Bob Bogdan suggests it's a bit like asking whether Tuesday is a good idea. We've all had good Tuesdays and bad Tuesdays. It all depends on what we make of Tuesday or any other day of the week. So it is with integration. It does not mean, "Do away with special services." It does not say, "Integrate, but do not give the necessary support services to the teachers to make it work." (Center for Human Policy, 1985, p. 19)

Strategies for Inclusion

The question is not "Do we teach all children together?" but rather "*How* do we teach all children together?" The remainder of this chapter presents suggestions for teaching in an inclusive manner. The suggestions are organized around three ideas: (a) Promote acceptance among all students; (b) modify curricula to promote inclusion; and (c) get support through collaboration.

Acceptance

In teaching diverse students, plan instruction that promotes acceptance, encompassing the acceptance of students of both genders, diverse races, cultures, or languages, or individual differences reflecting their challenging conditions. Teachers need to *plan* for promoting acceptance because acceptance rarely happens on its own. Specific strategies for promoting acceptance follow.

• Prepare an environment in which individual differences are respected and valued. "When class norms allow name calling, verbal harassment or poor sport behavior to go unchallenged, students learn to defend themselves from embarrassment by either attacking classmates first, choosing only 'safe' activities or withdrawing from participation altogether" (Griffin, 1989, p. 20).

In contrast, an atmosphere more accepting of individual differences is established when teachers

– challenge any disrespectful behavior toward other students and use positive language, free of sarcasm and derogatory comments;

– establish an atmosphere in which mistakes are permitted, acknowledging that they as teachers also make mistakes; and

– encourage students to attain their personal best.

• Confront differences by encouraging students to ask questions. Combat ignorance by encouraging discussions of differences in positive ways, rather than pretending no differences exist. Strategies that have worked for some teachers include providing opportunities for students of diverse races, cultures, and language to share, in a positive manner, information about their differences. The teacher plays a crucial role in this through *modeling* acceptance and showing interest in differences. A teacher might incorporate many dance styles in an aerobics lesson to show applications of fitness to dance. Or, the teacher might introduce and provide a role model for a sport or an activity that reaches beyond gender stereotypes to reinforce diversity. For example, female teachers can offer instruction in weightlifting; male teachers can offer instruction in field hockey.

Be sensitive to the fact that ignorance of other students' various challenging conditions can cause unnecessary concern, especially for young children. For example, classmates may not wish to stand next to a child with autism for fear they might ''catch'' it. Others might worry that the classmate with cerebral palsy may die from it. Class discussions facilitated by the instructor help reveal such concerns and provide the factual information that can quickly dispel unnecessary fears.

• Simulate challenging conditions. Provide typical students with the opportunity to assume a challenging condition for a few minutes or an entire day. Allow typical students to open a door while in a wheelchair, write while wearing oversize gloves, or read while wearing glasses coated with Vaseline to simulate physical, learning, or visual impairments. Taken alone, a Disability Awareness Day can suggest tokenism or patronization; but when a Disability Awareness Day serves as an introduction to inclusion that is modeled every day of the school year, it can be a powerful teaching tool.

• Provide positive role models. Invite positive role models to speak, demonstrate, or teach to the class or the entire school. Many athletes with challenging conditions are eager to describe their sports experiences to others. Contact one of the national sport organizations for athletes with disabilities (listed in adapted physical education texts) to identify athletes who live nearby; or show a film or videotape of a role model if a local athlete is not available. Similarly, positive role models among girls and women, people of diverse races, ages, and cultures, or those who speak languages other than English may be available and appropriate for promoting acceptance. Although much of contemporary culture focuses on highly visible persona such as super heroes, sports stars, and television stars, students may also respond positively to heroes who are not extraordinary. Look within the students' environment for role models whose circumstances and activities promote acceptance. For example, consider the school maintenance worker who does not speak English and has won medals through

competition in 10K road races in the Senior Games.

• Malicious or sexual harassment is illegal, adversely affects the learning climate, and is unacceptable behavior. Lead a discussion about why people tease and why they make derogatory comments about others. Help students realize that such behavior most likely reflects insecurity in the person who is harassing others.

• Identify and eliminate bias. The first step in eliminating bias is the recognition of bias in its many forms. Six prevalent forms of bias that might appear in materials, environment, and interactions are presented in Figure 4.2.

• Embark on a journey of self-examination. The preceding six suggestions may be helpful in establishing a classroom atmosphere that promotes acceptance, but efforts in all of the above areas can be quickly undone if teachers hold attitudes that are not accepting of individual differences. ''Unless there is willingness to risk the discovery of personal prejudices, there is no reason to expect physical education classes to be equitable'' (Griffin, 1989, p. 19). The grid presented in Table 4.1 is designed to help teachers evaluate their own attitudes regarding gender and race equity. Although acceptance is an important first step in promoting inclusion, curricular requirements also need to be examined to identify what aspects of the curriculum do and do not promote inclusion.

Modify Curricula

Griffin (1989) has conducted extensive research in gender equity in physical education classes. She has concluded that when the class exhibits the following characteristics, there is little likelihood of achieving equitable student participation.

1. An overemphasis on competition and competitive activities
2. A majority of class time spent in noninstructional game play
3. Inequitable and disrespectful interactions among students
4. Inequitable participation among students
5. Student ability is not taken into account in organizing instruction or game play (Griffin, 1989, p. 21)

''In contrast, there are also characteristics common to physical education programs that have successfully implemented equitable instruction within coed classes'' (Griffin, 1989, p. 21).

These characteristics include teachers who

1. are committed to making coed classes operate equitably;
2. work together to learn and try new activities;

Invisibility: Certain groups are underrepresented in curricular materials. The significant omission of women and minority groups has become so great as to imply that these groups are of less value, importance, and significance in our society.

Stereotyping: By assigning traditional and rigid roles or attributes to a group, instructional materials stereotype and limit the abilities and potential of that group. Stereotyping denies students a knowledge of the diversity, complexity, and variation of any group of individuals. Children who see themselves portrayed only in stereotypic ways may internalize these stereotypes and fail to develop their own unique abilities, interests, and full potential.

Imbalance/Selectivity: Textbooks perpetuate bias by presenting only one interpretation of an issue, situation, or group of people. This imbalanced account restricts the knowledge of students regarding the varied perspectives that may apply to a particular situation. Through selective presentation of materials, textbooks distort reality and ignore complex and differing viewpoints. As a result, millions of students have been given limited perspective concerning the contributions, struggles, and participation of women and minorities in our society.

Unreality: Textbooks frequently present an unrealistic portrayal of our history and our contemporary life experience. Controversial topics are glossed over and discussions of discrimination and prejudice are avoided. This unrealistic coverage denies children the information they need to recognize, understand, and perhaps some day conquer the problems that plague our society.

Fragmentation/Isolation: By separating issues related to minorities and women from the main body of the text, instructional materials imply that these issues are less important than and not a part of the cultural mainstream.

Linguistic bias: Curricular materials reflect the discriminatory nature of our language. Masculine terms and pronouns, ranging from *our forefathers* to the generic *he*, deny the participation of women in our society. Further, occupations such as *mailman* are given masculine labels that deny the legitimacy of women working in these fields. Imbalance of word order and lack of parallel terms that refer to females and males are also forms of linguistic bias.

Figure 4.2.   The forms of bias.
Note. From *Sex Equity Handbook for Schools* (pp. 72-73) by M. P. Sadker and D. M. Sadker, 1980, 1988, New York: Longman Company. Copyright 1980, 1988 by David Sadker. Reprinted with permission. David and Myra Sadker, American University, recently published *Failing at Fairness: How Our Schools Cheat Girls* (Touchstone Press), 1995.

3. are willing to learn and try new activities;
4. are willing to examine and change their own stereotyped expectations of students; and
5. have administrative support and staff development resources available for help in identifying and solving instructional problems. (Griffin, 1989, p. 21)

Inclusive and equitable curricula are essential in physical education. If a curriculum that is based on competition and noninstructional sports/game play does not lend itself to inclusion and equity, what curricula are inclusive and equitable? Begin with a curriculum that embodies developmentally appropriate physical education practices for children.

The physical education curriculum has an obvious scope and sequence based on goals and objectives that are appropriate for all children. It includes a balance of skills, concepts, games, educational gymnastics, rhythms and dance experiences designed to enhance the cognitive, motor, affective, and physical fitness development of every child. An inappropriate curriculum lacks developed goals and objectives and is based primarily on the teacher's interests, preferences, and background rather than those of the children. For example, the curriculum consists primarily of large group games. *All* children are involved in activities that allow them to remain continuously active. It is inappropriate for activity time to be limited because children are waiting in lines for a turn in relay races, to be chosen for a team, or because of limited equipment or playing games such as Duck, Duck, Goose. Children are not to be organized into large groups where getting a turn is based on individual competitiveness or aggressive behavior. Children are also not to be eliminated with no chance to reenter the activity or made to sit for long periods of time. Activities emphasize self-improvement, participation, and cooperation instead of winning and losing. Teachers

Table 4.1 Program Equity Assessment Grid

Program categories	Discriminatory	Biased	Fair	Affirmative
Student-to-student interactions	Students engage in name-calling and harassment based on gender/racial stereotypes	Gender/race-segregated groups chosen by students	Students work respectfully in mixed gender/race groups	Students choose mixed groups and monitor own stereotyped interactions
Teacher-to-student interactions	Teacher intentionally interacts differently with students based on race or gender	Teacher unintentionally interacts differently with students based on race or gender	Teacher monitors interactions with students to avoid gender/race-stereotyped interactions	Teacher interacts with students to intentionally envision inclusive ways to compete or cooperate in sport activities
Game play	Teacher sets up race- or gender-segregated class games or teams	Teacher allows student selected gender/race segregation in games or teams or allows inequitable participation in mixed game	Teacher monitors and redistributes inequitable participation or segregation by gender or race	Teacher takes action to help students envision inclusive ways to compete in sport activities
Instructional strategies	Teacher sets up gender- or race-segregated instructional groups	Teacher allows students to segregate instructional groups by race or gender; doesn't provide a variety of instructional tasks to match differing student abilities	Teacher organizes instruction to maximize successful learning for all students, taking ability into account	Teacher provides extra help, encouragement, and refinement for lower-skilled students
Curriculum	Classes segregated by gender; little variety in activities; different activities for girls and boys	Teacher allows segregated classes that result from setting up competing gender-stereotyped activity choices (floor hockey vs. gymnastics)	Teacher plans curriculum to encourage or require mixed gender class, a variety of activities are offered	Teacher plans curriculum to encourage or require participation in "cross-gender" activities
Teacher role modeling	Male and female teachers of different races rarely interact with each other, white males hold leadership positions on staff	Teachers only teach activities associated with their gender stereotype	All teachers work together collaboratively, teach a variety of activities, share leadership	Teacher intentionally develops teaching competencies in activities with other gender stereotypes

Discriminatory practices are actions and policies that intentionally use gender or race as salient and legitimate criteria to segregate or restrict participation. **Biased** practices are unintentional actions and policies that either allow or encourage the use of gender or race to segregate or restrict participation. Biased practices are often the result of inaction, but discriminatory practices are the result of intentional action. **Fair** practices are intentional actions and policies that require or encourage equitable participation, respectful interaction and individual achievement for all students, without regard to gender or race. **Affirmative** practices are intentional actions and policies designed to encourage students to move beyond their own gender or race-stereotyped expectations of themselves and others by providing extra opportunities and special reinforcement for student actions that run counter to gender and race activities.

Note. From "Assessment of Equitable Instructional Practices in the Gym," by P. Griffin, 1989, CAHPER Journal, **55**, pp. 21-22. Reprinted by permission.

are aware of the nature of competition and do not *require* higher levels of competition from children before they are ready. For example, children are allowed to choose between a game in which the score is kept and one that is just for practice. (adapted from COPEC, n.d., pp. 6-7, 12-13, 16)

Several curricula and materials provide excellent direction to teachers seeking to implement an inclusive and equitable curriculum consistent with COPEC's statement on developmentally appropriate physical education practices for children. At the preschool and elementary levels, the books *Follow Me* (Torbert, 1993) and *Follow Me Too* (Torbert & Schneider, 1993) provide activities that allow a variety of challenges within a single activity so children may enter play at their own comfort level. For elementary physical education, the book *Elementary Physical Education: Toward Inclusion* (Morris, 1980) provides games as well as a framework for modifying them to promote the active and successful participation of all students.

Movement education ideas have been available for nearly three decades; yet too often teachers, who may not be physical education specialists, slip into traditional games like kickball and relays. Solving movement problems allows for open-ended responses in a noncompetitive environment that accommodates individual differences. An example of an elementary text with movement education-oriented lesson plans is *Children Moving: A Reflective Approach to Teaching Physical Education* (Graham, Holt-Hale, & Parker, 1993). The *Leaps and Bounds* (Hawaii State Department of Education, 1982) video series also utilizes the movement education approach for primary grades. For elementary and secondary levels, an adventure-based education, such as Project Adventure (Rohnke, 1989), not only eliminates competition but actively promotes cooperation and trust. Use of such a curriculum can facilitate affirmative practices that encourage students to move beyond their own stereotypic expectations. Further curricular suggestions may be found in chapter 2.

When the activities offered in a program lack variety and flexibility, the same students experience success and the same students experience frustration unit after unit. There must be enough variety in curricular offerings so that every student can find an activity she or he enjoys and can participate in successfully. (Griffin, 1989, p. 20)

Develop thinking, meaning-centered, interconnected curricula through collaborating with teachers in other subject areas to make connections across the curriculum. Making these connections reinforces learning in both subject areas. For example, have students analyze their own or the squad's data by creating graphs and calculating percentiles and averages as part of the track unit.

Write articles about movement and sports stories. Learn the history or traditions of sport and activity throughout the world and across cultures. Debate issues of class and economics and discuss how public and personal sport issues affect people's lives. Think critically about what the Olympic movement 50 to 100 years from now should be like.

What about students who may have severe challenges? The above curricular examples may not be appropriate for these students. To accommodate all students, teachers can expand curricular options in physical education. Inclusion promises a basic change in regular physical education teachers' job descriptions. The assumption changes from one in which the regular physical education teacher is employed to deliver the ''normal'' curriculum to students—to the assumption that *the teacher is employed to teach curricula appropriate for each of the students placed in the class, and that the curricula may vary among students depending on their needs*. The need for more expanded curricula becomes especially clear when contemplating teaching a student with a severe challenge. When a noncompetitive curriculum with an emphasis on personal best and individualized instruction is already in place, it is easier to also include a student who learns at a different rate and in a different manner.

There are curricular options for regular physical education classes that may accommodate students with severe challenges—and other students who do not have identifiable disabilities but who are not experiencing success in the regular curriculum. These options are: the same curriculum, a multilevel curriculum, curriculum overlap, and alternate curriculum. The following outline is adapted from Giangreco, Cloninger, and Iverson (1990).

1. Same curriculum: ''Students who pose intensive challenges can participate in regular class activities by doing what all the other students are doing'' (p. 15). For example, all students pursue the same objective of swimming with or without flotation devices. This curriculum includes the student with intensive needs as well as the many typical youth who cannot swim due to lack of instruction or the opportunity to practice.

2. Multilevel curriculum: ''Multilevel curriculum/instruction occurs when students are all involved in a lesson within the same curriculum area but are pursuing different objectives at multiple levels, based on their individual needs'' (p. 15). For example, to improve cardiovascular endurance, a student

- who uses a wheelchair does laps around the hardtop to his or her capacity;
- with visual impairment chooses to jump rope in place without the need for any assistance;

- who enjoys jumping rope also selects this form of cardiovascular exercise, perhaps creating patterns or rhythms;
- with a short attention span works with a partner who provides prompts to keep the student running around the track;
- with cerebral palsy completes part of one lap around the track using a walker; and
- who excels in running completes several laps around the track.

All students are pursuing cardiovascular fitness outcomes, but at different levels within the same activity or lesson. Following the principle of natural proportions, it is likely there would only be one student with a severe challenge in any class. Adaptations for several students with a variety of challenges are provided in this section for illustration only.

3. Curriculum overlap: As mentioned in Giangreco, et al. (1990), curriculum overlap occurs when a group of students work in the same lesson but pursue different curriculum areas. For instance, during warmups, any of the following could occur:

- Most students complete the same warm-ups;
- Every student creates, defines, and refines a style of push-ups and practices one that is strength building;
- A student with cerebral palsy receives physical therapy from the therapist in the gymnasium during the warm-up time. This student does the specific exercise needed to promote range of motion, so not all students are following the same curriculum during warm-ups.

An example of curricular overlap during instruction in basketball skills follows:

- Most students practice dribbling and shooting;
- Highly skilled students practice dribbling and shooting while closely guarded;
- A student with a severe challenge who is working on the functional skill of walking while carrying an object practices during the basketball lesson by walking while carrying a basketball. (Block & Vogler, 1994)

In other lessons, the student with special needs may pursue other objectives such as communication, following directions, or moving in his or her personal space without touching others. "When curriculum overlap occurs, the regular class activity is primarily a vehicle used to attain other goals. This approach opens many opportunities for students to participate in classes previously considered 'inappropriate.' These settings are selected because they offer opportunities to address identified needs" (Giangreco et al., 1990, p. 15).

4. Alternate curriculum: "*Occasionally* students may need to pursue alternative activities if the regular class does not offer reasonable opportunities to address relevant learning outcomes through multilevel curriculum/instruction or curriculum overlapping" (Giangreco et al., 1990, p. 15). For example, during a paper and pencil test on fitness concepts, a student with a special need may instead practice the functional skill of crossing streets with the assistance of a paraprofessional. This alternative may be needed because the regular class does not offer sufficient opportunities to practice pedestrian skills. In most cases, the needs of this student can be met in the regular classroom with a commitment to creative planning and inclusive education. Alternate curriculum would only be used occasionally.

This section on curricular considerations concludes with three thoughts. The first concern is the use of physical education classes only for the attainment of social goals. There have been instances where students with challenges have been placed in regular physical education classes without the support systems necessary to achieve success. Such placements have been justified on the grounds that these students are in the class only for socialization. The teacher has been told not to be concerned if unable to teach these students any motor skills. Such practices and statements patronize students with severe challenges by dismissing their needs to develop motor skills and by not recognizing the contribution physical education makes toward a healthy, active lifestyle.

A second thought focuses on the partial participation, not exclusion, of students with challenges. The principle of partial participation states that just because a student may not be able to participate fully in all of the activities of the class does not justify the exclusion of the person from the class. Partial participation is an option. For example, a student with severe behavioral challenges who is easily distracted might be able to attend the regular physical education class for only a few minutes at a time. Rather than exclude the student from the entire class, this student could join the class for warm-up and cool-down activities but leave the gymnasium with a paraprofessional and follow an alternate curriculum for the middle of the lesson. Gradually, as the student becomes more accustomed to the gymnasium and the regular class, the length of time the student attends may increase.

The final thought considers the issue of class size. There are far too many instances where a single physical education teacher at the secondary level is assigned classes of 60 or more students, often with freshmen and seniors in the same class. Similar situations are all too common at the elementary level where two classes of 25 students each are combined for their physical education instruction. If 25 students are deemed the maximum class size for other instructional classes, then that should be the maximum for physical education classes as well. Sixty students are too many for instruction in physical education, regardless of what the learning characteristics of the students may be.

Large classes create unsafe and potential liability situations. Classes of this size also suggest the expectation that no significant instruction will occur, but rather only supervised recreation will take place. With regard to a student with a challenge, the focus becomes how to include that student in supervised recreation—because there is probably no instruction occurring for anybody. Advocacy for smaller classes that are better designed for instruction becomes critical. Thus, the third and final section of this chapter addresses how to get support through working with others and offers suggestions for how to advocate for necessary support systems.

Collaborate

As the composition of physical education classes becomes richer through diversity, changes become necessary in the way teachers and administrators approach teaching. Collaboration becomes more than just a nice idea. It becomes an essential strategy for meeting the needs of students. In physical education, there are a number of people who can collaborate with the regular physical educator to provide for the needs of all students. The first step the physical educator must take is to recognize that it is all right to ask for support and assistance.

There are many individuals with whom regular physical educators may wish to collaborate to provide for the needs of students:

1. Collaborate with an *adapted physical education resource specialist*, a person educated in adapting curricula and adapting teaching methods to meet the needs of students with challenges. Share ideas for adapting activities and for increasing the number of teachers in the gymnasium through the use of peer tutors, volunteers, paraprofessionals, or team teaching with an adapted physical educator.
2. Collaborate with the *students' other teachers*, who might have successful teaching methods and insights to share.
3. Collaborate with the students' *physical therapist or occupational therapist* and other health service providers, who can share suggestions regarding positioning, assistive devices, exercises, and so forth.
4. Collaborate with *school administrators* to brainstorm about support systems needed and how they might be provided.
5. Collaborate with *parents or caregivers*, who have rich stores of knowledge about their children's likes, dislikes, past experiences, and future aspirations.
6. Collaborate with *other students in the school*, who may serve as peer tutors.
7. Collaborate with teachers of English as a Second Language and other language specialists to use sheltered English programs, small group work with like-language learners, buddies as translators, teachers learning key words in other languages, and extra wait time to include students with diverse languages.

In addition to collaborating with others, physical educators may need direct assistance in the gymnasium. Paraprofessionals are one source of this assistance. Paraprofessionals are among the most reliable sources of assistance because they are employees, not volunteers. Although it may be more difficult to obtain the assistance of a paraprofessional because of cost factors, if a paraprofessional is needed in order for the student to participate safely and successfully in physical education, request the services of this individual through the IEP.

Sometimes a paraprofessional has already been assigned to assist the student throughout the school day. If the paraprofessional assists in all other classes except physical education (that time often serves as the paraprofessional's break period), do not accept the lack of a paraprofessional in physical education. The school district is obligated to provide the services listed on the IEP. If the child's IEP states that the child is to receive the assistance of a paraprofessional throughout the day, then this includes physical education. Request the paraprofessional and enlist the support of a parent or legal guardian in getting this help. The IEP is also the mechanism for making requests for any other support systems needed to make the inclusion of the child in regular physical education successful.

When the assistance of a paraprofessional is needed, state specifically what the paraprofessional is to do. It is also important to request the planning time to help the paraprofessional prepare for his or her role and responsibilities (Kelly, 1994). Avoid pointing out the student to the paraprofessional (or volunteer) with whom the person is to work, or talking about the student in the student's presence. Ask the paraprofessional to work with a group of students that coincidentally includes the student with the challenge that the paraprofessional is assigned to help.

Consider alternating tasks with the paraprofessional. After the teacher has led the lesson a few times, permit the paraprofessional to lead the lesson while the teacher assists individual students. This offers the paraprofessional the opportunity to assume additional responsibilities and allows the teacher to work individually with students. Alternating roles does much to foster excellent paraprofessional cooperation.

If integration is the goal, hold adult presence to a minimum when working with students. For errands, avoid sending an adult to accompany a student. Instead, send a friend. More interactions occur when peers accompany students. If the adult is necessary for safety, let the adult accompany the student and friend as an observer. Also, encourage students to travel in pairs rather than in larger groups throughout the school. Casual interactions among students occur more readily when there are just a few students who are not in the presence of adults. This suggestion applies to all groups within a school.

In addition to paraprofessionals, imaginative teachers have located other sources of assistance in the gymnasium. These include volunteers, caregivers, high school future teacher club members, other students who are peer coaches, retired people in the community, preservice physical education students, and classmates. When working with classmates, ask students in the class to help plan adaptations. Ask ''How can we make sure (student's name) is included in this lesson? How can we make (student's name) a meaningful part of this activity?'' To foster student friendships, speak in terms of friendships rather than peer tutor relationships.

Caregivers as Partners and Advocates

Inclusion does not work when students with special needs are simply dumped in a regular class with minimum support for the teacher. From this author's experience, there are more examples of students with challenges being dumped into regular physical education classes than examples of students being included through a thoughtful process that provides appropriate support systems to the teacher. Inclusion works, but it takes preplanning and commitment of personnel and resources. *Teachers and administrators can choose to be proactive and advocate for appropriate services.* Students' caregivers are important partners in efforts to advocate for appropriate services. Get to know the caregivers of students and enlist their help. Involved caregivers can make their children's needs known. Teachers and administrators who are knowledgeable about inclusion and the legal responsibility of the school district to provide quality physical education to these children can share this information with the children's caregivers. Caregivers need to be informed that they

have the right to provide input into their child's education through the IEP process and that they can speak with teachers, administrators, and members of the Board of Education.

In the best possible world, those making these efforts would be rewarded with the appropriate support systems needed to serve students. Realistically, however, teachers often find that sometimes appropriate support systems may not be forthcoming for various reasons. Change takes time. Bear in mind, however, that proactive efforts begun now may yield significant improvement in support systems 3 to 5 years from now.

Caregivers can request that support systems, such as the consultation services of an adapted physical educator or the assistance of a paraprofessional, be made available to their child's physical education teacher so that the child's needs and those of typical peers may be met in the regular physical education class. It is not necessary that all caregivers advocate for their children. A few articulate, determined caregivers can advocate for appropriate services for their children and, indirectly, for all children. These caregivers can set the precedent for providing support systems for inclusion.

Conclusion

In conclusion, the pendulum continues to swing along the educational continuum toward inclusion. Strategies such as promoting acceptance, expanding curricular options, and collaborating with others may help teachers as they instruct diverse students in physical education. Physical education instruction is at its best when it provides a welcoming and supportive educational environment, one that is respectful and appreciative of individual differences, and in which all students participate fully.

''. . . Inclusion emphasizes our commonalty and our sameness. We do not need to be viewed as so different that we cannot be educated together, through alternate methods perhaps, but all together in the same school and class'' (Craft, 1994, p. 55).

Acknowledgment

The author wishes to gratefully acknowledge the contribution of supporting information and context regarding issues of diversity in physical education provided by Phyllis Lerner, Staff Developer, interweave, 838 11th Street, Apt. 102, Santa Monica, CA 90403.

References

Block, M.E. (1994). *A teacher's guide to including students with disabilities in regular physical education.*

Baltimore: Paul H. Brookes.

Block, M., & Vogler, W. (1994). Inclusion in regular physical education: The research base. *Journal of Physical Education, Recreation, and Dance (JOPERD)*, **65**(1), 40-44.

Brown v. Board of Education, 347 U.S. 483 (1954).

Brown, L., Nisbet, J., Ford, A., Sweet, M., Shiraga, B., York, J., & Loomis, R. (1983). The critical need for nonschool instruction in educational programs for severely handicapped students. *Journal of the Association for the Severely Handicapped*, **8**, 71-77.

Center for Human Policy at Syracuse University. (1985). *Preparing for life: A manual on the least restrictive environment*. Prepared for the Technical Assistance Parent Programs (TAPP) Project, 19-21.

Civil Rights Act of 1964, Pub. L. No. 88-352, § 601, 78 Stat. 252 (1965).

Council on Physical Education for Children (COPEC) (no date). *Developmentally appropriate physical education practices for children*. Reston, VA: American Alliance for Health, Physical Education, Recreation and Dance.

Craft, D.H. (1994). Implications of inclusion for physical education. *Journal of Physical Education, Recreation and Dance (JOPERD)*, **65**(1), 54-55.

DePauw, K. (1986). Toward progressive inclusion and acceptance: Implications for physical education. *Adapted Physical Activity Quarterly*, **3**, 1-5.

Education Amendments of 1972, Pub. L. No. 92-318, § 901, 86 Stat. 235 (1973).

Education Amendments of 1974, Pub. L. No. 93-380, § 204, 88 Stat. 484 (1975).

Education of All Handicapped Children Act of 1975. *Code of Federal Regulations*. 34 CFR § 300.17. The Office of the Federal Register (1977).

Education of All Handicapped Children Act Amendments of 1986. *Code of Federal Regulations*. 34 CFR § 300.500. The Office of the Federal Register (1986).

Education of the Handicapped Act Amendments of 1990, Pub. L. No. 101-476, § 101.04, Stat. 1103 (1991).

Eichstaedt, C., & Kalakian, L. (1992). *Developmental/adapted physical education: Making ability count*. New York: Macmillan.

Giangreco, M., Cloninger, C., & Iverson, V. (1990). *C.O.A.C.H. - Cayuga-Onondaga assessment for children with handicaps* (6th ed.) (pp. 38-39). Stillwater: National Clearinghouse for Rehabilitative Training Materials, Oklahoma State University.

Graham, G., Holt-Hale, S., & Parker, M. (1993). *Children moving: A reflective approach to teaching physical education* (3rd ed.). Mountain View, CA: Mayfield.

Griffin, P. (1989). Assessment of equitable instructional practices in the gym. *The Journal of the Canadian Association for Health, Physical Education, and Recreation*, **55**(2), 19-22.

Kelly, L. (1994). Preplanning for successful inclusive schooling. *Journal of Physical Education, Recreation and Dance (JOPERD)*, **65**(1), 37-39, 56.

Leaps and Bounds. (1982). Honolulu: Hawaii State Department of Education.

Morris, D. (1980). *Elementary physical education: Toward inclusion*. Salt Lake City: Brighton.

Project SEE Legal Update. (1986). Sacramento: California State Department of Education.

Rohnke, K. (1989). *Cowtails and Cobras II*. Dubuque, IA: Kendall/Hunt.

Stainback, W., & Stainback, S. (1990). *Support networks for inclusive schooling: Interdependent integrated education*. Baltimore: Paul H. Brookes.

Torbert, M. (1993). *Follow me: A handbook of movement activities for children*. Available through the Leonard Gordon Institute for Human Development through Play of Temple University, 3306 Midvale Avenue, Philadelphia, PA 19129-1404.

Torbert, M., & Schneider, L. (1993). *Follow me too: A handbook of movement activities for three- to five-year-olds*. Menlo Park, CA: Addison-Wesley.

Appendix

Resources on Inclusion

Block, M.E. (1994). *A teacher's guide to including students with disabilities in regular physical education*. Baltimore: Paul H. Brookes.

This practical book provides step-by-step instructional and curricular strategies, along with games and activity modifications to include students with challenges in regular physical education classes.

Block, M.E. (1994). All kids can have physical education the regular way. In M.S. Moon (Ed.), *Making school and community recreation fun for everyone: Places and ways to integrate*. Baltimore: Paul H. Brookes.

Craft, D.H. (Ed.) (1994). Inclusion: Physical education for all. *Journal of Physical Education, Recreation and Dance (JOPERD)*, **65**(1), 22-56.

This feature provides an overview of the issue of inclusion along with information on making curricular modifications, promoting equal status relationships among peers, teaching collaboratively with others, research on inclusion, ideas on infusion, and experiences implementing inclusion in two schools.

Rainforth, B., York, J., & Macdonald, C. (1992). *Collaborative teams for students with severe disabilities*. Baltimore: Paul H. Brookes.

Stainback, S., & Stainback, W. (1985). *Integration of students with severe handicaps into regular schools.* Reston, VA: Council for Exceptional Children.

Stainback, S., & Stainback, W. (1992). *Curriculum considerations in inclusive classrooms: Facilitating learning for all students.* Baltimore: Paul H. Brookes.

The last three books listed and several other books and articles by Stainback and Stainback provide a wealth of information on issues related to inclusion. In most cases, physical education is not specifically addressed, so the reader must apply information addressing other subject areas to physical education.

The Association for Persons with Severe Handicaps (TASH) and its publication *Journal of the Association for Persons with Severe Handicaps (JASH)* have been at the forefront in the promotion of inclusive schools. This organization may be one of the single best resources for current progressive ideas on inclusion.

5

Securing Funding for Physical Education

Louis Bowers
University of South Florida

The first question to be answered in regard to securing external grant funds is "Who is eligible for grant funding?" Whether the funding is from a service club, corporation, foundation, or the state or federal government, the person applying for funding must have an affiliation with a nonprofit public or private university, college, community college, high school, middle school, elementary school, preschool, or other nonprofit agency. A grant is awarded not to an individual, but to the nonprofit agency through which the grant was submitted. The project director is, however, responsible for the expenditures of the project according to the guidelines of the funding agency.

Individuals who are not employed by a nonprofit agency but who have ideas for projects that have a potential for funding could either incorporate as a nonprofit agency or become affiliated with a nonprofit university, school system, or community agency. The salary of the originator of the project can be included in the grant budget and, if funded, can be paid for the duration of the grant project. Educational institutions are usually interested in considering the sponsorship of outstanding project proposals that would meet their priorities and programmatic needs to improve student learning and which would be paid for by external funds.

Due to educational budget cuts, and thus spending limitations, the need to secure outside funding for educational programs has increased greatly over the last several years. The result has been that the faculty in universities and colleges and teachers in school systems have been encouraged to seek external funding for the development of new programs in physical education, evaluation of instructional methods, the use of technology in physical education, and a variety of other educational endeavors that may not have been funded in the yearly budget.

Since there are relatively few educators who are experienced in securing grants, there are several existing myths in regard to grant proposals and the operations of the grant project.

| **Myth 1** | A person receiving a grant will be paid an enormous amount of money. |

Grant regulations do not permit personnel whose salaries are paid by grants to receive a salary higher than the salary normally paid by the university, college, or school system during the period of grant funding. Persons applying for grants as members of a nonprofit group must request a salary befitting the degrees, skills, and experience required for the position. Salaries requested in the budget are evaluated in regard to their appropriateness for work performed and their overall contribution to the cost effectiveness of the project. For this reason, inflated salaries would be detected. Inflated salaries would contribute negatively to the cost effectiveness rating for the project and reduce its chances of funding.

| **Myth 2** | People on grants work less. |

Those experienced with grants recommend that persons writing grant proposals should be careful because they might succeed in having them funded. This advice is based on the experience of being funded and then realizing that you must do everything you stated in the proposal in what now looks like a short amount of time. Usually teachers and administrators on grants work more hours because of the demands of the grant, which are sometimes in addition to some of their other teaching or administrative duties.

Myth 3	A quality grant can be written in one day.

It will take at least one day to secure the signatures of institutional or school system administrators that are necessary before the grant can be submitted to the funding agency. The serious planning and writing process, as well as requests for letters of support and cooperation, should begin at least six to eight weeks before the proposal is to be submitted. A well-written proposal usually requires five to six draft revisions, and each review and rewrite takes time. The exception to the above time line would be a shorter proposal submitted to a service club or local corporation.

Myth 4	Grants are like sweepstakes, which are based on luck.

Luck will not substitute for a well-written proposal with exciting new ideas that hold promise for needed educational improvements. When a proposal has the foregoing elements, demonstrates the existence of qualified personnel and facilities necessary to successfully complete the project, and is cost effective, it has a good chance of being funded. When deciding on the approach and style to be used in writing the proposal, it is important to consider the point of reference of the people who will be evaluating it. Grants competition is not a sweepstakes; a well-written proposal should leave very little to chance.

What Will Grant Funding Provide?

Grant proposals should be written only for projects that are important, for which there is a great need, that the proposer is capable of completing, and for which everyone involved is committed. Without these qualities, a proposal stands little chance of being funded or completed. One way to get an idea of the standard for funded proposals is to read a proposal that has been recently funded by the agency to which the proposal is to be submitted. The most direct way to obtain a proposal that has been funded is to request it from the agency that received the funding or from the funding agency itself.

Because all funding agencies have limited funds, they are most interested in funding projects that seek to answer questions important to the improvement of education, health, or general quality of life. Categories of funding for projects by federal and state governmental agencies include research and development of curriculum, evaluation of instructional strategies, program support, and use of technology in physical education, to name a few. Foundations tend to establish priorities not according to general categories, but rather in specific areas such as physical fitness, injury prevention, or physical education for students with disabilities. Eligibility for funding through foundations is sometimes limited to a geographical area or to those who are members of a specified group such as those who work for the company sponsoring the foundation.

Grant funding may provide partial payment of salaries and fringe benefits such as social security, medical insurance, and worker's compensation for personnel conducting the project. It may also include payment for scholarships, graduate assistantships, stipends, substitute payment for teachers in school systems, or support for university and college students. Funds may be provided for travel, telephone charges, postage, office rental, office supplies, and printing. The purchase of equipment can be included in the proposed budget if it can be shown that the equipment is essential to the success of the project and is not otherwise available within the school system, college, or university. For the most part, however, standalone equipment requests are not funded.

Grant funding may provide additional funds that an ongoing budget of an institution may not be able to provide. Some funding agencies, however, require that matching or partial funding of the project be provided by the agency submitting the proposal. This can be in-kind funding such as providing office space, telephones, or equipment for the project, or it might be direct matching funding such as payment of a percentage of the salary of personnel conducting the project.

It is important to read the grant guidelines carefully in advance in order to know which budget items will be funded and which expenditures are prohibited. Failure to read grant guidelines could result in having a grant proposal completed that cannot be submitted due to budgetary restraints.

Formulating the Grant Proposal Topic

It is important that a grant proposal topic be created and evaluated for eligibility for and probability of funding before beginning a search for a funding source. Valuable time should only be invested in searching for funding sources if the project has a reasonably high probability of being funded.

If the individual or group has not identified a topic for a project, a group "brainstorming" session could be helpful. In a brainstorming session, there is no criticism or judgment of ideas for topics put forth: Criticism or evaluation inhibits the creative process and should not occur during such a session. To stimulate project ideas, individuals in the group could ask questions such as "What improvements could we make in our curriculum?"; "How can we effectively use technology in our program?"; or "What educational questions do we need to have answered by research?" Thoughts of not being able to afford the project should be suppressed, for that is the purpose of grant funding. In the process of generating ideas, quantity is more important than quality, because among many ideas there should be at least one that can be funded.

All suggested topics for projects should be written as soon as they are voiced. Once a list of topics has been posted in the creative phase, it is time to enter the critical phase, in which the topics are evaluated and further developed. In this phase, the following questions must be answered:

1. Is the topic specific enough to be accomplished in a reasonable amount of time?
2. Are the objectives measurable so that the project can be evaluated?
3. Are the objectives attainable in a reasonable amount of time?
4. Is the topic one that focuses on important results?

If the answers to the above questions are negative, perhaps the topic needs to be narrowed, further developed, or refined in order to qualify for funding. Save the list of topics that were not selected for future review: Some topics deemed inappropriate may be more timely in the future. Think big in regard to planning a proposal, because the effort of writing a large budget grant is not that much greater than that needed to write a small budget grant. It is also relatively easy to scale back a project if sufficient funding is not available.

As you focus on finding a topic that is fundable, don't lose sight of the original intent of the team members. The team must be passionate about and committed to not only writing the proposal, but to carrying it out. Before seeking a funding source and writing the full proposal, it is necessary to write a one-page abstract of the proposal. Writing the abstract requires that the entire project be thought through, organized, and clearly explained. The one-page abstract will be a valuable asset in any case, because sometimes the submission of an abstract is required by a funding agency for initial consideration.

In addition to the preparation of the abstract, there should be a statement of the amount of time necessary to complete the project and an estimated budget for the duration of the project. This information becomes crucial as one begins the search for funding sources. Those funding sources whose limitations on the length and amount of funding are less than the level needed to complete the project need to be eliminated from consideration. Do not expect the funding agency to change their funding range and duration of funding in order to be able to fund your outstanding project.

Identifying the Funding Agencies

The general rule for success in seeking funding is that funding sources located nearer to the proposer have a higher probability of providing funding. Applying for funding from internal funding sources of one's university, the educational foundation of one's school system, or from a local service club or local foundation greatly narrows the competition and meets the priority of the agency for local awards. Submitting a proposal to a national foundation or to the U.S. Department of Education greatly increases the number of competitors and removes the geographical advantage.

Following the recommendation to apply to sources nearer to home, the first possible source of funding for physical educators would be internal grants within a school system, community college, or university. These grant opportunities are announced as mini grants or internal grants at least on a yearly basis. Although these grants are relatively small, ranging from $500 to $10,000, the amount needed may be within this range. Receiving one of these mini grants provides an excellent opportunity to build a professional track record for future funding.

Projects currently being supported by educational foundations in school systems include innovative use of technology, school drop-out prevention, involvement of families of at-risk students, student and faculty wellness programs, and innovative equipment grants. Guidelines for writing proposals from the Educational Foundation of one's school system should be obtained through the school principal and submitted with the principal's support. The principal's support will be most valuable in the successful completion of the project once it is funded. University and college faculty need to work with the support of their department chairpersons, college deans, and offices of sponsored research.

Selecting the Appropriate Funding Agency

The first consideration in selecting any type of funding agency is whether the proposal topic matches the funding agency's priorities. The proposal topic must clearly fit under the current priorities of one of the agencies, and preferably should match the top priority of an agency. If it is not clear whether the project fits the priorities of the service club, foundation, corporation, or government agency, a telephone call to the agency should answer the question. Be sure the project topic fits the interests of the funding agency before writing the proposal for the agency.

A second concern is whether the range of the amount of funding that can be provided by the agency is sufficient to support the proposed project. If the range of funding is from $5,000 to $10,000 with the average grant being $7,500, and your project requires more than $10,000, you need to look for another funding agency. Do not reduce the budget of your proposal in order to submit it to a particular funding agency unless you can appropriately reduce the scope of the project.

A third consideration is whether the funding agency's deadline for receiving grant proposals and the starting date for funding match the anticipated schedule of the proposed project. Should an agency's deadline for receiving grant proposals be only a few weeks away, there may not be enough time to prepare a quality proposal. If funding for a project begins January 1st (in the middle of the school year), but the project is planned to start in August (at the beginning of the school year), there will be no funding when it is initially needed. Since most agencies fund on a yearly basis, it may be necessary to wait until the next year to submit a proposal.

Whether the funding agency provides for 1, 2, 3, 4, or 5 consecutive years of funding must be a fourth consideration. If the time needed to complete the proposal calls for multiyear funding, and the funding agency will provide only one year of funding, an agency that supports multiyear funding must be found.

Finally, the guidelines of the funding agency need to be read carefully for any statements regarding geographical restrictions or funding eligibility being restricted to members of certain groups. Federal government grants are available to all members of nonprofit agencies who reside in the United States and its territories. State government grants, of course, are awarded to members of nonprofit agencies who reside within the individual states. However, national foundations and corporations, because they are private, can limit funding to persons who live in a certain section of the country or work for a designated company. Because funding restrictions eliminate many potential proposals, it is important to identify a funding agency whose restrictions, even if narrow, can accommodate your proposal.

If the proposal meets the criteria of the funding agency's priorities for funding, amount of funding, duration of funding, and geographical and group eligibility, then the project can be submitted and will be considered for funding by the agency.

It is not mandatory, but it is helpful to know the number of proposals received as well as the number of projects and the total dollars funded by the agency the previous year. The amount of funds available for the current year and the number of projects anticipated to be funded become important information when selecting one funding agency over another. Obviously, with all other factors being equal, the proposal writer will find the funding agency that funds a large number of projects or has a high ratio of funding to proposals submitted to be the most attractive. However, a proposal writer who really believes a project can be funded will not view getting funded as impossible even if submitting a proposal to an agency that funds only 10% of proposals received.

Funding Sources

The search for funding sources close to home first takes one to a local phone directory for the numbers of local service clubs such as Civitan, Rotary, Lions, Seratoma, or Elks. A phone call followed by a presentation to the membership of one of these clubs might provide an immediate answer to your funding needs. Appropriate thanks and recognition of the service club's grant will enhance the probability of future funding.

Each state has a directory that lists foundations that support funding within the state and their funding guidelines. These state foundation directories can be obtained at local libraries, school system grant offices, or at university offices for external funding. See the listing at the end of this chapter for additional funding resources.

Writing the Proposal

As reviewers of your grant proposal might have to read, rate, evaluate, and write comments for 10 or more proposals, it is important for the proposal to be concise, well organized, and clearly written. Some funding agencies provide their evaluation criteria in writing in advance to those who anticipate submitting proposals to them. The proposal is much easier to review if it is written in the format of the evaluation criteria.

A well-organized proposal with a table of contents makes it easy for the reviewer to find specific information related to the review and evaluation. Write to the individual reader using short, clear sentences typed in readable fonts. The easier the proposal is to review, the more pleased the evaluator will be. Having a reviewer have good feelings about your proposal is a definite plus.

If the guidelines for the proposal call for a 20-page narration of the grant, make sure your proposal is 20 pages or less. The grant may not be disqualified for being more than 20 pages, but it gives the reviewer more to read and raises the question as to why you could not stay within the guidelines of the funding agency.

The length of a proposal and the format for writing the proposal will vary from one agency to another. However, the following components are usually required regardless of the format.

Introduction

The introduction clearly establishes the purposes, goals, programs, and activities of the agency applying for funding. The clients or constituents served by the agency should also be identified, along with the agency's accomplishments. This section can be especially strong if statistics, quotes, or endorsements are provided to support claims about the effectiveness of the program. This support can help establish the overall credibility of the applying agency, and will be more convincing if previous achievements are for an area in which the funds are being sought. In summary, the introduction should be brief, attention-getting, and convincing in regard to the credibility of the agency requesting funding. The last statement in the introduction should provide a logical and smooth transition to the statement of purpose and need.

Statement of Purpose

The proposal should include a clear statement of the purpose of the project, preferably with input from its clients and beneficiaries. The purpose should be related to the philosophy and goals of the applying agency and also should be related to projects that the agency has previously completed: This shows the agency's prior interest in the topic as well as its capability. The project needs to be of reasonable dimensions so that it can be accomplished by the agency in the amount of time funded.

Statement of Need

The need for the project must be demonstrated in terms of student and community needs and not the need of the proposing agency to secure the funding. The need for the project must be great, and the result of meeting the identified need must produce important positive changes. The need for the project should be well established by statistical evidence, statements from authorities, or informed observations. It is wise to refrain from making unsupported assumptions related to the need for the project. If the project is designed to contribute to a local, state, or national need, the supporting evidence should be specific to the region.

Program Objectives

The objectives of the proposed project relate directly to the statement of purpose and need. Each objective needs to be stated as a positive outcome that is measurable. Quantifiable results will make it easier to evaluate the degree of achievement of each objective. The specific population that will benefit from the successful completion of each stated objective should also be identified.

Plan of Operation

The plan of operation should flow naturally from the stated purpose, needs, and objectives and should clearly describe the program of activities. It is most convincing to state reasons for selecting this program of activities to achieve the objectives. A schedule showing the sequence of activities and time line for the accomplishment of each objective demonstrates an understanding of each task necessary to accomplish each objective.

Expected accomplishments can be identified on a monthly basis as part of an organizational chart that also describes personnel who will be responsible for each program activity and the amount of time they will devote to each activity. The scope of activities must be supported by an appropriate quantity of assigned time and resources for the proposed project.

Quality of Personnel and Resources

Among the most important resources for a research or programmatic project are the qualifications of the key personnel involved in carrying out the project. A brief description of the broad capabilities of each member of the project team, such as degrees earned, years of teaching or research experience, and achievements in successfully completing other grant projects, should be included in the narrative. Brief statements regarding specific education, experience, or talents related to the current proposal will help convince the reviewer of the probability for success of the project. This information can be detailed further in an abbreviated vitae for each project staff member in an appendix.

It is important to understand that should the proposed project require unique skills or equipment not available to the project staff, contracting for the services of individuals with these skills and leasing necessary equipment is quite appropriate. Securing services or equipment only for the period of time each is needed by the project can be very cost effective as compared to purchasing the services or equipment for the duration of the project.

Other resources important to projects include available office, lab, and activity space, or specialized equipment necessary for conducting the project. A letter of support from the appropriate administrator assures the reviewer of the proposal that the space and equipment will be assigned to the project.

Finally, any established network through which the results of the project or programmatic materials developed by the project might be distributed should be described in detail as an existing resource.

Evaluation

A sound evaluation should present a plan for assessing the degree to which objectives of the project are met and the plan of operation is followed. The plan should specify who will be doing the evaluation and why they were chosen. Paying for the services of an evaluator external to the project can enhance the objectivity of the evaluation.

In a programmatic project, it is very important to develop a formative evaluation plan that provides for both assessment and modification of methods and strategies over the course of the project. The plan should clearly state the criteria for judging the success of the project objectives and describe how and when data will be gathered for the evaluation.

A summative evaluation should also be conducted to ascertain the effectiveness of the strategies employed to achieve these objectives. Standardized tests, instruments, or questionnaires should be described and included in the appendix in the event that the reviewer is not familiar with them. The process for the analysis of data should be clearly described and referenced. Any evaluation reports of the project that are to be produced and their method of distribution should also be described. Last, a diagram and flow chart should be included to provide a clear overview of the evaluation plan.

Budget

The budget clearly delineates which costs are to be supplied by the funding agency and which in-kind costs will be provided by the recipient of the grant. It is both honest and wise to request as near as possible the amount of funding necessary for successfully completing the project. Asking for less than is needed to score more points in cost effectiveness is not recommended, and neither is requesting more funding than is needed. If the project is funded for less than the amount requested, it may be necessary to reduce the scope of the project. Costs must be projected to include inflation which may occur before funding and during the project. A budget must be detailed and correct in every respect. Check your calculations several times for accuracy.

The budget explanation that follows the budget outline should provide a detailed account of how the funds requested will be expended. This section should leave no doubt in the reviewer's mind regarding the need for and appropriate expenditure of funds.

The salary section should specify the percentage of time for 9 or 12 months that each person will devote to the grant for each year of the project. A percentage breakdown of the fringe benefits for each person paid by the grant must also be provided.

The type of equipment to be rented or purchased needs to be listed and a description included of how it will be used in the project. If equipment is rented, show how many days it will be used and the cost savings of renting versus purchasing the equipment.

The name, location, and purpose of local, state, or national travel associated with the project for each person should be clearly explained, along with a statement about how this travel will benefit the purposes of the project.

The proposal should also explain the need for expense funds for office supplies, photocopying, telephones, and other necessities. Also included in this category are physical education activity items such as balls, striking implements, and self-testing apparatus.

Figure 5.1 presents a typical budget for a mini grant, and Figure 5.2 shows an example of a budget for a mid-sized grant proposal.

Indirect cost rates are set by the funding agency and are used by the university, school system, or nonprofit agency to provide office space, air conditioning, mail service, and accounting for grant expenditures. Some foundations, corporations, and state agencies do not allow indirect costs to be included in the budget request. Assurance that your institution, school, or nonprofit agency will accept a grant without indirect cost funds is important to have before the proposal is written.

Appendixes

Appendixes present an opportunity to include more detailed information supportive of the grant proposal. A brief vitae of proposed project personnel, statistics supporting the need for the project, evidence of previous success in related projects, and letters of support are appropriate for inclusion in appendixes. Reference to material in Appendix A, B, or C will allow the reviewer of the proposal the choice of reading the more extensive material.

A few strong letters of support are better than many weak ones. Strong letters of support should be solicited and included in the proposal. Potential supporters should be contacted by telephone and then be sent an abstract of the proposal with a letter suggesting the areas that you need them to address in their letter of support. Good sources for letters of support are state education agencies, institutions of higher education, professional associations, parent groups, and the ultimate beneficiary of the products of the projects such as teachers, students, or their families. Groups or individuals with whom you have completed previous projects are in a position to write particularly meaningful letters based on experience. Make sure letters of support are typed on letterhead and that the writers know your deadline for submitting the grant proposal well in advance.

Requested Budget

A. Salary

Substitute teacher for Project Director for 10 days at $50 per day	$500
Substitute teachers for 10 teachers to attend workshop for 10 days at $50 per day	$5,000

B. Workshop Materials

Purchasing books and videotapes	$2,000

C. Travel

In-county travel to school sites 600 miles at .20 per mile	$120
Travel to state conference 200 miles at .20 per mile	$40
Consultant travel 50 miles at .20 per mile	$10

D. Expense

Telephone and office supplies	$250

E. Other

Consultant for workshop for 10 days at $300 per day	$3,000

TOTAL DIRECT COST	**$10,920**

Figure 5.1.   Example of a mini-grant budget.

Reasons Why Proposals Are Not Funded

Here are 10 reasons why proposals for projects are not funded:

1. Writer did not follow guidelines provided by funding agency.
2. Proposal objectives do not match priorities for funding by the funding agency.
3. Proposal budget is not within range of funding available through the funding agency.
4. Need for project has not been documented properly.
5. Need does not strike reviewer as significant. The needs section failed to convince the reviewer that the proposal merited funding.
6. Proposal is poorly written and hard to understand.
7. Evaluation plan and procedure are inadequate.
8. Project objectives are too ambitious in scope to be accomplished during the funding period.
9. Proposed program has not been coordinated with other individuals and organizations working in the same geographical area.
10. Funding source has not been adequately informed about the capabilities of those submitting the proposal.

Steps in the Process of Securing a Grant

To summarize the process, here are the steps to take in obtaining a grant:

1. Utilize brainstorming sessions to create project topics.
2. Identify fundable projects.
3. Identify possible funding agencies.
4. Select the funding agencies with the highest probability for funding the project.
5. Prepare an abstract of the project.
6. Request letters of support for the proposal.
7. Write a draft of the proposal.
8. Have colleagues review the proposal.
9. After several rewrites, complete a final draft of the proposal.
10. Submit the proposal to the funding agency.
11. Negotiate funding of the project with the funding agency.
12. Begin work on the project.

Requested Budget

A. Salary

Project Director	$10,000
30% of time for 12 months to be devoted to project	
Project Assistant	$20,000
100% of 12 months devoted to project	

B. Fringe Benefits

Project Director	$2,700
27% of salary	
Project Assistant	$5,400
27% of salary	

C. Equipment $5,000

Purchase of two computers

D. Travel

Project Director's travel to national AAHPERD convention $950
Project Assistant's travel to state AAHPERD conference

E. Expense $1,500

Office supplies, copying

F. Other $500

Telephones

TOTAL DIRECT COST	**$46,050**
10% INDIRECT COST	**$4,605**
	$50,655

Figure 5.2. Example of a mid-sized grant proposal budget.

Appendix

National Directories of Funding Sources

Public Funding

Catalog of Federal and Domestic Assistance
Superintendent of Documents
U.S. Government Printing Service
Washington, DC 20402

Catalog of Federal Education Assistance Programs
Superintendent of Documents
U.S. Government Printing Service
Washington, DC 20402

Complete Grants Source Book
American Council on Education
One Dupont Circle
Washington, DC 20036

Disability Funding News
8204 Fenton St.
Silver Spring, MD 20910
301-588-6380

Guide to Federal Funding for Education
Education Funding Research Council
4301 N. Fairfax Dr.
Suite 875
Arlington, VA 22203-1627
703-528-1000

Foundation Funding

The next two directories are available from:

The Taft Group
12300 Twinbrook Parkway
Suite 450
Rockville, MD 20852
1-800-877-TAFT

Corporate Giving Yellow Pages

This is an easy-to-use guide to the contact people of the leading corporate giving programs and corporate foundations in America.

- Over 3,900 corporate direct giving programs and company-sponsored foundations
- Indexed by two-digit SIC code and headquarters/operating locations
- 420 pages

The Directory of Corporate and Foundation Givers

- 8,000 profiles of private foundations, corporate foundations, and corporate giving programs
- Top 10 grants for each foundation
- 3,000 pages in 2 volumes

Chronicle of Philanthropy
PO Box 1989
Marion, OH 43305-1989

The Foundation Center
79th Fifth Ave.
Department JG
New York, NY 10010

The Grantsmanship Center
PO Box 17220
1125 West 6th St.
5th Floor
Los Angeles, CA 90017

Research Grant Guides
Dept. 34
PO Box 1214
Laxahatchee, FL 33470

National Foundations With Educational Funding Priorities

Aetna Foundation, Inc.
151 Farmington Ave.
Hartford, CT 06156-3180

203-273-6382
Contact: Diana Kinosh, Management Information Supervisor

Alcoa Foundation
1501 Alcoa Building
Pittsburgh, PA 15219-1850
412-553-2348
Contact: F. Worth Hobbs, President
Giving primarily in geographic areas of company operation.

The Allstate Foundation
Allstate Plaza North
Northbrook, IL 60062
708-402-5502
Contacts: Alan Benedict, Executive Director;
Allen Goldhammer, Manager;
Dawn Bougart, Administrative Assistant

The Annenberg Foundation
St. Davids Center
150 Radnor-Chester Rd.
Suite A-200
St. Davids, PA 19087
Contact: Dr. Mary Ann Meyers, President

ARCO Foundation
515 S. Flower St.
Los Angeles, CA 90071
213-486-3342
Contact: Eugene R. Wilson, President

Bell Atlantic Charitable Foundation
1310 N. Courthouse Rd.
10th Floor
Arlington, VA 22201
703-974-5440
Contact: Ruth P. Caine, Director

The Bush Foundation
E-900 First National Bank Building
332 Minnesota St.
St. Paul, MN 55101
612-227-0891
Contact: Humphrey Doermann, President

Carnegie Corporation of New York
437 Madison Ave.
New York, NY 10022
212-371-3200
Contact: Dorothy W. Knapp, Secretary

The Coca-Cola Foundation, Inc.
PO Drawer 1734
Atlanta, GA 30301
404-676-2568

GTE Foundation
One Stamford Forum
Stamford, CT 06904
203-965-3620
Contact: Maureen Gorman, Foundation Vice
President, Secretary, and Director, Social
Responsibility, GTE Corp.

Hasbro Children's Foundation
32 West 23rd St.
New York, NY 10010
212-645-2400
Contact: Eve Weiss, Executive Director
Funding for children under the age of 12 with
special needs.

Hershey Foods Corporation Fund
100 Crystal A Dr.
Hershey, PA 17033
717-534-7574
Contact: M.L. Berney, Manager, Corporate
Contributions

The Hitachi Foundation
1509 22nd St. NW
Washington, DC 20037
202-457-0588
Contact: Robyn L. James

Knight Foundation
One Biscayne Tower
Suite 3800
Two South Biscayne Blvd.
Miami, FL 33131-1803
305-539-0009

Mattel Foundation
c/o Mattel Toys
333 Continental Blvd.
El Segundo, CA 90245
213-524-3530
Contact: Janice R. Nakayama, Administrator

McDonnell Douglas Foundation
PO Box 516, Mail Code 1001510
St. Louis, MO 63166
314-232-8464
Contact: Walter E. Diggs, Jr., President

RJR Nabisco Foundation
1455 Pennsylvania Ave. NW
Suite 525
Washington, DC 20004
202-626-7200
Contact: Jaynie M. Grant, Executive Director

Rockefeller Brothers Fund
1290 Avenue of the Americas
New York, NY 10104
212-373-4200
Contact: Benjamin R. Shute, Jr.,
Secretary-Treasurer

The Sears Roebuck Foundation
Sears Tower
Dept. 903-BSC 51-02
Chicago, IL 60684
312-875-8337
Contact: Paula A. Banks, President and
Executive Director

Toyota USA Foundation
c/o Corporation Tax Dept.
19001 South Western Ave.
Torrance, CA 90501
213-618-4727
Contact: Joe Tethrow

Dewitt Wallace-Reader's Digest Fund, Inc.
261 Madison Ave.
24th Floor
New York, NY 10016
212-953-1201
Contact: Jane Quinn, Program Director

The Skillman Foundation
333 West Fort St.
Suite 1350
Detroit, MI 48226

Robert Woods Johnson Foundation
Route 1 and College Road East
PO Box 2316
Princeton, NJ 08543-2316

Z. Smith Reynolds Foundation, Inc.
101 Reynolds Village
Winston-Salem, NC 27106-5199
919-725-7541
Contact: Thomas W. Lambeth, Executive
Director

Part II

Curriculum Resources and References

In this second half, we present tools for you to use in developing physical education curricula and instruction. The tools run from full state-level curriculum guides to listings of textbooks, trade books, equipment, and other supplementary teaching aids. They even include professional organizations that can provide assistance and training to teachers.

Part II begins with Bob Ritson's review of the curriculum guides of nearly all 50 states. For each state, he describes the format and content of the materials and evaluates their helpfulness in curriculum development.

Next comes Bonnie Mohnsen's review of some of the best commercially available teaching materials. Chapter 7 includes curriculum guides and lesson plans, student texts, and more high-technology aids such as videos, software, and interactive laser discs. To help instructors stay current, she also recommends professional journals and Internet connections.

In schools with integrated curricula, trade books can help teachers in both physical education and other subject areas to cross boundaries. In chapter 8, Patricia Bledsoe presents a lengthy annotated listing of books both for pleasurable reading and for learning sport skills, plus an assortment of records, audiocassettes, and videos.

Physical education activities also require equipment and related resources. Chapter 9 provides addresses for many equipment manufacturers, publishers, and non-profit organizations related to physical activity.

This final part of the book should give you leads on new resources to incorporate into your teaching. We hope that, when you put the two parts together, you find that you have all the information you need to design classes that meet your students' needs and teach them the joy of movement.

6

State-Level Curriculum Guides and Contacts

Robert Ritson
Oregon Department of Education

This chapter synthesizes state-level resources available for administrators, curriculum coordinators, curriculum writing teams, teachers, and students to use as they study, plan, and evaluate physical education programs. State-level program documents vary widely across the United States as to (a) how they address policy and procedural issues, (b) whether they are curriculum guides in and of themselves or "how to" documents for schools to develop their own curriculum guides, and (c) their method of organization. For example, some are organized by goals of instruction, some by student outcomes, and some by specific content (sport, dance, gymnastics, etc.). Some of the documents are inclusive, meaning that the state department of education has published one text for each program such as physical education or science; others are "first-step" documents, meaning that the state has published a content-rich document accepted by a state school board or other governing body as policy that provides a beginning to curriculum development; and still others are "backup" publications designed to aid in local program implementation.

Although a synthesis of this kind can provide a valuable service to the discipline, it can never be properly timed: States simply operate independently. Therefore, some documents reviewed were in draft form, some were "hot off the press," and some were from states that were restructuring due to reform legislation or accountability initiatives, and thus they may soon become obsolete. In addition, for one reason or another, some states submitted no documentation.

In order to define and plan the breadth and depth of a program, curriculum planners should decide on their baseline philosophy (be it developed or adopted) and consider the effects of federal mandates on program planning.

Two principles of federal mandate affect all physical education programs. The first is the original Public Law No. 94-142 (see chapter 4), which calls for free and appropriate public education for all children. This law places special emphasis on the inclusion of students with disabilities in regular physical education, in adaptive physical education programs as a second choice, or in another environment that is least restrictive. The second mandate is Title IX of the Education Amendments of 1972 and the accompanying regulation adopted in 1975 (see chapter 4). Title IX prohibits the separation of students by gender for any educational program, except on the few occasions where heavy contact or specialized ability grouping of students may be necessary.

Various other issues and considerations may affect program development: geographical location; preparation of teachers to deliver the program; access to and abundance of facilities and equipment; content delivery system (e.g., integrated, interdisciplinary, or isolated); ways in which resource allotments for physical education are balanced with those for other subject areas; average and range of performance of students in class; and time limitations and allotments available for lessons. Once all of the issues and factors mentioned thus far have been considered, a final step in program planning is evaluating whether or not the program can stand the test of its baseline philosophy: This philosophy must guide the planning if progress towards a comprehensive and progressive program is to occur.

In all of the documents submitted by the states, physical education is given its due as an integral part of school curricula: *No* state document suggests that physical education is a chance for children to have free play, and *no* state publication confuses physical education with recess or break time for students. Each publication reflects an instructional program designed to increase students' motor, fitness, and social skills, and each publication generally supports the philosophy of physical education as integral to, and integrating easily with, an overall school program that is rooted in what is best for the development of children and youth.

Many of the newer publications are beginning to address the concept of physical education as one of eight components included in a Comprehensive School Health Program (CSHP). The other seven components are health education; health services; nutrition services; counseling, psychological, and social services; healthy school environment; health promotion for staff; and parent and community involvement (Allensworth & Kolbe, 1987). In this view, physical education, with its emphasis on the overall health of the child, is a valuable part of a balanced and coordinated school health program.

Physical education programs should also focus on cognitive understandings concerning the development and improvement of motor performance so as to encourage students to participate in a variety of physical activities across their life spans. Most state publications reflect both a health emphasis and a cognitive focus for physical education.

As described in chapter 2, a document published by the National Association of Sport and Physical Education (NASPE) titled *Outcomes of Quality Physical Education Programs* (1992) describes the five qualities of a physically educated person: (a) skillful, (b) fit, (c) participative, (d) knowledgeable, and (e) valuing of physical activity. Some state publications were used in the development of the NASPE definition and outcomes; other publications, in turn, reflect the 1992 NASPE document. The NASPE publication, therefore, may be used as one means of reviewing state-level productions and not solely as a separate program development guide.

This chapter describes the resources provided by state departments of education upon request (as previously mentioned, not all of the states furnished publications). An earnest attempt was made to procure current publications from every state department of education. The documents are reviewed here on a state-by-state basis in alphabetical order. Each description was written not only using a set of criteria applied to all states, but also attempting to capture the uniqueness and creativity of each state's individual contribution. Table 6.1 is an overview of the guides reviewed in this chapter.

Table 6.1   State Curriculum Guides Reviewed

State name	Year of publication	Purpose	Organization
Alabama	1989	Local Curr. Develop.	Goals, Activities
Alaska	1986	Model Program	Topic, Obj., Act.
Arizona	1990	Comp. Health	Conceptual
Arkansas	1992	Guide to Requiremt.	Topics
California	1994	Local Curr. Develop.	Outcomes
Colorado	1991	School Reform	Outcomes
Connecticut	1981	Local Curr. Develop.	Outcomes
Delaware	1985	Local Curr. Develop.	Goals
District of Columbia	NA	not received	
Florida	1991, 1992	Local Curr. Develop.	Content/Outcome
Georgia	NA	not received	
Hawaii	NA	not received	
Idaho	1990	Local Curr. Develop.	Topics of Program
Illinois	1986	Guide to Requiremt.	Early Outcomes
Indiana	1993	Local Curr. Develop.	Proficiency Indic.
Iowa	1985	Assessment/Design	Goals/Objectives
Kansas	1990	Local Curr. Develop.	Toward Outcomes
Kentucky	1991	School Reform	Outcomes
Louisiana	1990	Local Curr. Develop.	Program Units
Maine	1991	Regs. & Grad. Stds.	Requirements

Table 6.1   *(continued)*

State name	Year of publication	Purpose	Organization
Maryland	1988	Technical Assist.	Goals Framework
Massachusetts	1982	Regulation & Assist.	Model Programs
Michigan	1991	School Reform	Core Outcomes
Minnesota	1992, 1989	School Reform	Outcomes/Assmt.
Mississippi	1986	Local Curr. Develop.	Goal, Skill, Concept
Missouri	1992	Curriculum Reform	Grad. Outcomes
Montana	1988	Guidance & Assist.	Concept Summaries
Nebraska	1992 (NASPE)	Define Program	Def./Outcomes
Nevada	1984	Regulatory	Course of Study
New Hampshire	1993	Regulatory	Topics in Subjects
New Jersey	NA, in process	not received	Content Standards
New Mexico	1992	State System Change	Discipline Based
New York	1986, 1988	Regs. & Guidance	Activity Type
North Carolina	1992, 1987	Local Curr. Develop.	Goals & Measures
North Dakota	NA	not received	
Ohio	NA	not received	
Oklahoma	1992	School Reform	Desired Competency
Oregon	1988	School Reform	Required Goals
Pennsylvania	1993	School Reform	Learning Outcomes
Rhode Island	1990	State Assessment	Results of Test
South Carolina	NA	not received	
South Dakota	Not identified	Local Curr. & Ins. Dev.	Scope & Sequences
Tennessee	NA	not reviewed	
Texas	NA	not reviewed	
Utah	1987	Req. Course Descrpt.	Numbered Stds.
Vermont	1986	Portray Framework	Sug. Learner Obj.
Virginia	1990	Local Curr. Develop.	Standard Obj.
Washington	1989	Local Prog. Imp.	Program Adm.
West Virginia	1992	Program of Study	Learning Outcomes
Wisconsin	1989	Local Prog. Develop.	Development Topic
Wyoming	Not identified	Regulatory	Min. Core Stds.

Alabama (1989)

The *Alabama Course of Study: Physical Education* requires school districts to develop local curriculum plans that include the state-prescribed content, and is designed to help each school district meet the needs of its population. The 90-page document consists of four major sections. The first section identifies 14 trends in physical education that teachers should consider, including integrating program parts, encouraging independence, and reducing gender bias.

At 56 pages, the second section, which describes the minimum content required of school physical education programs, is the publication's largest section. A full-page diagram contains the focus of the publication—types of activities to be offered in school programs—along with grade levels and five goal concepts (health-related fitness, motor-related fitness, cognitive development, affective development, and safety). Types of activities include movement skills and body management, rhythmic activities, stunts and tumbling, gymnastics, games and sports, personal fitness, lifetime activities, and so forth.

Full-page diagrams that frame the content for program planners are also included for each grouping of grade levels (K-2, 3-6, 7-8, and 9-12 [course required for graduation]). In addition to breaking down the required content according to grade levels, these diagrams convey the percentage of instructional time to be spent on each type of activity. This section concludes with a brief discussion about elective courses for high school students.

The third section contains the federal and state laws and the state resolutions related to physical education. The fourth section, entitled "Characteristics of an Effective Physical Education Program," states the legal authority with specific language and code numbers followed by an explanation of what each law or resolution entry means in practice. This section also contains 18 guiding principles of planning and teaching physical education that take the laws and resolutions into account. The appendixes include a glossary, time requirements for all subjects, and a page on study habits, homework, and student responsibility.

Alaska (1986)

The Alaska Department of Education's Office of Curriculum Services offers two publications: the *Alaska Elementary Physical Education Model Curriculum Guide* (2nd edition, 40 pages) and the *Alaska Secondary Physical Education Model Curriculum Guide* (2nd edition, 16 pages). These publications are intended to serve as models rather than mandates. The elementary guide describes grades 1 through 8 and is organized into grade-level sections (1-3, 4-6, 7-8); the secondary guide covers grades 9 through 12. Information on kindergarten can be seen in a separate document, the *Alaska Kindergarten Model Curriculum Guide*.

Both guides are parts of an entire curriculum series that include 10 subject areas. They have similar formats: Each guide includes a general preface, a 3-page preface specific to the subject area (this preface is the same in both documents), and a section organized into three columns—Topics/Concepts, Learning Outcomes/Objectives, and Sample Learning Activities—that is 30 pages long in the elementary guide and 13 pages long in the secondary guide.

Three themes organize the Learning Outcomes/Objectives and the Sample Learning Activities columns: fitness outcomes, motor skill development, and life skills development. Where skill themes are used as guidance for program planning in motor skill development, the general rubrics describing the "pre-control, control, utilization, and proficiency levels" are modified from

Graham (1987). Two of the three themes, fitness outcomes and motor skill development, are subdivided into performance, knowledge, and attitude components, each with two or more sample learning activities to illustrate and support the outcome or objective.

The secondary guide also contains two pages of major activity areas listed as suggestions for program development. The lists contain 14 team sports, 21 individual and dual activities, 11 aquatic activities, 11 rhythmic activities, and 16 outdoor activities appropriate for this region. Four activities are specifically highlighted as survival skills that should be taught either in the health curriculum or in the physical education curriculum.

Both documents include suggested percentages of educational outcomes presented in a histogram format by grade level. Outcomes are broken down into cognitive, psychomotor, and affective components, with the cognitive component being further broken down into six subsections as adapted from Bloom's taxonomy of cognition. The histogram is presented as a way to look at and understand the different taxonomic levels of thinking required to accomplish a particular objective.

Arizona (1990)

Physical education is one of 13 components of the *Arizona Comprehensive Health Essential Skills*. This document is a product of the state-mandated Comprehensive Health Essential Skills Committee, appointed in November 1988, and is intended to recognize the comprehensive nature of health education and physical education instruction within the context of a comprehensive health program.

The publication begins with a broad statement regarding children's health and its importance to their overall learning process. The 13 general areas of comprehensive school health concerns are defined briefly and then articulated into grade levels (K-3, 4-6, 7-8, 9-12), and subsections on "essential skills," "key indicators of student action," and "suggested evaluation" are provided for each of these levels.

The introductory remarks state, "Even though physical education is recognized as an essential skill area in comprehensive health, it has particular needs as a specialized area of school instruction" (p. ii). As an example, physical education is the only component of the 13 that provides alternatives to the traditional oral and written response techniques of evaluation. Each level offers from five to seven student essential skill goals (pp. 155-178). An appendix is included to enhance the physical education materials on teaching basic safety, building self-concept, developing social skills, understanding leisure activity, and equal opportunity. The physical education section ends with a brief section on the requisites for a successful program of physical education for all students.

Arkansas (1992)

The two documents analyzed for content and application bear the same title except for the indication of grade levels. The *Physical Education Course Content Guide* (grades 1-6) was published in 1992 to be in effect until 1997; the *Physical Education Course Content Guide* (grades 7-12) was originally published in 1987 and revised in 1990. The intent of the documents is to meet the state requirement to provide a framework for Arkansas schools that, once adopted, should be expanded by individual school districts to include additional resources, selection of teaching methodology, and coordination of evaluative techniques. In short, the guides do not offer much direction or initial work.

The 10-page elementary guide provides a grade-level articulation (for grades 1-6) of objectives organized under various content headings. Contrary to the advice of American Alliance for Health, Physical Education, Recreation and Dance (AAHPERD) test manuals, the fitness objectives listed for all grade levels identify a score "at or above the 25th percentile" on AAHPERD test items as a target for both health-related and skill-related fitness. Other objectives are listed in qualitative terms. The secondary document (also 5 pages long) targets the 50th percentile for fitness performance and evaluates other objectives in qualitative terms. What happens to students not performing at the 25th or 50th percentiles on fitness tests? The answer is not provided.

An activity menu of 42 types of movement activities that concludes both guides classifies movement forms as either health-related, skill-related, or lifetime. Analysis of this chart reveals either typographic errors or information that defies rationale (e.g., social dance, archery, and badminton are not included in the lifetime category).

Little correlation with current professional literature about the discipline is present in either document.

California (1994)

Physical Education Framework for California Public Schools: Kindergarten Through Grade Twelve, published by the California Department of Education, is based, at least in part, on the work done by the NASPE Outcomes project. There is very little left out of or questionable about this document: The authors have taken care to write clearly, succinctly, and with purpose. Of the publications reviewed in this study, this document is a standout, ranking in the top classification. Using the evaluation rubric (performance standard) of

0 to 6 presented in the text itself on pages 66-67, the publication rates a 6 (i.e., it "fully achieves the purpose of the task, while insightfully interpreting, extending beyond the task, or raises provocative questions").

The publication's vision for physical education promotes three goals. One goal deals with movement and knowledge about movement; the second aims for the development of self-image and personal development; and the third suggests learning about and through social interaction. No other state has taken the step that California has in deliberately making the development of fitness implicit in the language of the first goal, although the document goes on to explain that health-related fitness is not a direct goal of the program. Instead, fitness is considered a byproduct of a focus on moving and being responsible in and for one's own regular and vigorous movement. Clearly, California is saying that moving is an essential part of learning and growing and that quality physical education includes moving, understanding how to move, and understanding that frequent movement activities are essential for good health and for feeling positive about oneself and others.

Throughout the text, the idea emerges clearly from the publication that physical education can help children learn to reduce health risk factors with the cooperation of school, home, and community; by encouraging healthy lifestyles, it can reverse negative health trends. The document's presentation of the rationale and benefits of physical education is impressive, and could be very persuasive in any discussion with school board members, parents, and administrators when budgetary considerations lead to the inevitable question of whether this program is integral to the mission of schooling. The discussion continues to get better as California makes the point of creating an environment for the development, enhancement, and maintenance of a quality physical education program. Many issues like class size, certificated staff, staff development, equipment and supplies, and support for programs are dealt with succinctly and with aplomb.

Should physical education integrate with other subjects in school or be a separate and self-sustaining curriculum? Although this has long been a matter of debate, California has answered this question well. In this program, attainment of each goal involves expanding the disciplines of content to include motor learning, exercise physiology, health-related fitness, the humanities, psychology, and so forth. Quite sensibly, the approach works to integrate courses that college students take in preparation for teaching physical education.

After the disciplines are presented and discussed, grade-level guidelines are introduced using a theme approach for instruction and student learning. The sequence is logical and does not overburden students. The text mentions many examples of activities that are age appropriate and targeted toward the grade-level theme of the instruction.

The section on assessment presents a direction for current and future development of performance-based evaluation of student work, and could initiate a national agenda for assessment practices in physical education. Although performance-based assessment is not new in physical education, it is in many other subject areas; indeed, physical education has the opportunity to take the lead in what is being extolled as a more authentic way of assessing student work than other methods. The California *Physical Education Framework* has been worth the time it took to read and review.

Colorado (1991)

The curriculum efforts in the Colorado Department of Education's *Colorado Sample Outcomes and Proficiencies for Elementary, Middle, and High School Education* focus on supporting students' abilities to think critically and creatively, solve problems, and become active learners in a new educational direction that follows the sample program suggested by the national Association for Supervision and Curriculum Development (ASCD). The result of many state-wide discussions, the Colorado document's intent is to create a bridge between the traditional departmentalized curriculum and the emerging interdisciplinary curriculum.

A diagram (p. iii) presents 13 major content areas, stating that they are to be integrated so that students show progress toward meeting eight learner outcomes of aesthetic development, career development, communication, human relations and responsibility, multicultural understanding, physical and emotional health, reasoning and problem-solving, and scientific and technological development. However, the diagram offers little information about how this integration is to occur. The document defines four terms used throughout the outcomes-based curriculum context: *outcomes, assessment, standards,* and *accountability*. Brief sections describe how the same outcomes can be achieved while meeting the needs of students with disabilities as well as those of gifted, talented, and high ability students. The diagram lists dance and health education separately from physical education. The portion of the document that discusses physical education (pp. 70-79) matches 15 learner outcomes/content standards to the eight broad outcome categories previously mentioned. Benchmarks of assessment demonstrations are presented for each learner outcome/content standard at grades 4, 8, and 12. According to the document, Colorado plans next to develop evaluation standards and levels of proficiency that will accord with the assessment demonstrations and learner outcomes/content standards.

Connecticut (1981)

The State of Connecticut Board of Education's extensive (125-page) manual, *A Guide to Curriculum Development in Physical Education*, identifies the practical needs of curriculum designers and developers as well as content resources and technical assistance for the program innovators, namely teachers and coaches. The publication is intended to be a resource for the development of local physical education programs throughout the state. It is not, therefore, a state mandate, nor should it be confused with a course of study or a complete scope and sequence.

The *Guide's* 11 chapters provide information on topics ranging from the motor development principles of a 3-year-old to the high school towel service. Chapters 1 and 2 present trends in physical education and the foundations of physical education in the behavioral, biological, and physical sciences. Chapters 3 and 4 introduce concepts and recommendations for planning the scope and sequence of a program and designing it so that it meets the individual, group, and special needs of developing children and youth as its segments are implemented at 2-year intervals (from ages 3 to 18 years). These chapters describe characteristics of each age group as well as the needs, interests, and program implications for each chronological age category. The chapters also discuss the teaching philosophy, learning outcomes, and desirable experiences for each age category.

Common learning styles, instructional strategies, and the selection of appropriate measurement techniques are presented in chapters 5 and 6. Chapter 7 introduces the legal authority and program responsibility to provide for the needs of students with disabilities. Chapter 8 examines the legal requirements' implications for programs, and chapters 9 and 10 provide a thorough discussion of administrative procedures, facilities, equipment, and supplies, offering suggestions and recommendations. Chapter 11 briefly discusses the physical education program's connection with experiences outside of the classroom. The manual also includes 14 appendixes that support material from the chapters.

It was interesting to compare two appendixes, Learning Outcomes and Desirable Experiences, with those from more recent state publications, such as *Colorado's Learning Outcomes/Content Standards*. Although these states define "outcome" differently, many concepts are similar. Both have unique ideas for program development and for integration with other academic content.

The document concludes with footnotes, an extensive glossary of terms, and a bibliography organized by chapter.

Delaware (1985)

The Delaware Department of Public Instruction's 14-page *Physical Education Content Standards* lists instructional program provisions and student expectations organized in four grade-level categories (grades 1-3, 4-6, 7-8, and 9-12). Seven or eight goals of instruction appear for each grade category. Each of the student expectations is aligned to a single instructional goal. Verbs like *demonstrate, participate, perform,* and *express* dominate the column of student expectations and imply that the student is expected to be active. Although the number of goals and expectations varies from one grade category to another, the goals and expectations align developmentally across categories. One of the goals of instruction in each of the grade categories pertains to special physical education for students with special needs. The document provides no resource or program development assistance beyond the instructional provisions and statements of student expectations.

District of Columbia

No materials were received for this review.

Florida (1991 and 1992)

Pursuant to section 230.2319 of the Florida Statute, students in grades 6 through 8 are to receive instruction in subjects in physical education (among other subjects), with local school boards deciding on the time spent in physical education. The high school graduation requirement includes one-half credit in physical education focusing on the assessment, improvement, and maintenance of personal fitness.

Physical Education Curriculum Frameworks: Grades 6-8 includes an overview (5 pages) and a collection of 10 themes, each of which is designed to be the primary focus of instruction for an extended unit of instruction. These themes include the major concepts/content and intended outcomes that are to result from the student's work. The goal of the skill theme curriculum is the ability to use skills, or selected sets of skills, in a variety of contexts and situations. Some skill themes include adapted physical education Individual Education Programs (I.E.P.), two themes in physical fitness, body management, three themes on various manipulative skills, and comprehensive physical education 1, 2, and 3. Each theme has been developed into a course description.

The High School Overview (5 pages) contained in the *Physical Education Curriculum Frameworks: Grades 9-12, Adult* describes the philosophy of assisting students and adults to acquire the skills, knowledge, and motivation to incorporate physical activity into their daily lives. No individual high school is expected to include all of the 46 courses (which range from five courses for students with disabilities to fitness, team sport, individual and dual activity, gymnastics, recreational activities, outdoor education, and more). They are organized in the same way as the course descriptions for grades 6 through 8, identifying major concepts/content and then intended outcomes for students in grades 9 through 12 and adults.

The Florida Department of Education Bureau of Education for Exceptional Students has published a 147-page manual entitled *Perfect Harmony Reaching Out: An Extracurricular Fitness and Leisure Program for Individuals with Disabilities* (1992). It was developed by Florida State University and the Hernando County Schools to document a model for increased school and community intervention toward students with disabilities. The document describes how to get started, and includes information about volunteers, setting up courses, and making modifications to allow those with disabilities to interact with others in fitness and leisure activities. The document includes references, resources, and even a script for a skit to introduce the program and raise the awareness of audiences toward the problems of those with disabilities.

Georgia

We were unable to review the materials from Georgia.

Hawaii

No materials were received from the state of Hawaii for this review.

Idaho (1990)

Idaho's guide to physical education for grades K through 6 is uniquely titled *Nuts and Bolts and Climbing Ropes: Physical Education for Idaho Schools, Grades K-6.* Originally approved by the Idaho State Board of Education and printed in 1982, it was reprinted in 1984, 1987, and 1989. The 339-page document was developed to help Idaho schools plan and develop a viable, relevant physical education program that reflects the philosophy of lifelong, life-giving skills for all youngsters. A secondary level guide was not available for review.

The K-6 guide begins with a philosophy statement of skill development through participation in movement experiences. It continues with applications of movement principles, an accountability challenge in which the teacher provides sequential skills for students' mastery, and a legal and a professional challenge. No legal reference is listed, but the guide indicates that students should receive 150 minutes per week, 30 minutes per day of instructional physical education by well-trained personnel who are professionally inclined to seek continual inservice development.

The table of contents and the various sections are inconsistent with the page numbers, but the information included is cogent and in many respects still helpful. A guide to using a 116-item self-appraisal checklist with a Likert scale scoring tool is included for program analysis, followed by a bibliography listing two films and several books and kits. It is unclear whether the bibliography was used to develop the self-appraisal checklist or whether it was used as an additional resource. The self-appraisal checklist is followed by a score comparison chart. The program self-appraisal is unique among the state-level guides reviewed in this analysis.

Pages 13 to 171 review motor skills with sections on body awareness, stages of motor skill development, and 101 performance objectives of specific skills and their corresponding grade levels. The fitness section, which contains brief summary materials and has no color-coded grade-level activity samples, may not reflect the overall quality of the rest of the guide. The rhythms and dance section (pages 47-105) refers to several books in its description of creative dance and then lists 136 different codified movement dances. It also offers some descriptions, suggests appropriate grade levels, and includes the source of the recorded music. The gymnastics section contains a 10-page scope and sequence with hundreds of items, followed by sample grade-appropriate materials. The games sections, which could be more appropriately named "games and sports," contain a scope and sequence of lead-up games by grade level, followed by skill sets by sport and grade level, some skill tests, and sample grade-appropriate materials. The text concludes with a short section on suggested equipment needs and ideas for improvising various equipment and apparatus (13 pages).

Illinois (1986)

State Goals for Learning and Sample Learning Objectives: Physical Development and Health—Grades 3, 6, 8, 10, & 12 is one of the earlier outcomes publications. The state of Illinois has one of the most stringent requirements for physical education in the schools. As stated in the introduction, seven broad terminal goals (meaning what students should know and be able to do at the time of their graduation from high school as a result of their schooling) form the basis of the instructional program for all students.

The required program calls for daily classes that include vigorous activity and rigorous development of students' understanding of health concepts as well as of physical skills. Assessment is based on written tests, student projects, criterion-referenced observation, and class discussion. Like the Maryland publication, this document contains a section that repeats each goal outlined in the introduction and provides a summary of general knowledge and skills related to that goal. The next section articulates the sample learning objectives for each goal; this is followed by a brief section that lists the student learning outcomes in five other learning areas outlined in the *State Goals for Learning and Sample Learning Objectives* series. The concluding section includes questions about planning, funding, and testing.

Although most of this information is specific to Illinois, it could still be helpful to the state-level planner. The format employed by the document is effective at clarifying levels of sophistication expected for each goal so that readers clearly understand the intent of the goals framework. Most of the learning objectives are well written and are descriptive yet succinct. Although this document mixes the traditional with the new, it demonstrates a vision for the future of education, bridging separatist's verbiage to help break down some of the barriers between very traditional health education and physical education programs with newer ideas such as the focus on learning outcomes. Indeed, it implicitly encourages integration of the related and sometimes overlapping subject areas of physical education and health education.

Indiana (1993)

Indiana's 31-page publication, entitled *Physical Education Proficiency and Essential Skills Guide*, utilizes the NASPE Outcomes (1992) as a platform from which to provide guidance to schools and teachers in developing sound instructional practices, curriculum, and assessment of students and local physical education programs. The publication's proficiency statements are intended to serve as benchmarks for state-level decision making and local curriculum development, but the proficiency indicators are sample activities, skills, and behaviors for teachers and curriculum developers.

The list of essential skills follows the same format as the sample benchmarks of achievement from the NASPE Outcomes. These essential skills have been interpreted to provide, in general terms, the expectations for all students at transition points in school, namely at the end of grades K, 2, 4, 6, 8, 10, and 12.

Appendixes include Suggested Skills and Activities, Definition of Terms, Curriculum Planning General Suggestions, Recommendations for a High Quality Physical

Education Program, Parent/Community Involvement, Adaptive/Adapted Physical Education, Policies (i.e., guidance for local district policy development), Procedures, and Premises (for understanding the essential skills). Those using the document are encouraged throughout to access the services of a state-level consultant in physical education located at the Indiana State Department of Education.

Iowa (1985)

Iowa's 66-page document, *A Tool for Assessing and Designing a K-12 Physical Education Program*, was developed by a four-member writing team and reviewed by 12 selected physical education experts within Iowa. The section on philosophical considerations contains a rationale for physical education as well as a statement of beliefs and the goals and objectives for the local programs. The legal authority for the program is included.

This publication includes a fairly extensive physical education program assessment instrument as well as models of student performance expectations for teachers either to adopt or to use in developing appropriate local student performance expectations. The final section discusses program scope and sequence (including the development of a local scope and sequence) as well as time allotment, and provides an example of time percentages appropriate for specific activity types in the primary grades. The appendixes include a glossary of terms, completed samples of performance expectations in the cognitive, psychomotor/fitness, and affective domains, and district examples of a program scope and sequence.

The document also contains a user guide to a computer program available to supplement the written guide and to assist in shaping the local physical education program. An additional appendix contains a position statement written by the Iowa Association for Health, Physical Education, Recreation, and Dance. The document concludes with a bibliography of 28 entries, most of which are guides from other state departments of education.

Kansas (1990)

Healthy Lifestyles for Kansas Schools and Communities: The Role of the School Physical Education Program highlights the importance of physical education programs in developing healthy, physically active young people, and examines how these programs form a coordinated part of a complex and comprehensive school health approach. The 25-page document does not contain mandates; rather, it is intended to assist schools in improving their programs. The issue of healthy lifestyles

figures prominently throughout the document.

The first section elaborates on the philosophy that a quality physical education program supported through community recreation programs promotes an active lifestyle and contributes to the prevention of disease and the maintenance of positive mental health. The next section provides answers to 10 questions about the role of physical education programs. The issues covered include amount of time spent on physical education, time spent actively participating in tasks, preparation to perform lifetime physical activity skills, health-related versus skill-related fitness assessment, healthy attitudes, class size, equipment, coeducational classes, special needs legislation, community-based extensions of school programs, staff collaboration with others in the school and community, and teachers as models of healthy lifestyle practices. Trends for program development are identified and adapted (*Alabama Course of Study: Physical Education*, 1989).

The third section offers assistance in the development of a school/district physical education curriculum plan that includes a philosophy, program outcomes, course and grade-level outcomes, time allocations, and methods of evaluating and recording student progress towards the outcomes. The publication encourages curriculum designers to supplement the plan by adopting or creating an activity guide and a policies and procedures manual. NASPE's *Outcomes of Quality Physical Education Programs* (1992) are included as model outcomes for schools.

The document also includes a content model and a partial program checklist that teachers might use to self- or peer-evaluate the programs, and a reference list and appendixes provide resources for program development, implementation, and maintenance. The inclusion of an action photo of Arnold Schwarzenegger (Past Chair of the President's Council on Physical Fitness and Sport) to conclude the document tells a story all by itself.

Kentucky (1991)

Kentucky provided a brief portion (pp. 5-9) of *Kentucky's Learning Goals and Learner Outcomes* and a portion of its *Transformations: Kentucky's Curriculum Framework* (Volume I) for this analysis. The first document outlines six broad learning goals and 75 learner outcomes that take into account the assumption guiding the Kentucky Education Reform Act (KERA) that all students can learn. The goals and outcomes delineate what students should know and be able to do as a result of their school experience. Selected outcomes implicitly support the inclusion of physical activity as a general learning tool (e.g., 3.2-3.7 and 4.1-4.7) while others (2.31-2.35) are specific to a quality physical education program.

The second partial document includes and expands upon the first. The section on practical living skills (pp. 181-212) is designed to communicate methodological options to curriculum planners and teachers, and the ideas provided as learning links (connections to other outcomes) and related concepts (connections to subject content) help to focus and ultimately reach the outcomes. The document suggests applying more authentic (real life) learning and assessment. Ideas for incorporating the community further embrace curriculum reform. Sample activities are listed in order to encourage teacher creativity while articulating an understanding of what might be developmentally appropriate for the age level grouping from elementary to middle and high school.

The sections on applications across the curriculum are helpful to schools in transition from a course-oriented, traditional program to an outcomes-driven program (e.g., teaching various general education principles in a physical education context). The *Framework* is an important resource for Kentucky teachers working for this transition with cross-disciplinary, interdisciplinary, and integrated content that focuses on what students know and are able to do. The full *Framework* probably would have yielded a more positive review because a more complete curriculum balance might have been observed. The sections available for review demonstrate many connections to the current professional literature and aim for an education of the whole person.

Louisiana (1990)

The 51 authors contributing to the Louisiana Department of Education's 468-page *Physical Education and Recreation Curriculum Guide: Grades K-10* have created activity units in movement, physical fitness and fitness appraisal, dance, team sports, individual and dual sports, lifetime sports, park and recreational games, and outdoor adventure. The document's introductory pages provide the rationale, including research implications, for physical education competencies. The activity unit approach used in this document is traditional, but comprehensive, and the document includes a large variety of units. Louisiana's inclusion of the categories of park and recreational games and outdoor adventure is unique: Any mention of activities such as horseshoes, boating, paddle tennis, tether ball, angling and casting, fire building, knots and lashings, outdoor cooking, outings and trip preparation, gun safety, tents and shelters, and hiking was rare in other physical education programs reviewed.

A key to using the guide includes directions for how to read the enclosed scope and sequence and the activity units. Each unit contains an activity content outline,

required as well as elective performance objectives, suggested activities with methods and techniques, and finally a bibliography outlining books and materials available for each activity unit included in the guide.

Maine (1991)

Physical education instruction is required by state statute and outlined in two publications of the Department of Education, *Chapter 125—Regulations Governing Basic School Approval* and *Chapter 127—Instructional Requirements and the Graduation Standard*. In these publications, physical education is designed to promote physical wellness, self-esteem, sportsmanship, and interpersonal relationships through sequential instruction of a variety of activity forms and movement concepts. The documents also help clarify Maine's requirements for an elementary course of study and for the inclusion of one full credit of physical education in the secondary school program and diploma requirements.

Maine also has a two-page outline of physical education certification endorsement requirements for teachers seeking to educate students in grades K-12. These three documents contain information about requirements only; they provide no information about program planning, staff development, implementation, or assessment.

A draft copy of the *Guidelines for Programming in Adapted Physical Education* (no date of publication) was the only form of technical assistance included in materials sent for this review. This manual is designed to foster the development of procedures and practices for the implementation of an adapted physical education program. It includes an introduction that reiterates the elementary and secondary course of study required by Maine law and explains that all Maine students are entitled to an appropriate physical education, whether it is regular or modified, including adapted, physical education.

This publication uses "adapted physical education" as an umbrella term for a wide range of delivery models and gives examples of instances where these models would apply (remediation, disability, and short term injury or illness). The 28-page document also includes screening and assessment processes, a discussion of physical education in the IEP process, and programming for students who have special needs but do not require an IEP. Finally, the document suggests procedures for implementing an adaptive physical education program. Six appendixes include definitions of exceptional students, a description of the least restrictive educational alternative, major requirements of Public Law 101-476 and of Public Law 93-112, section 504, some assessment tools, and sample physician referral letters.

Maryland (1988)

The state of Maryland's *Physical Education: A Maryland Curricular Framework* provides school districts with technical assistance in physical education. The vintage of the Maryland document is not apparent, as it anticipates the intent of the NASPE Outcomes of 1992. The presentation of the materials is classy, progressive, and thorough, and the team of writers and reviewers reads like a list of who's who in physical education.

The publication's three-goal approach (i.e., fitness, movement skills, and affective qualities) is effective at providing exactly what the title implies: a curriculum framework. The goals are expanded into subgoals and student expectancies. The goal orientation is expressed in matrixes that provide usable information for teachers. One example shows what instructional vehicles (e.g., sports or dance) are best with what level of student and in what kind of balance.

Maryland's document does not quit there, as those of many states have done. It also includes illustrative objectives, or benchmarks (as they are referred to most often), after grades 2, 5, 8, and 12. These benchmarks are followed by a guide for curriculum specialists and teachers to use in developing new curricula. This guide is easy to follow, with examples that show exactly how local curriculum can match the state goals. Instructional units are explained and examples provided that fit right into today's thinking on various approaches to education generally and to physical education specifically.

Although assessment is mentioned and elaborated upon briefly, this is the weakest part of the document. On the other hand, the appendixes shed new light on some of the materials contained in the body of the text, thus adding depth to the document and the reader's understanding of it. One appendix discusses what parts of the framework are necessary to meet the state-required "expected outcomes" included in a resource paper published in 1981, which makes Maryland a pioneer in the outcomes movement. Much of what is written would be embraced today as cogent and current.

This publication, assessment notwithstanding, is among the strongest reviewed in terms of continuity, ease of use, and its view of the big picture. It should be on the short list of resources for the next steps of physical education curriculum building at the national, state, and local levels.

Massachusetts (1982)

The purpose of physical education in the Commonwealth of Massachusetts is to promote the physical well-being of all students. The Commonwealth of Massachusetts Department of Education's 30-page booklet, entitled *Physical Education: 1. Laws and regulations; 2.*

Guidelines for Adapted Physical Education; and 3. Chapter 622 [Massachusetts law prohibiting discrimination] and Title IX [from the Federal Code] as They Relate to Physical Education and Athletics, contains technical assistance narrative mixed with regulation. The document provides resources and contacts throughout Massachusetts, with the idea that the document's impact will be expanded through district and school programs.

Selected resources include suggested forms useful within the program (listing of school health care contacts, accident recording form) and reaching outside the program (parent letter concerning placement, three physician referral letters, and a physician direction form). The text includes direct contacts and notes describing 18 promising programs in adapted physical education (annotated) and 8 coeducational programs. The document concludes with resource contacts in the Massachusetts Department of Education and the Massachusetts AHPERD section on adaptive physical education.

Michigan (1991)

The Michigan State Board of Education's 70+-page working paper, *Model Core Curriculum Outcomes*, includes current dialogue on restructuring education, much like the documents reviewed from Colorado, Kentucky, and a few other states. Michigan includes a brief background discussion of the legislation behind the school restructuring and nine underlying principles guiding assessment, curriculum, and delivery development. Broad student outcomes are listed in terms of what is defined as the "capable" person: learning over a lifetime; applying knowledge in diverse situations; making decisions for successful living; being a caring, sensitive, and flexible person; being a creative and innovative person; being an effective communicator; and being a competent and productive person.

Beyond the broad outcomes, Michigan has developed a state model for a core curriculum. This model lists a set of content disciplines and a set of local core curriculum responsibilities that include determining the courses, materials, and sequence. The document illustrates how the core curriculum is developed in a matrix of process skills organized according to disciplinary and interdisciplinary outcome areas. Physical education and health are listed together, as are mathematics and science.

The core curriculum outcomes for physical education are then grouped conceptually by fundamental motor skills, cognitive concepts, physical fitness, body control skills, sports and leisure skills, and effective personal and social skills. The conceptual grouping in the outcomes section is then broken down into specific demonstrations of student competence at three different levels of schooling. The lists of competency statements seem to apply only to physical education, for they do not appear to be connected to the underlying principles, process skills, and broad outcomes of Michigan's general approach to core curriculum and outcomes as espoused earlier in the document.

Minnesota (1989 and 1992)

The most comprehensive set of materials reviewed was from Minnesota. This is a guide that could, and does, assist local program development; it could be helpful to other states as well. In 78 pages, *Outcome Competencies and Assessment Strategies for Physical Education* (1992) provides direction for districts and schools to follow in structuring programs. This reader found a one-page discussion of the six-step process of writing the document, contained in the introductory information, to be quite useful: It offered a glimpse of the rigor applied to program development, and also provided a bridge to reader "ownership" of the ideas.

Minnesota's vision of a physically educated person is based on fitness, self-image, and social behaviors. In contrast to the NASPE definition, Minnesota makes no reference to the acquisition and refinement of motor skills, but identifies perceptual motor and object manipulation—locomotor and nonlocomotor—as the first two areas of study. The areas of study follow a traditional grouping: In addition to the two areas already mentioned, they are rhythm and dance, health-related physical fitness and wellness, group and team sports, individual sports and recreational activities, outdoor education, and aquatics.

In the 1989 document, *Model Learner Outcomes for Physical Education* (92 pages), each area of study identifies the appropriate 32 "essential" learner outcomes from a list of 83 "model" learner outcomes. Competency samples are aligned with assessment samples, which are written in terms of Bloom's taxonomy of cognitive skills. The 1989 document's fourth chapter, "Transposing Model Learner Outcomes Into Curriculum," is indicative of the complexity of program and curriculum development seen throughout the publication. Although organized and well-written, it would still seem somewhat overwhelming to a local program developer or a team of teachers on release time for the development process. The reader comes away with a sense of knowing only the complexity of curriculum development without knowing what an actual program might look like.

State guide developers would find the two-document set valuable and inclusive, and would see it as an asset to their bookshelves. Indeed, both documents must be present for the reader to understand the approach. Each

is laden with acronyms that are introduced at one time or another throughout the documents. Minnesota is eager to share these documents, emphasizing that they are available both in hard copy and on computer disk from the designated state department of education specialist assigned to physical education.

Mississippi (1986)

In *Mississippi Curriculum Structure — Philosophy, Goals, Skills, and Concepts for Curriculum Development and Instructional Planning: Health and Physical Education* (1986; 6th printing 1992), the section on health education information is separate from that on physical education. However, they share the basic charge to teach motor skills, knowledge, and attitudes vital to the development of a healthy, active lifestyle and to include options to school districts for allowing graduation credits (grades 9-12) based on the Carnegie Unit.

The introduction and formats for the health education and physical education sections are similar. The eight goals of physical education listed vary in conceptual sophistication and assessment criteria (e.g., demonstrate, understand, participate, develop, etc.). A general grade-level organizer is useful from a curriculum developer's perspective and follows an "introduction — mastery continuum" designation for skill and knowledge expansions. Content scope (somewhat useful) and sequence (of little use) is organized into activity categories (basic movements, low organized games, lead-up games, sports, rhythms, gymnastics, health-related fitness, and aquatics) by the grade-level indicators of introduction and mastery.

The document presents four levels (scenarios) of offering a program in health and physical education so that participating Mississippi school districts can select from a range that meets the law and fits their own school culture. Due to the age of the document, it does not reflect the current trends in physical education articulated in the NASPE Outcomes (1992).

Missouri (1992)

Like other states, Missouri is in the throes of converting the elementary and secondary school system from a focus on the processes of education to one on the valued outcomes of education. The 14-page draft, *A Proposal to Implement Outcome-Based Graduation in Missouri High Schools: Moving to Outcome-Based Education*, is articulate and provides direction for curriculum reform. (In fact, the last page is an invitation, written by the state department of education, to review the document.) The first page discusses the traditional system and makes direct arguments for a change to an outcome-based system in physical education and other subject areas. The rest of the document describes five general outcomes and the 25 programmatic outcomes. All have extended definitions organized in bullet lists under each outcome.

It is clear from all of the outcomes that Missouri is embracing the notion of a performance-based assessment system and of integrated instructional models as it progresses toward educational and cultural restructuring in its schools. In the category of outcomes entitled "Physical, Emotional, and Social Well-Being," the document identifies many themes of physical development, structure, functions, and changes of the human body in its discussion of topics of disease, injuries, and health care issues, all of which are knowledge based. A bullet under one programmatic outcome is a direct quote from one of the 20 outcomes in the *NASPE Outcomes of a Physically Educated Person* (1992) related to the "costs, benefits, and obligations associated with regular participation in physical activity" (p. 3). The second programmatic outcome in this same category introduces the skills and behaviors of a graduating student. Psychomotor skill in various settings and participation in health-enhancing leisure-time activity are mentioned.

As is to be expected in a cross-disciplinary model, physical education is not explicitly identified as a program, but it exists implicitly as a context for learning many of the outcomes listed. It will be important to follow the development of the Missouri system in its coming stages. Although it is interesting to read about the "what" of education, at this stage, the "how" and "what if" questions have not been answered. This material would be of value to states moving toward an outcomes-based system so that they could compare the outcome language, level of sophistication, and number of outcomes with that of their own developing programs. It would be of little or no value to disciplinary-based programs.

Montana (1988)

Montana in Action: Physical Education Curriculum Guide: Grades K-12 is a collaborative effort of the Montana Office of Public Instruction and the Montana AHPERD. The 100-page manual is in its second printing. It does not take the place of local curriculum development but enhances the process with suggestions, ideas, and encouragement toward sequential and health-enhancing skill building—and a lifetime of activity-conscious attitudes for all Montana students. The philosophy behind this program emanates from the research of the discipline itself, the health community, the medical

literature, and local adaptation.

True to the mission of being a guide to self-development in improving physical education programs, the text is divided into three helpful sections: managing the system, instructional programs, and supplemental programs. The first section, about managing the system, discusses topics of public relations, organizational patterns, administration, safety, and evaluation. The inclusion of graphics, which say more than straight text, is refreshing and provides variety on the page; information presented in an outline format, including subtopics, provides a hierarchy for concept development and understanding.

The section on instructional programs introduces the content options of the adapted and the elective program. Programs begin with an understanding of the importance of learning to move and of being fit; they continue through the three domains of learning—cognitive, affective, and psychomotor—and promote an interdisciplinary approach. The sequences of particular content are presented so that they provide enough information for motivation but, holding true to the mission of the text, they would require some expansion by practicing teachers for implementation.

The supplemental program section, although brief, provides practical guidance for the reader and user.

Overall, the manual is to be used, not read in a single sitting. It summarizes voluminous disciplinary content into an understandable and usable package that is an asset to program developers.

A second folder included for review, *Health Enhancement: A Design for Montana's Future*, introduces an interdisciplinary approach toward health and physical education that focuses on learner outcomes instead of adhering to a time/unit accreditation model. The health enhancement program (HEP) is designed to present a more holistic approach to teaching and learning the health and physical education curriculum.

Nebraska (1992)

Nebraska has no standards of its own for physical education. The state provided a copy of the NASPE *Outcomes of Quality Physical Education Programs* (1992) for review.

Nevada (1984)

The state of Nevada documents its physical education program in two publications, the *Elementary Course of Study* and the *Nevada Secondary Course of Study*. The elementary document lists physical education as one subject among eleven, and the secondary document lists physical education as one of eight required subjects (six more subjects are listed as electives within the course of study at the high school level).

The documents include three statutes pertaining to both courses of study. One of these states, ''Every teacher in the public schools shall enforce the course of study as prescribed by law'' (p. 3) (NRS 391.260). The courses of study are considered to be established standards for Nevada school students. A rationale is provided that addresses the value and need for the physical education program in each course of study.

Both documents supply a program overview. The elementary course of study provides state mandates requiring that specific objectives be met upon completion of kindergarten and of grades 3, 6, and 8. The secondary course of study lists requirements for graduation, outlining six categories of mandated student objectives: understanding and realizations, physical conditioning, rhythms, individual and dual sports, team sports, and the fitness course.

New Hampshire (1993)

As of this writing, a physical education curriculum guide is being developed but has not been released. However, New Hampshire sent its 50-page rule, ''PART Ed306 Minimum Standards for Public School Approval'' (with appropriate statutory authority), for review. Although many states allow course content to be decided upon at the local level, New Hampshire includes course content in the administrative rule (law) of the state.

This publication lists and describes learner enablement and course content for 10 elementary, middle, and junior high school subjects out of a total of 11 required subjects and an elective category. Allocating the balance of the elementary school day over the year is a responsibility of local districts. In middle and junior high school, the allotment of time for physical education is a minimum of 35 hours for the school year. High schools have a minimum standard of one credit (from a total of 19-3/4) for graduation. Although the document lists health education information separately from the physical education information, some of the content overlaps, allowing for some degree of integration to occur across subject areas and course design.

Topics in the physical education curriculum appear to be consistent with those in many other states, and are traditional to a certain extent. Although somewhat consistent with the NASPE Outcomes (1992), no reference or wording demonstrates a connection with the national definition. The elementary school programs seem to emphasize movement skill acquisition, but fitness becomes the emphasis in the middle school and junior high school programs, and the high school programs balance fitness and cooperative and recreational

activities. The three main areas of instruction include (a) movement activities designed to improve fitness; (b) movement activities such as dance, rhythm, dramatics, and gymnastics; and (c) cooperative and recreational activities such as bowling, archery, tennis, cycling, and fishing. The high school program focuses on understanding the importance of and adhering to participation in physical activity and fitness, and it is worth noting that the high school program also identifies the learning of outdoor recreational activities (seven elective courses) as a viable course construct.

New Jersey

Because its curricular materials were still being developed as of this writing, the Garden State was unable to provide any state-level documentation for the discipline of physical education for this review. A draft of content standards has been approved for dissemination but has not yet been adopted by the state school board. A recently completed second project that will go into effect in the 1995-96 school year encompasses the core course proficiencies of students in grades 9 through 12 that met high school graduation requirements.

New Mexico (1992)

The State Board of Education has initiated a student-centered framework for system-wide educational change in New Mexico to provide a broad program in which the disciplinary frameworks (areas of competency) relate to standards of excellence for all New Mexico students. Among the eleven competency frameworks presented in the 23-page *New Mexico Competency Frameworks* are many with traditional titles, but ''Interscholastic Education/Activities'' and ''Employability/Life Skills'' indicate some new areas that are, however, beyond the scope of this physical education review.

The physical education competency framework begins with the definition of a physically educated person (NASPE, 1992) and adds a sixth component, namely, ''Explores occupational opportunities.'' This framework discusses competency in terms of domain-specified learning topics (cognitive, affective, or psychomotor) for students. The document is a glimpse at the big picture across the entire curriculum in a system that is undergoing reform. The listings provide some direction but little initiative, guidance, or commentary on procedures for developing or implementing state or local programs.

New York (1986 and 1988)

New York provides two documents for understanding, developing, and implementing complete programs in physical education. *Physical Education Syllabus: Grades K-12* (1986) is a 56-page manual that contains state laws and regulations; the Regent's goals; scope and sequence of inclusive subtopics for physical education; guidelines for developing a program from scratch; and articulation, evaluation, and integration of course content, which is defined as the "art and science of human movement." The 47-page manual, *Physical Education Guide: Grades K-12* (1988), includes ideas and suggestions to assist educators in planning, teaching, and evaluating the physical education program at the local level. Extensive planning and refining of the product is evident throughout both documents.

Although not labeled as outcomes as in current vernacular, the K-12 program focuses on the student's demonstration of nine personal living skills. These include both quantitative and qualitative skills such as cardiovascular fitness, musculoskeletal fitness, cooperation, risk taking, safety, initiative, leadership and followership, trust, and respect. Sample activities range from those stressing a very traditional skills approach to those favoring more conceptual ideas for movement and developmental approaches for opportunistic learning.

The guide is organized by activity type (rhythms and dance, games and sports, etc.) and is formatted to include ideas for safety. Valuable sections include matrices of how sample activities lead to the personal living skills and questions for evaluative purposes written in the context of three domains of learning. This publication also includes some ideas on teaching students with disabilities, grading for credit, and finding further resources that can assist in the development of a comprehensive program.

The manuals deserve applause for being a joint effort of the university system and the state department of education. They are useful, easy to understand, and present an organized and comprehensive approach to program development, implementation, and evaluation. These manuals could be useful to professionals outside as well as inside the state of New York. A page in the syllabus describing how physical education is implicit in each one of the Regent's goals for total education is especially noteworthy. It is unfortunate that this link between physical education and the general curriculum is often missed by state-level documentation, because exploration of this link could prove to be of vital importance to public awareness and understanding of the dynamic changes that have occurred in physical education over the past 20 years.

North Carolina (1987 and 1992)

A draft copy of the state publication, *North Carolina Teacher Handbook: Physical Education Overview and K-3 Major Emphases* (dated 07/29/92), was received for review and commentary. At first glance, it appears to be a primary level document because of its graphics and subtitle, *K-3 Physical Education: A Strong Foundation for Our Children's Future*. However, the document moves quickly into a comprehensive program of K-12 physical education for all students.

The six program goals making up North Carolina's definition of a physically educated person are designed to be inclusive of students with disabilities and other special needs. Three goals deal with skill, fitness, and knowledge for participation in physical activities. The other three goals emphasize the development of a positive self-image, responsible social behavior, and awareness and respect for cultural diversity through participation in physical activity. Four vehicles of instruction (skills/subject area) are used to further define specific competency goals, objectives, and sample measures: dance, gymnastics, games, and movement exploration.

The format for this 127-page publication is easy to grasp, and many of the sample measures, written in behavioral terms, outline student activities clearly. However, there is a danger that a classroom teacher or a physical education specialist could misuse this document by simply pulling suggested activities out of the text without reading the material concerning the sequencing of the activities. Although this is not the intended use, the lack of a section on whom the text was designed for and how it should or could be used makes the document confusing.

Furthermore, the document is replete with behavioral objectives. One would never have to write another such objective: They are all here! In addition, although the scripted presentations for teacher use in class may be helpful to the novice teacher, they encourage teachers to simply read the information to students.

On the other hand, the use of the instructional vehicles is impressive, providing continuity and a focus on learning motor behavior as opposed to a focus on preparation for athletics in the upper grades. The emphasis on primary children's physical education is also laudable, as it integrates movement and skills approaches well. This publication, although incomplete in its present form, is a resource of some depth and it is on its way to becoming a valuable, applicable curriculum.

North Carolina also provided *Physical Education at Work: Innovative K-12 Physical Education Ideas* (1987) as part of the information packet for review. In this pamphlet, some of the best teachers in the state present the "best" and the "promising" ideas for physical education. This brief document would be valuable to innovative teachers or to teachers wishing to try something new and exciting. Each activity listed includes a contact's name and address to foster better connections and statewide unity. This unique document is an excellent innovation.

North Dakota

No materials were received from the state of North Dakota for this review.

Ohio

Sources in Ohio report that all curriculum guidance documents are being revised and are thus unavailable for this review. However, progress is being made toward board approval and state implementation.

Oklahoma (1992)

Oklahoma, an outcomes-approach state, was mandated to write desired competencies for students in public schools and to suggest how these competencies might be centered upon various skills and knowledge rather than be constrained by a traditional course unit structure. The resulting six-part series, entitled *Learner Outcomes: Oklahoma State Competencies* (for grades 1, 2, 3, 4, 5, and 6-12), develops 10 subject areas. A short introduction precedes the comprehensive health and physical education section. Although the two curricular areas appear together under this section heading, they are discussed separately throughout the rest of the document.

The physical education component of the comprehensive health and physical education section quotes the NASPE definition of a physically educated person (1992) and continues with physical education learner outcomes for grades 1, 2, 3, 4, 5, and 6-12. These learner outcomes are the examples of benchmarks contained in the NASPE document. Although laudable in researching the NASPE effort, the Oklahoma documentation does not maintain the integrity of the NASPE project's middle section, namely, the section providing the 20 outcome statements that provide focus for a K-12 program of student progress toward the desired outcomes. Important concepts were dropped.

Oregon (1988)

The Beaver State's comprehensive *Common* (meaning required in all districts) *Curriculum Goals in Physical Education* are published in a matrix format that includes 3 goal areas, 12 goals, and grade-level expectancies coupled with appropriate essential learning skills of general education. The aim is to show how physical education is an integral part of general education. Each goal area is preceded by a concept paper designed to give focus and clarity to curriculum specialists and to those teachers on assignment specifically to flesh out the local curriculum. The document itself is somewhat cumbersome for teachers to use "as is" in curriculum planning or in the classroom, and has been criticized for trivializing the subject area into little boxes rather than presenting a flowing sequence of skill progress and behaviors becoming of a physically educated person.

The three goal areas—Expressive and Efficient Movement, Fitness, and Personal Responsibility and Social Behavior—are each subdivided by a number of goals, with four goals in the first area, three in the second, and five in the third. These goals serve as targets for assessment of students and programs at grades 3, 5, 8, and 11. Each grade-level expectancy is formatted in terms of student achievement, and all of them combined comprehensively cover the subject area.

The document also contains a very useful bibliography annotated by some of the best physical education teachers in the state. In the annotations, these teachers extol the benefits of the resource, note where they found it, and describe how the resource has changed their thinking, planning, teaching, and assessment of student performance. The document concludes with a physical education logo for teachers to use when making posters for the gymnasium or handouts for student consumption; the logo can also be used in student newsletters or in any other place where physical education could get visibility.

Pennsylvania (1993)

The student learning outcomes received for this review (Section 5.202 of Chapter 5 dated January 15, 1993) were adopted by the Commonwealth of Pennsylvania's State Board of Education and were scheduled to proceed to the House and Senate Committees on Education and the Regulatory Review Commission prior to being published as final regulations in the *Pennsylvania Bulletin*. The ten outcome areas included are broken down into 55 student targets. The State Board has premised each learning target with the inclusive phrase, "All students . . . ."

The physical education and health component includes six statements encouraging the integration of these two subject areas. Many of the other areas covered in the outcomes also include meaningful overlap with what might be described as health or physical education, further implying an overall integrated approach on how students demonstrate what they know and are able to do. Further development from Pennsylvania should put the commonwealth into the classification of other "outcomes" states such as Oregon, Kentucky, Colorado, and Oklahoma. It seems clear that Pennsylvania intends further publications as school reform and curricular restructuring occurs.

Rhode Island (1994)

The state of Rhode Island provided *Reaching for High Standards: Student Performance in Rhode Island*, a 41 page booklet of the results of their Spring, 1994 statewide testing effort. Although interesting, it contains no information about the state's physical education program. However, the booklet does include the results of Rhode Island's health knowledge tests. Physical fitness test results were included until 1992, but are no longer provided.

South Carolina

No information was received for review.

South Dakota (no date listed)

Each of South Dakota's volumes in their two-volume *Guide for Instruction in Physical Education* (one for grades K-6 and one for grades 7-12) provides a 19- to 20-page detailed overview of the scope and sequence of a total physical education program. However, the guide itself is much more than an overview. Each volume is about 300 pages long, and includes sequences, line drawings, progressions, sample lessons, collections of activities, and programmatic assistance. Both are resources with depth and character that provide many options for teachers to select and conduct a variety of approaches toward a physical education program. The state has gone to great expense and time to create a guide that is directed toward local curriculum planners and especially teachers.

It is clear that the guide owes much to an activity-based skill development approach. Acknowledgments were offered to Maryland and Minnesota for assistance and partnership in the development of the manuals. Although the table of contents hits the highlights, it is not very helpful in locating specific topics. An index would help readers in finding some types of assistance in these volumes.

It is interesting that, although the text is entitled as a guide for "instruction," very little space is devoted to instructional methodology; rather, almost all of the

document is devoted to the content. Although the "what" (content) of physical education is presented in an organized, referenced, and sequenced manner, the "how" (instruction) is blatantly overlooked, or assumed, or perhaps presented in another venue. The addition of teacher tips, hints, and formal instructional options could enhance an already good guide.

Tennessee

No information was received for review.

Texas

No information was received for review.

Utah (1994)

The *Healthy Lifestyles Core Curriculum* is a compilation of course outlines that delineate how education is to respond to the student's need for learning in the health education and physical education disciplines. Although the State Board of Education has developed what appears to be an integrated approach to the two subject areas, it has maintained a separation between health education and physical education in the course outlines. These include a narrative description of the core program in health education or movement/fitness (not physical education), the numbered core standards of the course (behavioral antecedent of all standards is "the student will. . ."), and the numbered objectives (descriptions of actions and activities in which the students participate).

Inferences throughout the document indicate that these are state-mandated course descriptions. Because the course descriptions are succinct and clearly written, there should not be much confusion about the expectations of teachers and how they are to plan; the expectations of students and descriptions of their learning targets are equally well defined. Beyond the course descriptions, however, the document offers no assistance in building a program and no information about instructional approach alternatives, evaluation techniques, and reporting procedures or other related issues. The text provides a way of organizing state policy but offers no new or interesting information on content or methodology.

Vermont (1986)

The "Physical Education Framework" is a single wall chart (22" x 17") that portrays suggested learner objectives in a matrix of four student grade levels and five strands of student qualities that can be developed through physical education. The strands cover physical fitness, social interaction, affective qualities, motor skills, and knowledge. Each of the four grade categories includes from 31 to 45 suggested learner objectives that are intended to be the basis for local decision making and curriculum building. The objectives range from concise and measurable to vague (e.g., "Expand principles of locomotion, nonlocomotion, and manipulative skill") or even inaccurately placed (e.g., "Display a positive attitude toward physical activity" was listed in the physical fitness strand instead of in the affective qualities strand). The knowledge strand objectives consistently require only low cognitive functioning.

Despite these problems, the one-page format allows presentation of the big picture without the reader's having to thumb through page after page of material. It seems that the prudent and conscientious teacher would use this chart with other teachers to build local curriculum, and then post it so that other teachers, as well as students and parents, could see it and ask questions about it. It might also be useful for the teacher to refer to it often in class as a constant reminder of how the lessons each day fit into the rest of the school year, and how the activities of each grade level fit in with those of the other grade levels.

Virginia (revised 1990)

The Commonwealth of Virginia's 23-page *Standards of Learning Objectives for Virginia Public Schools: Physical Education* is a set of student learning objectives organized by grade level and by three topic areas: personal wellness, body management, and either educational game skills (grades K-5) or sports and leisure (grades 6-12). There are 13 to 17 objectives per grade level. Because no other information is provided beyond the objectives themselves, it is difficult for a teacher (or a reviewer) to know whether these are mandated or simply offered as guidance for local curriculum development.

Each standard is written like a minimum competency, for example: "Hold a balanced position demonstrating muscle tension" (grades 1-8). Beyond the standard is a statement description that generalizes an emphasis for instruction. The one corresponding to the example above is "The emphasis is static balance activities." Many of the standards call for a specific response from students (e.g., "Jump and land, absorbing force"), but others ask the student to perform general skill sets (e.g., "Perform jump rope activities with a long or short rope"). This disparity may lead to some confusion of program balance if not addressed by a local curriculum development team.

The conciseness and readability of the standards would be helpful to those engaging in the art and science of building a curriculum. Along with their brevity, the fact there are comparatively few standards listed per grade level makes the program scope achievable, though limited. This text is not, and was not intended to be, a program in itself; however, the document could aid physical education specialists and classroom teachers in organizing for more complete program development. In summary, the best aspect of this state document is its compact usability; it could use other process-oriented documentation to assist with local program development.

The Commonwealth also publishes similar documents for the Health Curriculum (provided for review) and for other subject areas (not provided).

Washington (1989, reprinted in 1992)

The state of Washington's 280-page comprehensive guide to the development of local programs of physical education at all grade levels, the *Guidelines for Student Outcomes K-12: Physical Education*, is thorough in its approach, broadly representative of Washington teachers and administrators, and carefully presented as a result of an extensive field test across Washington schools for a 4-year test period. The publication provides an implementation approach rather than the approach usually taken by states, which is to provide goals and other documentation so that districts and schools can expand and fill in gaps to develop local programs. Indeed, it is clear that a district could, in effect, tear the cover off of this document and replace the cover with one of its own for local school board approval. The fact that the document has gone through an original development and review process, as well as a field test and revision, suggests that local ownership of this final product may be a realistic, economical, and efficient way of gaining direction for a complete program. The only steps left seem to be (a) staff development and ownership and (b) a process for continuous improvement.

The text contains all aspects of documentation helpful for developing a program, including a lengthy bibliography containing references for expanding on program depth that is rich and deep in its own right. The goals of the program are progressive and current. If there is a criticism of the text, it would be that it takes a seemingly traditional approach to the content, focusing on the development of skills for specific sports, specific dances, games, and so forth. This can be seen, for example, in the primary grades' "instructional" orientation to movement exploration, teaching for discovery, educational gymnastics, rudimentary manipulative skills, dance making, interpretive/imitative/associative movement skill and analysis, individual and group movement creativity, and other areas.

Particularly impressive, however, is the 86-page section dealing with physical education for students with disabilities. The depth of coverage and disciplinary integrity concerning this aspect of a complete physical education program was not evident in other state documents. The program guidance offered to adapt instruction and curriculum to the needs of students with disabilities is sensitive and directional for the teacher, administrator, and program developer. Other states could benefit by acquiring and adapting this information to address the federal mandates of the original Public Law #94-142 and the more recent legislation of the Americans With Disabilities Act (1990).

A second publication provided for review, the 39-page booklet *Physical Education Guidelines for School Administrators* (1989), is unique in that the target audience is administrators rather than program developers and teachers. Where information focusing on the administrator is usually buried in the text of a larger general document, a part of this booklet's value is that it concentrates this information in a separate source. Some of the information is included in other state publications.

The booklet is written to empower administrators to know about and be able to engage teachers and others in a process of continuous improvement of local programs. The administrator's role in supporting a quality program in physical education is clear and is presented concisely. The administrator's guidance and direct supervision is shown to be imperative for effective program development, implementation, and evaluation.

These two texts complement each other and demonstrate thoughtful design. The list of contributors is impressively long and warrants mention in recognition of the many hours of discussing, organizing, writing, editing, reviewing, and consensus building that must have taken place. This review is more lengthy than others. It must be! There is simply more meat on the bone. The quality and unique aspects of the documents deserve special attention, as they are among the better publications for the many reasons listed above.

West Virginia (1992)

The three *West Virginia Programs of Study: Instructional Goals and Objectives* manuals frame nine subject areas to guide local program development in the counties of West Virginia. Early childhood education is the focus of one manual; middle childhood education and adolescent education are the focuses for the other two. Introductory information regarding the authority and scope of the document precedes the guiding principles for curriculum development and the implementation of the instructional goals and objectives.

Physical education and health are two of the nine subject areas. Levels are presented that coincide with the grade-level groupings K-4, 5-8, and 9-12. Each level contains 17 to 24 learner outcomes, all beginning with, ''The learner will . . .'' However, the document does not make clear where the goals and objectives are: It must be assumed that the term ''outcome'' is synonymous with goal, or perhaps objective. Each level begins with a brief narrative that is helpful, seems sequenced appropriately, and is different enough from other levels that each level has its own identity.

The outcomes themselves are presented in a list. They range from specific skill sets (e.g., locomotor movements and safety rules and hazards) to concepts of questionable measurability for an outcome statement (e.g., ''Participate in low organized games''; ''Engage in activities involving cooperation''). Although they do describe a program, they appear random and incomplete. In addition, there is little continuity or sequencing among items on the list.

These documents provide little technical assistance for instruction and no assistance for staff development. Although they make reference to quality through standards, no reference to standards appears in the various program areas. The West Virginia publications reviewed lack quality in relation to documents from many other states.

Wisconsin
(1985; third printing 1989)

Wisconsin's *A Guide to Curriculum Planning in Physical Education* is one of the finer resources for curriculum builders, and is excellent for staff development activities as well. It presents difficult concepts clearly, in a concise manner. The manual offers an easy-to-follow process that allows the user to enter at almost any step in the journey of curriculum development. It flows through eight well-written chapters and has a set of appendixes that provide sample forms and reports useful to teachers and administrators. The artwork, from the full-color cover to the children's art present throughout, complements the written material, which is of the highest caliber. The materials are written as step-by-step instructions so that the publication can be used by a novice, while its depth is attractive to the expert. The text does not directly impose a particular philosophical direction but suggests ways of developing one at the local level.

Wisconsin is to be congratulated. This manual is valuable to the school district embarking on curriculum writing, and developers will probably still be referring to the manual through completion of the curriculum process. If the manual has a shortcoming, it is well hidden. It will be interesting to see how the manual is revised in coming years, given the curriculum movement to an outcome base. The writing team will have a hard time coming up with many improvements. This manual is the standard by which other state department publications are, or should be, judged!

Wyoming (no date available)

Chapter VI, School Accreditation was provided for review. No publication date was provided with the list of policies. The rules and regulations pertain to the evaluation and accreditation of public schools (K-12). Wyoming's intention is to provide minimum standards with which public schools must comply.

Physical education is mentioned, by title only, among 11 subject areas in Section 7, Common Core of Knowledge. Section 8, Common Core of Skills, mandates that school districts have the responsibility to set performance standards. These core skills include problem solving, interpersonal communications, keyboarding and computer applications, critical thinking, creativity, and life skills (which must include cardiopulmonary resuscitation, or CPR). No guidance is provided to schools and districts as to how they should develop programs. Performance standards that cross match the knowledge areas and skill topics must be standardized locally.

It would be interesting to review how Wyoming regulates schools and districts regarding Sections 7 and 8 (plus the sections on district performance standards and school performance standards) of the code. The policies place maximum authority on schools, without any state-level assistance or guidance; schools also do not have to document that any of the policies established by the regulatory agency are met by districts. The policies, if implemented as required, would produce valuable information for the nation regarding the setting of performance standards for all students. The information provided, that is to say "state policy," is not useful to physical education program developers. It may prove more interesting and beneficial to review the materials of selected Wyoming school districts directly than it is to seek information through the Wyoming Department of Education.

Conclusion

A synthesis of the analyses above indicates that states, in general, consider physical education to be an important subject for students to learn in schools. Although some states are following a traditional activity approach to providing guidance for program development and delivery (meaning that they discuss what is to be taught), many are taking a more contemporary goals/student outcomes approach (meaning that they discuss what students are to learn).

There is work to be done by some states that have placed a low priority on physical education or perhaps, for one reason or another, have allowed their materials to become outdated. Many of the state documents borrowed elements from other state documents. Indeed, there seems to be some cooperation among states that have shared materials; it was somewhat surprising, however, that there was not more evidence of sharing of materials and collaborative efforts. In instances where states did share, proper acknowledgment and citation were given early and thoroughly.

The majority of states were more than willing to provide materials for review. The availability of state level curriculum and policy guides should prove of value to program planners at the school, district, county, and state levels.

References

Allensworth, D.D., & Kolbe, L.J. (1987). The comprehensive school health program: Exploring an expanded concept. *Journal of School Health*, **57**(10), 409-412.

Graham, G., Holt/Hale, S., & Parker, M. (1987). *Children moving* (2nd ed.). Mountain View, CA: Mayfield.

NASPE. (1992). *Outcomes of quality physical education programs*. Reston, VA: NASPE Outcomes Committee.

See Appendix for bibliographic information on all state publications mentioned in this chapter.

Appendix

Physical Education Curriculum Guide Sources

This listing was updated just before publication. Some curriculum guides included here were not available at the time the review in the chapter was done.

Alabama

Division of Student Instructional Services
Coordinator, Curriculum Development/Courses of Study
State Department of Education

Gordon Persons Office Building
50 North Ripley Street
Montgomery, AL 36130-3901
205-242-8059

Alabama Course of Study: Physical Education. Bulletin 1989, No. 25, 90 p. $3.00.

Alaska

Division of Educational Program Support
Administrator, Office of Curriculum Services
State Department of Education
Goldbelt Building
P.O. Box F
Juneau, AK 99811
907-465-2841, Fax 907-463-5279

Alaska Elementary Physical Education Model Curriculum Guide. (1986). 2nd Edition. 40 p.

Alaska Secondary Physical Education Model Curriculum Guide. (1986). 2nd Edition, 16 p.

Arizona

Education Services
Instructional Technology
State Department of Education
1535 West Jefferson
Phoenix, AZ 85007
602-542-2147

Arizona Comprehensive Health Essential Skills. (1990). Includes essential skills for physical education. 185 p.

Arkansas

Instructional Services
Coordinator, Curriculum, and Assessment
State Department of Education
Four State Capitol Mall
Room 304 A
Little Rock, AR 72201-1071
501-682-4558

Physical Education Course Content Guide (Grades 1-6). (1992). 10 p.

Physical Education Course Content Guide (Grades 7-12). (1987). 5 p.

California

State Department of Education
Bureau of Publications

State Department of Education
P.O. Box 944272
721 Capitol Mall
Sacramento, CA 94244-2720
916-445-1260

Physical Education Framework for California Public Schools: Kindergarten Through Grade Twelve. (1994). 92 p.

Colorado

State Department of Education
201 East Colfax Avenue
Denver, CO 80203-1705
303-866-6806

Colorado Sample Outcomes and Proficiencies for Elementary, Middle, and High School Education. (1991). Includes outcomes and proficiencies for physical education. 162 p.

Connecticut

Program and Support Services
Division of Curriculum and Professional
   Development
State Department of Education
P.O. Box 2219
165 Capitol Avenue
State Office Building
Hartford, CT 06106-1630
203-566-8113

A Guide to Curriculum Development in Physical Education. (1981). 125 p.

Note: The Connecticut State Department of Education is currently revising its curriculum framework for physical education.

Delaware

Instructional Services Branch
State Director, Instruction Division
State Department of Public Instruction
P. O. Box 1402
Townsend Building, #279
Dover, DE 19903
302-739-4647

Physical Education Content Standards. (1985). 95-01/85/12/02. 12 p.

District of Columbia

District of Columbia Public Schools
The Presidential Building
415 12th Street, N.W.
Washington, DC 20004
202-724-4222

Florida

Curriculum Support Services
Bureau of Elementary and Secondary Education
State Department of Education
Capitol Building, Room PL 116
Tallahassee, FL 32301
904-488-6547

Perfect Harmony Reaching Out: An Extracurricular Fitness and Leisure Program for Individuals with Disabilities. (1992). 147 p.

Physical Education Curriculum Frameworks: Grades 6-8. (Rev. 1991). 26 p.

Physical Education Curriculum Frameworks: Grades 9-12, Adult. (Rev. 1991). 92 p.

Georgia

Office of Instructional Programs
Director, General Instruction Division
State Department of Education
2066 Twin Towers East
205 Butler Street
Atlanta, GA 30334
404-656-2412

Physical Education Curriculum Guide: Grades K-4. (1991). Appleworks version 1 diskette set ($12.00) or IBM WordStar version 1 diskette set ($4.00).
Physical Education Resource Guide: Grade 1. (1992). Appleworks version 5 diskette set ($20.00) or IBM WordStar version 2 diskette set ($8.00).
Physical Education Resource Guide: Grade 2. (1992). Appleworks version 3 diskette set ($12.00) or IBM WordStar version 1 diskette set ($8.00).
Lifetime Physical Fitness Resource Guide: Grades 9-12. (1992). Appleworks version 5 diskette set ($20.00) or IBM WordStar version 2 diskette set ($8.00).

Hawaii

Office of Instructional Services
Director, General Education Branch
Department of Education

1390 Miller Street, #307
Honolulu, HI 96813
808-396-2502

Idaho

Chief, Bureau of Instruction/School Effectiveness
State Department of Education
650 West State Street
P.O. Box 83720
Boise, ID 83720-0027
208-334-2165

Nuts and Bolts and Climbing Ropes: Physical Education for Idaho Schools, Grades K-6. (1990). 339 p.

Illinois

School Improvement Services, Curriculum Improvement
State Board of Education
100 North First Street
Springfield, IL 62777
217-782-2826, Fax 217-524-6125

State Goals for Learning and Sample Learning Objectives. Physical Development and Health: Grades 3, 6, 8, 10, 12. (1986). 78 p.

Indiana

Physical Education Consultant
Office of Program Development
State Department of Education
Room 229, State House
100 North Capitol Street
Indianapolis, IN 46024-2798
317-232-9157

Physical Education Proficiency and Essential Skills Guide. (1993). 31 p.

Iowa

Division of Instructional Services
Bureau Chief, Instruction, and Curriculum
State Department of Education
Grimes State Office Building
Des Moines, IA 50319-0146
515-281-8141

A Tool for Assessing and Designing a K-12 Physical Education Program. (1985). 66 p.

Kansas

Program Specialist, Health, and Physical
  Education
Educational Assistance Section
State Department of Education
120 East Tenth Street
Topeka, KS 66612
913-296-6716

Healthy Lifestyles for Kansas Schools and Communities: The Role of the School Physical Education Program. (1990). 25 p.

Kentucky

Office of Learning Programs Development
Division of Curriculum
State Department of Education
Capitol Plaza Tower
500 Mero Street
Frankfort, KY 40601
502-564-2106

Kentucky's Learning Goals and Learner Outcomes

Transformations: Kentucky's Curriculum Framework (Volume I). (1993). 280 p.

Louisiana

Office of Academic Programs
State Department of Education
P.O. Box 94064
Baton Rouge, LA 70804-9064
Elementary Education 504-342-3366
Secondary Education 504-342-3404

Physical Education and Recreation Curriculum Guide: Grades K-10. (1990). Bulletin No. 1597. 468 p.

Maine

Bureau of Instruction
Director, Division of Curriculum
State Department of Education
State House/Station No. 23
Augusta, ME 04333
207-287-5800

Chapter 125—Regulations Governing Basic School Approval. (April 1991). 21 p.

Chapter 127—Instructional Requirements and the Graduation Standard (November 1991). 13 p.

Guidelines for Programming in Adapted Physical Education (1991).

Maryland

Bureau of Educational Development
Division of Instruction, Branch Chief, Arts
  and Sciences
State Department of Education
200 West Baltimore Street
Baltimore, MD 21201
410-333-2307

Physical Education. A Maryland Curricular Framework. (1988). 42 p.

Massachusetts

State Department of Education
350 Main Street
Malden, MA 02148-5023
617-388-3300, ext. 118

Physical Education: 1. Laws and regulations; 2. Guidelines for Adapted Physical Education; and 3. Chapter 622 [Massachusetts law prohibiting discrimination] and Title IX [from the Federal Code] as They Relate to Physical Education and Athletics. (1982). 30 p.

Michigan

Instructional Specialists Program
State Board of Education
P.O. Box 30008
Lansing, MI 48909
517-373-7248

Model Core Curriculum Outcomes. (1991). Includes educational outcomes for physical education and health. 73 p.

Minnesota

Minnesota Curriculum Services Center
State Department of Education
712 Capitol Square Building
550 Cedar Street
St. Paul, MN 55101
612-296-2358

Model Learner Outcomes for Physical Education. (1989). 92 p.

Outcome Competencies and Assessment Strategies for Physical Education. (1992). 78 p.

Mississippi

Bureau of Instructional Services
State Department of Education
P.O. Box Office 771
Jackson, MS 39205-0771
601-359-2791

Mississippi Curriculum Structure — Philosophy, Goals, Skills, and Concepts for Curriculum Development and Instructional Planning: Health and Physical Education. (1986; 6th printing 1992). 33 p.

Missouri

Department of Elementary and Secondary
    Education
Curriculum Services
P.O. Box 480
Jefferson City, MO 65102
314-751-0682

A Proposal to Implement Outcome-Based Graduation in Missouri High Schools: Moving to Outcome-Based Education. (1992). 14 p.

Montana

Department of Accreditation and
    Curriculum Services
Curriculum Assistance and Instructional
    Alternatives
Office of Public Instruction
State Capitol Room 106
Helena, MT 59620
406-444-5541

Montana in Action: Physical Education Curriculum Guide: Grades K-12. (1988). 100 p.

Health Enhancement: A Design for Montana's Future. (1990).

Nebraska

State Department of Education
301 Centennial Mall, South
P.O. Box 94987
Lincoln, NE 68509
402-471-4816

The Nebraska State Department of Education follows the NASPE outcomes, guidelines, and developmental approaches to physical education.

Nevada

Instructional Services Division
Director, Basic Education Branch
State Department of Education
Capitol Complex
400 West King Street
Carson City, NV 89710
702-687-3136

Elementary Course of Study. (1984). Includes scope and sequence for physical education. 65 p.

Nevada Secondary Course of Study. (1984). Includes scope and sequence for physical education. 72 p.

New Hampshire

Division of Instructional Services
General Instructional Services Administrator
State Department of Education
101 Pleasant Street
State Office Park South
Concord, NH 03301
603-271-2632

PART Ed306 Minimum Standards for Public School Approval. (1993). 50 p.

New Jersey

Division of General Academic Education
Department of Education
225 West State Street
CN 500
Trenton, NJ 08625-0500
609-984-1971

New Mexico

Learning Services Division
Instructional Materials
State Department of Education
Education Building
300 Don Gaspar
Santa Fe, NM 87501-2786
505-827-6504

New Mexico Competency Frameworks. (1992). Provides "Competencies by Subject Area," including physical education. 23 p.

New York

State Education Department
111 Education Building
Washington Avenue
Albany, NY 12234

The University of the State of New York
The State Education Department
Publications Sales Desk
518-474-3806

Physical Education Guide: Grades K-12. (1988). 47 p.

Physical Education Syllabus: Grades K-12. (1986). 56 p.

North Carolina

Publications Sales Desk
Department of Public Instruction
Education Building
301 North Wilmington Street
Raleigh, NC 27601-2825
919-715-1299

North Carolina Teacher Handbook: Physical Education Overview and K-3 Major Emphases. [Draft 7/29/92]. 127 p.

North Dakota

Office of Instruction, Supplies
State Department of Public Instruction
600 East Boulevard Avenue
Bismarck, ND 58505-0164
701-224-2272

Physical Education Curriculum Development Guide K-12. (1992). 106 p.

Ohio

State Department of Education
65 South Front Street
Columbus, OH 43215-4183
614-466-3304

Curriculum documents are being revised.

Oklahoma

School Improvement/Standards Division
Instructional Programs
Department of Education
2500 North Lincoln Boulevard
Oklahoma City, OK 73105-4599
405-521-3361

Learner Outcomes. Oklahoma State Competencies, Grade One. (1992). Includes learner outcomes for physical education. 90 p. $3.00.

Learner Outcomes. Oklahoma State Competencies, Grade Two. (1992). Includes learner outcomes for physical education. 90 p. $3.00.

Learner Outcomes. Oklahoma State Competencies, Grade Three. (1992). Includes learner outcomes for physical education. 92 p. $3.00.

Learner Outcomes. Oklahoma State Competencies, Grade Four. (1992). Includes learner outcomes for physical education. 98 p. $3.00.

Learner Outcomes. Oklahoma State Competencies, Grade Five. (1992). Includes learner outcomes for physical education. 98 p. $3.00.

Learner Outcomes. Oklahoma State Competencies, Grades Six-Twelve. (1992). Includes learner outcomes for physical education. 337 p. $3.00.

The cost for the complete set of state competencies is $13.00.

Oregon

Publications Sales Clerk
State Department of Education
255 Capitol Street, N.E.
Salem, OR 97310
503-378-3589

Common Curriculum Goals in Physical Education. (1988). 35 p. $3.00.

Pennsylvania

Office of Elementary and Secondary Education
Bureau of Curriculum and Academic Services
Bilingual Education Section
State Department of Education
333 Market Street
Harrisburg, PA 17126-0333
717-787-1890

Regulations of the State Board of Education of Pennsylvania. Chapter 5 Curriculum. (1993). Includes student learning outcomes for wellness and fitness. 8 p.

Rhode Island

State Department of Education
22 Hayes Street

Providence, RI 02908
401-277-2031

The Rhode Island Department of Education now has available learning outcomes for subject areas.

South Carolina

State Department of Education
Rutledge Building
1429 Senate Street
Columbia, SC 29201
803-734-8492

South Dakota

Office of Educational Services
Division of Education
Department of Education and Cultural Affairs
700 Governor's Drive
Pierre, SD 57501
Elementary Curriculum 605-773-3782
Secondary Curriculum 605-773-4670

A Guide for Instruction in Physical Education, Grades K-6. (no date). 299 p.

A Guide for Instruction in Physical Education, Grades 7-12. (no date). 283 p.

Tennessee

Curriculum and Instruction
8th Floor, Gateway Plaza
710 James Robertson Parkway
Nashville, TN 37243-0379
615-741-0874

Tennessee Comprehensive Curriculum Guide, Grades K-8. (1992). Contains guidelines for physical education. 194 p.
Physical Education Curriculum Guide, Grades K-12. (no date). 190 p.

Texas

Texas Education Agency
1701 North Congress Avenue
Austin, TX 78701-1494
512-463-8985

State Board of Education Rules for Curriculum— Essential Elements. (1991). Includes physical education. AD202101. 545 p.

Utah

Office of Instructional Services
Curriculum
State Office of Education
250 East 500 South
Salt Lake City, UT 84111
801-538-7774

Healthy Lifestyles Core Curriculum. (1994).

Vermont

Basic Education
Curriculum and Instruction Unit
State Department of Education
120 State Street
Montpelier, VT 05620-2501
802-828-3111

Framework for the Development of a Physical Education Scope and Sequence K-12. (1986). 17 in. x 22 in. folded sheet.

Virginia

Instruction and Personnel
Administrative Director of General Education
Department of Education
P.O. Box 2120
101 North 14th Street
Richmond, VA 23216-2120
804-225-2730

Standards of Learning Objectives for Virginia Public Schools: Physical Education. (Rev. 1990). 23 p.

Washington

Curriculum, Student Services and Technology
Curriculum
Office of Superintendent of Public Instruction
Old Capitol Building
Legion and Franklin
P.O. Box 47200
Olympia, WA 98504-7200
206-753-6727

Guidelines for Student Outcomes K-12: Physical Education. (1985, rev. 1989, reprinted 1992). CSST/606/ 92. 280 p.

Physical Education Guidelines for School Administrators. (1989). 39 p.

West Virginia

Division of Instructional and Student Services
State Department of Education
1900 Kanawha Boulevard, East
Charleston, WV 25305
304-348-7805

West Virginia Programs of Study: Instructional Goals and Objectives. Early Childhood Education K-4. (1992). Includes physical education program of study. 132 p.

West Virginia Programs of Study: Instructional Goals and Objectives. Middle Childhood Education 5-8. (1992). Includes physical education program of study. 181 p.

West Virginia Programs of Study: Instructional Goals and Objectives. Adolescent Education 9-12. (1992). Includes physical education program of study. 268 p.

Wisconsin

Publication Sales
State Department of Public Instruction
125 South Webster Street
P.O. Box 7841
Madison, WI 53707
608-266-2188

A Guide to Curriculum Planning in Physical Education. (1985, 3rd printing 1989). Bulletin No. 6230. 134 p.

Wyoming

Division of Certification, Accreditation, and
    Program Services
School Improvement Unit
State Department of Education
Hathaway Building
2300 Capitol Avenue, 2nd Floor
Cheyenne, WY 82002-0050
307-777-6808

The Wyoming State Department of Education does not produce curriculum frameworks for physical education.

7

Recommended Curriculum Materials to Enhance Student Learning

Bonnie S. Mohnsen
Orange County Department of Education, Costa Mesa, California

This chapter contains an annotated listing of publications on curriculum and instruction; curriculum guides; textbooks for students; publications on specific content areas and teaching ideas; supplemental materials including instructional television programs, videos, laser discs, and computer software; and resources for staying current in the field including periodicals and the information superhighway. These references will assist curriculum developers and teachers in designing and providing quality physical education programs for students.

Specific references were selected to demonstrate the variety among and within categories, to highlight *current* resources, and to document publishers active in the discipline of physical education. A few references are older than the others, but have proven their worth over time. Although the references included are specific to physical education, general education references can also be very beneficial when the concepts are applied to the development of curriculum, instructional strategies, and assessment techniques for the physical education program.

Publications on Curriculum Development and Instructional Strategies for Teachers

This section contains publications on curriculum and instruction, since several authors address both issues in the same textbook. The information contained in the curriculum publications gives the reader a strong foundation in curriculum development, but that contained

in the instruction publications presents a wide variety of instructional strategies with which to implement the curriculum. The publications listed here are typically used as textbooks for preservice teachers. However, these publications will also be appreciated by those writing curriculum and seeking alternative strategies for instruction. The publications represent a variety of current curriculum design models as described in chapter 2.

K-12 Materials

Adapted Physical Education: A Comprehensive Resource Manual of Definition, Assessment, Programming, and Future Predictions, by Paul Bishop, Editor (Kearney, NE: Educational Systems Associates, 1988), 308 p. ISBN 1-878276-01-8. Available from Educational Systems Associates, Inc., PO Box 96, Kearney, NE 68847 for $40.00.

Grades K-12. This is a comprehensive text on adapted physical education with chapters authored by the leading experts in the field. The major sections include an overview of the manual, an introduction to adapted physical education, student identification, student programming, and predictions about the future of adapted physical education in the United States. The student programming section is especially appropriate for both adapted physical educators and regular physical educators, covering a variety of skills and activities ranging from individual, dual, and team sports to folk dancing and aquatics, and providing suggestions for integrating students with exceptional needs into the regular physical education program.

• • •

A Teacher's Guide to Including Students With Disabilities in Regular Physical Education, by Martin E. Block (Baltimore: Paul H. Brookes, 1994), 276 p. ISBN 1-55766-156-1. Available from Paul Brookes Publishing Co., PO Box 10624, Baltimore, MD 21285-0624 for $37.00.

Grades K-12. This is an excellent ''up-to-date'' text that takes a new look at physical education instruction for students with disabilities. Appropriate for both adapted and regular physical education teachers, it addresses the life-long recreational environments for the student with disabilities and then designs a physical education program that prepares the student for that environment. The guide provides real-life case examples, step-by-step instructional and curricular strategies, and a variety of activity modifications to meet the student's needs within a regular physical education setting without accentuating differences.

• • •

Basic Stuff Series I, by Pat Dodds, Editor (Reston, VA: American Alliance for Health, Physical Education, Recreation and Dance, 1987), 45-110 p. ISBN 0-88314-024 through 0-88314-029. Available from American Alliance for Health, Physical Education, Recreation and Dance (AAHPERD), 1900 Association Drive, Reston, VA 22091 (out of print).

Grades K-12. Series I consists of six booklets (*Exercise Physiology*, *Kinesiology*, *Motor Learning*, *Psycho-Social Aspects of Physical Education*, *Humanities in Physical Education*, and *Motor Development*) that represent the subdisciplines of physical education. Each booklet covers the central concepts for that subdiscipline, and collectively these booklets present the body of knowledge for physical education. Each concept is accompanied by an explanation and examples. These concepts can be used when developing a conceptually based K-12 physical education curriculum. Sample lesson plans showing how to deliver these concepts in K-12 classes are included in Series II; see under ''Curriculum Guides and Lesson Plans.''

• • •

The Curriculum Process in Physical Education, by Ann E. Jewett, Linda L. Bain, & Catherine D. Ennis (Dubuque, IA: Brown, 1995), 401 p. ISBN 0-697-16825-5. Available from Wm. C. Brown Publishers, 2460 Kerper Boulevard, Dubuque, IA 52001 for $46.15.

Grades K-12. This textbook provides a comprehensive look at the curriculum process in physical education. The book is divided into four major sections.

The first section provides the theoretical basis and introduces five of the major curriculum models (sport education, fitness education, movement analysis, developmental, and personal meaning) utilized in physical education curriculum development. The second section addresses the process of developing curriculum, including understanding the school setting, legal requirements, approaches to curriculum development, change issues, developing goals and objectives, and selecting and sequencing educational activities. The third section provides numerous examples of how each of the five curriculum models can be applied in a variety of educational settings. The last section discusses curriculum evaluation, including issues and concerns. This book contains excellent information and is one of only a few that deal exclusively with curriculum.

• • •

Designing the Physical Education Curriculum, by Vincent Melograno (Dubuque, IA: Kendall/Hunt, 1985), 447 p. ISBN 0-8403-3488-5. Available from Kendall/Hunt Publishing Company, 2460 Kerper Boulevard, Dubuque, IA 52004-0539. New edition is in press with Human Kinetics, but price is not yet available.

Grades K-12. In this text, Melograno describes a curriculum design process that leads the reader from content goals and organizing centers through entry level assessment, learning objectives, learning experiences, and learner evaluation to program assessment and revision. This is a very detailed design book with a new edition scheduled to be published by Human Kinetics.

• • •

Teaching Physical Education, by Muska Mosston & Sara Ashworth (New York: Macmillan College, 1994), 263 p. ISBN 0-02-384183-4. Available from Macmillan College Publishing Company, New York, NY 10022 for $38.00.

Grades K-12. This is a classic text that describes, in detail, what it terms the Spectrum of Teaching Styles. The Spectrum, created by the authors, addresses the relationship between the teacher, the learner, and the tasks they each perform. The Spectrum covers styles running from the highly ''teacher-structured'' command style through practice, reciprocal, self-check, inclusion, guided discovery, convergent discovery, divergent production, individual program-learner's design, and learner-initiated styles to the ''maximum student independent'' style of self-teaching. Many lesson examples are provided for each style. The authors are quick to remind the reader that one style is not necessarily better than any other; rather, each has its own appropriate place in the learning spectrum. This is the definitive book on teaching styles.

• • •

Moving Into the Future: National Standards for Physical Education, a Guide to Content and Assessment, by National Association for Sport and Physical Education (St. Louis: Mosby, 1995), 125 p. Stock Number 304-10083. Available from AAHPERD, 1900 Association Drive, Reston, VA 22091-1599 for $22.00.

Grades K-12. This book contains the seven national physical education standards along with sample benchmarks and assessment examples for grades kindergarten, 2, 4, 6, 8, 10, and 12.

• • •

Outcomes of Quality Physical Education Programs, by National Association for Sport and Physical Education (Reston, VA: AAHPERD, 1992), 22 p. Stock Number 304-10035. Available from AAHPERD, 1900 Association Drive, Reston, VA 22091-1599 for $8.00.

Grades K-12. This booklet contains the definition and outcomes of the physically educated person along with examples of grade-level benchmarks. The outcomes material was developed by the NASPE Outcomes Committee and reviewed by over 500 professionals. It provides direction to districts and schools developing curriculum.

• • •

Teaching Physical Education for Learning, by Judith E. Rink (St. Louis, MO: Times Mirror/Mosby College, 1992), 348 p. ISBN 0-8016-4136-5. Available from Times Mirror/Mosby College Publishing, 11830 Westline Industrial Drive, St. Louis, MO 63146 for $33.95.

Grades K-12. This textbook focuses on assisting readers who wish to improve their teaching skills in order to become effective teachers. It is one of the few instruction books to be based on current research from both the motor learning and teaching behavior areas. The textbook is divided into two major parts. Part 1 identifies the major components of the instructional process, including organizing the learning environment, presenting progressive learning tasks to students, and providing feedback. Emphasis is placed on different instructional strategies and content analysis and development. Rink proposes the concept of breaking content down into its component parts—extension, refinement, and application—and provides examples on how to teach each aspect. Part 2 focuses on collecting and interpreting data on the teaching process.

• • •

Developing Teaching Skills in Physical Education, by Daryl Siedentop (Mountain View, CA: Mayfield, 1991),

343 p. ISBN 0-87484-899-7. Available from Mayfield Publishing Company, 1240 Villa Street, Mountain View, CA 94041 for $35.95.

Grades K-12. This text is based on the research that has been conducted on effective teaching (general education and physical education) over the past 20 years. It focuses on critical characteristics of effective teaching in general as opposed to a particular style of teaching. This third edition is divided into four parts: the systematic improvement of teaching skills, management and discipline, effective teaching, and issues and concepts (liability, teacher organizations, improving one's effectiveness) that are important to teachers. The emphasis here is on the process of teaching, not on how to teach skills and activities.

• • •

Program Design in Physical Education, by Paul Vogel & Vern Seefeldt (Indianapolis: Benchmark, 1988), 152 p. ISBN 0936157-29-1. Available from Benchmark Press, Inc., 8435 Keystone Crossing, Suite 175, Indianapolis, IN 46240 for $15.00.

Grades K-12. This is a brief guide to developing and evaluating exemplary programs in physical education. Components include program design, outcomes, goals, objectives, organization of curriculum, effective instruction, developing resource materials, evaluating student status and progress, and evaluating program effectiveness. The appendixes contain a variety of sample forms and checklists to assist teachers and departments in the process of improving their programs.

Materials for Specific Grade Levels

Developmental Physical Education for Today's Children, by David L. Gallahue (Dubuque, IA: Brown and Benchmark, 1993), 616 p. ISBN 0-697-14208-6. Available from Brown and Benchmark Publishers, 2460 Kerper Boulevard, Dubuque, IA 52001 for $36.00.

Elementary. This publication is written from a developmental perspective and emphasizes the need to provide activities based on each child's developmental level rather than on chronological age or grade level. This developmental approach delineates skills by initial, elementary, and mature levels; it also provides visual descriptions, teaching tips, strategies, skill and movement concepts, and guided discovery activities. The author takes an eclectic approach to curriculum models in physical education, attempting to merge the more traditional activity orientation to elementary school physical education with the newer movement education perspective. One of the major strengths of the text is that Gallahue places an emphasis on cognitive development, stressing children's understanding of the "why" behind what they are doing.

The text is divided into five parts—The Learner, The Teacher, The Program, The Skill Themes, and The Program Strands. The Learner addresses developmental physical education, movement skill acquisition, fitness components, cognitive learning, affective behavior, growth and development, and children with disabilities. The Teacher addresses effective teaching, positive discipline, teaching styles, and legal liability. The Program focuses on the development of curriculum, planning the lesson, content areas, and program assessment. The Skill Themes, like those in other elementary method books, include stability, locomotor movement, manipulative skills, stunts and tumbling, apparatus use, disc (i.e., Frisbee), basketball, soccer, softball, and volleyball. The book concludes with the Program Strands, which cover vigorous activity, perceptual-motor skills, creative dance, folk and square dance, and cognitive learning. The book provides a comprehensive overview of elementary physical education.

● ● ●

Teaching Children Physical Education: Becoming a Master Teacher, by George Graham (Champaign, IL: Human Kinetics, 1992), 174 p. ISBN 0-87322-340-3. Available from Human Kinetics Publishers, Inc., PO Box 5076, Champaign, IL 61825-5076 for $20.00.

Elementary. This text is designed for the pedagogy course of the American Master Teacher Program (AMTP). It focuses entirely on successful teaching skills and techniques used by master teachers. The publication is clearly written and is easy to understand. The author uses examples and an accompanying study guide to ensure that the material is understood by the reader.

Chapter topics include planning to maximize learning, creating an atmosphere for learning, minimizing off-task behavior and discipline problems, getting the lesson started, instructing and demonstrating, motivating children to practice, observing and analyzing, developing the content, providing feedback, questioning and problem solving, building positive feelings, assessing children's progress, and continuing to develop as a teacher. The author also suggests that the readers videotape themselves and use the book's videotape analysis sections to examine and reflect on their own teaching. Successful completion of all courses and requirements in the program leads to certification as a Master Teacher of Children's Physical Education.

Also available from Human Kinetics is the AMTP Course Instructor Video, which presents examples of the 17 teaching techniques covered in this book.

Each technique is illustrated through examples from actual teaching situations, allowing instructors to discuss the techniques and show how they can be used in the teaching process.

A recent addition (1994) to the AMTP are five companion books: *Teaching Children Movement Concepts and Skills: Becoming a Master Teacher* by Craig Buschner, *Teaching Children Dance: Becoming a Master Teacher* by Theresa Purcell, *Teaching Children Gymnastics: Becoming a Master Teacher* by Peter Werner, *Teaching Children Games: Becoming a Master Teacher* by David Belka, and *Teaching Children Fitness: Becoming a Master Teacher* by Tom and Laraine Ratliffe. Each book is approximately 140 pages long and sells for $14.00. The books cover the why and how of teaching children these various content areas.

Each of the books described in the previous paragraph is organized into two parts. The first part covers the importance of the content area, tailoring the content area to fit your teaching situation, incorporating the content area into your program, principles for teaching the content area, and assessing children's progress in the content area. The second part is devoted to developmentally appropriate learning experiences in the content area, with several learning experiences per grade level. Each of these books also has a 30-minute companion video available for $19.95 that illustrates condensed lessons that provide examples of how to effectively teach children the content area.

● ● ●

Children Moving: A Reflective Approach to Teaching Physical Education, by George Graham, Shirley Holt-Hale, & Melissa Parker (Mountain View, CA: Mayfield, 1993), 553 p. ISBN 1-55934-130-0 (book only) and ISBN 1-55934-304-4 (book and lesson plans). Available from Mayfield Publishing Company, 1240 Villa Street, Mountain View, CA 94041 for $47.95 or $52.72 for book and accompanying lesson plans; see description under "Curriculum Guides and Lesson Plans."

Elementary. This text uses a skill themes approach to teaching children motor skills through developmentally appropriate activities. The authors use a movement analysis framework that includes locomotor, nonmanipulative, and manipulative skills and emphasizes space awareness, relationships, and effort. The strength of this text lies in its presentation of skills. Each skill is delineated by precontrol, control, utilization, and proficiency with appropriate practice activities for each level. Teaching skills are stressed as much as content in order to help teachers increase their effectiveness. Examples of extending, refining, and applying cues are also provided for each skill activity.

The themes include space awareness, effort concepts, relationships, traveling, chasing-fleeing-dodging, jumping and landing, balancing, transferring weight and rolling, kicking and punting, throwing and catching, volleying and dribbling, striking with rackets and paddles, and striking with long-handled implements. These themes are followed by chapters on teaching through games, dance, and gymnastics. The book concludes with a look at the future of elementary physical education. Holt-Hale's accompanying lesson plan book is described under the ''Curriculum Guides and Lesson Plans'' section.

• • •

Instructional Strategies for Secondary School Physical Education, by Joyce M. Harrison & Connie L. Blakemore (Dubuque, IA: Brown, 1992), 596 p. ISBN 0-697-10115-0. Available from Wm. C. Brown Publishers, 2460 Kerper Boulevard, Dubuque, IA 52001 for $28.05.

Grades 6-12.   As the name implies, this text introduces the reader to a variety of instructional strategies and styles for teaching middle school and high school physical education. The authors first take a look at understanding the learner and the process of learning before providing information on writing objectives and planning units and lessons. This book covers both management and instruction with a focus on how to teach. The strength of the text lies in its many excellent instructional examples using different activities and sports. The book concludes with a brief introduction to curriculum development. Readers should be aware that there are some rather traditional references to coeducational physical education, ability grouping, and activities for shortened days.

• • •

Goals and Strategies for Teaching Physical Education by Donald R. Hellison (Champaign, IL: Human Kinetics, 1985), 172 p. ISBN 0-931-250-74-9. Available from Human Kinetics Publishers, Inc., PO Box 5076, Champaign, IL 61825-5076 for $18.00.

Grades 6-12.   This is an instructional book that addresses the development of social and self-esteem goals based on the needs and values of students. Hellison introduces five developmental levels designed to change students' attitudes and behaviors. The five levels are irresponsibility, self-control, involvement, self-responsibility, and caring. Using five interactive strategies (teacher talk, modeling, reinforcement, reflection time, and student sharing), students are encouraged to move from one level to the next. The majority of the text is spent elaborating on the five levels, beginning with self-control, and explaining how the five general interactive strategies can be used with students at each of these levels.

The ideas can be used in many programs, but some teachers have found the book especially helpful in alternative settings.

• • •

Meeting Needs and Pleasing Kids: A Middle School Physical Education Curriculum, by Christine Holyoak & Herman Weinberg (Dubuque, IA: Kendall/Hunt, 1986), 135 p. ISBN 0-8403-4186-5. Available from Kendall/Hunt Publishing Company, 2460 Kerper Boulevard, Dubuque, IA 52004-0539 for $17.95.

Grades 6-8.   This short text offers a unique approach to the middle school physical education curriculum by organizing the learning experiences and concepts around a skill theme model based on student need. The seven themes developed in the book are locomotor skills, throwing and catching, striking with body parts, striking with implements, body management, physical fitness, and processing. For each theme, the authors discuss the crucial elements, give suggested progressions and activities that will contribute to the development of the theme, and provide sample lesson plans. The book ends with some suggested instructional approaches to ensure the success of the curriculum. This publication forms the basis for the middle school physical education textbook series described in the section on ''Textbooks for Students.''

• • •

Elementary Physical Education Methods, by Daryl Siedentop, Jacqueline Herkowitz, & Judy Rink (Englewood Cliffs, NJ: Prentice-Hall, 1984), 491 p. ISBN 0-13-259382-3. Available from Prentice-Hall, Inc., Englewood Cliffs, NJ 07632 for $58.00.

Grades K-6.   The aim of this text is to blend research on effective teaching and classroom management with the experience of successful practitioners. This text consists of four parts. The first part examines research and theory on the role of movement, learning movement skills, affective development, efficiency of movement, growth, physical fitness, and perceptual-motor development. The second part focuses on pedagogical techniques, including planning, climate, management, inclusion, and current concepts. Movement education forms the third part, which includes games skills, educational gymnastics, and educational dance. The last part addresses the culture of games and activities, including gymnastics, major sports, aquatics, traditional dance, and adventure activities.

This is a very comprehensive approach to elementary physical education, providing readers with a background in curriculum and instruction in physical education and a discussion of how to teach a variety of activities and skills. The strength of this text lies in its description of the major task, extension, and refinement for a variety of motor and movement skills. There is no accompanying lesson plan book.

• • •

Physical Education: Teaching and Curriculum Strategies for Grades 5-12, by Daryl Siedentop, Charles Mand, & Andrew Taggart (Mountain View, CA: Mayfield, 1986), 443 p. ISBN 0-87484-592-0. Available from Mayfield Publishing Company, 1240 Villa Street, Mountain View, CA 94041 for $39.95.

Grades 5-12. One of only a few books that effectively covers both curriculum and instruction, it is especially effective in describing curricular models, including multiactivity physical education, fitness, sports education, wilderness sports and adventure education, social development, and conceptually based programs. The instruction side of the book addresses managing the program, planning units and lessons, discipline, effective teaching strategies, and current issues in teaching (safety, coeducational teaching, grading). The book gives a good overview of quality physical education in secondary schools.

• • •

Physical Education for Children: Concepts Into Practice, by Jerry R. Thomas, Amelia M. Lee, & Katherine T. Thomas (Champaign, IL: Human Kinetics, 1988), 256 p. ISBN 0-87322-175-3. Available from Human Kinetics Books, PO Box 5076, Champaign, IL 61820 for $30.00.

Grades K-8. Information is provided on how to create a physical education program based primarily on the developmental design model. The authors have adapted this model to include content from traditional and movement education programs. This book is based on research from motor learning and development, exercise physiology, and sport psychology. It provides information on children's growth and development, how to measure and improve physical fitness, motor skill development, psychosocial factors (cooperation, encouragement, self-esteem) related to movement, planning and organizing a class in physical education, mainstreaming students, observation skills, facilities and equipment, and evaluation. Lesson plans that accompany this text are described in the "Curriculum Guides and Lesson Plans" section.

• • •

Instructional Design for Teaching Physical Activities: A Knowledge Structures Approach, by Joan N. Vickers (Champaign, IL: Human Kinetics, 1990), 298 p. ISBN 0-87322-226-1. Available from Human Kinetics Publishers, PO Box 5076, Champaign, IL 61825-5076 for

$42.00.

Grades 6-12. This book describes the Knowledge Structure Model for teaching complex skills. This design model sets the stage and theoretical framework for the "Steps to Success" activity series described in the "Publications on Specific Content Areas and Teaching Ideas" section. The author explains how the subject matter of any sport or activity is structured and how the structure can be used as a basis for teaching.

The model is based on the fields of cognitive psychology, sport sciences, instructional design, and computing science. Eight modules are used in implementing the model, and they are described in detail: creating a personalized knowledge structure, analyzing learning environments, analyzing learners, developing a scope and sequence, writing objectives, determining evaluation, designing learning activities, and making real-world applications. The book helps teachers effectively design learning progressions for sport-specific curricula.

Curriculum Guides and Lesson Plans

Commercial curriculum and lesson guides provide sources of instructional ideas, skill analysis and progression, activities, lead-up games, and sample drills. In most cases complete lesson plans are presented. These resources should be used as samples for educators training in physical education and as actual lesson plans for classroom teachers who are still in the process of learning about teaching physical education.

Grades K-12 Commercial Curriculum Guides and Lesson Plans

Basic Stuff Series II, by Norma Carr, Editor (Reston, VA: AAHPERD, 1987), 125-180 p. ISBN 0-88314-364-X, 0-88314-365-8, 0-88314-366-6. Available from AAHPERD, 1900 Association Drive, Reston, VA 22091 (out of print).

Grades K-12. Series II consists of three booklets (*K-3, 4-8, 9-12*) that provide sample lessons based on the concepts addressed in Series I (see under "Publications on Curriculum Development and Instructional Strategies for Teachers"). Personal fitness, skillful movement, and joy, pleasure, and satisfaction are identified as the three goal areas. Selected concepts from Series I have been identified to meet the three goals, and active learning experiences are suggested. Curriculum materials, including worksheets and lab experiences, are provided.

Elementary Commercial Curriculum Guides and Lesson Plans

On the Move: Lesson Plans to Accompany Children Moving, by Shirley Holt-Hale (Mountain View, CA: Mayfield, 1993), 553 p. ISBN 1-55934-130-0. Available from Mayfield Publishing Company, 1240 Villa Street, Mountain View, CA 94041 for $17.95.

Elementary. This guide includes 81 sample elementary lessons based on the textbook *Children Moving: A Reflective Approach to Teaching Physical Education* by Graham, Holt-Hale, & Parker. A skill themes approach is used to teach children motor skills in developmentally appropriate activities. Each lesson contains a focus, a subfocus, an objective(s), a list of materials and equipment, the organization/management of the lesson, an introduction, content development, a closure, and a reflection that requires the teacher to review the amount of learning that occurred during the lesson.

All activities in each lesson support the focus of that lesson, providing maximum participation, high time on task, and a high success rate. The lessons are based on ideas that have been successfully used by Holt-Hale for enhancing children's motor skill development, fostering positive attitudes toward physical activity, and developing an awareness and understanding of concepts associated with physical fitness and wellness. Elementary physical education specialists may find this book particularly helpful because it contains sample lessons on which to build daily lessons.

• • •

Elementary Physical Education Curriculum Series, by Don Morris & Craig Cunningham (Encino, CA: 21st Century Education, 1990), pages vary by level. Available from 21st Century Education Enterprises, 16650 Morrison Street, Encino, CA 91436 for $79.95 each.

Elementary. This series consists of four binders of lesson plans: Kindergarten, 1st and 2nd Grade, 3rd and 4th Grade, and 5th and 6th Grade. Each binder contains eight units—one unit per month—with sufficient lesson plans to cover an entire year.

The binders for kindergarten and 1st and 2nd grade contain units on introductory activities, locomotor activities, manipulative eye-hand activities, manipulative eye-foot activities, balance, jump rope, rotary motion, and dance. The binder for 3rd and 4th grade contains units on introductory activities, manipulative eye-hand activities, manipulative eye-foot activities, jump rope, net games, dance, rotary motion, and frisbees. The binder for 5th and 6th grade contains units on introductory activities, jump rope, basketball, international games, volleyball, dance, track, and softball.

The units on introductory activities present activities that the children can play during recess time, rules for the games, safety procedures, exercises, and daily procedures for physical education. Each binder also contains a section on exercises called the "huff and puff" section. The lesson format includes purpose, equipment, location, huff and puff exercises, instructional focus, skill practice and organizational pattern, and cool down and close. The instructional focus section provides the lesson's objective in simple terms so that it can be read to the students, and also includes a description of the skill that can be read during the demonstration.

Several of the lessons take a guided discovery approach, increasing students' higher level thinking skills along with their motor skill development. Each binder also includes evaluation procedures for each unit; equipment, music and video lists with prices; inclement weather lessons; nutrition and tobacco- and substance-avoidance lessons; and teaching techniques and management strategies. Containing daily lessons, this package is especially effective with classroom teachers who have very little experience with physical education; however, the binder for 5th and 6th grade does place students into traditional sports earlier than is recommended in current professional literature.

• • •

Quality Daily Physical Education: Lesson Plans for Classroom Teachers, by Robin D. Reese (Dubuque, IA: Kendall/Hunt, 1990), 336 p. for 1st/2nd, 560 p. for 3rd/4th, and 656 p. for 5th/6th. ISBN 0-8403-5815-6. Available from Kendall/Hunt Publishing Company, 2460 Kerper Boulevard, Dubuque, IA 52004-0539 for $43.95 for 1st/2nd grade and $59.95 for the others.

Elementary. This is a comprehensive, three-volume (grades 1-2, 3-4, 5-6), year-long series of detailed daily physical education lesson plans for classroom teachers and specialists. These lessons are developmental and have been successfully field tested by the author. The sequential curriculum provides time to develop social skills in a movement setting while focusing on health-related physical fitness, movement concepts, movement patterns, rhythm and dance, sport-related skills, and tumbling.

Most lessons include recommended or required facilities and equipment, topics for classroom discussion, lesson theme(s), an introductory activity, flexibility exercises, muscular endurance exercises, aerobics, an activity description, and a culminating activity. Each lesson is designed for maximum participation and success in a cooperative and supportive learning environment. Sample forms, station ideas, certificates, equipment lists, ideas for homemade equipment, and sample rules are also provided.

● ● ●

Every Child a Winner, by Susan Rockett & Martha Owens (Ocilla, GA: Every Child a Winner, 1980), pages vary by level. Available from Every Child a Winner, Box 141, Ocilla, GA 31774 for $10.00 (Level I and III) and $8.00 (Level II).

Grades K-8.   Although this series has a publication date of 1980, it is a National Diffusion Network project that has withstood the test of time. Approximately 180 lessons are provided at each of three levels representing kindergarten through 8th grade. The lesson plans, based on the movement education approach to physical education, focus on the concepts of space awareness, body awareness, quality of movement, and relationships. Behaviorally stated objectives are provided, and each lesson builds on the previous ones.

Content areas include creative dance, creative games, and educational gymnastics. The instructional strategy used throughout the program is guided discovery, which subscribes to the philosophy that, within the boundaries of safety, there is no wrong way to move. Each lesson provides a series of questions that teachers can use as stimuli for student movement experiences. Sample questions include: "Can you find your personal space?", "Can you strike your hands together?", and "Working alone in your space, can you select a yarn ball and use light force to strike your ball in a low level?"

Although comprehensive in its coverage of movement education and the development of fundamental motor skills, the program developers do not directly address fitness; instead, they believe that fitness is a by-product of a high quality physical education experience. This series is especially effective for elementary physical education specialists who understand the mechanics of movement and motor skills and are capable of guiding students to discover the correct techniques.

● ● ●

Physical Education for Children: Daily Lesson Plans, by Jerry R. Thomas, Amelia M. Lee, & Katherine T. Thomas (Champaign, IL: Human Kinetics, 1988), 1088 p. ISBN 87322-176-1. Available from Human Kinetics Books, PO Box 5076, Champaign, IL 61820 for $48.00.

Grades K-8.   The *Daily Lesson Plans* put the information from the *Physical Education for Children* textbook into action. There are 376 lesson plans with each lesson requiring 30 minutes to implement. The lesson plans are divided into four developmental levels (K-1, 2-3, 4-5, 6-8), and use illustrations to demonstrate instructional ideas. Each lesson includes objectives, equipment needs, safety tips, warm-up activities, skill development activities (fitness, gymnastics, games and sports, and rhythmic activities), teaching cues and directions, and concluding activities. Plans for making equipment, evaluation forms, and resources for rainy-day classroom activities are also provided. The lessons are easy to follow, and classroom teachers will find them easy to implement.

Textbooks for Students

The idea of using student textbooks for physical education is a relatively new one and, as of now, is confined to middle and high school. Although one usually associates textbook use with an image of rows of students all reading simultaneously, this is not the strategy used in physical education. Current methodologies include using the textbook as a resource to be read the night before a new skill is introduced, having students consult the textbook when developing a project, and including reading as one station in a circuit to reinforce a particular concept. Notice that in each of these scenarios the amount of activity time is not reduced. Students, in fact, will benefit more from the activity time in class, because they will already understand the concept or skill to be practiced.

General Middle School

Australian Physical Education—Book 1, by Bernie Blackall (South Melbourne: MacMillan Company of Australia, 1986), 219 p. ISBN 0-333-41548-5. Available from MacMillan Company of Australia, 107 Moray Street, South Melbourne 3205.

Grades 5-8.   Designed for students in middle school, this book covers basic anatomy, nutrition, and physical fitness. The book then presents 14 different sports and activities, including track and field (called athletics), Australian rules football, ball handling, baseball and softball, basketball, bat tennis, cricket, gymnastics, hockey, netball, rugby, soccer, volleyball, and water activities. The chapter on ball handling is especially effective in covering throwing, catching, kicking, punching, bowling, heading, pitching, and hitting. Each chapter contains a description of the activity, rules, skills, and safety issues.

Short-answer questions, word searches, and crossword puzzles can be found at the end of each chapter.

• • •

Australian Physical Education—Book 2, by Bernie Blackall & Damien Davis (South Melbourne: MacMillan Company of Australia, 1987), 326 p. ISBN 0-333-45080-9. Available from MacMillan Company of Australia, 107 Moray Street, South Melbourne 3205.

Grades 5-8.   The second in the Australian textbook series for middle/junior high school, this textbook addresses health education and physical education. In terms of physical education there are chapters on fitness and on each of 26 different activities, including archery, track and field (athletics), Australian rules football, badminton, baseball and softball, basketball, cricket, European handball, flying disc sport, golf, gridiron football, fitness centers and gyms, gymnastics, hockey, korfball, soft lacrosse, netball, soccer, speedaway, squash, swimming, table tennis, tennis, tenpin bowling, touch rugby, and volleyball. As in Book 1, each chapter contains a description of the activity, rules, skills, and safety issues, but here they are at a more advanced level. Each chapter concludes with a quiz. This is one of only two series currently available for middle school students in physical education.

• • •

Middle School Physical Education, by Gary B. Spindt, William H. Monti, Betty Hennessy, Christine Holyoak, & Herman Weinberg (Dubuque, IA: Kendall/Hunt, 1992), 112 p. for Teacher's Resource Book, 225 p. for each Student Text, 150 p. for each Portfolio, and 150 p. for each Teacher's Edition. ISBN 0-8403-7162-4 for Teacher's Resource Book, 5333-2 Student Text for Moving With Confidence, 5334-0 Physical Education Portfolio for Moving With Confidence, 5910-1 Teacher's Edition for Moving With Confidence, 5911-X for Student Text for Moving With Skill, 5912-8 for Physical Education Portfolio for Moving With Skill, 5913-6 for Teacher's Edition for Moving With Skill, 5914-4 for Student Text for Moving as a Team, 5915-2 for Physical Education Portfolio for Moving as a Team, 5916-0 for Teacher's Edition for Moving as a Team. Available from Kendall/Hunt Publishing Company, 2460 Kerper Boulevard, PO Box 539, Dubuque, IA 52004-0539 for $39.90 for Teacher's Resource Book, $14.90 for each Student Text, $5.90 for each Portfolio, $29.90 for each Teacher's Edition.

Middle School.   This program consists of three comprehensive physical education textbooks, *Moving With Confidence-Step 1*, *Moving With Skill-Step 2*, and *Moving as a Team-Step 3*, designed developmentally for middle school students in grades 6th through 8th. The teacher's edition for each level includes margin notes that direct teacher actions. The student portfolio for each grade level contains classroom, laboratory, and field activities for students to complete in and outside of class. There is also a teacher resource book covering all three levels that includes chapter tests and suggested activities. Step 1 focuses on the development of confidence and self-esteem. Step 2 focuses on developing and improving physical skills to achieve personal best. Step 3 focuses on the use of personal skills to develop prosocial skills and teamwork. Each textbook emphasizes the pursuit of excellence, physical fitness, movement skills and qualities (including techniques, movement patterns, biomechanics, and offensive and defensive strategies), self-image, and prosocial skills. These textbooks are primarily designed to accompany a conceptually based physical education program. This is one of only two series currently available for middle school students in physical education.

General High School

Physical Education: Theory and Practice, by Damien Davis, Tom Kimmet, & Margaret Auty (South Melbourne: MacMillan Company of Australia, 1986), 453 p. ISBN 0-333-43021-2. Available from MacMillan Company of Australia, 107 Moray Street, South Melbourne 3205.

High School.   The most comprehensive student textbook available for physical education, this textbook was written for Year 12 in Australia. Divided into six parts, it covers all the subdisciplines of physical education in its 51 chapters. The parts include anatomy and physiology, exercise physiology, biomechanics, motor learning, history, and sociology. Each chapter contains information, worksheets, and laboratories to assist students with understanding the material. This book is designed for conceptually based physical education programs.

• • •

Physical Activity and Sport for the Secondary School Student, by Neil J. Dougherty IV, Editor (Reston, VA: AAHPERD, 1993), 394 p. ISBN 0-88314-526-X. Available from AAHPERD, 1900 Association Drive, Reston, VA 22091 for $24.95.

Secondary.   This is a comprehensive student textbook on contemporary physical activities and sport concepts. It is organized by activity, with sections on skills and techniques, safety, scoring, rules, etiquette, strategies, equipment, and related terminology. This textbook is designed for multiactivity physical education programs.

• • •

Moving for Life, by Gary Berg Spindt, William H. Monti, & Betty Hennessy (Dubuque, IA: Kendall/Hunt, 1991), 115 p. for Teacher's Guide, 229 p. for Student Textbook, 150 p. for Portfolio I, 103 p. for Portfolio II. ISBN 0-8403-4608-5 for Teacher's Guide, 5330-8 for Student Textbook, 5331-6 for Physical Education Portfolio I, 5332-4 for Physical Education Portfolio II. Available from Kendall/Hunt Publishing Company, 2460 Kerper Boulevard, PO Box 539, Dubuque, IA 52004-0539 for $39.90 for Teacher's Guide, $24.90 for Student Text, and $5.90 for each Portfolio.

High School. This is a comprehensive physical education textbook designed to teach high school students the cognitive and physical skills necessary to become physically educated adults. This textbook and the middle school physical education textbooks described under the middle school section comprise Kendall/Hunt's Essentials of Physical Education Program. A textbook, two portfolios, and a teacher's guide complete the package.

The textbook focuses on physical fitness, biomechanics, movement patterns, motor learning, prosocial skills, self-image, pursuit of excellence, and lifetime activity. The portfolios provide classroom, laboratory, and field activities that enable students to explore, practice, and apply the concepts described in the student text. The teacher's guide supplies notes, answers to study questions in the textbook, and chapter tests. The textbook is designed primarily to accompany a conceptually based physical education program.

Secondary Fitness

Fitness for Life, by Charles B. Corbin & Ruth Lindsey (Glenview, IL: Scott, Foresman, 1990), 232 p. ISBN 0-673-29575-3 for Teacher's Resource Book, 29576 for Teacher's Annotated Edition, and 29578-8 for Student Book. Available from Scott, Foresman and Company, 1900 East Lake Avenue, Glenview, IL for $21.15 hard bound, $11.50 soft bound, $16.90 Teacher's Edition, and $25.68 Teacher's Resource Book.

Grades 7-12. This textbook provides a concept approach to fitness covering both health-related and skill-related physical fitness. Students learn how they can achieve a personal level of fitness through an understanding of why fitness is important, what their own fitness needs are, and how to maintain fitness for a lifetime. The book includes fitness activities that assist the student in relating concepts to their personal fitness. Specific information on principles of fitness, cardiovascular fitness, strength, muscular endurance, flexibility, body composition, warm up,

nutrition, stress, consumer issues, and planning and evaluating exercise programs is included.

The Teacher's Resource Book provides blackline masters, worksheets for self-evaluation activities, reinforcement sheets on chapter concepts, and chapter quizzes. The annotated teacher's edition includes background notes, teaching strategies, safety, research data, professional articles, flexible management schedules, vocabulary lists, and suggestions for individualizing instruction. This was one of the first student textbooks available on this subject and it has been updated to withstand the test of time.

• • •

Personal Fitness and You, by Roberta Stokes & Clancy Moore (Winston-Salem, NC: Hunter Textbooks, 1993), 215 p., 106 p. for laboratory activities, and 252 p. for teacher's edition. ISBN 0-88725-064-5. Available from Hunter Textbooks, Inc., 823 Reynolda Road, Winston-Salem, NC 27104 for $23.96, $29.56 for Teacher's Edition, and $25.00 for Resource Book.

Grades 7-12. This book covers an introduction to fitness, fitness evaluation, principles of training, flexibility, cardiovascular fitness, muscular strength and endurance, nutrition, weight control, stress, exercising safely, planning an exercise program now and in the future, and consumer awareness for high school students. The laboratory activities are especially effective at reinforcing the information in the textbook. These are ''hands-on'' activities, most of which involve actual physical activity.

The teacher's edition provides motivational ideas and tips, a sample course outline, suggested student projects, games and activities for fitness, performance standards, suggested instructional materials (films, videos, equipment, records, tapes, books, software), answers to chapter review questions, sample black line masters (for overheads), and chapter tests. Readers should be aware that the grading policy suggested in the Teacher's Edition is based on traditional grading that includes dressing out and showering. Despite the grading policy, this is an excellent text for students.

• • •

Personal Fitness: Looking Good/Feeling Good, by Charles S. Williams, Emmanouel G. Harageones, DeWayne J. Johnson, & Charles D. Smith (Dubuque, IA: Kendall/Hunt, 1992), 277 p. for Student Text, 122 p. for Student Activity Handbook, 312 p. for Teacher's Edition, and 499 p. for Teacher's Resource Book. ISBN 0-8403-5134-8 for Student Text, 5135-6 for Student Activity Handbook, 5136-4 for Teacher's Edition, and 7214-0 for Teacher's Resource Book. Available from Kendall/Hunt Publishing Company, 4050 Westmark

Drive, PO Box 1840, Dubuque, IA 52004-1840 for $21.90 for Student Text, $7.90 for Student Activity Handbook, $39.90 for Teacher's Edition, and $45.90 for Teacher's Resource Book.

Grades 9-12. The Student Text covers an introduction to fitness, components of fitness, goal setting for teenagers, guidelines for exercise, principles of training, flexibility, cardiovascular fitness, muscular fitness, nutrition, body composition and weight control, stress, consumer issues, evaluation of activities, and designing a fitness program for high school students. The student text is accompanied by a "hands-on" Student Activity Handbook that includes 51 different activities to reinforce and apply the fitness concepts.

The annotated teacher's edition includes a teacher guide that addresses the following: features of the program, implementing the program, planning the program, fitness assessment, helping students set goals and develop exercise prescriptions, students with special needs, grading procedures, health, environmental and safety considerations, and planning for emergencies. Annotations include teacher objectives, teaching notes and strategies, and answers to study questions. The Teacher's Resource Book includes the following for each chapter: bulletin board ideas, transparency blackline masters, learning activities to reinforce fitness concepts, and a chapter test including answers.

Publications on Specific Content Areas and Teaching Ideas

This section includes publications to assist teachers with developing their own lesson plans. Detailed information is provided about content areas (such as aquatics, team sports, gymnastics, dance), concepts (such as biomechanics, exercise physiology, motor learning), and teaching ideas. Resources are also included for establishing a safe environment in the physical education class and on the playground, and for promoting physical education programs.

K-12 Resources

Teaching Strategies for Improving Youth Fitness, by Charles B. Corbin & Robert P. Pangrazi (Reston, VA: AAHPERD, 1994), 250 p. Stock No. A-566-9. Available from AAHPERD, PO Box 385, Oxon Hill, MD 20750-0385 for $26.00.

Grades K-12. This text is now the reference manual for the new cooperative health-related venture between the National Association for Sport and Physical Education (NASPE) and the Cooper Institute for Aerobics Research. Their joint program, the new Physical Best, incorporates the educational materials available from NASPE and AAHPERD with the fitness test items and software available from the Cooper Institute for Aerobics Research. The publication provides information about the Fitnessgram assessment program (described on p. 128) as well as ideas on how to include fitness instruction in the physical education curriculum.

Included are ideas and activities for improving students' fitness and understanding of the fitness cognitive concepts. The program is also available as educational kits (Physical Best Educational Kit) for grades K-6 and 6-12 for $45.00 each. Each kit includes the textbook; teaching idea cards; posters; and reproducible masters of a class record, a student contract, an activity log, and a report card sheet. Two videos (Physical Best: Integrating Concepts with Activities for Grades K-6 and for Grades 6-12) are also available for $24.00 each.

• • •

Changing Kids' Games, by G.S. Don Morris & Jim Stiehl (Champaign, IL: Human Kinetics, 1989), 160 p. ISBN 0-87322-187-7. Available from Human Kinetics Publishers, PO Box 5076, Champaign, IL 61825-5076 for $14.00.

Grades K-12. The Games Design Model described in this book assists teachers with analyzing and adapting games. By modifying the games kids already play, teachers can better meet the needs, abilities, interests, and skill development of students. The Games Design Model uses the variables of purpose, players, movements, objects, organization, and limits for teachers and students to adapt games. Many examples are provided.

• • •

Sport and Physical Education Advocacy Kit, by National Association for Sport and Physical Education (Reston, VA: AAHPERD, 1994) 122 p. Stock Number 304-10056. Available from AAHPERD, 1900 Association Drive, Reston, VA 22091 for $37.50.

Grades K-12. This notebook is designed to assist physical education teachers and other interested people in promoting physical education programs to parents, community members, media personnel, other educators, and legislators. The packet contains sample press releases, reference materials, survey results, promotional ideas, and sample speeches. Also available from AAHPERD are a variety of brochures that can be distributed at community events. These brochures include: (1) *Required: Quality Daily Physical Education* (stock number 304-10034 for $5.00 per package of 50), which contains NASPE's position statement on the value and importance of physical education programs along with objectives, program design, and desired student goals; (2) *The Physically Educated Person* (stock number 304-10032 for $5.00 per package of 50), which summarizes the work of the NASPE Outcomes Project; and (3) brochures on ''developmentally appropriate practices'' and ''guidelines for physical education programs'' at the elementary, middle school, and high school levels. A 12-minute video on quality physical education entitled *Making the Case for Quality Daily Physical Education* (stock number 304-10020 for $15.00) rounds out the complete package.

• • •

Encyclopedia of Line Dances: The Steps That Came and Stayed, by Ollie May Ray (Reston, VA: AAHPERD, 1992), 176 p. ISBN 0-883145-00-6. Available from AAHPERD Publications, 1900 Association Drive, Reston, VA 22091-1599 for $26.00.

Grades K-12. This manual provides music, history, formation, steps, and directions for over 90 separate solo and line dances that can easily be taught in physical education. This reference is particularly valuable for teachers with limited experience teaching dance.

• • •

A Manual for Tumbling and Apparatus Stunts (8th ed.), by Otto E. Ryser & James R. Brown (Dubuque, IA: Brown, 1990), 260 p. ISBN 0-697-07170-7. Available from Wm. C. Brown Company Publishers, 2460 Kerper Boulevard, Dubuque, IA 52001 for $20.00.

Grades K-12. After providing an introduction to gymnastics that includes teaching coeducational classes, safety, spotting, and conditioning, this manual describes all of the stunts taught in a physical education class. The stunts are organized by simple stunts, tumbling stunts, static balance, pyramids, floor exercise, pommel horse, parallel bars, vaulting rings, low horizontal bar, high horizontal bar, balance beam, and uneven parallel bars. This reference is particularly valuable for physical educators with limited experience teaching tumbling and gymnastics. This is an excellent resource that approaches the subject from a teaching perspective instead of a coaching perspective.

• • •

Public Playground Handbook for Safety (Washington, DC: U.S. Consumer Product Safety Commission, 1990). Available from U.S. Consumer Product Safety Commission, Washington, DC 20207 for free.

Grades K-12. This is a technical brochure that provides safety guidelines for construction, installation, and maintenance of playground equipment. Recommendations are also provided for the layout of playgrounds and ground covering for maximum protection of children during falls.

Elementary Resources

Peaceful Playgrounds, by Melinda Bossenmeyer (Byron, CA: Front Row Experience, 1989), 50 p. ISBN 0-915256-27-4. Available from Front Row Experience, 540 Discovery Bay Boulevard, Byron, CA 94514 for $6.95.

Elementary. This publication is designed for elementary school teachers and administrators to use in setting up their recess and lunch programs. The author addresses five principles for establishing peaceful playgrounds: consistent set of rules, solutions to conflicts, game markings on the blacktop and grass areas, necessary equipment available, and consistent expectations on the part of school staff members. A variety of playground games are explained, including necessary equipment, the objective of the game, and skills that are practiced by playing the game. Appendixes include award samples, safety issues, equipment recommendations, and game and field markings. This is an excellent resource for developing recess and lunch programs; however, the suggested games for these ''play periods'' should not be confused with suggested activities for physical education.

• • •

Health Related Physical Fitness, by Clayre K. Petray, Sandra L. Blazer, & Kelly McWilliams, Illustrator (Edina, MN: Bellwether, 1991), 263 p. ISBN 0-8087-3383-4. Available from Bellwether Press, Burgess International Group, Inc., 7110 Ohms Lane, Edina, MN 55435 for $21.95.

Elementary. This book is designed to help physical education specialists and classroom teachers incorporate health-related physical fitness into their existing physical education programs. The organization is clear and easy to follow. The authors cover the frequency, intensity, and time (FIT) concepts along with principles for exercising before proceeding to a comprehensive coverage of each area of health-related fitness (flexibility, cardiorespiratory endurance, body composition, and muscular strength and endurance) that includes cognitive concepts, assessment, and exercises for children. The book also provides a framework for the entire physical education program, including scheduling, safety, discipline, keeping students active, public relations, and the role of fitness in the overall program.

• • •

Upper Elementary Children Moving and Learning, by

Rae Pica (Champaign, IL: Human Kinetics, 1993), 136 p. ISBN 0-87322-468-X. Available from Human Kinetics Publishers, PO Box 5076, Champaign, IL 61825-5076 for $69.00 (includes three-ring notebook and 2 cassettes).

Elementary. This complete movement education program contains over 120 outstanding problem-solving and guided discovery movement ideas and activities in 40 lesson plans. In a content area where upper elementary classroom teachers and physical education specialists alike need assistance, this is an excellent resource. For each problem-solving and guided discovery activity, the resource contains possible student responses to assist teachers when facilitating their students toward all possible movement solutions. Rae Pica has also developed *Moving and Learning* resources for toddlers, preschoolers, and early elementary children.

• • •

P.E. Teacher's Skill by Skill Activities Program: Success-Oriented Sports Experiences for Grades K-8, by Lowell F. "Bud" Turner & Susan Lilliman Turner (West Nyack, NY: Parker, 1989), 260 p. Available from Parker Publishing Company, West Nyack, NY 10995 for $27.95.

Elementary. The Turners take a threefold approach to teaching basic game skills: success-oriented, skill-oriented, and interdisciplinary. Activities include basketball, football, soccer, softball, volleyball, conditioning, gymnastics, tennis, and track and field. Each unit includes an introduction, word search of basic terms, skills (goals, performance tips, and desired competencies), equipment needs, and tasks for practice and mastery of the skill. Each unit concludes with a circuit training plan that includes all of the skills identified in the unit, motivators (that challenge the students with a "Can you?" approach), and lesson extensions that relate the activity to other areas of the curriculum.

Secondary Resources

Principles of Safety in Physical Education and Sport, by Neil J. Dougherty IV, Editor (Reston, VA: AAHPERD, 1994), 256 p. ISBN 0-88314-556-1. Available from AAHPERD, 1900 Association Drive, Reston, VA 22091 for $35.00.

Secondary. Provides safety factors to consider when teaching sport and physical activities. The book begins with information on the extent of injuries in physical education and sport, the legal issues regarding safety, administering the safety program, and establishing first aid and sport safety policies. Checklists, outlines, and expert commentary furnish information for developing safety guidelines by activity. This is an important book to consult prior to establishing curriculum, unit, and lesson plans for physical education.

• • •

Teaching Team Sports: A Coeducational Approach, by Joan A. Phillip & Jerry D. Wilkerson (Champaign, IL: Human Kinetics, 1990), 320 p. ISBN 0-87322-259-8. Available from Human Kinetics, PO Box 5076, Champaign, IL 61825-5076 for $29.00.

Secondary. The strength of this book is found in chapters 2 and 3. Chapter 2 covers mechanical principles (center of gravity and balance, force, Newton's laws of motion, levers, etc.) from a practical standpoint with application to teaching secondary students. Chapter 3 describes and analyzes each fundamental movement using the mechanical principles defined in chapter 2. Part 2 addresses specific sports, including basketball, field hockey, flag or touch football, soccer, softball, speedball, and volleyball. The history, purposes and values, rules, and teaching progressions are given for each activity. The authors describe how to analyze and teach each skill by breaking it down into its fundamental body movements. Drills, along with common movement problems and suggestions, are also provided.

• • •

Cowstails and Cobras II: A Guide to Games, Initiatives, Ropes Course, and Adventure Curriculum, by Karl Rohnke (Hamilton, MA: Project Adventure, 1989), 210 p. ISBN 0-8403-5434-7. Available from Project Adventure, PO Box 100, Hamilton, MA 01936 for $14.95.

Secondary. This book forms the basis of an adventure-based curriculum for physical education. It covers the philosophy and goals of Project Adventure, which emphasizes that individuals are more capable than they perceive themselves to be. The games, initiatives, and ropes course activities provide individuals with the opportunity to try new experiences in a supportive atmosphere. The activities promote the participants' sense of confidence in themselves and in others. Some activities require agility and physical coordination, but others require problem solving and group cooperation. The process for the activities is outlined: group formation, selecting activities, briefing the group, leading the group, and debriefing the group. Sample curriculum models are provided for elementary, middle school, high school, and higher education. Project Adventure publishes a number of books, but this is the one to get you started.

• • •

Individualizing Physical Education: Criterion Materials, by Dorothy Zakrajsek & Lois A. Carnes (Champaign, IL: Human Kinetics, 1986), 251 p. ISBN 0-87322-045-5. Available from Human Kinetics Publishers, Inc., PO Box 5076, Champaign, IL 61820 for $25.00.

Secondary. Targeting the middle school level, this book explains task learning experiences (sequential activities that lead the learner from a basic skill level to application of the skill in a game situation) for selected fundamental skills, rhythmic gymnastics, tumbling, gymnastics, track and field, badminton, tennis, basketball, flag football, soccer, softball, and volleyball. The skill analysis for each activity is especially effective. The strength of this book lies in its examples of various kinds of tasks sheets for each of the activities.

• • •

Steps to Success Activity Series, various authors (Champaign, IL: Human Kinetics, 1989-1993), pages vary. Available from Human Kinetics Books, PO Box 5076, Champaign, IL 61825-5076 for $13.95-$15.95 for student books and $19.95 for teacher books.

Secondary. The books in this series are based on Joan Vickers' *Instructional Design for Teaching Physical Activities,* which is described under "Publications on Curriculum Development and Instructional Strategies for Teachers." The books provide teachers with resources for use in a high school activity program. For each activity, two books are offered, one on technique and the other on instruction. The technique books provide instruction in the basic skills, applying the latest information from the areas of biomechanics, kinesiology, exercise physiology, motor learning, sport psychology, cognitive psychology, and instructional design.

The instructional books provide carefully sequenced instructional design suggestions for learning the activity along with proven drills for practicing single-skill and multiple-skill combinations. Current activity offerings include alpine skiing, archery, bowling, golf, Nordic skiing, racquetball, self-defense, soccer, social dance, softball, swimming, table tennis, tennis, volleyball, and weight training. The technique books can be used as high school textbooks for junior and senior semester-long classes on the activities listed above.

Supplemental Materials

Several types of instructional materials—instructional television, videos and laser discs, and technology devices and software—are described in this section. Instructional television refers to broadcasts used during the instructional period to reinforce concepts. Specific instructional television shows are described in this section; however, sporting events and commercial programs can be used to reinforce concepts. For example, certain episodes from "Wonder Years," "Full House," and "Afterschool Specials" have information or ideas appropriate for physical education.

Videos and laser discs can be used in ways similar to instructional television. The advantage of laser discs is that a particular segment can be accessed within 1-3 seconds without having to go through an entire videotape to find the information needed for the lesson. When using instructional television, videos, and laser discs, video clips should be selected to demonstrate a particular skill or concept; the entire episode or tape should not be shown at one time.

When selecting instructional television programs, videos, or laser discs, make sure the models represent males and females from different ethnicities. Also, be sure the images accurately depict the skill technique being demonstrated and that an explanation is included describing the technique and biomechanics.

Technology includes a variety of electronic devices including digital blood pressure meters, body composition analyzers, heart monitors, and computers. The first three devices assist the teacher with collecting personal data on students more efficiently. For example, with the Futrex Bodyfat Analyzer, the user simply places a wand on the biceps and the device calculates the percentage of body fat. The use of computers can be categorized by the intended purpose of the software into three major areas: teacher utility, computer-assisted instruction, and computer-assisted assessment. Teacher utility software assists the physical education teacher in becoming more efficient. Word processing, database, and spreadsheet programs form the backbone of utility software for all teachers. For physical educators specifically, software that analyzes fitness scores is very popular.

Computer-assisted instructional software for physical education is in its infancy; however, commercial vendors are beginning to develop software for the consumer market, and physical educators can take advantage of some of these programs. This type of software provides instruction for students on techniques, fitness concepts, and biomechanical principles. Physical educators should also look at software available for history, science, and health classes that may have portions applicable to physical education, such as ErgoMotion from Houghton Mifflin for science, which contains a section on biomechanics. An interactive laser disc system connects a laser disc player to a computer so that at specific points in the software, video images are displayed to reinforce concepts or ideas. Digitized video, in which video images are stored as computer files, is also used in software programs providing "live action" visual images for the learner. However, these files require a tremendous amount of storage space and are typically found in programs stored on CD-ROM (Compact Disc-Read Only Memory).

Computer-assisted assessment refers not only to grading programs, but also to ideas for using the computer in authentic assessment. Generic programs, such as Grady Profile from Software for Teachers and programs designed specifically for physical education that contain a portfolio section, are incorporating the concepts of authentic assessment. Authoring programs, such as HyperCard for the Macintosh, HyperStudio for the Apple or Macintosh, and LinkWay Live for the IBM and compatibles, also allow students to set up electronic portfolios on the computer that include written assignments along with captured stills or video images of themselves. The computer should be set up as a station or resource for use during or after the class period.

The specific resources below are samples of outstanding videos, laser discs, instructional television programs, and computer software programs on the market.

Instructional Television and Videos

K-12 Television and Videos

Assessment of Fundamental Motor Skills, by Arlene A. Ignico (Madison, WI: Brown and Benchmark, 1994). Twelve videotapes. Available from Brown and Benchmark Publishers, 25 Kessel Court, Madison, WI for $35.00 each (discounts for the series are available).

Grades K-12. This video series assists teachers with improving their observation skills. Separate videos are available for running, jumping, hopping, sliding, galloping, leaping, skipping, striking, throwing, kicking, catching, and dribbling. For each fundamental motor skill, performance criteria are identified and illustrated through an adult model. Samples of student performance are then provided with a query as to whether a particular performance criterion has been met. Viewers are given the opportunity to respond, and then feedback is provided. As a result of using these videos, teachers should be able to identify performance criteria and to observe and detect errors in performance at various developmental levels. This video series can also be used with secondary students to help them provide peer and cross-age tutorials in motor skills.

• • •

Juggling Star, by Jugglebug (Champaign, IL: Human Kinetics, 1992), 28 minutes. Available from Human Kinetics, PO Box 5076, Champaign, IL 61825-5076 for $17.95.

Grades K-12. This is a motivational and entertaining video set to music that teaches students to juggle.

Progressing quickly through one and two balls, the video focuses on step by step instructions for three- and four-ball tricks. Also available are *Juggletime*, which focuses on juggling scarves and is aimed at younger students, and *Juggler's Jam*, which focuses on advanced juggling tricks using rings, clubs, and other manipulatives.

• • •

The Jump Rope Primer Video, by Ken M. Solis & Bill Budris (Champaign, IL: Human Kinetics, 1991), 32-minute video. Available from Human Kinetics, PO Box 5076, Champaign, IL 61825-5076 for $34.95.

Grades K-12. This video is a companion to *The Jump Rope Primer* book; however, the video can stand alone as an instructional resource. The video covers the history of rope jumping, benefits, types and appropriate length of jump ropes, preferred floor surfaces, appropriate attire, class design, games, and rope skills. The video begins with a section on jumping properly without a rope and progresses through intermediate and advanced skills using short and long ropes. Included in the video are choreographed routines that will help to motivate students.

Elementary Television and Videos

Leaps and Bounds (Honolulu: Hawaii State Department of Education, 1982), sixteen 15-minute programs. Available from Agency for Instructional Television, Box A, Bloomington, IN 47402-0120 for $125 per program.

Grades K-3. The series includes lessons on body awareness and control, locomotor skills, creative movement, tumbling, apparatus, rope jumping, underhand throw and catch, overhand throw and ball dodging, projecting the ball, kicking, and striking. In each session, there is a demonstration of specific skill areas using a small group of students followed by a public school physical education class involved in activities based on the skills presented in the first part. Students are encouraged to try the skills after seeing their peers mastering them on television.

• • •

All Fit With Slim Goodbody, by Slim Goodbody (Champaign, IL: Human Kinetics, 1987), fifteen 15-minute programs on three videotapes. Available from Human Kinetics, PO Box 5076, Champaign, IL 61825-5076 for $195.00 including three videotapes and the teacher's guide.

Elementary. This program series, available through instructional television and from Human Kinetics, consists of the following lessons: Lifetime Fitness, Cardiorespiratory Fitness, Strength and Endurance,

Flexibility, Body Composition, Fitness, Training Principles, Warm-up/Cool-down, Speed and Power, Coordination and Agility, All Fit Workout, Body Design, Balance, Posture, and Stress and Relaxation. It is designed for children in grades two through five to help them improve their overall level of fitness. The series helps children identify and develop fitness skills, and also helps them develop a positive attitude toward themselves and others. Each program combines participatory elements as well as cognitive information. An accompanying *Teacher's Guide* provides a program summary for each lesson including the main concept, objectives, and vocabulary. Also included are previewing activities, post-viewing activities, and master activity sheets. Although this series is several years old, it is still highly recommended; however, there are a few contraindicated exercises (double leg lifts, curl ups with hands behind neck) of which teachers will need to be aware.

● ● ●

Step by Step for Kids, by Slim Goodbody (Champaign, IL: Human Kinetics, 1994), 40 minutes. Available from Human Kinetics, PO Box 5076, Champaign, IL 61825-5076 for $24.95.

Elementary. In this 2-part video, Slim discusses safety measures for using steps, teaches individual steps, and leads students through several step aerobic routines. The themes for the routines include dinosaurs, the old west, ball skills, and language arts. Part 1 introduces the aerobic routines along with instructions, and Part 2 takes the students through each aerobic routine without detailed instructions.

Secondary Television and Videos

The World of Volleyball (North Palm Beach, FL: Athletic Institute, 1992), 30 minutes. Available from Human Kinetics, PO Box 5076, Champaign, IL 61825-5076 for $29.95.

Secondary. This video reviews the rules of volleyball and then demonstrates the proper techniques for serving, passing, setting, spiking, blocking, and digging. The video also explains how to correct common errors and offers training tips from Olympic athletes. This video is best used in segments to introduce and demonstrate each new skill before students have an opportunity to practice.

● ● ●

The Science and Myths of Tennis, by Vic Braden (Coto de Caza, CA: Vic Braden Communications, 1992), 48 minutes. Available from Human Kinetics, PO Box 5076, Champaign, IL 61825-5076 for $39.95.

Secondary. As physical educators begin to bring the concept-based physical education curriculum into

their classes, this is an excellent video illustrating how physics applies to physical activity. Not only does this video provide information on tennis skills, it also illustrates several biomechanic principles. Twenty commonly asked questions about tennis are analyzed using statistics, timed experiments, and slow motion graphics, including the use of tight or loose strings for power, how to calculate ball speed, and the real value of follow-through. The end of the video contains a quick answer to each of the twenty questions explored during the video. Vic Braden also produces other videos on tennis, skiing, volleyball, badminton, and the learning of motor skills.

● ● ●

"He Coulda' Been Great" (Charleston, WV: Cambridge Career Products, 1989), 35 minutes. Available from Cambridge Career Products, PO Box 2153, Charleston, WV 25328 for $49.95.

Grades 9-12. This video covers anatomy, conditioning, risk factors, and injury management related to knee injuries from playing football, although the concepts presented can be applied to joints other than the knee as well as to other sports. Strength, flexibility, agility, and injury reduction exercises are demonstrated and analyzed for safety. Also included are several exercises that should be avoided (full squats, duck walk, hurdler stretch, knee sitting) due to their potential for causing injury to the player. Although this video targets competitive football, it is well done and could be used in a high school fitness unit or sports medicine class.

● ● ●

Teaching Lifetime Fitness, by David Laurie & Charles Corbin (Manhattan, KS: Audio Visual Designs of Manhattan, 1993), ten 20-minute videos. Available from Audio Visual Designs of Manhattan, 2208 Fort Riley Boulevard, Manhattan, KS 66502 for $79.95 per video or all 10 for $699.95.

Secondary. This is a series of 10 videos for use in teaching fitness concepts to secondary school students. Each video contains current conceptual information as well as discussion questions that can be used in class for student participation and cooperative learning. The 10 videos are separated into two packages. Package A contains "Climbing the Fitness Stairway," "Introduction to Physical Fitness," "Preparing for Exercise," "Fitness, Exercise, and Good Health," and "How Much is Enough." Package B contains "Cardiovascular Fitness," "Building Cardiovascular Fitness," "Muscle Fitness," "Flexibility," and "Body Fatness." The videos can be used as a supplement to the *Fitness for Life* high school textbook by Charles Corbin and Ruth Lindsey.

• • •

Golf with Al Geiberger (San Francisco: SyberVision, 1989), 60-minute video and four 60-minute audio cassettes. Available from SyberVision, One Sansome Street, Suite 1610, San Francisco, CA 94104 for $89.95.

Secondary. In the 1970s, SyberVision Systems used a Stanford University researcher's findings on visual learning to develop a sports teaching technique known as "neuro-muscular training." SyberVision found that players who concentrated on images of perfectly executed fundamentals showed marked improvement. The images triggered nerve impulses that were stored and later retrieved as "muscle memory." This golf video provides images of Al Geiberger demonstrating the perfect drive, pitch, chip, and putt. His rhythm becomes part of the mental timing. This publisher also provides videos for tennis, racquetball, bowling, soccer, basketball, baseball, softball, and so forth.

• • •

P.E. TV (Knoxville, TN: Whittle Communications, 1994). Available from Whittle Communications, 333 Main Street, Knoxville, TN 37902-1897 for $50.00.

Secondary. This series is comprised of thirty-two 12-minute video multimedia programs and an accompanying 175-page manual on physical education and the benefits of being physically active. The series is designed so that one 12-minute program is shown at the beginning of each week and followed up by activities during the week to reinforce the concepts from the show. Weekly topics range from Health-Related Fitness Foundations (cardiovascular endurance, flexibility, etc.) to Performance Training (agility, coordination, and balance) to Sports and Dance (moving the body through space) and Mastery (the challenge to reach a personal best). Included with the program is a new fitness evaluation, homework assignments, and handouts that further illustrate the concepts covered in the lesson. The program emphasizes that all students, not just gifted athletes, can be successful in physical education.

• • •

Personal Fitness: Looking Good/Feeling Good, by Charles S. Williams, Emmanouel G. Harageones, De-Wayne J. Johnson, & Charles D. Smith (Dubuque, IA: Kendall/Hunt, 1993). Available from Kendall/Hunt Publishing Company, 4050 Westmark Drive, PO Box 1840, Dubuque, IA 52004-1840 for $239.90 for Video Package (ISBN 0-8403-8095-X), $89.90 for Teacher's Video (7487-9), $179.90 for Student Videos (8243-X).

Secondary. This video series is a companion to the *Personal Fitness: Looking Good/Feeling Good* textbook program. The teacher's video helps teachers implement the program and addresses the following: how to get started, suggested instructional sequence for each chapter, teaching strategies for classroom instruction and laboratory activities, suggestions for such issues as homework, fitness assessment, and student evaluation, and ideas for marketing a fitness education program. The 14-part student video program uses real-life scenarios to motivate and introduce students to the major concepts of each chapter. Titles of the student videos: "Looking Good-Feeling Good," "Components of Fitness," "Goal Setting for Teenagers," "Guidelines for Exercise," "Principles of Training," "Flexibility," "Cardiovascular Fitness," "Nutrition," "Body Composition and Weight Control," "Stress," "Consumer Issues," "Evaluation of Activities," and "Designing Your Own Program."

Technology and Computer Software

Using Technology in Physical Education, by Bonnie Mohnsen (Champaign, IL: Human Kinetics, 1995), 168 p. ISBN 0-87322-661-5. Available from Human Kinetics Publishers, Inc., PO Box 5076, Champaign, IL 51820 for $14.00.

Grades K-12. This is an introductory textbook for physical educators. It covers the use of video cassette players and recorders, camcorders, computers, laser disc players, and other technology specifically in physical education. Other technologies addressed include heart monitors, electronic blood pressure devices, and body composition analyzers. The information on computers ranges from teacher utility software to computer-assisted instruction and computer-assisted assessment. There is also a chapter on accessing electronic bulletin boards and using electronic mail. The final chapter offers readers a view of the future, in which technology will be integrated into every physical education class.

Teacher Utility Software

MacFitness Report 3.0 (Cerritos, CA: Bonnie's Fitware, 1995). Available from Bonnie's Fitware, 18832 Stefani Avenue, Cerritos, CA 90703 for $75.00. Macintosh version.

Ages 5-18. Contains a pretest and post-test program aligned with AAHPERD's Physical Best and Prudential's Fitnessgram test items. The pretest program prepares and prints individual reports showing score, minimum standards, whether standards are met or not met, and suggested improvement, and it provides room for students to set goals. It also prints a summary report showing all students, scores, and averages. The post-test program prepares and prints individual reports showing pretest and post-test scores, minimum competency, and met/not met for each test. A statistics screen shows the average for each test item and the number of students passing the minimum competency for 5 tests out of 5 tests, 4 out of 5, 3 out of 5, 2 out of 5, 1 out of 5, and 0 out of 5.

• • •

Health Related Physical Fitness Student Profile (Hastings, MN: CompTech Systems Design, 1984). Available from CompTech Systems Design, PO Box 516, Hastings, MN 55033 for $49.95. Apple version.

Student Profile I is for ages 6 to 12 and Student Profile II is for ages 13 to 17. This software is designed especially for students to learn more about their own physical well-being. Students can enter their own personal data acquired from the AAHPERD Health Related Fitness tests. Once data are entered, students receive a personal fitness prescription. Personal data are analyzed using national standards, and a comparison chart is displayed. Students can choose to print out the recommended exercise prescription.

• • •

Fitnessgram (Dallas, TX: Cooper Institute for Aerobics Research, 1994). Available from Cooper Institute for Aerobics Research, 12330 Preston Road, Dallas, TX 75230 for $6.00 for the software and $10.00 for the manual. IBM, Apple, and Macintosh versions.

Grades K-12. Fitnessgram is a youth fitness testing and reporting system. It provides feedback to students, teachers, and parents through an informative, personalized report card. A comprehensive awards program, designed to emphasize and reward exercise behavior, is an important component of the program. The test items are health related, and analysis is based on health standards established for each age and sex. Each student is compared to the standards and not to each other. Pre and post scores can be viewed on a single printout. Although the software costs only $6.00, the reports must be printed out on special cards that are available for $22.00 for a box of 200 cards and $60.00 for a box of 600 cards. A special enrollment package is available for $76.00 and includes 600 cards, software, a computer reference manual, a test administration manual, calipers, pacer tape, a lap counter, curl-up measuring strips, and an awards sample kit. This program is endorsed by the National Association for Sport and Physical Education (NASPE).

Computer-Assisted Instructional and Assessment Software

MacFootball Rules Game (Cerritos, CA: Bonnie's Fitware, 1991). Available from Bonnie's Fitware, 18832 Stefani Avenue, Cerritos, CA 90703 for $50.00. Macintosh version.

Secondary. This software teaches and reinforces students' understanding of flag football rules through a game simulation. Students choose from 5-yard, 10-yard, and 15-yard questions. They receive four questions (downs) in which to move the ball across the next quarter line. If they are successful, they receive a "first down" with four more opportunities to advance the ball. If unsuccessful, possession of the ball transfers to the opponent. Crossing the goal line awards the student or team six points.

• • •

MacHealth-Related Fitness Tutorial and Portfolio (Cerritos, CA: Bonnie's Fitware, 1993). Available from Bonnie's Fitware, 18832 Stefani Avenue, Cerritos, CA 90703 for $100.00. Macintosh version.

Secondary. This tutorial covers the five components of health-related fitness: cardiorespiratory endurance, muscular strength, muscular endurance, flexibility, and body composition. Also included are FIT (frequency, intensity, time) concepts, principles of exercise, dangerous and safe exercises, and warm-up and cool-down procedures. Students create their own fitness portfolios containing fitness scores, selected exercises, and the opportunity to describe their understanding of the concepts and principles related to fitness.

• • •

MacVolleyball Complete: Tutorial and Portfolio (Cerritos, CA: Bonnie's Fitware, 1995). Available from Bonnie's Fitware, 18832 Stefani Avenue, Cerritos, CA 90703 for $100.00. Macintosh version.

Secondary. This program provides information on each of the eight subdisciplines of physical education (exercise physiology, motor learning, biomechanics, psychology, growth and development, aesthetics, sociology, and historical perspectives) as they relate to the learning of volleyball. Teachers and students can access and interact with the information to increase their understanding of volleyball skills, the game, offensive and defensive strategies, training guidelines, and teamwork. Students create their own volleyball portfolios demonstrating their understanding of volleyball.

• • •

Heart and Fitness (Hastings, MN: CompTech Systems Design, 1983). Available from CompTech Systems Design, PO Box 516, Hastings, MN 55033 for $79.95. Apple version.

Secondary. This program covers basic information on how the heart works, how to determine pulse, and the relationship between exercise and good health. The software package also includes a stethoscope, student activity book, and training charts.

● ● ●

John Rae—Survival Series (Hastings, MN: CompTech Systems Design, 1985). Available from CompTech Systems Design, PO Box 516, Hastings, MN 55033 for $99.00. Apple version.

Secondary. This simulation presents Arctic Explorer John Rae and his actual adventures. The program reinforces basic first aid concepts, orienteering, and outdoor survival skill activities. Students learn through problem solving how to build a snowhouse, determine longitude and latitude, plot a bearing, and identify wildlife. In order to complete the Arctic trek, the student must make correct decisions based on real-life situations.

● ● ●

Physics of Sport—Basic Motor Learning (Hastings, MN: CompTech Systems Design, 1980). Available from CompTech Systems Design, PO Box 516, Hastings, MN 55033 for $49.95 for software only and $150.00 for Activity Kit. Apple and IBM versions.

Secondary. This program introduces the basics of internal and external timing and their relation to sport skills. Through computer animation and simulation, students are introduced to each motor learning concept. Striking skills such as how to swing a bat to meet the ball are used, as well as long jumping examples. The content correlates with the Basic Stuff series from AAHPERD. The activity kit includes a comprehensive curriculum guide, Physics of Sport software, and a battery-operated digital timer that measures reaction time in hundredths of a second.

● ● ●

The Outdoor Athlete (Evergreen, CO: Cordillera Press, 1992). Available from Cordillera Press, PO Box 3699, Evergreen, CO 80439 for $39.95. Macintosh version.

Secondary. This CD-ROM combines text, Quick-Time video, and interactive files for journal-keeping. It is based on Steve Ilg's book *The Outdoor Athlete*, and in many instances comes across as information meant for a linear (book) format. However, it does provide video clips of each exercise presented. In addition, it features training programs for cross-country skiing; technical rock and ice climbing, mountaineering and backpacking; kayaking, windsurfing and other water sports; and mountain biking.

● ● ●

Body and Mind (Tallahassee, FL: Fitness Lifestyle Design, 1993). Available from Fitness Lifestyle Design, Inc., 2317 Eastgate Way, Tallahassee, FL 32308 for

$229.95 single unit ($689.85 for 5-unit Lab Pack, $1379.70 for 10-unit Lab Pack). Macintosh version.

Secondary. This software is designed especially to help students practice real-world tasks in developing a personal fitness program by reinforcing and applying fitness concepts. Eight client case studies provide examples for problem-solving activities. The personal track supports self-assessment, goal-setting activities, and fitness planning. The exercise planner allows students to simulate and model alternative fitness plans. The program immediately displays the consequences of adding exercises, deleting exercises, or changing the overload variables. This is one of the few software programs available for physical education that is based on the constructivist instructional design model, helping the student construct knowledge based on personal experience.

● ● ●

The Total Heart (Eagan, MN: IVI, 1993). Available from IVI Publishing, 1380 Corporate Center Curve, Suite 305, Eagan, MN 55121 for $59.95. IBM and Macintosh version.

Secondary. This CD-ROM provides a comprehensive examination of the heart including anatomy, normal heart, heart disease, reducing risk, heart tests, treatments, cardiology, drug directory, and emergency. It includes text, dictionary links, 3-D video animations, and audio effects to convey the information. The hypermedia approach allows users to find the information important to them. There is also a "notes" section that lets the user keep track of personal health history. The information for this CD-ROM was adapted from William Morrow and Company's *Mayo Clinic Heart Book*. Although under most circumstances book adaptations are considered a poor use of a CD-ROM, the publishers of this program have done an outstanding job of adapting the book to a new medium.

● ● ●

Interactive Guide to Volleyball (Renton, WA: SISU Software). Available from SISU Software, PO Box 2305, Renton, WA 98056 for $55.00. Windows and Macintosh.

Secondary. This CD-ROM provides text, graphics, and video clips on the history of volleyball, officiating, strategies (6-2, 4-2, 5-1), and skills. Skills include the dig, block, attack, pass, serve, and set. Each skill is broken down with detailed explanations and video clips. The CD-ROM also contains a multiple choice quiz and a reference section that includes court information, glossary, and rules. Although this CD-ROM provides comprehensive coverage of volleyball, the interactivity is limited to students choosing what they will view. Students do not create or demonstrate their learning except to answer multiple choice questions in the quiz section.

Interactive Laser Disc Technology

I'm Special Production Network (Tampa, FL: University of Southern Florida). Available from Lou Bowers, University of Southern Florida. Interactive Laser Disc Software for the IBM.

Various grade levels. This project was funded by the United States Office of Special Education and produced by the School of Physical Education, Wellness, and Sport Studies at the University of Southern Florida in collaboration with WUSF-TV in Tampa. It was designed to increase the number of university physical education professors knowledgeable in regard to the potential instructional uses of interactive videodisc technology and skilled in the design and production of interactive videodisc learning programs. Four adapted physical education videodisc projects were developed:

- The Adapted Physical Education Developmental Model (Dr. Robert Arnold and Dr. Nelson Ng, Slippery Rock University), which details an approach to implement a developmental physical education program for children with psychomotor deficiencies based on motor, sensory, and sensory-motor developmental progressions.

- The Analysis of Catching Skills (Dr. Diane Craft and Dr. Michael Kniffin, SUNY College at Cortland), which is designed to prepare teachers to analyze the skills of catching. The program describes the correct performance points of catching, identifies the performance of students with disabilities and discrepancies compared to a mature model for catching, and demonstrates appropriate progressions and activities to improve catching performance

- Conflict Resolution (Dr. Michael Loovis and Dr. Richard Hurwitz, Cleveland State University), which prepares teachers of physical education to utilize listening and communication skills to avoid or resolve conflict situations with students demonstrating disruptive behavior.

- Sports for All (Mr. Terry Terry and Mr. Mike Milligan, Message Makers, and Dr. Gail Dummer, Michigan State University, Lansing, Michigan), which is designed to prepare counselors to work with persons with disabilities by showing them how to assess and select appropriate competitive or recreational sport opportunities to meet individuals' personal needs and interests.

Physics of Sport (Seattle, WA: Videodiscovery). Available from Videodiscovery, 1700 Westlake Avenue North, Suite 600, Seattle, WA 98109-3012 for $289 or $338 with software. Interactive Laser Disc Software for the Macintosh.

Secondary. The laser disc package includes a bar-coded student handbook and teacher's guide, a directory of images, and a detailed record of over 20 athletic events. A software program can also be purchased; however, the program is directed toward physics instruction and is not taken from a physical education perspective.

Staying Current

In order to stay up-to-date on current trends in the profession, teachers need access to the most current research and ideas. Books are typically published 2 years after they are written, which makes the information at least 3 years old when it is read. More current information is obtained through journals and telecommunications.

Journals are typically published by professional associations and offered as part of a membership package. However, some professional associations provide their publications to nonmembers for a fee. Some publishers also produce periodicals when they determine that a need exists.

Even more current information can be obtained through telecommunications. With a computer and modem, teachers can dial up electronic information sites and access information that is updated regularly. Journals and telecommunications are described in this section.

Periodicals

Journal of Physical Education, Recreation and Dance (Reston, VA: AAHPERD). Available from AAHPERD, 1900 Association Drive, Reston, VA 22091 for $65.00/year institutional rate.

Grades K-12. Provides articles on current issues, new methods, trends, and materials in physical education, athletics, recreation, and dance. Articles focus on theory and practice, applied research, model programs, and professional preparation and development. Published nine times each year.

• • •

Research Quarterly for Exercise and Sport (Reston, VA: AAHPERD). Available from AAHPERD, 1900 Association Drive, Reston, VA 22091 for $70.00 institutional rate.

Grades K-12. Provides original research on exercise and sport reviewed by a board of researchers.

Four regular issues and a supplement are published annually.

● ● ●

Strategies: A Journal for Sport and Physical Education (Reston, VA: AAHPERD). Available from AAHPERD, 1900 Association Drive, Reston, VA 22091 for $35.00 or $15.00 with membership/year.

Grades K-12. Provides practical information and ideas that work in elementary and secondary physical education classes. Published eight times per year.

● ● ●

Update (Reston, VA: AAHPERD). Available from AAHPERD, 1900 Association Drive, Reston, VA 22091 for $45.00 institutional subscription rate.

Grades K-12. Provides news related to the association for education professionals in health, physical education, athletics, dance, recreation, and leisure (AAHPERD). It includes legislative developments, professional news and activities, association features, professional job placement, and a calendar of events. Special features explore current concerns of all movement-related professionals. Published eight times per year.

● ● ●

Journal of Teaching in Physical Education (Champaign, IL: Human Kinetics). Available from Human Kinetics Publishers, Inc., PO Box 5076, Champaign, IL 61825-5076 for $36.00 per year.

Grades K-12. This publication provides a forum for discussion and research articles that focus on the teaching process and teacher education in physical education. This journal is published four times a year (October, January, April, and July).

● ● ●

Teaching Elementary Physical Education (Champaign, IL: Human Kinetics). Available from Human Kinetics Publishers, Inc., PO Box 5076, Champaign, IL 61825-5076 for $18.00 per year.

Elementary. This publication provides elementary physical educators with practical articles on topics such as instruction, curriculum, class management, inclusion, fitness, professional issues, physical education news, and opinions from educators. New resources are described and important events listed. The newsletter is published six times a year (September, October, November, January, March, and May).

● ● ●

Teaching Secondary Physical Education (Champaign, IL: Human Kinetics). Available from Human Kinetics

Publishers, Inc., PO Box 5076, Champaign, IL 61825-5076 for $18.00 per year.

Secondary school. This newsletter provides information and a communication link for secondary (middle and high) school physical education specialists. Topics covered include advocacy, assessment technology instruction, games, class management, inclusion, fitness, tips from teachers, opinion pieces, news from the field, and listings of new resources and upcoming events. This periodical is published six times a year (September, October, November, January, March, and May).

Telecommunications

California Physical Education Electronic Web Home Page

Grades K-12. This electronic information system is devoted entirely to physical education. Access is available through the URL (universal resource locator) address http://www.coreplus.calstate.edu/pedadm/. There are several main menu items for the board, including Current News, Calendar of Events, Curriculum Share, Lesson Plan Share, Resources, California Association for Health, Physical Education, Recreation, and Dance (CAHPERD) Information, Assessment, and Research Works. Also available are connections to other web pages related to physical education, located around the world.

● ● ●

Internet

Grades K-12. The Internet is a network of networks connecting thousands of computers. Anyone with an electronic mail address, acquired through a commercial or non-commercial service linked to Internet, can communicate with anyone else with an electronic mail address. In addition, there are numerous information sites (with new ones arriving daily) that can be accessed ranging in topics from education to hobbies. For more information or a listing of the most current information sites, there are several books on the Internet from which to choose, including *Zen and the Art of the Internet* by Brendan P. Kehoe (Prentice Hall, Englewood Cliffs, NJ, 1993) and *Way of the Ferret* by Judi Harris (ISTE, Eugene, OR, 1994). Make sure when purchasing a book about the Internet to get a current copyright date so that you will have an up-to-date listing of resources.

8

Children's Books for Physical Education

Pat Bledsoe

Downey Unified School District, Downey, California

This chapter describes a selection of trade books, that is, books that are available through bookstores and libraries, that facilitate the infusion of physical education into the school curriculum. These books help teachers highlight aspects of physical education in literature and capture the interest of students in physical education and sports. For instance, sports figures can have a great impact on students, motivating them to find out more about individual athletes, sports, or related topics.

The books listed in this chapter are organized under the following headings:

- **Joy, Pleasure, and Satisfaction.** These books focus on self-management, goal setting, humanitarianism, and psychology.
- **Skillful Moving.** This section lists books on motor learning, motor skills, and biomechanics. Authors present varied approaches to learning sport skills.
- **Dance.** These are books on rhythm and dance for grades K through 12.
- **Gymnastics.** This section includes books on tumbling, apparatus, and related activities not addressed in the previous categories.
- **Historical Perspectives.** This last section focuses on the evolution of many current activities, as well as on the traditions of sports.
- **Multicultural.** This section furnishes titles on cultural and global activities.
- **Personal Fitness and Physical Fitness.** These are books on fitness and exercise physiology.

With these trade books, the physical education teacher is able to collaborate with colleagues who have expertise in language arts, history/social science, and other subject areas. By collaborating, teachers create a "whole language" and literature-based instructional model, one that has become common in today's elementary schools. This instructional model provides an easy crossover for the elementary school teacher who has to teach physical education, and it also gives the secondary school teacher a new look at physical education in literature.

With the changing times, teachers now need more assistance in understanding other cultures. One way to do this is through physical education and related literature. Books that describe sports and games played in other cultures or provide biographies of athletes from other cultures can provide students with some insight into those cultures. And if these books also help students understand the history and ritual of a sport, they will be better able to understand and appreciate the sport.

These trade books help students and teachers develop a physical education vocabulary and explore the literary aspects of movement. Through these books, readers are exposed to different points of view on fair play, cooperation, competition, and other themes that can be further investigated and discussed in the classroom. My intent is to provide teachers with physical education resources that are developmentally appropriate and culturally specific. I hope that you will enjoy using the books as much as I have enjoyed reviewing them.

This chapter also contains an annotated list of tapes and records that will enhance your physical education program. They are listed by record company under various categories. Labeling indicates those that are available in both English and Spanish.

Joy, Pleasure, and Satisfaction

This section is a collection of books that relate stories demonstrating the mental and emotional aspects of physical education. Watching a child move is fascinating. In a decision to move, the child is often motivated by a feeling of joy. Satisfaction emerges when a goal or expectation has been met. The themes in this section are motivation and self-management, goal setting, humanities, and psychology. The books are categorized according to sport topics.

Baseball and Softball

The Atami Dragons, by David Klanz (New York: Scribner's, 1984). ISBN 0-684-18223-8.

> *Grades 6-8, fiction.* After the death of Jerry's mother, his father takes the family to Japan for a summer. In Japan, Jerry suffers from boredom and loneliness until he discovers the local high school baseball team. With this discovery, his summer changes for the better. The author shows how team support can help one cope with grief and loneliness.

● ● ●

The Baltimore Orioles, by James R. Rothaus (Mankato, MN: Creative Education, 1986).

> *Grades 6-9, nonfiction.* James Rothaus traces the history and spirit of the Baltimore Orioles, providing an in-depth look at the team. Rothaus has also written books on the Boston Red Sox, the Atlanta Braves, and the Chicago Cubs. These books have beautiful pictures of the teams and give great information about the players, the managers, and plays performed by the teams.

● ● ●

Baseball in April and Other Stories, by Gary Soto (San Diego: Harcourt Brace Jovanovich, l990). ISBN 0-15-205720-4-x.

> *Grades 4-6, nonfiction.* This book consists of 11 short stories focusing on the everyday adventures of Latino young people growing up in Fresno, California. The author shares aspects of the lives of the Latino youngsters and helps other students understand the struggles and fun many young people experience growing up.

● ● ●

Baseball Ballerina, by Kathryn Cristaldi (New York: Random House, 1992). ISBN 0-679-81734-4.

> *Grades 1-2, fiction.* A baseball-loving girl worries that the ballet class her mother forces her to take will ruin her reputation with the other members of her baseball team. This is an excellent resource to help children understand how various activities can help develop movement skills and strengthen overall performance.

● ● ●

Baseball Fever, by Johanna Hurevity (New York: Morrow, 1981). ISBN 0-688-00710-4.

> *Grades 4-5, fiction.* Ten-year-old Ezra tries to convince his scholarly father that his baseball fever is not wasting his mind. Ezra and his dad take a trip to the Baseball Hall of Fame. Ezra uses a chess game to work out a way he and his father can compromise on Ezra's love for baseball and his responsibilities in daily life. Ezra not only helps his father understand his passion for baseball; he also shows other students how to solve problems when they have differences of opinion. This book can promote good discussions and writing.

● ● ●

Baseball, Football, Daddy and Me, by David Friend (New York: Viking Penguin, 1990). ISBN 0-670-82420-8.

> *Grade 1, fiction.* A little boy and his father enjoy a full assortment of sporting events together. This is a wonderful book for sharing with children the large assortment of sporting events that are available for them to play and watch. The pictures are particularly interesting for children.

● ● ●

Baseball Kids, by George Sullivan (New York: Dutton, Cobblehill Books, 1990). ISBN 0-525-65023-7.

> *Grades 2-3, nonfiction.* The author profiles 12 boys, ages 11 to 13, who play baseball. He reveals their likes and dislikes, favorite plays, and individual views of the game. The pictures in this book are of actual boys playing baseball. This is a great resource to promote discussion of how people feel about sports.

● ● ●

Baseball Legends, by Jim Murray & Earl Weaver (New York: Dutton Books, 1990).

This collection of biographies of baseball's greatest players offers captivating portraits that will appeal to baseball lovers of all ages. Each volume contains fascinating information about pivotal games that helped shape the careers of the players. The volumes, filled with black-and-white photographs and career statistics, provide information about numerous baseball greats. Following is a list of a few of the biographies: Ernie Banks, Bob Gibson, Stan Musial, Tom Seaver, Duke Snider, Ted Williams, and Hank Aaron.

● ● ●

Bear-ly Bear-able Baseball Riddles, Jokes, and Knock-Knocks, by Mort Gerbery (New York: Scholastic, 1989). ISBN 0-590-42583-8.

Grades 1-3, fiction.   The author uses bears to show the humor in baseball from all angles. Through the world of baseball, students are entertained, and reading is made enjoyable.

● ● ●

The Berenstain Bears Go Out for the Team, by Stan and Jan Berenstain (New York: Random House, 1991). ISBN 0-394-0338-6.

Grades 1-3, fiction.   Brother and Sister Bear are such good baseball players that Papa Bear decides they should try out for the Bear Country Cub League. The Berenstains have a terrific way of showing how students can participate in the same sport and work together.

● ● ●

The Biggest Victory, by Alfred Slote (New York: Lippincott, 1972). ISBN 0-397-31252-0.

Grades 6-8, fiction.   The only thing Randy enjoys about baseball is having it over with so he can go fishing, but his father insists that he participate on the school team. This story addresses how to deal with a difference in parent and child attitudes toward different sports, and why a child may be urged to participate in a particular sport.

● ● ●

The Case of the Missing Babe Ruth Baseball, by Lucinda Landon (Boston: Bantam-Skylark Book, Little, Brown, 1989). ISBN 0-553-15690-x.

Grades 3-6, fiction.   Meg Machintosh loves being a detective. Alice asks Meg to help find who stole her treasured baseball that was autographed by Babe Ruth. This is an enjoyable mystery book for students.

● ● ●

Casey at the Bat, by Ernest Lawrence Thayer (Boston: David R. Goding, 1988). ISBN 0-8-7923-772-8.

Grade 1, fiction.   This book has beautiful pictures to illustrate the poem of ''Casey at the Bat.'' This resource demonstrates the spirit of our national pastime. It is a definite must in the classroom.

● ● ●

"Casey at the Bat," A Ballad of the Republic Sung in the Year 1888, by Ernest Lawrence Thayer (New York: G.P. Putnam's Son, 1988). ISBN 0-399-21585-9.

Grades 3-5, fiction.   This is the popular narrative poem about a celebrated baseball player who strikes out at the crucial moment of a game. The pictures are very interesting and can help motivate personal creations in an art class. Students may learn to recite the poem during baseball season. This book will help

students gain an appreciation for the pressures and achievements of sports figures, and can also help link poetry, art, and movement.

● ● ●

Con Mi Hermano, por Eileen Row (New York: Bradbury Press, 1991). ISBN 0-02-777373-6.

Grades 1-2, fiction, Spanish.   A little boy admires his big brother and aspires to be like him. This book relates team building in basketball to building a family unit. This book can be used to initiate good discussions on the responsibilities of group membership.

● ● ●

The Diamond Champs, by Matt Christopher (Boston: Little, Brown, 1977). ISBN 0-316-13972-6.

Grades 3-4, fiction.   An aura of intrigue surrounds a baseball coach obsessed with the idea of turning a bunch of hand-picked beginners into champions in one season. Christopher has written many stories that revolve around sports. This story relates how a coach, through hard work, can help a team become successful. This is a very humorous story.

● ● ●

Elmer and the Chickens vs. the Big League, by Brian Mc Connachie (New York: Crown, 1992). ISBN 0-517-57616-3.

Grades 1-2, fiction.   A barnyard becomes a stadium, and chickens become outfielders, when young Elmer imagines himself the star of a major league baseball game. This is an enjoyable book that demonstrates how a team can work together.

● ● ●

Frank and Ernest Play Ball, by Alexandra Day (New York: Scholastic, 1976). ISBN 0-590-42548-x.

Grades 2-3, fiction.   An elephant and a bear take over the management of a baseball team for one night and learn about cooperation, responsibility, and baseball lingo. This book has great pictures, and students enjoy reading it.

● ● ●

Grandmas at Bat, by Emily Arnold Mc Cully (New York: Harper Collins, 1993). ISBN 0-06-021031-1.

Grades 1-2, fiction.   Pip's two grandmothers, who cannot agree on anything, take over coaching her baseball team and create chaos. From this chaos the team learns strategies to straighten out the mess. This book can provide material for discussions on group problem-solving.

● ● ●

Grandma's Baseball, by Gavin Curtis (New York: Crown, 1990). ISBN 0-517-57389-x.

Grades 1-3, fiction. A young boy learns to see beyond his grandmother's grumpiness when she comes to live with his family following her husband's death. The young boy gains this insight when he discovers his grandmother's love for baseball and learns the story behind her interest in it. This is a good resource to show children that other relatives may be interested in sports, and that common interests such as baseball can help in learning more about each other.

● ● ●

Hang Tough, Paul Mather, by Alfred Slote (New York: J.B. Lippincott, 1973). ISBN 0-397-31451-5.

Grades 6-8, fiction. A baseball pitcher with a serious blood disease is determined to get in as much time on the mound as possible. This book is a great resource to help children understand the feelings of physically challenged individuals and to appreciate the courage it takes to overcome obstacles.

● ● ●

Happy Birthday, Little League, by Gerald Newman (New York: Franklin Watts, 1989). ISBN 0-531-10678-x.

Grades 2-4, nonfiction. Gerald Newman discusses the history and structure of the 50-year-old Little League by describing the various participants and the levels and types of competition. The real-life pictures and history of the Little League provide students with important background information and help them understand the purpose and development of Little League.

● ● ●

Here Comes the Strike Out, by Leonard Kessler (New York: Harper & Row, 1965). Library catalog number 65-10728.

Grade 1-2, fiction. Every time Bobby comes up to bat the other team yells, ''Here comes the strikeout!'' Bobby's friend Willie shows Bobby how to improve his baseball skills. This is an excellent resource to promote a discussion on perseverance.

● ● ●

The Hit Away Kid, by Matt Christopher (Boston: Little, Brown, 1988). ISBN 0-316-13995-5.

Grades 3-4, fiction. Barry Mc Gree, hit-away batter for the Peach Street Mudders, enjoys winning so much that he has a tendency to bend the rules. The dirty tactics of the pitcher on a rival team give him a new perspective on sport ethics. This is a great resource to promote discussions on sport ethics and to explore changes in ethical behavior over time in different sports, including those seen on television.

● ● ●

The Home Run Trick, by Scott Corbitt (Boston: Little, Brown, 1973). ISBN 0-316-15693-0.

Grades 3-4, fiction. The Panthers try desperately to lose a baseball game when they find out the winners must play a girls' team called the Taylorville Tomboys. See what kind of superb plays are worked out between the two teams. This resource provides a great opportunity to explore the roles of girls in sport.

● ● ●

Jason and the Baseball Bear, by Dan Elish (Boston: A Bantam Skylark Book, 1992). ISBN 0-553-15878-3.

Grades 4-6, fiction. Jason Munson is the only fourth-grader on his little league team. Because he's the youngest, he doesn't get to play very much. Jason's good friend, Whitney, helps him out. The story demonstrates how a boy and a girl can work together to improve skills and attitudes.

● ● ●

The Kid From Tomkinsville, by John R. Tunis (San Diego: Gulliver Books, Harcourt Brace Jovanovich, 1987). ISBN 0-15-200500-5.

Grades 7-12, fiction. As the newest addition to the Brooklyn Dodgers, young Roy Tucher's pitching helps pull the team out of a slump. When a freak accident ends his career as a pitcher, he must try to find another place for himself on the team. The author explores the feelings of his characters as they face unexpected changes in their hopes and dreams. Other books by the same author are *Keystone Kids* and *Rookie of the Year*.

● ● ●

The Kid Who Only Hit Homers, by Matt Christopher (Boston: Little, Brown, 1972). ISBN 74-169006.

Grade 3-4, fiction. Sylvester looked like a poor prospect for the Redbirds baseball team at their first practice. He was pretty bad at the bat and even worse in the field. He is ready to give up playing altogether until he meets a stranger, Mr. George Baruth, who loves baseball just as much as Sylvester does. This is an entertaining story of the rise of a phenomenal young baseball player who does not give up in his desire to play. This resource demonstrates the importance of asking for help when it is needed.

● ● ●

The Littlest Leaguer, by Syd Hoff (New York: Scholastic, 1976). ISBN 0-590-05385-x.

Grades 2-3, fiction. Harold is the smallest player in his Little League. However, his coach shows him how to be a top player in spite of his size. The author captivates young readers and challenges them to be the best they can be. This is a good book to have in a library for general reading and enjoyment.

• • •

Matt Garan's Boy, by Alfred Slote (New York: Lippincott, 1975). ISBN 0-397-31617-8.

Grades 4-6, fiction.   A major leaguer's son feels threatened when a girl tries out for his baseball team and his divorced mother becomes interested in the girl's father. This story can help students identify and deal with feelings that surface when new people and changes enter their lives.

• • •

Matt's Mitt & Fleet-Footed Florence, by Marilyn Socks (New York: E.P. Dutton, 1988). ISBN 0-525-44450-5.

Grades 2-3, fiction.   In the first of these two baseball stories, the mitt that Matt's errant uncle gives him at his birth possesses unusual qualities that shape Matt's life. In the second story, the fleet-footed star of the North Dakota Beavers meets her match when she encounters Yankee catcher Fabulous Frankie. These tales of baseball capers are made enjoyable by their characters and plots.

• • •

Men at Work: The Craft of Baseball, by George F. Will (New York: Macmillan, 1990). ISBN 0-06-097372-2.

Grades 9-12, nonfiction.   George F. Will, news columnist and political commentator, gets behind the scenes to reveal the American "national pastime" in ways that will surprise even the most avid lover of the game. Will travels to the dugouts and the locker rooms to interview dozens of players in order to accurately describe their exciting craft.

• • •

Mice at Bat, by Kelly Oechsli (New York: Harper & Row, 1986). ISBN 0-06-024623-5.

Grade 1, fiction.   When the human baseball game is over, two teams of mice take over the ball park to play their own championship ball game. Through the mice characters, the author motivates children to develop interest in the game of baseball.

• • •

My Greatest Day in Baseball, by Elliot Cohen (New York: Simon & Schuster, Books for Young Readers, 1991). ISBN 0-671-70440-0.

Grades 6-12, fiction.   The author has collected exciting stories of the game from the following baseball stars: Hank Aaron, George Brett, Jose Canseco, Will Clark, Tug Mc Graw, Kirby Puckett, Ryne Sandberg, Ozzie Smith, Robin Young, and many more. This is a great way to witness baseball's most historic

moments through the eyes of the players who made baseball happen. This terrific book helps teachers with the historical aspects of baseball, and students can learn about the top players that influenced the game.

• • •

Nate the Great and the Stolen Base, by Marjorie Weinman Sharmat (New York: Coward Mc Cann, 1992). ISBN 0-698-20708-4.

Grades 2-3, fiction.   Nate the Great investigates the mysterious disappearance of the purple plastic octopus that his baseball team uses for second base. Because there are many creative ways for students to solve the mystery, this cute story can motivate students to rewrite the ending.

• • •

Play Ball Zackary!, by Muriel Blaustein (New York: Harper & Row, 1988). ISBN 0-06-020543-1.

Grades 1-3, fiction.   Zackary, the Cub Scout tiger cub, is good at art and reading but not at sports. However, he manages to show his athletic father that they can still do things together. This is a delightful story to help children who are not athletically inclined understand the importance of trying to do one's best.

• • •

Players of Cooperstown, Baseball's Hall of Fame, by David Nemec (Lincolnwood, IL: Publications International, 1992). ISBN 1-56173-2303.

Grades 4-12, nonfiction.   Induction into the Baseball Hall of Fame is the single greatest accolade a player can receive. This book shares the drama and excitement of baseball's historic figures through stunning pictures of players in the Cooperstown Baseball Hall of Fame. Player profiles are accompanied by outstanding pictures of related memorabilia.

• • •

Ronald Morgan Goes to Bat, by Patricia Reiley Giff (New York: Puffin Books, 1990). ISBN 0-14-050669-1.

Grades 1-2, fiction.   Although he can't hit or catch, Ronald Morgan loves to play baseball. See how Ronald changes his game in order to become a good player. This book addresses determination, working out, and practicing to become the best you can. This book helps children learn not to give up at the first failure.

• • •

Sam Saves the Day, by Charles E. Martin (New York: Greenwillow Books, 1987). ISBN-688-06814-6.

Grades 1-2, fiction.   Sam has a busy summer: After traveling, he helps his neighbor take in his lobster traps, and goes on to help his island baseball team win a game. The key character provides a good role model to help demonstrate positive free time activities other than watching television.

● ● ●

Shoeless Joe, by W.P. Kinsella (New York: Ballantine Books, 1982). ISBN 0-345-34256-9.

Grades 7-12, fiction.   The author is the winner of a Houghton Mifflin Literary Fellowship Award. This enchanting novel about the power of dreams that transform reality focuses on a man, a baseball team, and life decisions.

● ● ●

The Spy on Third Base, by Matt Christopher (Boston: Little, Brown, 1988). ISBN 0-316-13996-3.

Grades 3-4, fiction.   A third baseman is sick with anxiety about whether or not to help his team by using his knack for knowing where the batter is going to hit the ball. This is a good general book for pleasure reading.

● ● ●

Stealing Home, by Mary Stolz (New York: Harper Collins, 1992). ISBN 0-06-021154-7.

Grades 3-4, fiction.   When Thomas' great Aunt Linzy writes that she's coming to Florida, both Thomas and his grandfather suspect her visit is going to be a long one: They are concerned about her lack of patience with baseball and fishing. However, they manage to have an interesting visit. This story promotes discussions on compromise and how members of a group can work together to make decisions.

● ● ●

Supercharged Infield, by Matt Christopher (Boston: Little, Brown, 1985). ISBN 0-316-13983-1.

Grades 6-8, fiction.   Penny Farrell, captain and third base player of the Hawks softball team, tries to uncover the reason for the strange behavior of two teammates who have suddenly turned into super athletes. If students like detective stories, this book will lead them on an adventure that could be particularly motivating during the softball season.

● ● ●

Take Me Out to the Ball Game, by Maryann Kovalshi (New York: Scholastic, 1993). ISBN 0-590-45638-5.

Grades 1-2, fiction.   Jenny and Joanne love baseball, and Grandma's always game for an adventure in the setting celebrated by the traditional baseball song. The pictures are beautiful and display the baseball stadium with all the trimmings.

● ● ●

Tony and Me, by Alfred Slote (New York: Lippincott, 1974). ISBN 0-397-31507-4.

Grades 6-8, fiction.   Tony, a star athlete, befriends Bill and gives hope to Bill's losing baseball team. However, Tony has a problem, which forces Bill to make some tough decisions. This book contains some great lessons on making tough decisions and helps middle school students learn the process of decision making.

● ● ●

The True Francine, by Marc Brown (Boston: Little, Brown, 1981). ISBN 0-316-11212-7.

Grades 2-3, fiction.   Francine and Muffy are good friends until Muffy lets Francine take the blame for cheating on a school test. As a result, Francine is not allowed to play softball. This book deals with honesty in the classroom and in games. It provides an excellent resource to discuss peer pressure, taking the blame for your best friend, and fair play in life and sports.

● ● ●

What Kind of Baby-Sitter Is This?, by Dolores Johnson (New York: Macmillan, 1991). ISBN 0-02-747846-7.

Grades 1-3, fiction.   Kevin intensely dislikes the idea of having a baby-sitter. That is, until the unconventional baseball-loving ''Aunt'' Lovely arrives to change his mind: He finds out this baby-sitter really loves baseball.

● ● ●

Wild Pitch, by Matt Christopher (Boston: Little, Brown, 1980). ISBN 0-316-14019-8.

Grades 3-4, fiction.   Eddie doesn't like the idea of girls playing baseball in his league, but when one of his pitchers injures a girl, he reconsiders his views and changes his attitudes. This story can help students learn to give other students a chance before developing attitudes that can be hurtful.

● ● ●

The Year Mom Won the Pennant, by Matt Christopher (Boston: Little, Brown, 1968). ISBN 68-11110.

Grades 3-4, fiction.   The Thunderballs need a coach badly, but Nick Vassey's mother is not what they have in mind. Yet she is the only parent who volunteers to coach, and without a coach there can be no team. The Thunderballs are bewildered; Nick is mortified; and their arch rivals, the Tornadoes, howl with glee. The author is able to help boys understand that women can coach teams and do a great job. This is a great resource to help discuss the male domination of many sports and how hard it is for women to get opportunities in some sports.

Basketball

The Basket Counts, by Matt Christopher (Boston: Little, Brown, 1968). ISBN 68-21168.

Grades 3-4, fiction.   When it comes to basketball, there are many famous players whom students admire. In this story, Mel Jensen finds out it's not easy to play basketball with the Titans: It's pretty hard to score when most of the players never pass the ball to him. But Mel and his friend Cotton keep trying, and they get better and better. Before long, the two boys become two of the Titans' most valuable players. This story leads to good discussions on perseverance and initiative.

• • •

Leprechauns Don't Play Basketball, by Debbie Dadey (New York: Scholastic, 1992). ISBN 0-590-44822-6.

Grades 3-4, fiction.   In this humorous story, readers experience a season with a Leprechaun coach and the third grade teacher, Mrs. Jeepers. Could it be that the coach and Mrs. Jeepers have met before? How will the season end? This is a superb story to be read during the winter basketball season.

• • •

Magic Johnson, Basketball's Smiling Superstar, by Rick L. Johnson (New York: Dillon Press, Macmillian, 1992). ISBN 0-87518-553-3.

Grades 3-12, nonfiction.   This is a biography of the star guard for the Los Angeles Lakers who shocked fans by retiring in 1991 because he had contracted the HIV virus. He discusses the importance of AIDS education and living a careful life. As a role model, Magic Johnson has inspired many young people to play basketball and go after their dreams.

• • •

Michael Jordan, Basketball Skywalker, by Thomas R. Raber (New York: Lerner, 1992). ISBN 0-8225-9625-3.

Grades 4-13, nonfiction.   This biography discusses the childhood, education, basketball career, and personal life of Michael Jordan, hero in the basketball world. This is a good story to help motivate people to move towards their dreams and goals, and it makes for very enjoyable reading.

• • •

The Moves Make the Man, by Bruce Brooke (New York: Scholastic, 1984). ISBN 0-590-43198-6.

Grades 5-8, fiction.   This story is about Jerome Fox Worthy. His nickname is "the Jayfox," and he can handle anything when it comes to basketball. The Jayfox meets the moody and mysterious Bix Rivers, an outstanding athlete. Can the Jayfox convince Bix he'll never win at hoops or anything else in his life if he doesn't learn the moves? Find out what happens. This story leads to discussions and writing on teamwork, fair play, and the value of someone who believes in you.

• • •

Nancy Lieberman, Basketball Magic Lady, by Betty Millsaps Jones (New York: Harvey House, 1980). ISBN 0-8178-0009-3.

Grades 8-12, nonfiction.   This book deals with Nancy Lieberman's struggles as a member of the "Lady Monarch" basketball team and a competitor in the 1980 Olympics. This is a great resource for talking about women in sports and about the feelings and effort that go into competition at the Olympics. This is an excellent book for promoting discussions and stories on gender equity, hard work, and competition.

• • •

Rebound Caper, by Thomas J. Dygard (New York: Morrow, 1983). ISBN 0-688-01707-7.

Grades 5-8, fiction.   High school basketball player Gary Whipple, known for his mischievous pranks, creates a sensation when he switches from the boys' team to the girls' team. The author's creative way with sports subjects motivates students to read.

• • •

Taking Sides, by Gary Soto (San Diego: Harcourt Brace Jovanovich, 1991). ISBN 0-15-284076-1.

Grades 5-12, fiction.   Fourteen-year-old Lincoln Mendoza, an aspiring basketball player, must come to terms with his divided loyalties when he moves from the predominantly Latino inner city to a predominantly white suburban neighborhood. This book can help initiate writing and discussions that encourage students to investigate and reflect on personal loyalties towards groups of people.

• • •

Tournament Upstart, by Thomas J. Dygard (New York: Morrow, 1984). ISBN 0-688-027610-x.

Grades 5-8, fiction.   This story is about Floyd Bentley, the new young coach of the Cedar Grove High School basketball team. The Cedar Grove High "Falcons," a team from the Ozark foothills, challenge big city schools for the state championship. Find out how the Falcons overcome their opponents from larger schools while overcoming their own insecurities as well. This story can help students learn how to deal with feelings of insecurity.

Boxing

Joe Louis, Heavyweight Champion, by Robert Jakouben (New York: Chelsea House, 1990).

Grades 4-6, nonfiction. This biography of Joe Louis describes his youth in a Detroit ghetto, his rise to heavyweight champion and major sports hero, and his role in destroying myths related to racial stereotypes. The Black American of Achievement Award was presented to the author of this book.

• • •

Muhammad Ali, by Norman Macht (New York: Chelsea Juniors, 1993). ISBN 0-7910-1760-5.

Grades 3-4, nonfiction. A biography of the famous boxer Muhammad Ali. This book emphasizes his career as a role model and a great fighter.

Combative Sports

Combat Sports, by Robert Sandelson (New York: Crestwood House, 1991). ISBN 0-89686-668-8.

Grades 4-8, nonfiction. In a matter-of-fact way, the author describes the history, rules, and great moments of the Olympic combat sports of boxing, fencing, judo, and wrestling. The book's pictures are very attractive and informative, helping the reader understand and appreciate Olympic combat sports.

Football

Backfield Package, by Thomas J. Dygard (New York: Morrow Junior Books, 1992). ISBN 0-688-11471-7.

Grades 5-8, fiction. Four high school friends decide to go to the same college so that they can continue playing football together. However, the wisdom of their decision is called into question when one of them begins to receive attention as a star quarterback. Dygard is an outstanding writer of sport stories for youth. Students can relate to this story and learn how to deal with a friend's success. This is a good book to promote discussion on friendship.

• • •

Bo Jackson: A Star for All Seasons, by John Dwaney (New York: Walker and Company, 1992). ISBN 0-8027-8178-0.

Grades 6-12, nonfiction. This book is a biography of the first person to play on both a major league baseball team and a professional football team.

• • •

The Dynasties of Football Heroes, by Jonathan Bliss (New York: The Rourke Corporation, 1992). ISBN 0-86593-156-9.

Grades 6-10, nonfiction. The author examines the few teams in professional football who have consistently had championship seasons and excelled on the field.

• • •

Football Kids, by George Sullivan (New York: Cobblehill Books, 1990). ISBN 0-525-65040-7.

Grades 4-8, nonfiction. The author profiles seven high school boys who play football, revealing their likes and dislikes, favorite plays, and individual views of the game. This is a motivating book to help students understand many aspects of the game.

• • •

Football's Cunning Coaches, by Nathan Aaseng (New York: Lerner, 1981). ISBN 0-8225-1065-0.

Grades 6-12, nonfiction. The author describes the highlights of the lives of seven professional football coaches: Paul Brown, Vince Lombardi, Tom Landry, Don Shula, Bud Grant, George Allen, and Chuck Noll. This book is a wonderful resource for understanding how these coaches became legends.

• • •

Football's Daring Defensive Backs, by Nathan Aaseng (Minneapolis: Lerner, 1984). ISBN 0-8225-1335-8.

Grades 5-8, nonfiction. The author presents brief biographies of eight defensive backs: Lester Hayes, Nolon Cromwell, Mel Bount, Miles Haynes, Pat Thomas, Everson Walls, Gary Fench, and Ronnie Lott. This book provides great information about these football players, and helps students appreciate how difficult a position defensive back is to play.

• • •

Football's Winning Quarterbacks, by Nathan Aaseng (Minneapolis: Lerner, 1980). ISBN 0-8225-1062-6.

Grades 6-12, nonfiction. The author provides brief biographies of 10 professional quarterbacks: Fran Tarkenton, Roger Staubach, Bob Griese, Ken Stabler, Terry Bradshaw, Archie Manning, Ken Anderson, Bert Jones, Dan Fouts, and Jim Zorn.

• • •

Forward Pass, by Thomas J. Dygard (New York: Morrow Junior Books, 1989). ISBN 0-688-07961-x.

Grades 5-8, fiction. To improve his struggling football team's chances of winning, Coach Gardner brings in a new wide receiver, Jill Winston. Jill Winston's got what it takes to win, but when the rival team shouts foul game, the officials start checking rule books to see if she can play. Read about the compelling personal conflicts of all involved when students of one gender begin to participate in sports traditionally played by the other gender.

• • •

The Great Quarterback Switch, by Matt Christopher (Boston: Little, Brown, 1989). ISBN 0-316-13903-3.

Grades 3-4, fiction. Twelve-year-old Michael, confined to a wheelchair after an accident, uses mental telepathy to communicate football plays to his quarterback twin brother Tom. Suddenly, he finds himself on the field in his brother's place. This book helps students to understand the emotions that a physically challenged person must go through. Excellent classroom discussion can result from this story.

• • •

Halfback Tough, by Thomas J. Dygard (New York: Morrow, 1986). ISBN 0-688-05925-2.

Grades 5-8, fiction. Joe Atkins, a new student, is a "tough guy" at Graham High. Joe joins the football team and begins to change his outlook as he becomes involved in the game, gains self-esteem, and makes new friends.

• • •

Kick, Pass, and Run, by Leonard Kessler (New York: Harper & Row, 1981). ISBN 0-06-023160-2.

Grades 1-2, fiction. After observing a football game played by boys, a group of animals organizes teams to play the game. This story about animals playing football is enjoyable reading for this grade level.

• • •

Quarterback Walk-on, by Thomas J. Dygard (New York: Morrow, 1982). ISBN 0-688-01065-2.

Grades 5-6, fiction. When the fourth-string quarterback for a Texas college team suddenly finds himself the starter for the upcoming Saturday's game, he creates a plan that helps the team win. The book helps students look at alternative ways to solve problems.

• • •

Running Scared, by Thomas J. Dygard (New York: Morrow, 1977). ISBN 0-688-22103-3.

Grades 7-12, fiction. A football coach whose job is on the line discovers a talented quarterback who is afraid to run. The author provides exciting, vivid play-by-play descriptions that bring football fields alive. Readers will become engrossed, sharing the moments of gloom and triumph.

• • •

Strategies of the Greatest Football Coaches, by Hank Nuwer (New York: Watts, 1988). ISBN 0531-10518-0.

Grades 4-6, nonfiction. This book discusses the careers of coaches whose innovative strategies changed the game of football. Included are such famous coaches as John William Heisman, Knute Rockne, Vince Lombardi, Bear Bryant, and Tom Landry. This is an excellent resource for students to learn football strategies from the perspectives of different coaches.

• • •

The Super Book of Football, by J. David Miller (New York: Sports Illustrated for Kids, The Time Magazine Co., 1990). ISBN 0-316-57370-1.

Grades 6-12, nonfiction. This book traces the history of football, discusses superbowl championships, and highlights college and professional record holders. It is packed full of information and is a great reference source on the game of football.

• • •

Tackle Without a Team, by Matt Christopher (Boston: Little, Brown, 1989). ISBN 0-316-14067-8.

Grades 4-5, fiction. Unjustly dismissed from the football team for drug possession, Scott learns that only by finding out who planted the marijuana in his duffel bag can he clear himself with his parents and the team. This is a good book to help students analyze problems associated with drug use.

• • •

The Tampa Bay Buccaneers, by James R. Rothaus (Mankato, MN: Creative Education, 1986). ISBN 0-88682-050-2.

Grades 6-9, nonfiction. James Rothaus traces the history and spirit of the youngest team in the NFL, providing an in-depth view of the Buccaneers. He has also written books about other NFL teams, including the Indianapolis Colts, Cincinnati Bengals, and Dallas Cowboys. All of his books are terrific resources for learning about the NFL teams. The pictures are dynamic and colorful.

• • •

Winning Kicker, by Thomas J. Dygard (New York: Morrow, 1978). ISBN 0-688-22140-8.

Grades 5-8, fiction. The author has an interesting way of relating the struggle of girls who join football teams. An uproar is created when a girl succeeds in making the high-school football team. This entertaining sports story depicts a situation that is occurring more and more frequently in school sports, and is presented here from the point of view of the embattled coach. Boys and girls will empathize with the coach as he copes with trouble on and off the field. Plenty of game action and a satisfying conclusion add up to a great novel for young persons.

Golf

Hispanics of Achievement: Lee Trevino, by Thomas W. Gilbert (New York: Chelsea House, 1992). ISBN 0-7910-1256-5.

Grades 9-12, nonfiction. A biography of the acclaimed Mexican American golfer Lee Trevino. This book highlights his unique ability to make fans feel part of the action through sharing his tremendous enjoyment of golf and his witty sense of humor.

Ice Hockey

Face-off, by Matt Christopher (Boston: Little, Brown, 1972). ISBN 78-189258.

Grades 3-4, fiction. When Scott Harrison joins the Golden Bears hockey team, he learns not only that he loves to play hockey, but also that he is "puck shy": He is afraid that the puck will fly off the ice and strike him in the face. Because of this fear, he ruins some plays, much to the disgust of his teammates. This story tells of Scott's efforts to overcome his fear of the puck and win the respect of the team. This is an interesting story to help students learn skills for team building and overcoming fears.

● ● ●

The Hockey Machine, by Matt Christopher (Boston: Little, Brown, 1986). ISBN 0-316-14055-4.

Grades 3-4, fiction. Abducted by a "fan" and forced to become a member of a professional junior hockey team, thirteen-year-old star center Steve Crandall quickly realizes that he must play not only to win but to survive.

● ● ●

Ice Magic, by Matt Christopher (Boston: Little, Brown, 1973). ISBN 0-316-13958-0.

Grades 3-4, fiction. The twin boys' toy hockey game seems to be magic: It plays games identical to the real ones before the real ones even happen. This is a good mystery book for fun reading.

Olympics

The Complete Book of the Winter Olympics, 1994, by David Wallechensky (New York: Little, Brown, 1993). ISBN 0-316-92081-9.

Grades 7-12, nonfiction. This may be the most comprehensive and interesting book ever written about the Winter Games. Everything one might want to know is here, including the statistics for every event, the stories of the athletes about their events, and the rules for the various sports.

● ● ●

Great Summer Olympic Moments, by Nate Aaseng (Minneapolis: Lerner, 1990). ISBN 0-8225-1536-9.

Grades 3-6, nonfiction. This book shares with younger readers the unusual and memorable athletic performances that have taken place in the history of the summer Olympics.

● ● ●

Great Winter Olympic Moments, by Nate Aaseng (Minneapolis: Lerner, 1990). ISBN 0-8225-1535-0.

Grades 3-6, nonfiction. Aaseng's book sums up information on winter Olympic sports. Some of the sports highlights are Sonja Henie, figure skater; Andrea Mead Lawrence, alpine skier; Toni Saibe, slalom racer; Valino Huhtala, cross-country relay skier; Lydia Skoblekova, speed skater; and other winter Olympic champions.

● ● ●

Quest for Gold, The Encyclopedia of American Olympians, by Bill Malton & Ian Buchanan (New York: Leisure Press, 1993). ISBN 0-88011-217-4.

Grades 7-12, nonfiction. The authors have compiled a wonderful collection on athletes who have participated in the Olympics, and provide readers with biographical information on each U.S. Olympic athlete. The United States has enjoyed a great deal of success at Olympic competitions, having produced the most Olympic athletes, the most Olympic gold medalists, and the most Olympic medalists. This book tells about the Olympians and their quests for the gold.

Also see the listings for *An Approved History of the Olympic Games; A New True Book: Olympics; Olympic Games in Ancient Greece; The Olympics: A History of the Modern Games;* and *U.S. Olympians* under Historical Perspectives.

Soccer

Dulcie Dando, Soccer Star, by Sue Stop (New York: H. Holt, 1992). ISBN 0-8050-2413-1.

Grade 2, fiction. Dulcie, a talented soccer player, shows that girls are just as capable as boys when she's given the chance to play on the school team during a big game. This remarkable story demonstrates that both boys and girls can successfully play sports.

● ● ●

Kyle Rote, Jr.: American Born Soccer Star, by Edward F. Dolan Jr. & Richard B. Lyttle (Garden City, NY: Doubleday, 1979). ISBN 0-385-14098-3.

Grades 4-8, nonfiction. This story is about Kyle Rote, Jr., son of the great football superstar Kyle Rote. The son is the first American to win the "Most Valuable Player" award in professional soccer. This is the story of a great young athlete and the support that he receives from his father.

• • •

Old Turtle's Soccer Team, by Leonard Kessler (New York: Greenwillow Books, 1988). ISBN 0-688-07157-0.

Grades 1-2, fiction.   Under Old Turtle's guidance, the animals learn how to play soccer and appreciate the meaning of fair play. The pictures and story lead to wonderful discussion for students in primary grades who need help in understanding fair play.

• • •

Pele, Soccer Superstar, by Louis Sabin (New York: G.P. Putnam's Sons, 1976).

Grades 6-12, nonfiction.   A biography of Pele, the Brazilian soccer star who has achieved international fame because of his athletic achievements.

• • •

Soccer Duel, by Thomas J. Dygard (New York: Morrow, 1981). ISBN 0-688-00366-4.

Grades 6-8, fiction.   A former football star finds he must share the spotlight with other players when he decides to play soccer. This is an enticing story for middle school, or junior high school, students. It can help them understand team responsibility, working together, and sharing success.

• • •

Soccer Sam, by Jean Marzollo (New York: Random House, 1987). ISBN 0-394-88406-x.

Grades 2-3, fiction.   The author has written a delightful story about a group of second-graders and soccer. Marco is Sam's cousin. Marco is a soccer star, so he teaches Sam and his friends how to play soccer. This is a story about sports, friendships, and some really funny second-grade surprises.

Sport Stories

Bart Conner, Winning the Gold, by Bart Conner (New York: Warner Books, 1985). ISBN 0-446-51333-4.

Grades 7-12, nonfiction.   This story describes the efforts put forth by Bart Conner to win a gold medal in gymnastics in the 1984 Olympics. This is a phenomenal tale of one man's personal triumph that can truly inspire students.

• • •

Confessions of a Fast Woman, by Lesley Hazleton (New York: Addison Wesley, 1992). ISBN 0-201-62481-8.

Grades 8-12, nonfiction.   This is an inspirational story. Lesley Hazleton has driven race cars and tinkered with engines. She takes us on a hot, smart, high-speed trip through the hard-edged world of fast cars. Her book describes the transformation that can happen to a person when driving a fast car.

• • •

Dare to Dream, by Tim Daggett with Jean Stone (New York: Wynwood Press, 1992).

Grades 6-12, nonfiction.   This is Tim's own account of growing up as a single-minded individual who dares to pursue his dream. This is a motivating story for all ages.

• • •

The Funniest Moments in Sports, by Human L. Masin (New York: M. Evans, 1974). ISBN 0-87131-152-6.

Grades 5-12, nonfiction.   This book displays a wonderful sense of humor regarding baseball, football, basketball, golf, hockey, and gymnastics. It is a great collection of sports anecdotes that shares the humor in sports with students.

• • •

Fun Sports for Everyone, by Gail Anderson Myers (Philadelphia: The Westminster Press, 1985). ISBN 0-664-32720-6.

Grades 8-12, nonfiction.   Today, sports are for everyone, male and female, younger and older, short and tall, strong and weak. This book describes sports for the person who sometimes feels like a ''klutz'' as well as for the highly skilled athlete.

• • •

Great Latin Sports Figures, The Proud People, by Jerry Izenberg (New York: Doubleday, 1976). ISBN 0-385-11117-7.

Grades 8-12, nonfiction.   From a perspective of sociology in physical education, Jerry Izenberg tells the stories of famous Latino athletes and their struggles to break into the sports world in the U.S. The backgrounds and experiences of the athletes vary greatly, and their strong spirits and special courage make their stories worthwhile reading. The sports figures are Roberto Clemente, baseball player; Chi Chi Rodrigues, golfer; Canonero II, jockey; Lee Trevino, golfer; Gaspar Ortega, boxer; Zoil Versalles, baseball player; and Rod Carew, baseball player. This is a great reference book for students to learn about these role models in sports.

• • •

Guinness Book of Sports Spectaculars, by Norris Mc Whister (New York: Sterling, 1981). ISBN 0-8069-0222-1.

Grades 4-12, nonfiction.   The author presents a collection of unusual and outstanding sports facts and feats. This book is enjoyable to read and is very informative.

Hopscotch, Hangman, Hot Potatoes, & Ha Ha Ha: A Rulebook of Children's Games, by Jack Maguire (New York: Simon & Schuster, 1992). ISBN 0-671-76332-6.

Grades 3-12, nonfiction.   The author has compiled playing rules for more than 250 games and sports for children of every age. This book includes indoor, outdoor, party, travel, water, memory, and card games. There are games to play on grass, on the pavement, on steps and stoops, inside houses for rainy days and parties, and while traveling. Step-by-step instructions and rules for each game are provided with clear diagrams and line drawings.

The Norton Book of Sports, edited by George Plimpton (New York: Norton, 1992). ISBN 0-393-03040-7.

Grades 7-12, nonfiction.   When it comes to popularity among Americans, enthusiasm for sports is right up there with "mom" and "apple pie." From this long love affair with games has sprung literature that includes fiction, nonfiction, and poetry. George Plimpton, America's troubadour of sports and its most famous amateur participant, has compiled the best collection of sports literature yet to appear. This is an excellent resource for short stories that deal with sports.

Playgrounds, by Gail Gibbons (New York: A Holiday House Book, 1985). ISBN 0-8234-0553-2.

Grades K-1, nonfiction.   This book introduces the various types of playground equipment, including swings, slides, and sandboxes, as well as games and toys that may be enjoyed at the playground. This is an excellent source for children to become familiar with the safe use of playground equipment.

The Random House Book of Sport Stories, by L.M. Schulman (New York: Random House, 1990). ISBN 0-394-82874-7.

Grades 4-8, fiction.   The author presents a collection of sport stories by such authors as Ernest Hemingway, Ring Lardner, and John Updike. These storytellers have found sports a fertile field in which to root their work. The stories present a sense of going to the limit to live life at its peak.

Safety at the Playground, by Joseph De Varennes (Toronto: Grolier, 1988). ISBN 0-7172-2472-4.

Grades K-1, nonfiction.   This picturesque book describes elements of all the safety rules that should be followed on a playground. A badger family, the Badgersons, helps the reader find out about playground safety.

Sport and Recreation Fads, by Frank W. Hoffmann, Ph.D. & William G. Baily, M.A. (New York: Harrington Park Press, 1991). ISBN 0-91-8393-92-2.

Grades 6-12, nonfiction.   This is an encyclopedia of delightful information, from Hank Aaron's home run records to yo-yos and Wrestle Mania, from artificial turf to volleyball. It has all the stories of the side shows and main events of American popular culture. This book is enjoyable to read and is a must for sport buffs.

The Stinky Sneakers Contest, by Julie Anne Peters (Boston: Little, Brown, 1990). ISBN 0-316-70214-5.

Grades 2-3, fiction.   Earl and Damian jeopardize their friendship when they compete in a contest to see who has the smelliest sneakers. This is a good resource to initiate discussion about competition and fair play. This story provides a good example of the negative effects of cheating.

The World's Best Sports Riddles and Jokes, by Joseph Rosenbloom (New York: Sterling, 1988). ISBN 0-8069-6337-0.

Grades 3-4, fiction.   The author presents hundreds of riddles and jokes relating to football, baseball, weight lifting, karate, croquet, and other sports. This is a wonderful book to have in a collection of humor.

Swimming

Cannonball Chris, by Jean Margollo (New York: Random House, 1987). ISBN 0-394-88512-0.

Grades 1-2, fiction.   Chris tries to overcome his fear of jumping into deep water in time for the second grade swimming party. Primary students will enjoy reading this book. The story will help younger students overcome their fear of jumping into the pool—under adult supervision, of course.

In Lane Three, Alex Archer, by Tessa Duder (Boston: Houghton Mifflin, 1989). ISBN 0-395-50927-0.

Grades 6-8, fiction.   Fifteen-year-old Alex struggles to overcome personal trauma and hardship as she competes with her arch rival for a place on the New Zealand swimming team that will participate in the 1960 Olympic Games in Rome. Even though this book was written about the 1960 Olympic Games, the story, feelings, and struggles depict what many athletes go through today. Many spin-off activities can be created from this story.

● ● ●

The Twenty-One-Mile Swim, by Matt Christopher (Boston: Little, Brown, 1979). ISBN 0-316-13979-3.

Grades 3-4, fiction. With remarks about his small stature and poor swimming skills ringing in his ears, the son of Hungarian immigrants begins to train for the 21-mile swim across a nearby lake. His strong determination and effort to complete the 21-mile swim offers young readers an excellent example of perseverance.

Tennis

Althea Gibson, Tennis Champion, by Tom Biracree (New York: Chelsea House, 1989). ISBN 1-55546-654-0.

Grades 4-8, nonfiction. Althea Gibson is a talented athlete who has used her talents in many ways. She is the first African American woman to win the tennis competition at Wimbledon, and opened the door for African American participation in the game. She also launched a professional golf career. She remains an inspiration to all athletes.

● ● ●

Famous Women Tennis Players, by Trent Trayne (New York: Dodd, Mead, 1979). ISBN 0-396-07681-5.

Grades 4-8, nonfiction. Trent Trayne captures the lives of eleven of the all-time celebrated women tennis players. The players are Suzanne Lenglen, Helen Willie, Helen Jacobs, Alice Marble, Maureen Connolly, Althea Gibson, Virginia Wade, Margaret Court, Evonne Goolagong, Billie Jean King, and Chris Evert. This is an excellent book to help students understand the struggles that the top tennis players face. It also provides a good historical perspective of women in sports.

● ● ●

King! The Sports Career of Billie Jean King, by James and Lynx Haem (New York: Crestwood House, 1981).

Grades 4-6, nonfiction. This is a biography of Billie Jean King, the famous tennis champion. King's work has helped achieve equality in tennis, and has elevated the women's game to an important pro sport. This book is an important resource to help children understand the struggle that women have gone through to succeed in sports today.

● ● ●

The Pigeon With the Tennis Elbow, by Matt Christopher (Boston: Little, Brown, 1975). ISBN 0-316-13966-1.

Grades 3-4, fiction. While playing in a tennis tournament, Kevin O'Toole meets a talking pigeon who turns out to be his great uncle. This great uncle gives him effective tennis tips. This is a humorous story for young readers.

● ● ●

Rosemary Casal, The Rebel Rosebud, by Linda Jacobs (St. Paul: EMC Corporation, 1975). ISBN 0-88436-167-5.

Grades 4-8, nonfiction. Rosemary was called Rosebud and she became a rebel in the tennis world. This book describes how she became the first woman touring professional in tennis history and helped increase the earnings available to women in tennis competitions.

● ● ●

Winners on the Tennis Court, by William G. Glichman (New York: Watts, 1978). ISBN 0-531-02912-3.

Grades 4-8, nonfiction. The author discusses the lives and careers of six young tennis champions. Included are Evonne Goolagong, Jimmy Connors, Bjorn Borg, Arthur Ashe, Chris Evert, and Billie Jean King.

● ● ●

Winning Men of Tennis, by Nathan Aaseng (Minneapolis: Lerner, 1989). ISBN 0-8225-1068-5.

Grades 4-8, nonfiction. The author discusses the careers of outstanding tennis players Bill Tilden, Pancho Gonzales, Guillermo Vilas, and John Mc Enroe. This is another exceptional book, which discusses the heroes in men's tennis and their exceptional efforts in the competitive world of the game.

● ● ●

Winning Women of Tennis, by Nathan Aaseng (Minneapolis: Lerner, 1981). ISBN 0-8225-1067-7.

Grades 4-8, nonfiction. Brief biographies of eight famous women on the international tennis scene including Helen Willie, Althea Gibson, Margaret Smith Court, Billie Jean King, Chris Evert Lloyd, Evonne Goolagong, Martina Navratilova, and Tracy Austin. This is another good selection on women in tennis.

Also see the listing for *Famous Firsts in Tennis* under Historical Perspectives.

Track

Babe Didrikson, Athlete of the Century, by R.R. Knudson (Toronto: Viking Penguin, 1985). ISBN 0-670-80550-5.

Grades 3-4, nonfiction.   This is a biography that emphasizes the early years of Babe Didrikson. Didrikson broke records in golf, track and field, and other sports at a time when there were few opportunities for female athletes. Babe Didrikson was a very talented, dynamic woman who showed her strength in sports and life in general. Many lessons can be generated by this book.

● ● ●

Field Day, by Nick Butterworth and Mick Inkpen (New York: Delacorte Press, 1991). ISBN 0-385-30328-9.

Grade 1, fiction.   Parents and children participate in the field day races. This is a good resource for a teacher to help students set up a field day. The pictures are helpful and illustrate different field day races.

● ● ●

Jesse Owens, by Tony Gentry (New York: Chelsea House, 1990). ISBN 0-7910-0247-0.

Grades 6-12, nonfiction.   A biography of the track and field star who won gold medals in the 1936 summer Olympic Games. The ''Black American of Achievement'' award was given to the author for this book. Jesse Owens was an amazing athlete. This book provides a great historical perspective of race relations and the international political aura of the Olympic Games in Germany in 1936.

● ● ●

A Picture Book of Jesse Owens, by David A. Adler (New York: Holiday House, 1992). ISBN 0-8234-0966-x.

Grades 4-6, nonfiction.   A simple biography of the noted African American track star, who competed in the 1936 Berlin Olympics. This is an excellent historical perspective and allows comparisons of how athletes trained in 1936 versus how they train today.

Books Written in Spanish

El Cuento de los Osos Bailarines, by Ulrich Mihr (Compton, CA: Santillana, 1990). 4549-5 PB.

Grade 1, fiction.   This is a story about the Dancing Bears. It is autumn, a bad season for street artists and dancing bears. Atta Troll and Muma Troll decide to go with their trainers to spend the winter in Paris.

● ● ●

Patito Aprende a Nadar, by Rosalinda Kightley (Compton, CA: Santillana, 1990). ST146 HB.

Grade 1, fiction.   A touching group of baby animals forms new friendships with each other as they learn about the natural world around them.

See also the listings for *Con mi Hermano* under Joy, Pleasure, and Satisfaction (Baseball and Softball); *Puedo Ser Jugador de Beisbol* under Skillful Moving (Baseball); and *Biblioteca Grafica Artes-Marciale* and *Biblioteca Grafica Gymnasia* under Historical Perspectives.

Skillful Moving

Skillful moving deals with the notion that a student becomes an independent learner by understanding how to regulate and modify personal ways of moving based upon an understanding of motor skill development. In this section, the reader will find books on biomechanics, motor skills, motor learning, and on regulations and strategies pertaining to specific sports. A wide variety of material related to the study of human movement is included.

Archery

Archer's Digest, by Roger Combs (Northbrook, IL: DBI Books, 1991). ISBN 0-87349-114-9.

Grades 7-12, nonfiction.   This is a wonderful resource. The author has provided a comprehensive guide on the new developments, new materials, new technology, and new products that have come along by the hundreds. Some aspects of archery have seen dramatic growth in popularity: There has been an increase in participation in target archery, especially field archery, and in all types of realistic three-dimensional target shooting. Some tournaments offer tens of thousands of dollars in cash and product prizes for competitors. These shoots have become big business.

● ● ●

Archery-Steps to Success, by Kathleen M. Haywood & Catherine F. Lewis (Champaign, IL: Leisure Press, l989). ISBN 0-880-11-324-3.

Grades 7-12, nonfiction.   The authors provide a unique guide designed to maximize the reader's progress in archery. The book's development of progressive steps for learning archery is a breakthrough in sport skill instruction. Some important factors are the explanation of the concept or skill, the identification of the correct technique, and the instruction on how to correct common errors.

Badminton

Badminton, A Complete Practical Guide, by Pat Davis (London: David and Charles, 1988). ISBN 0-1753-9228-X).

Grades 6-12, nonfiction. The author has called upon his wide experience and knowledge of badminton, not only as a player but as a coach, official, and journalist, to produce what can be truly described as a complete guide to the sport. The author offers clear explanations of basic strokes and simple tactics for beginners and average players; for top club and County players, the book points out ways in which they can raise their play up to championship level.

Baseball

At the Ball Park, by Ken Robbins (New York: Penguin Books, 1988). ISBN 0-670-81600-0.

Grades 1-2, nonfiction. This book's hand-tinted photographs and simple text recreate the fun and excitement of a day at a baseball game. This resource can help student spectators follow the action in baseball games.

• • •

The Baseball Book, by Zander Hollander (New York: Random House, 1990). ISBN 0-679-81055-2.

Grades 3-8, nonfiction. An alphabetically arranged reference book of baseball's great moments, stars, teams, techniques, language, and anecdotes. This is a marvelous resource for students because of its wealth of information about baseball.

• • •

Baseball Is Our Game, by Joan Downing (Chicago: Children's Press, 1982). ISBN 0-516-03402-2.

Grade 1, nonfiction. This pictorial introduction to baseball is a great way to show young students the many aspects of the game.

• • •

Baseball's All-Time All-Stars, by Jim Murphy (New York: Clarion Books, a Houghton Mifflin Company, 1984).

Grades 4-8, nonfiction. The author presents two hypothetical "all-time, all-star" teams chosen from the best players in baseball history, with research to support his choices. He judges the players on many skills, including hitting, run production, base-running, and so on. Murphy pays particular attention to how these players played their positions in the field. This is an excellent resource for readers to learn how to improve their game.

• • •

Baseball Techniques in Pictures, by Michael Brown (New York: Putnam, 1993) ISBN 0-399-51798-7.

Grades 3-12, nonfiction. This book provides easy-to-follow instructions for playing a better game of baseball. This detailed source book is replete with helpful line drawings and clear explanations of all the game skills. It addresses defensive and offensive skills, with terrific discussions on techniques that will give a team the winning edge.

• • •

Baseball Tips, by Dean Hughes & Tom Hughes (New York: Random House, 1993). ISBN 0-679-83642-x.

Grades 4-6, nonfiction. A beginner's guide to baseball basics with tips on how to hit, run bases, field, throw, and sharpen skills through practice.

• • •

Careers in Baseball, by Howard J. Blumenthal (Boston: Little, Brown, 1993). ISBN 0-316-10095-1.

Grades 4-6, nonfiction. Blumenthal introduces and explains a variety of jobs available in baseball, on and off the field. The jobs include broadcaster, computer analyst, sports reporter, trainer, sports photographer, scout, umpire, stadium entertainer, and many more. This book provides an excellent discussion of many careers related to baseball, and explains how to work towards some of these positions. This is a super resource for students.

• • •

The First Book of Baseball, by Marty Appel (New York: Crown, 1988). ISBN 0-517-56726-1.

Grades 4-6, nonfiction. The author has been involved with baseball for more than 20 years. In this book, he draws on his expertise to explain important facts about baseball, including its history.

• • •

I Can Be a Baseball Player, by Carol Greene (Chicago: Children's Press, 1985). ISBN 0-516-01845-0.

Grade 1, nonfiction. The author provides details of most aspects of major league baseball teams, including positions, camps, trainers, scouts, and the efforts needed to play. This is an excellent resource for students to understand all of the concepts of baseball. The pictures are very helpful. This book also has been translated into Spanish (see *Puedo Ser Jugador de Beisbol* later in this section).

• • •

The Kids' Complete Baseball Catalogue, by Eric Weimer (Englewood Cliffs, NJ: Julian Messner, 1991).

Grades 4-8, nonfiction. A guide for locating information services, products, and other materials related to baseball.

• • •

A Major League Way to Play Baseball, by Bob Carroll (New York: Simon & Schuster Books for Young Readers, 1991). ISBN 0-671-70441-9.

Grades 3-4, nonfiction. This book provides an introduction to baseball in a ''question and answer'' format. This is an exceptional book to help children find answers to their own questions about baseball and how it is played.

• • •

The Official Baseball Hall of Fame Answer Book, by Mark Alvarez (New York: Little Simon, Simon & Schuster Inc., 1989). ISBN 0-671-67377-7.

Grades 4-8, nonfiction. For baseball buffs from eight to eighty. The author has captured fun, facts, activities, biographies, trivia, and many interesting facts related to baseball.

• • •

Puedo Ser Jugador de Beisbol, por Carol Greene (Chicago: Children's Press, 1988). ISBN 0516-31845-4.

Grade 1, nonfiction. This is a translation of the English book *I Can Be a Baseball Player* (listed earlier). The author describes the work and training of a professional baseball player and discusses the organization of baseball teams and the rules of the game. This is a wonderful resource guide for the bilingual classroom.

Basketball

Basketball, Multiple Offense and Defense, by Dean Smith (New Jersey: Prentice-Hall, 1981). ISBN 0-13-072090-9.

Grades 6-12, nonfiction. This book is a guide to the importance of mental attitude. It describes how to use mental attitude as a tool to foster confidence in individual players and in the team as a whole, regardless of the style of offense and defense used in basketball.

• • •

Basketball Rules in Pictures, by A.G. Jacobs (New York: Putnam, 1989). ISBN 0-399-51842-8.

Grades 4-8, nonfiction. The author has provided a complete guide to the official rules of basketball. This is perfect for players, coaches, and fans at all levels. Included are the rules for free throws, shooting fouls, and penalties; the approved method of passing and dribbling; and offensive and defensive strategies, including zone defense.

• • •

Coaching Girls' Basketball Successfully, by Jill Hutchison (Champaign, IL: Leisure Press, 1989) ISBN 0-88011-343-x.

Grades 6-12, nonfiction. The author has created a book that gives the reader the fundamentals of basketball and the techniques for teaching them.

There are over 50 drills and activities for teaching the players the skills and strategies it takes to win.

• • •

A Parents Guide to Coaching Basketball, by John P. Mc Carthy, Jr. (Virginia: Betterway, 1990). ISBN 1-55870-170-2.

Grade 6-12, nonfiction. Even though this is a parents guide, it is an excellent resource for students. The author has included many creative tips and suggestions, personal anecdotes, and instructions, as well as scores of photographs and illustrations, to help both parents and children visualize the techniques needed to succeed in basketball.

• • •

Practical Modern Basketball, by John Wooden (New York: Macmillan, 1988). ISBN 0-02-429470-5.

Grades 6-12, nonfiction. This book is based on John Wooden's experiences as a player and a coach, as well as his studies of publications on playing and coaching the game. He has attended numerous coaching clinics and talked about basketball with many players and coaches. The book also covers the fundamentals and style of team play, and includes the author's ideas for teaching and coaching the wonderful sport of basketball.

• • •

Sports Illustrated Basketball-The Keys to Excellence, by Neil D. Isaacs & Dick Motta (New York: Sports Illustrated, 1988). ISBN 0-452-26207-0.

Grades 9-12, nonfiction. The author draws on Dick Motta's years of experience in the game of basketball to give an excellent guide to the fundamentals of play strategies for coaches; in addition, the book offers viewing tips for spectators and other valuable information. A terrific book for students to use as a reference.

Fencing

Fencing Is for Me, by Art Thomas (Minneapolis: Lerner, 1982). ISBN 0-8225-1129-0.

Grades 4-8, nonfiction. The text and photographs follow Kevin as he learns the sport of fencing, covering equipment, style, and techniques in the process. This book is superb in its demonstration of the art of fencing.

Field Hockey

Field Hockey Is for Me, by Susan Preston-Mauls (Minneapolis: Lerner, 1984). ISBN 0-8225-1141-x.

Grades 3-4, nonfiction.   Allison discusses her experiences in learning the basic rules and techniques of field hockey.

Footbagging

Footbagging, by Larry Dane Brimner (New York: Watts, 1988). ISBN 0-531-10477-x.

Grades 4-12, nonfiction.   This book introduces the various games played with a footbag. It includes instructions on basic moves and kicks, tips on strategies, and a guide to clubs and competitive events.

Football

De-Fense!, by Doug Marx (Vero Beach: The Rourke Corporation, Inc., 1992). ISBN 0-86593-152-6.

Grades 6-9, nonfiction.   The author describes football defense positions such as linebacker and cornerback, discusses effective defense strategies, and notes outstanding defense players in the history of the sport.

● ● ●

The First Book of Football, by John Madden (New York: Crown, 1988). ISBN 0-517-56981-7.

Grades 9-12, nonfiction.   Football and television superstar John Madden explains the fundamentals of football, and includes comments on what makes football great and ways to watch a game.

● ● ●

Know Your Game, Football, by Marc Bloom (New York: Scholastic, 1990). ISBN 0-590-43312-1.

Grades 6-12, nonfiction.   The book can help the reader learn football basics, including the rules of the game, playing positions, appropriate equipment, winning skills, how to keep in shape, and proper nutrition.

● ● ●

The Official Pro Football Hall of Fame Answer Book, by Joe Horrigan (New York: Simon & Schuster, 1990). ISBN 0-671-68695-4.

Grades 5-8, nonfiction.   This book provides great opportunities to test or add to one's knowledge of the exciting game of football. It features profiles of players, fascinating facts, entertaining trivia, and games and puzzles.

● ● ●

The Story of Football, by Dave Anderson (New York: Morrow, 1985). ISBN 0-588-05634-2.

Grades 7-12, nonfiction.   The author introduces the reader to all of the famous players and coaches, as well as to football's fundamentals: rushing, passing, pass-receiving, kicking, blocking, defense, and coaching.

Frisbee

Frisbee, by Dr. Stancil E.D. Johnson (New York: Workman, 1975). ISBN 0-911104-53-4.

Grades 8-12, nonfiction.   Frisbee is more than a game, sport, or pastime: It is a fantasy of unencumbered flight. The free spirit of Frisbee gives sport a new awareness. It is a fresh form of play, where the joy is in the doing, and where the mind and body interact with nature.

Golf

40 Common Errors in Golf and How to Correct Them, by Arthur Shay (Chicago: Contemporary Books, 1978). ISBN 0-8092-7827-8.

Grades 9-12, nonfiction.   This book tells the reader about errors in golf (which are demonstrated by Arthur Shay) and displays pictures on how to correct them. The pictures and descriptions are very clear, making this a good resource for the beginner.

● ● ●

Power Swing in 15 Days, by Walter Ostroshe & John Devaney (New York: Putnam, 1993). ISBN 0-399-51797-9.

Grades 7-12, nonfiction.   If you're one of those people who would love to hit the ball harder and longer while still maintaining accuracy, this is the book for you. Learn quick techniques and use easy-to-follow instructions for developing the power swing.

Ice Hockey

Illustrated Hockey Dictionary for Young People, by Henry Walker (New York: Harvey House, 1977). ISBN 0-8178-5472-x.

Grades 4-6, nonfiction.   The author uses humorous, informational illustrations and text that will serve to settle arguments among hockey enthusiasts of all ages. Details of the game, plays, positions, techniques, rules, teams and leagues, scoring, statistics, and much more are provided. This book will heighten the drama and thrills of hockey for participants and spectators alike.

● ● ●

Playing Hockey, by Chuck Solomon (New York: Crown, 1990). ISBN 0-517-57414-4.

Grades 1-2, nonfiction. The author follows young ice hockey players in text and photographs as they practice and play on outdoor ponds and in city leagues. The pictures are very helpful in aiding readers to develop an understanding of this sport.

Ice Sports

Ice Skating Basics, by Norman Mac Lean. (Englewood Cliffs, NJ: Prentice-Hall, 1984). ISBN 0-13-448762-1.

Grades 8-12, nonfiction. The author provides an introduction to the basic techniques of ice skating and includes information on equipment, exercise, and training for competitive events. This is another excellent resource guide for students.

● ● ●

The Illustrated Encyclopedia of Ice Skating, by Mark Heller (New York: Paddington Press, 1979). ISBN 0-448-22427-5.

Grades 4-12, nonfiction. With hundreds of clear diagrams, photographs, and facts, the author provides a definitive reference work on figure skating, pair skating, ice dancing, touring, and speed skating. Complete explanations of every ice rink sport include curling, eisschiessen, brandy, and ice hockey. This is a full, complete guide for the ice skater. Rule changes and judging procedures are also addressed.

● ● ●

Picture Library, Ice Sports, by Norman Barrett (New York: Watts, 1988). ISBN 0-531-10627-6.

Grades 1-2, nonfiction. This book gives the history of ice sports and describes such sports as figure skating, ice dancing, speed skating, ice hockey, ice racing, curling, and ice boating. This book is a wonderful resource for a historical perspective on ice sports.

● ● ●

The Skaters Handbook, by John Misha Petkivich (New York: Scribner's, 1984). ISBN 0-684-180162.

Grades 4-8, nonfiction. Every figure skater, from those just starting out to competitors working their way to the top, can use this informative guide. It describes in detail the learning and testing programs sponsored by the major skating associations, and discusses the requirements and scheduling of competitions from the local level up to the national and Olympic levels.

● ● ●

Sports World Skating, by Donna Bailey (Austin, TX: Steck-Vaughn, 1991). ISBN 0-8114-2854-0.

Grade 1, nonfiction. The author highlights aspects of the skating sports including figure skating, speed skating, ice hockey, and ice shows. Detailed pictures support the topical areas.

Karate

Karate, by Larry Bremmer (New York: Watts, 1988). ISBN 0-531-10480-X.

Grades 8-12, nonfiction. The exact origin of karate is a mystery. It is known to have existed thousands of years ago in India, where, according to folklore, weaponless warriors single-handedly defended themselves on the battle field. This wonderful book enhances understanding of this method of self-defense. Quality pictures help the reader visualize the style and movements of karate.

● ● ●

Secrets of Championship Karate, by Karyn Turner with Mark Van Schuyver (Chicago: Contemporary Books, 1991). ISBN 0-8092-4052-0.

Grades 7-12, nonfiction. There are hundreds of karate books on the market that teach everything from strategies to stances, but this is the first book that teaches everything you need to know to become a karate champion. Turner presents a formula for tournament success.

● ● ●

Winning Karate, by Joseph Jennings (Chicago: Contemporary Books, 1982). ISBN 0-8092-5800-5.

Grades 6-12, nonfiction. The author has thoughtfully conceived a no-nonsense step-by-step guide to mastering the art of karate. This is done by incorporating a clear, concise text with 425 action photographs displaying exact body positions and perfect form.

Lacrosse

Basic Lacrosse Strategy, by Henry E. Flanagan, Jr. & Robert Gardner (Garden City, NY: Doubleday, 1979). ISBN 0-385-14001-0.

Grades 3-4, nonfiction. This book outlines fundamental lacrosse offensive and defensive strategies and describes maneuvers that develop individual stick skills.

Racquetball

Racquetball Basics, by Tony Baccaccio (Englewood Cliffs, NJ: Prentice-Hall, 1979). ISBN 0-13-129585-3.

Grades 3-5, nonfiction. The author describes and explains the fundamentals of racquetball. The pictures help the reader understand the basics of the sport.

The Racquetball Book, by Margaret Poynter (New York: Simon & Schuster, 1980). ISBN 0-671-33014-4.

Grades 6-12, nonfiction.   The author introduces the game of racquetball and describes the equipment, clothing, rules, and techniques. Information is provided about a number of champion players.

• • •

Racquetball: Steps to Success, by Stan Kittleson, Ph.D. (Champaign, IL: Human Kinetics, 1992). ISBN 0-88011-440-1.

Grades 8-12, nonfiction.   This book will help the reader become a master player. The teacher's text helps the reader to design personal strategies. The pictures and explanations are helpful in learning racquetball.

Running

Cross-Country Running, by Marc Bloom (Mountain View, CA: World, 1978). ISBN 0-89037-092-3.

Grades 8-12, nonfiction.   Running began with cross-country. It is a natural yet misunderstood sport, too often treated either like a step-child of track or road racing or as a conditioner for other sports. Cross-country running is special because it follows neither artificial tracks nor engineered roads. This is a wonderful resource guide with helpful hints for the cross-country runner.

Snow Sports

Cross-Country Skiing, by Pat Tharnton (Port Colborne, Ontario, Canada, Beaverbooks, 1978). ISBN 0-8092-7557-0.

Grades 7-12, nonfiction.   This book takes the mystery out of Nordic skiing. It contends that there is only one way to teach this sport successfully: Cut through the frills and go back to the basics. This approach gives any beginner the information needed to cross-country ski at a personal pace.

• • •

Picture Library, Snow Sports, by Norman Barrett (New York: Watts, 1987). ISBN 0-531-10353-6.

Grades 1-2, nonfiction.   This book provides a look at the winter sports of ski jumping, alpine skiing, downhill racing, slalom, freestyle, cross-country, ski jumping, bobsleds, toboggans, and sleds. It also describes the history of snow sports.

• • •

Sports World Skiing, by Donna Bailey (Austin, TX: Steck-Vaughn, 1991). ISBN 0-8114-2856-7.

Grade 1, nonfiction.   This book provides an introduction, in simple text and photographs, to the techniques and equipment of skiing. The pictures, taken at a ski resort, help a beginner better understand the sport.

Soccer

The Grass of Another Country, by Christopher Merrill (New York: Holt, Rinehart & Winston, 1993). ISBN 0-8050-2771-8.

Grades 9-12, nonfiction.   The book describes the timeless beauty of the world's most popular sport. Merrill reveals soccer artistry and athletic grace. He follows soccer to towns throughout the world.

• • •

How to Understand Soccer, by Ross R. Olney (New York: Lothrop, Lee & Chopart, 1978). ISBN 0-688-41840-6.

Grades 4-8, nonfiction.   This book contains helpful information about the game of soccer, covering laws, penalties, signals, tips on equipment, and exercises. It also includes playing techniques and features great moments with famous players.

• • •

Our Soccer League, by Chuck Solomon (New York: Crown, 1988). ISBN 0-517-56956-6.

Grades 1-2, nonfiction.   This book describes how the Falcons and the Sluggers, two pony club soccer teams, play. It shows pictures and describes the actions of the team members as they prepare for and play the big game.

• • •

Soccer: From Neighborhood Play to the World Cup, by Caroline Arnold (New York: Watts, 1991). ISBN 0-531-20037-x.

Grades 6-12, nonfiction.   The author describes how to play the game, including the various rules, positions of players, and skill for each position required. This book presents a brief history of soccer from the days of the Romans to the present day World Cup Championships.

• • •

Soccer Basics, by Alex Yannis (Englewood Cliffs, NJ: Prentice-Hall, 1982). ISBN 0-13-815290-x.

Grades 5-10, nonfiction.   This book provides basic explanations of concepts and techniques. The book describes how soccer is played, the playing positions, strategies and tactics, scoring, coaching, and where to play. The author also provides a short history of soccer.

• • •

Soccer for Young Champions, by Robert J. Antonacci & Anthony J. Puglisee (New York: McGraw-Hill, 1978). ISBN 0-07-002147-3.

Grades 4-12, nonfiction. This book presents the history, rules, and techniques of soccer, including drills and advice on keeping score. The author provides suggestions for involving physically challenged persons in the sport.

• • •

Soccer Is for Me, by Lowell A. Dickmeyer (Minneapolis: Lerner, 1978). ISBN 0-8225-1076-1.

Grades 1-3, nonfiction. Todd plays for a youth soccer team called the Dolphins. In this book, he discusses skills he has learned and describes games his team has played.

• • •

A Sports Illustrated for Kids Book: Make the Team Soccer, by Richard J. Brenner (New York: Time Magazine, 1990). ISBN 0-316-10751-4.

Grades 5-12, nonfiction. This book provides instructions for improving soccer skills. The author discusses dribbling, heading, play making, defense, conditioning, mental attitude, and ways to handle problems with coaches, parents, and players. This book also includes background on the history of soccer.

• • •

Sports Illustrated Soccer: The Complete Player, by Don Herbst (New York: Sports Illustrated, 1988). ISBN 0-452-26206-2.

Grades 4-12, nonfiction. This superbly written book is designed to meet the needs of players and coaches in the United States. The book goes from basic ball skills to tips on pursuing a college soccer scholarship.

• • •

Winning Ways in Soccer, by Janet Grosshandler (New York: Cobblehill Books, Dutton, 1991).

Grades 1-3, nonfiction. The book displays text and photographs that illustrate how soccer is played, how players learn skills, and how they develop attitudes of fair play.

Swimming

Sports World Swimming, by Donna Bailey (Champaign, IL: Steck-Vaughn, 1991). ISBN 0-8114-2852-4.

Grade 1, nonfiction. The author focuses on a girl and her classmates as they learn to swim and dive.

The author highlights the types of strokes, professional competition, and water sports. The pictures are enjoyable for young readers.

Tennis

Famous Firsts in Tennis, by Joseph J. Cook (New York: G.P. Putnam's Sons, 1978). ISBN 0-399-6-1111-8. This book is out of print, but may be available in the library.

Grades 4-8, nonfiction. Persons who care about the game of tennis will be interested in the author's analysis of the playing styles of the great competitors of yesterday and today. Joseph Cook describes how tennis started as a game for the rich, and then became a game played and enjoyed by just about everyone.

• • •

Go for It-Tennis for Boys and Girls, by Bill Gulman (New York: Marshall Cavendish, 1988). ISBN 0-942545-88-5.

Grades 4-8, nonfiction. This book describes the history and current teams, leagues, and championships of tennis. It provides helpful instructions on how to play the game. The author has captured the art of tennis in this book.

• • •

Tennis Anyone?, by Dick Gould (Mountain View, CA: Mayfield, 1993). ISBN 1-55934-168-8.

Grades 9-12, nonfiction. This book is very helpful for students, teachers, and coaches. It offers an array of skills and drills to meet the needs of the novice as well as of the advanced player, and includes great coaching hints.

• • •

A Tennis Guide to the USA, by Dick Zeldin (New York: Watts, 1980). ISBN 0-531-09922-9.

Grades 4-12, nonfiction. This book is a directory of tennis. It provides the locations and information for most meets in the United States. This book also discusses the different types of playing surfaces and suggests tips on the most effective way to play on them.

• • •

Use Your Head in Tennis, by Bob Harman, with Keith Monroe (New York: Thomas Y. Crowell, 1974). ISBN 0-690-00584-9.

Grades 8-12, nonfiction. There is a lot more to tennis than hitting the ball with all your might and hoping to gain a point. Yet thousands play this hit-and-miss game without ever knowing how much more fun planned strategy can be. This book demonstrates how thinking and court strategy can easily compensate for tiring muscles and lack of a cannon-ball serve. It will teach the reader how to determine if one is stroking the ball against the racket, how to anticipate an opponent's next move, and a host of other helpful techniques that will improve one's game and add to the fun of playing.

• • •

You Can Teach Your Child Tennis, by Carol Kleiman (New York: Consumer Publishing Division of CBS, 1979). ISBN 0-445-04403-9.

This is a guide to giving your child or your students the gift of tennis. The book shares good strategies for beginning as well as advanced players. The pictures help the child or student better understand the skills of tennis.

Volleyball

Volleyball Is for Me, by Art Thomas (Minneapolis: Lerner, 1980). ISBN 0-8225-1094-4.

Grades 3-4, nonfiction.   The author follows Marta, a member of a volleyball team, as she learns volleyball fundamentals including serving, blocking, spiking, and passing.

Wrestling

Take It to the Mat, by Bobby Douglas (Ames, IA: Sigler Printing and Publishing, 1992). ISBN 0-9635812-0-1.

Grades 8-12, nonfiction.   The purpose of this book is to point out the key components of the techniques of mat wrestling. The author has presented the holds in a step-by-step progression, along with drills and counters.

• • •

Wrestling for Beginners, by Tom Jarman and Reid Hanley (Chicago: Contemporary Books, 1983). ISBN 0-8092-5656-8.

Grades 8-12, nonfiction.   The author provides the novice wrestler with the techniques that serve as the foundation for all conditioning maneuvers, holds, takedowns, counters, strategy, and pinning combinations. It is a wonderful resource.

Dance

Dance addresses the style, rhythm, self-expression, and aesthetics of movement. Included are forms of dance, such as ballet, and simple rhythmic activities and games. **American Indian Dance Steps, Rhythms, Costumes, and Interpretations**, by John L. Sequires & Robert E.

Mc Lean (New York: Ronald Press, 1963). Library of Congress Catalog Card number 63-19746.

Grades 1-12, nonfiction.   This book shares 23 dances of various Native American nations. It provides directions to help readers make inexpensive yet authentic Native American dance apparel. Each dance is presented as close to the original style as possible, according to the knowledge and understanding of the authors.

• • •

Amy, the Dancing Bear, by Carly Simon (New York: Doubleday, 1989). ISBN 0-385-26637.

Grades 1-3, fiction.   This is a warm and charming story about Amy, a bear. She dances the night away in an enchanting twilit ballroom. See how she ends her day. The illustrations in this book are delightful.

• • •

The Art of Making Dances, by Doris Humphrey (Pennington, NJ: Princeton Book, 1987). ISBN 0-87127-158-3.

Grades 9-12, nonfiction.   The author presents modern dance as theater. The book contains a short history of dance and various chapters that discuss design, dynamics, and rhythm of dance. Also included is a checklist of completed dances for dancers' use.

• • •

Astaire Dancing, by John Mueller (New York: Knopf, 1985). ISBN 0-396-51654-0.

Grades 7-12, nonfiction.   The author analyzes Astaire's entire filmed dance career. There are 31 chapters, one for each of his musical films. The author has provided incisive evaluations of the scripts and musical scores and of Astaire's partners and his supporting casts.

• • •

Ballet for Boys and Girls, by Katharine Sholey Walker & Joan Butler (Pennington, NJ: Prentice-Hall, 1979). ISBN 0-13-055574-6.

Grades 1-5, nonfiction.   The author discusses ballet techniques, costumes, and stories of famous ballet stars from all over the world.

• • •

The Ballet - Student's Primer, by Ambrose (New York: Bonanza Book, 1988). ISBN 0-517-66913-7.

Grades 3-12, nonfiction.   The author reviews the ''bare bones'' of ballet in all forms, from exercise to performance. This is a good resource book for teachers.

• • •

Barn Dance, by Bill Martin, Jr. & John Archambault

(New York: Henry Holt, 1986). ISBN 0-8050-0799-7.

Grades 1-6, fiction. Unable to sleep on the night of a full moon, a young boy follows the sound of music across the fields and finds an unusual barn dance in progress. The pictures are incredible and capture the fun and excitement of a barn dance.

● ● ●

The Bear Dance, by Chris Riddle (New York: Simon & Schuster, Simon & Schuster Books for Young Readers, 1990). ISBN 0-671-70974-7.

Grades 1-3, fiction. Jack Frost brings gray winter to a forest where it has always been summer. A young girl brings sunlight back by engaging Mr. Frost in a vigorous Bear Dance. There is a cooperative game called ''Jack Frost'' that could accompany the reading of this book.

● ● ●

Bill and the Google-Eye Goblins, by Alice Chertte (New York: Lathrop, Lu and Chopart Books, 1987).

Grades 1-2, fiction. A young man who loves to dance is captured by the goblins beneath the hill. He must challenge them to a dance contest in order to escape. The story is very entertaining for the young reader.

● ● ●

Color Dance, by Ann Jonas (New York: Greenwillow Books, 1989). ISBN 0-688-05990-2.

Grades 1-3, nonfiction. Three dancers show how colors can combine with dance to create different color patterns and visuals for the audience. This book can give students a different perspective on how to use color and dance.

● ● ●

The Complete Guide to Modern Dance, by Don Mc Donagh (New York: Doubleday, 1976). ISBN 0-385-05055-0.

Grades 7-12, nonfiction. This book provides a brilliant and comprehensive examination of one of the most popular and vital theatrical arts in the United States. Modern dance is placed in the context of the changing cultural patterns of 20th-century America. The author examines the interaction between modern dance and music in general. He also analyzes over 225 dances and provides information on the origins of each. This is a magnificent reference book for modern dance.

● ● ●

Dance, by Shan Finney (New York: Watts, 1983). ISBN 0-531-04525-0.

Grades 5-8, nonfiction. This book presents an overview of dance, including folk, social, dramatic, and aerobic dancing. Finney discusses dancing on the stage, in television, and in films, and highlights careers in dance therapy and professional dance.

● ● ●

The Dance of Africa: An Introduction, by Lee Warren (Englewood Cliffs, NJ: Prentice-Hall, 1972). ISBN 0-13-196733-9.

Grades 4-8, nonfiction. This book describes many African dances and discusses their origins and their significance as reflections of almost every aspect of African life.

● ● ●

Dance Away, by George Shannon (New York: Greenwillow Books, 1982). ISBN 0-688-00838-0.

Grades K-1, fiction. Rabbit's dancing saves his friends from becoming Fox's supper. The author introduces his readers to different dance steps that the Rabbit uses to save his friends.

● ● ●

Dancing With the Indians, by Angela Shelf Medearis (New York: Holiday House, 1991). ISBN 0-8234-0893-0.

Grades 3-5, nonfiction. This is an interesting story of a black family who watches and attends a Seminole celebration. The family joins and learns several exciting dances that help them understand the ways and culture of the Seminole people. This is a unique story with a multicultural focus.

● ● ●

The Eentsy, Weentsy Spider Fingerplay and Action Rhymes, by Joanna Cole & Stephanie Calmenson. (New York: Mulberry Book). ISBN 0-688-10805-9.

Grades K-4, fiction. This book provides a collection of play rhymes intended to be accompanied by finger play and other physical activities.

● ● ●

Frogs and the Ballet, by Donald Elliott (Boston: Gambit, 1979). ISBN 0-87645-0990.

Grades 1-3, fiction/nonfiction. The author uses frogs to illustrate traditional dance poses. In a charming manner, the author demonstrates how much work, practice, dedication, and skill results in the seemingly effortless movement on the stage that weaves the great tapestries of Classical Ballet.

● ● ●

The Greatest Tap Dance Stars and Their Stories 1900-1955, by Rusty E. Frank (New York: Morrow, 1990). ISBN 0-688-08949-6.

Grades 7-12, nonfiction. The author has compiled an incomparable memory book that includes the most comprehensive listing of tap acts, recordings, and films for these 55 years. A terrific resource.

• • •

Humpry, the Dancing Pig, by Arthur Getz (New York: Dial Press, 1980).

Grade 1, fiction.   Because of his desire to be slim like a cat, Humpry begins to dance his weight away. This is an enjoyable story about determination.

• • •

I Feel Like Dancing: A Year with Jacques d'Amboise and the National Dance Institute, by Steven Barboza (New York: Crown, 1992). ISBN 0-517-58454-9.

Grades 2-3, nonfiction.   The author describes the experiences of students during the year they spent as members of Jacques d'Amboise's National Dance Institute.

• • •

Jacques' Jungle Ballet, by Karen Lavat (New York: Holt, 1989).

Grade 1, fiction.   Despite discouraging words from family and friends, Jacques the elephant pursues his dream of becoming a ballet dancer. This is a terrific read-aloud story to initiate discussions of pursuing one's dream.

• • •

Jazz Dance Class-Beginning Thru Advanced, Gus Giordano (Pennington, NJ: Princeton Book, A Dance Horizons Book, 1992). ISBN 0-87127-182-6.

Grades 7-12, nonfiction.   The author introduces jazz terms and accurate body placement. The author believes it is crucial that choreography be created for the entire body, even finger positions, so that the student acquires the jazz style. Beginner, intermediate, and advanced levels cover warm-up, barre work, aerobic endurance, turns, leaps, and jazz combinations. The exercises can also be read individually, for reference, because they include counts, specific body movements, and, as a separate item, arm movements. Over 500 photographs illustrate how to execute each dance movement.

• • •

Josephine Baker, by Alan Schroeder (New York: Chelsea House, 1991). ISBN 0-7910-1116-x.

Grades 7-12, nonfiction.   This book is a biography of the African American singer and dancer who achieved fame in Paris in the 1920s and was awarded the French Legion of Honor for her work during World War II. Josephine Baker received the Black Americans of Achievement Award.

• • •

Katherine Dunham, Dancer and Choreographer, by Jeannine Dominy (New York: Chelsea House, 1993).

ISBN 0-7910-1148-8.

Grades 4-8, nonfiction.   This interesting book shares information about and achievements of Katherine Dunham, an African American dancer and choreographer. This book presents interesting insights into the training methods of dancers.

• • •

Lili at Ballet, by Rachel Isadora (New York: G.P. Putnam's Sons, 1993). ISBN 0-399-2242-8.

Grades 1-2, fiction.   Lili dreams of becoming a ballerina and goes to her ballet lessons four afternoons a week. This book is an exceptional book for children to become familiar with ballet.

• • •

Pretend You're a Cat, by Jean Marzollo (New York: Dial Books for Young Readers, 1990). ISBN 0-8037-0773-8.

Grades K-1, fiction.   This book's beautiful pictures capture rhyming verses with movement: Suggested actions include to purr like a cat, scratch like a dog, leap like a squirrel, and bark like a seal. A young reader will surely enjoy learning different locomotor movements through this book.

• • •

Ragtime Tumpie, by Alan Schroeder (Boston: Jay Street Books, 1989).

Grades 2-3, nonfiction.   Tumpie is a young African American girl who will later become famous as a dancer with the performer Josephine Baker. Tumpie longs to find the opportunity to dance amid the poverty and vivacious street life of St. Louis in the early 1900s. This is a historical and very motivational story for students.

• • •

Satomi Ichikawa: Dance, Tanya, by Patricia Lee Gouch (New York: Philomel Books, 1989). ISBN 0-399-21521-2.

Grades 1-2, nonfiction.   Tanya loves ballet dancing, repeating the moves she sees her older sister using when practicing for class or a recital. Soon Tanya is old enough to go to ballet class herself. The author has the ability to convey the ideas of keeping dreams and being patient.

• • •

Sometimes I Dance Mountains, by Byrd Baylor (New York: Scribner's, 1974). ISBN 684-13440-3.

Grades 1-2, nonfiction.   The author is able to portray a simple yet eloquent vision of young dancers. Baylor invites the reader to join her to dance mountains and whirlwinds, slow things and fast things, and open and closed things. Every dance is a new dance for a special moment.

● ● ●

Song and Dance Man, by Karen Ackerman (New York: Dragonfly Book, Alfred Knopf, Random House, 1988). ISBN 0-679-81995-9.

Grades 1-6, fiction.   Enjoy the fun of the Dance Man through this story of Grandpa. Grandpa opens an old trunk, pulls out his top hat and gold-tipped cane, and suddenly a Vaudeville man appears in Grandpa's place. He glides across the stage doing the old soft-shoe for his favorite audience, his grandchildren. This Caldecott Medal book can inspire art, tap dance, and soft-shoe dance lessons.

● ● ●

Square Dancing Everyone, by Bob Osgood (Charleston, NC: Hunter Textbooks, 1987).

Grades 7-12, nonfiction.   This book explains the development of, the basic movements of, and suggested dance drills for both traditional and contemporary square dance.

● ● ●

Two Young Dancers, by Alexandra Collard (New York: Julian Messner, 1984).

Grades 5-10, nonfiction.   Two 15-year-old American ballet students, a boy and a girl, discuss their training, their lives, their experiences as performers, and their hopes for ballet stardom.

● ● ●

An Usborne Guide to Ballet, by Annabel Thomas (London: Usborne, 1986).

Grades 2-6, nonfiction.   The author captures ballet with beautiful pictures. She leads the reader from the structure of the ballet company to famous choreographers, ballet stories, dancers, and ballet adventures.

Gymnastics

Gymnastics is a sport that combines flexibility, exercise, strength, and rhythm through patterned routines. These routines are done on the floor and on specialized equipment, and the floor exercises are usually accompanied by music. The equipment used can be a pommel horse, rings, vaulting horse, parallel bars, horizontal bar, asymmetric bars, and a beam.

There are three specialized areas of gymnastics:

● *Artistic gymnastics.* Artistic gymnastics is often referred to as Olympic gymnastics. It is competitive and is governed by the International Federation of Gymnastics (FIG). There are separate sections for males and females. The males work on six pieces of apparatus:

floor, pommel horse, rings, vault, parallel bars, and horizontal bar. The females work on four pieces of apparatus: vault, asymmetric bars, beam, and floor.

● *Rhythmic gymnastics.* Rhythmic gymnastics is a sport specifically for females. It is dance-oriented and requires that the gymnast work with small hand apparatus such as the ball, rope, hoop, ribbon, and clubs. Many rhythmic gymnasts perform a free exercise, and they also often perform in pairs and trios as well as groups.

● *General gymnastics.* This kind of gymnastics is noncompetitive. It encompasses the whole range of age groups under the umbrella of what could be termed gymnastics for leisure.

Better Gymnastics: How to Spot the Performer, by William T. Boone, Ph.D. (Mountain View, CA: World, 1979). ISBN 0-89037-127-x.

Grades 7-12, nonfiction.   This book is a wonderful guide for the instructor and coach in the proper teaching of gymnastics. The author provides directions on spotting the moves of gymnasts. A variety of suggestions are included for class, procedures, club organization, program planning, and proper training. An order of progression from simple to complex skills aids the teaching of gymnastics.

● ● ●

Everybody's Gymnastics Book, by Bell Sand & Mike Conklin (New York: Watts, 1983). ISBN 0-684-18091-x.

Grades 7-12, nonfiction.   This book provides a complete illustrated guide to gymnastics performance, instruction, history, and organization. It includes a directory of quality gymnastic training programs. The Hall of Fame, Olympics, and World Championships are highlighted.

● ● ●

Gymnastic, #1 The Beginners, by Elizabeth Levy (New York: Scholastic, 1988). ISBN 0-590-41562-x.

Grades 3-5, fiction.   The new gymnastic club promised to be terrific. Cindi, Lauren, Darlene, and Jodi knew they'd be friends from the day they first met. Coach Harmon said they would be in a real gymnastics meet right away, even if they were only beginners. Now they have to learn how to become a team. The story follows the girls as they train for this meet.

● ● ●

Gymnastics, by Tony Murdock & Nik Stuart (New York: Watts, 1985). ISBN 0-531-10022-7.

Grades 2-9, nonfiction.   This book was written to help aspiring young gymnasts of either gender who are either thinking of taking up the sport or who have just started on preparation work, training, and basic movements to develop their skills and advance. The step-by-step illustrations make this book a great resource for a teacher or coach.

• • •

Gymnastics, by Tony Murdock & Nik Stuart (New York: Watts, 1989). ISBN 9-531-10770-1.

Grades 3-6, nonfiction. This book was written to help aspiring young gymnasts. The step-by-step illustrations make this book a great reference to assist students in learning and enjoying gymnastics.

• • •

Rhythmic Gymnastics: The Skill of the Game, by Jenny Bott (Marlborough, England: Crowood Press, 1989). ISBN 1-85223-208-0.

Grades 6-12, nonfiction. This text builds on the basic skills of rhythmic gymnastics and gives ideas for class work, group work, and partner work. The pictures help the reader understand the skills and movements of this sport. This movement form can appeal to students of all levels of ability.

Historical Perspectives

The books in this section enhance the education of our students in physical education. Learning the history of an activity and participating in games and dances from the past can help students discover more about their heritage. Their knowledge of how past events have influenced the present can help students recognize the importance of preparing today to meet the goals they have set for themselves. The history of physical education blends naturally with the curriculum in history and social science. Sociological development is reflected in a society's participation in various physical activities. A current awareness of the importance of all aspects of health (physical, mental, and social) has extended the benefits of physical education beyond physical training. Reflecting ancient Greek philosophers, current practices promote a sound mind in a sound body within a sound social environment.

An Approved History of the Olympics Games, by Bill Henry (Los Angeles: Color Graphics, 1981). ISBN 0-9606628-0-4.

Grades 6-12, nonfiction. Bill Henry conducted his arduous research in order to write the true story of the Olympics after serving as Sport Technical Director of the summer Olympic Games. This is a marvelous collection of information about the history of the Olympics and about what goes on behind the scenes of the Olympic Games.

• • •

Biblioteca Grafica Artes-Marciale, by Norman Barrett (New York: Watts, 1990). ISBN 0-531-07902-3.

Grades 3-6, nonfiction, Spanish. This book, written in Spanish, describes karate, kung-fu, tae kwon do, boxing, archery, and the history of martial arts.

• • •

Biblioteca Grafica Gymnasia, by Norman Barrett (New York: Watts, 1991). ISBN 0-531-07906-6.

Grades 3-6, nonfiction, Spanish. This book, written in Spanish, explains the skills performed in gymnastics and provides a history of the sport.

• • •

Black Dance in America, by James Hackins (New York: Crowell, 1990). ISBN 0-690-0467-x.

Grades 5-10, nonfiction. This book describes the history of African American dance, from its beginnings in the ritual dances of African slaves through tap and modern dance to break dancing. The text includes information about influential dancers and dance companies.

• • •

The Concise Encyclopedia of Sports, by Keith W. Jennison (New York: Grolier of Canada, 1970).

Grades 8-12, nonfiction. This book provides detailed information on the history, development, and rules of more than 50 sports that engage the attention of millions of people throughout the world. The author provides sport instruction, capsule biographies of hundreds of famous sports figures, and many helpful charts, diagrams, and photographs.

• • •

Famous Firsts in Tennis, by Joseph J. Cook (New York: G.P. Putnam's Sons, 1978). ISBN 0-399-61111-8. This book is out of print, but it may be possible to find it in a library.

Grades 4-8, nonfiction. Everyone who cares about tennis will be interested in the author's analysis of the playing styles of the great competitors of yesterday and today. Joseph Cook describes how tennis started as a game for the rich, and became a sport played and enjoyed by just about everyone.

• • •

The Games They Played - Sports in History, by Richard B. Lyttle (New York: Mc Clelland & Stewart, 1982). ISBN -0-689-30928-7.

Grades 4-12, nonfiction. Historical perspectives are important in physical education. This book helps students understand archeological evidence that reveals how individual and team sports and games have been used for diversion since prehistoric times. The book includes individual events such as sport wrestling, boxing, chariot races, fencing, lance and sword, and archery, and team games such as lacrosse, court games, and polo.

• • •

The Greatest Sports Stories Never Told, by Bruce Nash & Allan Zullo (New York: Simon & Schuster, 1993). ISBN 0-671-75938-8.

Grades 4-6, nonfiction. The authors have compiled 34 stories from various sports, and feature professionals and amateurs. These are stories that few fans know about: the baseball player who was able to hit three home runs to encourage a sightless boy about to undergo surgery; the boxer who was knocked down 27 times in one match, but refused to give up; the golfer who had just teed off and was forced to stop playing to save a boy's life. There is an enthusiastic tone in this book, and students will enjoy these unusual stories.

• • •

A Hard Road to Glory: A History of the African American Athlete Vol. 1 (1819-1919): Vol. 2 (1919-1945): Vol. 3 (1946-1986) by Arthur Ashe, Jr. (New York: Warner Book, 1988). ISBN 0-446-71006-7.

Grades 3-12, nonfiction. This book, written by the famous athlete Arthur Ashe, Jr., provides a remarkable comprehensive history of African American athletes. The author collected information from family archives, personal interviews with many sports heroes and legends, dusty attics and closets, files in athletic department basements, and any other source he could think of. This collection includes three volumes of valuable American history.

• • •

A Hundred and Fiftieth Anniversary Album of Baseball, by Harvey Frommer (New York: Watts, 1988). ISBN 0-531-105888-1.

Grades 3-6, nonfiction. This book provides the history of the popular American sport from the end of the 19th century to the 1980s. The author discusses the impact of changing times on the sport of baseball.

• • •

Interference: How Organized Crime Influences Professional Football, by Dan E. Moldea (New York: Morrow, 1989). ISBN 0-688-08303-x.

Grades 6-12, nonfiction. This book describes how organized crime influences professional football. This is a richly documented study of the shocking degree of unethical play involved in the popular sport. The author provides an in-depth look at the mob's multimillion-dollar gambling and drug empire as it has thrived upon the institution of professional

football. This book can help initiate discussions related to ethics in the world of sports.

• • •

Medieval Games: Sports and Recreation in Feudal Society, by John Marshall Carter (New York: Greenwood Press, 1992). ISBN 0-313-25699-3.

Grades 6-12, nonfiction. The author provides the reader with a wealth of knowledge about sports and recreation in Medieval times. Topics such as sports and war, sports and art, sports violence, and other related issues are included in a chronological framework from 800 to 1300.

• • •

A New True Book: Olympics, by Dennis B. Fradin (Chicago: Children's Press, 1983). ISBN 0-516-01703-9.

Grade 1. The author briefly describes the development of the Modern Olympic Games beginning with a single 200-meter race run in Olympia, Greece in 774 BC as part of the Ancient Olympic Games.

• • •

Nineteenth Century American: The Sports, by Leonard Everett Fisher (New York: A Holiday House Book, 1980). ISBN 0-8234-0419-6.

Grades 3-12, nonfiction. This book deals with the spirit and development of athletic competitions in 19th-century America. Physical skill, strength, and stamina were qualities sought in the games Americans played. The sports addressed are polo, croquet, tennis, golf, gymnastics, boxing, football, lacrosse, bicycling, and crew.

• • •

Olympic Games in Ancient Greece, by Shirley Gulbok & Alfred Tamarin (New York: Harper & Row, 1976). ISBN 0-06-022-47-3.

Grades 6-12, nonfiction. In ancient Greece, the Olympic Games were the supreme test of skill for young athletes. The history of the Olympic Games is connected to the history of ancient Greece. Using the Games as a vantage point, the authors review 10 centuries of Greek history and legends to provide this remarkable collection of historical information.

• • •

The Olympics: A History of the Modern Games, by Allen Guttmann (Chicago: University of Illinois Press, 1992). ISBN 0-252-01701-3.

Grades 8-12, nonfiction. The book includes interesting perspectives on individual competitions. An early marathon through the streets of Paris, for example, brought complaints from the U.S. team that the course had been designed to allow French contestants to take shortcuts. Guttmann also provides insight into the behind-the-scenes maneuvering involved in site selection and shares little-known facts about the history of the Games and about International Olympic Committee leaders.

● ● ●

The Royal Ballet, by Alexander Bland (New York: Doubleday, 1981). ISBN 0-385-17043-2.

Grades 4-12, nonfiction. The author has compiled a wonderful history of the first 50 years of the Royal Ballet. The text provides a concise and clear picture of the glory and hard times of the Royal Ballet.

● ● ●

The Sporting News: First Hundred Years 1886-1986, by Lowell Reidenbaugh (New York: Sporting News, 1985). ISBN 0-89204-204-4.

Grades 6-12, nonfiction. Join a 100-year trip down memory lane through the views of "Sporting News." Discover how the great sport of baseball, chronicled through the Spinht family weekly newspaper, impacted society during economic depression, wars, and times of peace.

● ● ●

U.S. Olympians, by Zachary Kent (Chicago: Children's Press, 1992). ISBN 0-516-06659-5.

Grades 4-6, nonfiction. A tremendous amount of effort is evident in the author's attempt to document the history of U.S. participation in the Olympic Games from 1896 to 1992.

● ● ●

Webster Sports Dictionary, by Merriam-Webster (New York: Merriam-Webster, 1976). ISBN 0-87779-067-1.

Grades 3-12, nonfiction. The terms in this dictionary are used by participants, broadcasters, sports writers, officials, and spectators in various sports. This book is a great resource for the classroom or library.

Multicultural

This section includes books to help readers understand and foster cultural pluralism in an interdependent world. Multicultural education is a structured process designed to foster understanding, acceptance, and constructive relations among individuals of different cultures. The process addresses ethnic, racial, religious, linguistic, socio-economic, and gender differences. Multicultural education builds on an awareness of one's own cultural heritage, and promotes understanding and respect for other cultures. The process promotes social and communication skills that help one function effectively in multicultural environments. Books in this section support the process of multicultural education.

Adventures in Storytelling, Double Dutch, and the Voodoo Shoes: A Modern African American Urban Tale, by Warren Colman (Chicago: Children's Press, 1991). ISBN 0-516-05133-4.

Grades 1-3, fiction. See how creative two girls become as they compete in a double dutch jump rope contest to prove who is the best jumper. The author includes storytelling activities and a list of books on storytelling and folktales.

● ● ●

Anna Banana 101 Jump-Rope Rhymes, by Joanne Cole (New York: Beech Tree Books, 1989). ISBN 0-688-08809-0.

Grades 1-6, fiction. An illustrated collection of jump rope rhymes arranged according to the type of jumping they are meant to accompany.

● ● ●

Arroz-Con Leche Popular Songs and Rhymes From Latin America, by Lulu Delacre (New York: Scholastic, 1989). ISBN 0-590-41886-6.

Grades K-8, nonfiction. Latin American folklore is rich in children's songs, games, and rhymes. Many of these activities were brought from Spain and, with time, blended with the local customs of each country. That is why we find children from different locales singing versions of songs like "Arroz Con Leche." This book acquaints readers with the warmth and charm of songs and rhymes from an oral tradition.

● ● ●

Children's Games From Many Lands, by Nina Millen (New York: Friendship Press, 1965). This book is out of print, but may be available in libraries, library Card number 65-24039.

Grades 8-12, nonfiction. The children of some countries play much more often than children in other countries. In some places children do not have time for play because they have to work at an early age in order to aid their families in earning a living. The desire to play is there, but the youngsters may have little time or energy for games because of family situations. This collection will provide a historical perspective and an understanding of the play of students in other countries.

● ● ●

Games Children Play Around the World: Games With Sticks, Stones, and Skills, by Ruth Oakley (New York: Marshal Cavendish, 1989). ISBN 1-85435-079-x.

Grades 1-6, nonfiction. This book provides the background and instructions for playing hopscotch, jacks, and a variety of games played with sticks, stones, and marbles. This is a terrific collection of games from around the world.

● ● ●

Hopscotch Around the World, by Mary Lankford (New York: Morrow Junior Books, 1992). ISBN 0-688-08419-2.

> ***Grades K-8, nonfiction.***   This book contains a zesty collection of 19 hop-scotch games from all over the world. Rules and patterns are clearly provided for many versions of the game including Italian, Chinese, and Nigerian. Readers are encouraged to develop variations of their own.

● ● ●

International Games, by Valjean Mc Lentghan (Milwaukee: Raintree Children's Books, 1978). ISBN 0-8172-1162-4.

> ***Grades 2-3, nonfiction.***   The author has compiled a collection of 20 games from countries around the world. The book provides complete instructions on how to play each game. Countries represented include Norway, Greece, Brazil, South Africa, Canada, Guatemala, Denmark, and Italy.

● ● ●

Jamaica Tag-Along, by Juanita Havell (Boston: Houghton Mifflin, 1989). ISBN 0-395-49602-1.

> ***Grades K-3, fiction.***   Jamaica wants to play basketball at the playground with her big brother, Ossie. "I don't want you tagging along," he states. She watches Ossie, Jed, Buzz, and Maurice shoot baskets. This story can help initiate discussions on fair play, skill ability, and cooperation.

● ● ●

Miss Mary Mack and Other Children's Street Rhymes, by Joanna Cole and Stephanie Calmenson (New York: Morrow Junior Books, 1990). ISBN 0-688-09749-9.

> ***Grades 1-2, fiction.***   Drawing on memories from their own childhoods, the authors provide a collection of rhymes used in street games. Basic instructions for the activities are included. This is a wonderful resource to introduce children to street games and help youngsters invent their own street games.

● ● ●

Skipping to Babylon: A Collection of Skipping Rhymes, by Carole Tate (New York: Oxford University Press, 1985). ISBN 0-19-278206-1.

> ***Grades 1-3, fiction.***   The author takes the reader on a jumping adventure with jump rope rhythms through different places, ending up in Babylon. The pictures help motivate students in a jumping program which can take place anywhere. The students will

enjoy the new rhythms in this book.

Also see the listings for *Taking Sides* under Basketball and *Baseball in April and Other Stories* under Baseball/Softball (both in the section Joy, Pleasure, and Satisfaction).

Personal Fitness and Physical Fitness

Research and practices in physical fitness have drastically changed in recent years. It is important for children to create healthful patterns of living that include vigorous activities. It is never too late to establish personal fitness goals. This section provides information and motivation to begin personal fitness programs.

ACSM Fitness Book, by American College of Sports Medicine (Champaign, IL: Leisure Press, 1992). ISBN 0-88011-460-6.

> ***Grades 7-12, nonfiction.***   This book, written by a group of exercise science professionals, addresses cardiorespiratory fitness, muscle strength and endurance, flexibility, and healthy body composition. This resource can help individuals create an exercise program that leads to a healthy lifestyle.

● ● ●

The Adventure of Albert the Running Bear, by Barbara Isenberg & Susan Wolf (New York: Clarion Books, A Houghton Mifflin Company, 1982). ISBN 0-89919-113-4.

> ***Grades 1-2, fiction.***   Albert is a running bear that lives in a zoo. He escapes from the zoo, encounters a series of mishaps, and finally finds himself running a marathon. This cute story leads to discussions about nutrition and exercise. A stuffed toy of Albert, The Running Bear, is available to add to the enjoyment of the book.

● ● ●

Albert the Running Bear Gets the Jitters, by Barbara Isenberg & Susan Wolf (New York: Clarion Books, 1985). ISBN 0-89919-517-2.

> ***Grades 1-2, fiction.***   Albert has the jitters while getting ready for a race. The students will enjoy this delightful story, and learn how to deal with jitters before a big event.

● ● ●

Bear and Duck on the Run, by Judy Delton (Niles, IL: Albert Whitman, 1984). ISBN 0-8075-0594-3.

> ***Grades 1-3, fiction.***   Duck tries to get Bear to join him in running every day, but Bear is very uncooperative. This story leads to good discussions on fair

play and on how to deal with uncooperative students in sports.

● ● ●

The Beauty of Running, by Barron (New York: Harcourt Brace Jovanovich, 1980). ISBN 0-15-111401-3.

Grades 8-12, nonfiction.   The author writes beautifully about one woman's perspective on how she got involved in a running program and how it changed her life. This is an inspiring story to motivate persons to begin an exercise program.

● ● ●

Bodies in Motion, Finding Joy in Fitness, by Gilad Jankowicz & Ann Marie Brown (San Francisco: Foghorn Press, 1992). ISBN 0-935701-55-9.

Grades 7-12, nonfiction.   This book promotes pursuing one's personal best and having fun doing it. The authors emphasize the need for a good nutrition and exercise program to add life to one's years. Workout information is provided for aerobics, progressive flexibility, workout conditioning, weight lifting, swimming, and water aerobics. This is a great resource for secondary students.

● ● ●

Bunnies and Their Sports, by Nancy Carlson. (New York: Puffin Books, 1987). ISBN 0-14-05-617-9.

Grades K-1, fiction.   This illustrated book explains the basic types of exercise. Bunnies involved in jogging, swimming, and exercising at a gym help children better understand the values of exercise.

● ● ●

The Complete Waterpower Workout Book, by Lynda Huey & Robert Forster, P.T. (New York: Random House, 1993). ISBN 0-679-74554-8.

Grades 8-12, nonfiction.   Millions of people are discovering the benefits of working out in water. Working against water provides natural resistance that allows a healthier, more balanced workout than possible on land. This book describes water workout programs for fitness, injury prevention, and healing.

● ● ●

Encyclopedia of Modern Bodybuilding, by Arnold Schwarzenegger with Bill Dobbins (New York: Simon & Schuster, 1985). ISBN 0-671-63381-3.

Grades 9-12, nonfiction.   The ultimate book on bodybuilding is written by the world's ultimate bodybuilder, Arnold Schwarzenegger, and Bill Dobbins. Here are the basic concepts on training principles, contest preparation, and diet and nutrition. The book describes the history of bodybuilding and its growth as a sport. An analysis of the muscles of the body and techniques to increase muscle growth is included.

● ● ●

Everybody's Aerobic Book, by Dorie Krepton & Donald Chu (Mankato, MN: Bellwether Press, 1986). ISBN 0-8087-5621-4.

Grades 7-12, nonfiction.   This book is intended to serve the needs of the person involved in aerobic conditioning. The book attempts to cover all facets of an aerobic exercise program. One of the helpful features of this book is the concept of self-assessment. The ability to evaluate one's starting level provides an important reference point to measure change and improvement. The concept of joint mobility, as opposed to flexibility, is an interesting shift in emphasis.

● ● ●

Exercise, What It Is, What It Does, by Carola S. Trier (New York: Greenwillow Books, 1982). ISBN 0-688-00950-6.

Grades 7-12, nonfiction.   The author does a wonderful job of emphasizing the importance of exercise, and gives instructions for several exercises to be done alone or with a friend. The pictures support the text explanations of the exercises.

● ● ●

Exercise (The Healthy Body Series), by Don Nardo (New York: Chelsea House, 1992). ISBN 0-7910-0457-0.

Grades 9-12, nonfiction.   The author examines the benefits of exercise and explores the subject of physical fitness. The book provides a history of physical conditioning through the years. The pictures enhance the text to help the reader understand the applications of physical conditioning.

● ● ●

Forty Common Errors in Running and How to Correct Them, by Arthur Shay with Dr. Noel D. Nequin (Chicago: Contemporary Books, 1979). ISBN 0-8092-7370-5.

Grades 6-12, nonfiction.   This book shares some of the knowledge accumulated by Dr. Noel Nequin, ''The Running Doctor,'' about 40 common errors of running. The errors address facets such as starting out, conditioning, stride, hazards, and knowing one's limits. The pictures help illustrate the common errors.

● ● ●

If It Hurts Don't Do It, by Peter Francis, Ph.D. & Lorena Francis, Ph.D. (Rocklin, CA: Prima, 1988). ISBN 0-9144629-48-4.

Grades 7-12, nonfiction.   This is an exciting program for pain-free, injury-free, life-long fitness. The reader will leave with a good sense of what constitutes a balanced exercise program.

• • •

Jump! The New Jump Rope Book, by Susan Kalb-fleisch (New York: Morrow, 1985). ISBN 0-688-06930-4.

>   *Grades 3-12, nonfiction.* The author has compiled a great introduction to rope jumping with instructions for easy and advanced skills. The illustrations make it easy to follow each skill needed to jump rope. Because patterns from basic to complicated are provided, this book is a challenge for everyone who uses it.

• • •

Loudmouth George and the Big Race, by Nancy Carlson (Minneapolis: Bellwether Press, 1983). ISBN 0-87614-215-3.

>   *Grade 1, fiction.* George brags, procrastinates, and offers excuses instead of training for the big race. His friends in the race train every day and invite George to help. On race day, George is embarrassed because he is out of shape and his lack of training is apparent. This book is an excellent source for teaching students the value of training and of setting and working towards goals.

• • •

The Marathon Rabbit, by Mike Eagle (New York: Holt, Rinehart & Winston, 1985). ISBN 0-03-00405802.

>   *Grades 1-2, fiction.* A rabbit wants to run with people in a 26-mile marathon race around the city, and he has quite an adventure. This is an enjoyable story for students.

• • •

Modern Sports Science, by Larry Kettelkamp (New York: Morrow, 1986). ISBN 0-688-05494-3.

>   *Grades 6-12, nonfiction.* This book describes how the body functions during athletic performances in various sports. The author discusses the progress made in understanding muscle mechanics, body metabolism, peak performance, stress, mind and body relationships, and what is needed to become proficient in any sport.

• • •

Norma Jean, Jumping Bean, by Joanna Cole (New York: Random House, 1987). ISBN 0-394-88668-2.

>   *Grades 1-2, fiction.* Norma Jean, whose love of jumping might be a bit excessive, stops her favorite activity after her friends complain. However, participation in the school Olympics demonstrates that there is a time and place for jumping.

• • •

Ropics: The Next Jump Forward in Fitness, by Ken M. Solis, M.D. (Champaign, IL: Human Kinetics, 1992). ISBN 0-88011-444-4.

>   *Grades 7-12, nonfiction.* The author shows how Ropics can help any person master an amazing number of challenging jump rope techniques. Necessary skills are provided step by step to help the reader reap the benefits and fun of jump ropes.

• • •

Running: A Celebration of the Sport and the World's Best Places to Enjoy It, by John Schubert (New York: Random House, 1992). ISBN 0-679-02376-3.

>   *Grades 8-12, nonfiction.* Well-known sports author John Schubert brings to life the joys and frustrations every runner has experienced. This book demonstrates how the sport can invigorate the body, inspire self-confidence, and heighten appreciation of the world we live in.

• • •

Swimming for Total Fitness, by Jane Katz, Ed. D. (New York: Doubleday Books, 1992). ISBN 0-385-46821-0.

>   *Grades 6-12, nonfiction.* This book will help nonswimmers learn and will help swimmers sharpen their strokes. It provides conditioning information, including dozens of workouts of gradually increasing difficulty.

• • •

Tai-Chi: 10 Minutes to Heaven, by Chiu Siew Pang & Goh Eve Hock (Reno, NV: CRCS, 1985). ISBN 0-916360-30-x.

>   *Grades 7-12, nonfiction.* This very informative book answers key questions and provides a basic understanding of Tai-Chi, an excellent form of exercise.

• • •

Ultimate Fitness, by David Luna (Santa Monica, CA: Roundtable, 1989). ISBN 0-915677-38-3-5.

>   *Grades 7-12, nonfiction.* The author demonstrates his personal prescription for a healthier lifestyle by combining diet, attitude, and fitness techniques. The reader will learn how to establish a personalized program from beginning to advanced levels. Some of the exercise components include multifaceted exercise, heavy and light workouts, breathing, concentration, and goal setting.

• • •

Walking for Health, by Mark Buchlin (Garden City, PA: Rodale Press, 1992) ISBN 0-87596-165-7.

>   *Grades 8-12, nonfiction.* This book, the most complete guide ever written on the subject, is a practical encyclopedia on walking for health.

• • •

Wesley Paul, Marathon Runner, by Julianna A. Fogel

(New York: J.B. Lippincott, 1979). ISBN 0-397-31845-6.

Grade 1, nonfiction.   The author highlights the life of a Chinese American runner, Wesley Paul, who had a record-breaking performance in the New York City Marathon at the age of nine. He dreamed of competing in the Olympics. This is a wonderful story that young students can relate to and from which they can learn a few training techniques.

Records, Cassettes, Videos

Educational Activities, Inc.

P.O. Box 87
Baldwin, NY, 11510
1-800-645-3739 Fax 515-623-9282

Key

AR=LP Record
AC=Cassette
CD=Compact Disc

All the records include instructions.

Readiness Skills

Body Jive, by Ambrose "Braz" Brazelton
AR 96 or AC 96, Grades 3-6.

This recording provides an exciting variety of activities that include identification of body parts, reciprocal and opposite actions, the introduction of anatomical names, coordination of movements, and structured and participant-created skills. Listening and cognitive skills are sharpened by means of mental sequencing and retention. The activity, "Obey the Previous Command" is guaranteed to keep students constantly alert! All activities are geared for the classroom and need little space.

● ● ●

Can a Cherry Pie Wave Goodbye? Learning Through Music and Movement, by Hap Palmer
AR 520 or AC 520, Grades K-2.

This fun-filled, sprightly album is geared to the primary grades and English as a Second Language (ESL) students. Children acquire essential vocabulary and make it their own through singing and total movement participation. This new recording features call and response songs, listening, opposites, counting, and color reinforcement. The songs are "Let's All Clap Our Hands Together," "Bean Bag Alphabet Rag," "Parade of Colors II," "Weekly Rap," "Can a Cherry Pie Wave Goodbye?," "Put a Little Color on You," "Pocket Full of B's II," "Quick Color," "Animal Quiz Part I," "Animal Quiz Part II," and "Steppin' Out on the Town II."

● ● ●

Getting to Know Myself, by Hap Palmer
AR 585 or AC 585, Grades K-2.

This excellent "introduction to learning" covers awareness of body image and the body's position in space, identification of body parts, objects in relation to body part, body part identification, movements of the body, laterality of body, feelings, and moods. The songs are "Feelings," "Sammy Touch," "Shake Something," "The Circle," "Turn Around," "Circle Game," "Left and Right," "Be My Friend," "Change," and "What Do People Do?"

● ● ●

Learning Basic Skills Through Music, by Hap Palmer
Volume I (Black Jacket) AR 514 or AC 514, Spanish Version AR 531 or AC 519, Grades K-2.

Numbers, colors, the alphabet, and body awareness are all presented in a happy, rhythmic teaching program. Preschoolers and early primary children from all backgrounds can participate with success. Songs include "Colors," "Marching Around the Alphabet," "Put Your Hands Up in the Air," "The Number March," "Growing," "This Is the Way We Get in the Morning," "Birds," "What Are You Wearing?" "The Elephant," and "What Is Your Name?"

● ● ●

Learning Basic Skills Through Music, by Hap Palmer
Volume II (Red Jacket) AR 522 or AC 522, Spanish Version AC 632 or AC 632, Grades K-2.

The popular Hal Palmer style continues with this cheerful recording that includes game songs that teach about colors, numbers to 20, subtraction, and telling time. There are also two reading-readiness game songs. The songs include "Lucky Numbers," "Parade of Colors," "Paper Clocks," "Triangle, Circle, or Square," "Take Away," "Something That Begins Like," "One Shape, Three Shapes," "Partners," "Let's Hide the Tambourine," and "Let's Dance."

● ● ●

Sensorimotor Training in the Classroom, by Linda Williams and Donna Wemple
Volume 1, AR 532 or AC 532, Grades K-3.

This well-rounded selection of perceptual activities helps to develop directionality, basic movement, physical fitness, ocular training, and auditory discrimination. Included are songs, cheers, folk music, chants, popular music, and poems. Everything is suited for use in the limited space of a classroom.

Volume 2, AR 566 or AC 566, Grades K-3.

Focusing on new and appealing activities, Volume 2 helps to develop form perception, listening skills, body awareness, physical fitness, and coordination.

Relaxation

Quiet Places, Instrumental Music for Rest and Relaxation, by Hap Palmer
AR 689 or AC 689, CD 689, Grades K-5.

Here is a calming alternative to our fast-paced age of technology. This collection of all original instrumental music composed by Hap Palmer features the natural sounds of acoustic instruments such as harp, violin, viola, cello, flute, oboe, bassoon, clarinet, acoustic guitar, classical guitar, piano, and French horn. The guide includes a listing of the instruments used with each song as well as pictures of the featured instruments. Valuable for rest time, slow stretching, yoga, mirroring, and tension and release of specific muscle groups, the collection also serves as an introduction to the orchestra. These melodies, played with a variety of soothing sounds, will appeal to listeners of all ages. The songs evoke a tapestry of tranquil images as the titles suggest: ''Star Gazing,'' ''Snowfall,'' ''Twilight Sea,'' ''Misty Moonlight,'' ''Peaceful Cove,'' ''Smooth Sailing,'' ''Awakening,'' ''A Tender Moment,'' ''Sierra Sunrise,'' ''Fern River,'' ''Serenity,'' and ''Touching Clouds.''

• • •

Sea Gulls-Music for Rest and Relaxation, by Hap Palmer
AR 584 or AC 594, Grades K-4.

Teachers will find the record useful for slow motion activities, story time, and whenever soothing music is appropriate. The songs are ''Savannah,'' ''Sea Gulls,'' ''Noonie's Lullaby,'' ''Summer Rain,'' ''Misty Canyon,'' ''Morning Gold,'' ''Sweetwater Springs,'' and more.

Movement Exploration

Creative Movement and Rhythmic Exploration, by Hap Palmer
AR 533 or AC 533, Grades K-3.

Creative movement, mimetics, and basic skills are brought together with exciting songs that provide actions, images, and challenges that children can work on in their own ways (without demonstration). Lyrics explore ways to move, shapes, sounds, and colors. The songs are ''Moving Game,'' ''Fishing Trip,'' ''Colored Ribbons,'' ''Teacher Who Couldn't Talk,'' ''Percussion Instruments,'' ''Grandpa,'' ''Fast and Slow March,'' ''Out to the Country,'' and ''How Many Ways.'' Part 2 consists of instrumental versions of these songs.

• • •

Mod Marches, by Hap Palmer
AR 527 or AC 527, Grades K-3.

Collections of well-known tunes set to march tempos. March figures are included in the guide, progressing from easy to more difficult. The songs are ''It's a Small World,'' ''Yellow Submarine,'' ''Gentle on My Mind,'' ''Penny Lane,'' ''Happy Together,'' ''Love Is Blue,'' ''Ob-La-Di, Ob-La-Da,'' ''Sgt. Pepper's Lonely Hearts Club Band,'' ''Lodi,'' and ''Let It Be.''

• • •

Movin', by Hap Palmer
AR 546 or AC 546, Grades K-2.

A fully instrumental variety of musical moods, from symphony to rock and from classical to pop, make this an album that makes students want to move, explore, create, interpret, and enjoy themselves. The songs are ''Movin','' ''Funky Penguin,'' ''Midnight Moon,'' ''Tipsy,'' ''Enter Sunlight,'' ''Jamaican Holiday,'' and ''Far East Blues.''

Thinking Skills

Feelin' Free: A Personalized Approach to Vocabulary and Language Development, by Hap Palmer
AR 517 or AC 517, Grades K-2.

Games, movement, and music are combined to help students think, put together, and use language to describe people, places, situations, numbers, and more. The songs are ''Bumpity Bump,'' ''Who Wants to Touch and Be Touched?,'' ''Feelin' Free,'' ''Rockin' Hula,'' ''It's Just Fun,'' ''Pat-Pat,'' ''Make Up a Name,'' ''Numbers Can Tell a Lot About You,'' ''Questions I,'' and ''Questions II.''

• • •

Ideas, Thoughts, and Feelings, by Hap Palmer
AR 549 or AC 549, Grades K-2.

Provides experiences for discovery, problem solving, and independent thinking. All children will gain confidence as they respond to Hap's catchy questions. The songs are ''Everybody Has Feelings,'' ''Can You Guess What I Am?,'' ''Building Bridges,'' ''Find a Way,'' ''Follow Along,'' ''I Like Me,'' ''Letter Sounds (A-M and N-Z),'' ''Move Around the Room,'' ''Making Friends,'' ''I Don't Like Me,'' and ''Things I'm Thankful For.''

Rhythms

Children's All-Time Rhythm Favorites, by Jack Capon & Rosemary Hallum, Ph.D.
AR 630 or AC 630, Grades K-3.

Wonderful favorite children's dances and singing games, both old and new, that will never go out of style. Easy to learn and fun to do. Fits right in with early childhood core curriculum, physical fitness objectives, and multicultural goals. Useful for ESL. The songs are ''Hokey Pokey,'' ''Dance Little Bird,'' ''Patty Cake Polka,'' ''Chicken Fat,'' ''La Raspa,'' ''Dancin' Duck,'' ''Magic Ball,'' ''Limbo,'' ''Bunny Hop,'' ''If You're Happy,'' and more!

• • •

Motor Fitness Rhythm Games, by Jack Capon & Rosemary Hallum, Ph.D.
AR 97 or AC 97, Grades K-3.

The activities are designed for simplicity so that students and teachers can do them easily and well, with positive feelings and a high success rate. At the same time, they help build motor fitness and psychomotor coordination. The songs are ''Pink Panther,'' ''Ice Castles Theme,'' ''All Aboard!,'' ''Person to Person,'' ''Cowboy Slap Game,'' ''Whole Lotta Shakin','' ''Mr. Motor Mouth,'' ''Happy Sticks,'' and more!

• • •

Perceptual-Motor Rhythm Games, by Jack Capon & Rosemary Hallum, Ph.D. with special material by Henry ''Buzz'' Glass
AR 50 or AC 50, Grades K-3.

Perceptual motor experiences are combined with fun-filled ''learning through movement'' activities set to appropriate music. All games have been field tested for effectiveness in many different schools and workshops. Easy to introduce to your class, the activities do not require partners or constant teacher direction (the leader may be a paraprofessional, parent, or student). The songs are ''Love Is Blue,'' ''Hey, Look Me Over,'' ''Wheels,'' ''Electronic Music,'' ''Raindrops Keep Falling on My Head,'' ''Shoemakers Dance,'' ''Miss Frenchy Brown,'' and more!

• • •

Rhythms on Parade, by Hap Palmer
AR 633 or AC 633, Grades K-2.

Celebrate the joys of rhythm with this unique collection of songs. Children explore basic musical concepts through a colorful assortment of playful images. The songs are ''Rhythms on Parade,'' ''Woodpecker,'' ''Jingle Bell Bees,'' ''Five,'' ''Tap Your Sticks,'' ''Bean Bag Shake,'' ''The Mice Go Marching,'' ''Sounds Around the World,'' ''Mother Goose Has Rhythmical Rhymes,'' ''Kris Kringle's Jingle Bell Band,'' and ''Roller Coaster.''

• • •

This Is Rhythm, by Ella Jenkins
AR 45028 or AC 45028, Grades 2-6.

This recording helps youngsters hear rhythm in everyday sounds and introduces wood and tone blocks, rhythm sticks, conga drums, maracas, and five other instruments. Songs include: ''Let's Build a Rhythm,'' ''Hear That Train,'' ''Mexican Hand Clapping Song,'' ''Little Red Caboose,'' ''My Dog Has Fleas,'' and more!

Manipulatives

Rhythm Stick Activities, by Henry ''Buzz'' Glass & Rosemary Hallum, Ph. D. with special materials by Jack Capon
AR 55 or AC 55, Grades K-3.

Used creatively, rhythm sticks, whether they be rolled up newspapers, cardboard tubes, or short wooden dowel sticks, can help children develop perceptual motor skills. This recording and manual provide music, directions, and new ideas for using rhythm sticks. Activities include gross and fine movements, body image, following directions, and coordination skills. Songs include ''Do Your Own Thing,'' ''Basketball Style,'' ''Shoemaker Dance,'' ''Come Play the Stick Games, African Style,'' ''Stick Jive,'' ''Puppet Dance,'' ''Circle Follow the Leader,'' ''Pass the Stick,'' and more!

• • •

Streamer and Ribbon Activities, by Henry ''Buzz'' Glass & Jack Capon
AR 578 or AC 578. Complete Kit (Cassette, Guide, and 12 Ribbon wands is Set 578, Grades 1-6.)

This new approach to the traditional Chinese Ribbon Dance combines modern, folk, and soul music with the excitement and beauty of flowing streamers. There are over 10 activities that you can easily adapt to the needs of students preschool and up, including students with special challenges and the gifted. These activities do not require the use of partners, thus allowing individuality to surface. Children thoroughly enjoy these innovative physical experiences, which exercise the entire body. If you do not have streamers, you can make them by attaching various lengths (depending on size and skill of students) of 1 to 1-1/2'' width crepe paper to paper towel holders or wooden dowels 15 inches in length.

Action Games

It's Action Time-Let's Move!, by Henry ''Buzz'' Glass
AR 79 or AC 79, Grades K-3.

This record features happy singing action activities that give opportunities for creativity, movement exploration, and sensory motor activities. Directions are easy to follow. Vocals and music are on one side; the other side has music only and is adaptable to use of manipulatives.

● ● ●

Rainy Day Record, by Henry "Buzz" Glass & Rosemary Hallum, Ph.D.
AR 553 or AC 553, Grades K-3.

Educationally sound, "sure fire" classroom-tested activities that really involve the children. Included are action songs, games, clapping games, chanting, dances, and participation stories. Activities range from active to calming and can be done sitting, standing in place, or moving. Brief teaching directions are on the record. Children enjoy the *Rainy Day Record* activities so much that they want to do them even on sunny days! The songs are "It's Raining," "Go-Go," "Saturday Johnny," "Move It Now," and more.

Dance

Around the World in Dance, New Folk Dances for Early Childhood, by Henry "Buzz" Glass & Rosemary Hale, Ph.D.
AR 542 or AC 542, Grades K-3.

Includes a variety of dance experiences for the young child. Fresh, lively, and easy to teach, children from all environments will enjoy these dances with their different accents and vibrations that represent a living heritage of our cultural blend. The songs are: "Hornpipe," "Mowrah Cawkah," "Cherkessia," "Hokey Pokey," "Cissy, Come Dance With Me," "Rabbit and the Fox," and "Bingo."

● ● ●

Get Ready to Square Dance, by Jack Capon & Rosemary Hallum, Ph.D.
AR 68 or AC 68, Grades K-3.

Students learn the fundamentals of square dance and the value of listening, following directions, cooperation, taking turns, and rhythmic response. Eight easy, pleasant songs and movement games teach only one or two basic calls at a time, allowing gradual mastery. Once learned, all the basic calls are used in two simple, complete square dances. Songs include: "Cotton-Eyed Joe," "Oh Belinda," "Turkey in the Straw," "Shoo Fly," "Irish Washer-Woman," "Comin' Round the Mountain," "Hinkey Dinkey," and "Captain Jinks."

● ● ●

Learning by Doing, Dancing, and Discovering, by Henry "Buzz" Glass
AR 76, Grades K-3.

A variety of proven dances that are easily taught, fun to do physically, musically exciting, and innovative. Movement, body image, ethnic appreciation, spatial awareness, and social growth are the objectives of this album.

Fingerplays and Handplays

Clap, Snap, and Tap, by Ambrose "Braz" Brazelton in cooperation with Gabe DeSantis
AR 48 or AC 48, Grades 3-6.

Motor activities stimulate the sensorimotor growth of elementary school youngsters. These activities are geared for classrooms and need little space. Various types of music are utilized to motivate the students. Finger snapping, rhythmic hand and arm movements, finger exercises, cooperative cross hand patting, and various other exercises are included with songs such as "Clap-Snap-Pat," "Hand Jive," "Pattycake Partners," "Marching Fingers," "Pound and Resound," and other patterning activities.

● ● ●

Finger Games, by Linda Williams & Donna Wemple
AR 506, Grades K-3.

Rhythmic verses combined with hand motions are designed for enjoyment by all children. Complete instructions for activities are on the record. Songs include: "Ten Little Soldiers," "Here's a Cup," "Look at Me," "Knock-Knock," "Grandmother's Glasses," "Carpenter," and "Open Them-Shut Them."

● ● ●

Fingerplay Fun!, by Rosemary Hallum, Ph.D.
AR 529 or AC 529, Grades K-3.

Fingerplays are fun and also help children develop finger-hand coordination and auditory sequencing and memory. Traditional fingerplays from folk heritage as well as new fingerplays are included. Complete, easy-to-follow directions are given on the record. The guide includes words, directions, and suggestions for extending the fingerplays to creative dramatics, flannelboard, rhythms, and art. Songs and themes include: "Stop-Look and Listen" (Safety), "My Hands Upon My Head" (Body Parts), "Five Little Chickadees" (Counting/Subtraction), "Open Them-Shut Them" (Traditional), "Eency Weency Spider" (Singing Game), and more!

● ● ●

Fingerplays and Footplays for Fun and Learning, by Rosemary Hallum, Ph.D. & Henry "Buzz" Glass
AR 618 or AC 618, Grades K-3.

These charming fingerplays and footplays are fun to do with children. A combination of traditional and new, all activities are presented in a bright, up-to-date style with original music. They are valuable for fine motor coordination, memory training, and oral language development. Directions are on the recording, so the activities are easy to learn and are helpful for students learning to speak English. Songs include: "Penguins," "Two Little Blackbirds,"

"Footplay," "Peanut Butter," "New Pease Porridge Hot," "I'm a Little Teapot," "The Wheels on the Bus," "Five Little Monkeys," "New Shoes," "I Have Ten Little Fingers," "Johnny Work With One Hammer," and "Where Is Thumbkin?"

• • •

Hand Jivin', by Jill Gallina & Michael Gallina, M.A., Consultant
AR 95 or AC 95, Grades 3-6.

Stimulating activities help develop finger, hand, and arm dexterity and coordination. The original upbeat music encourages children to respond enthusiastically to a variety of body coordination activities and it enhances body awareness, eye-hand coordination, auditory perception, auditory memory, and patterning. The fun songs include: "Hand Jivin'," "Hand Rag," "Clap Your Hands to a Groovy Beat," "Finger Play Songs," "The Mirror Game," "Our Two Hands," "Making Pizza," and more!

Fitness Activities

Aerobics Dances for Kids, by Henry "Buzz" Glass & Rosemary Hallum, Ph.D.
AR 93 or AC 93, Grades K-3.

Students begin with a warm-up to increase their heart rates to a training level. The dancing then maintains the elevated heart rate. Between dances are suggested movement activities that lead to the next dance. A final cool-down then reduces the heart rates. Music with voice cues is on one side of the record, and music only is on the other side. An illustrated manual with easy-to-follow directions is included. Songs are: "The Little Man From Mars," "Four Wall Game," "Kangaroo," "Jumping Little Jerry," "Walking the Square," "Jello," "Scarecrows," "Fiddle Around," "Popcorn," "Scritchy Scratchy," "The Child Is Down," "Reach for It," and more!

• • •

Fitness Fun for Everyone, by Arden Jervey
HYR 24, Grades K-3.

Many activities are set to simple, appealing, well-known melodies that children instinctively enjoy. Clear and concise instructions are followed by song-and-action activities designed to develop legs, arms, shoulders, waist, abdomen, feet, and back. One side has music only. A completely illustrated manual is provided.

• • •

Get Fit While You Sit, by Ambrose "Braz" Brazelton with Gabe DeSantis
AR 516 or AC 516, Grades 3-6.

This album provides muscle strengthening, fitness, and coordination activities that can be done at a desk.

The material is presented in a manner that enhances listening skills, auditory perception, and memory. A complete, illustrated manual is included.

Combinations

Individualization in Movement and Music, by Henry "Buzz" Glass & Rosemary Hallum, Ph.D. (Edith Hom Newhart, Consultant)
AR 49 or AC 49, Grades K-3.

Action songs, chants, games, dances, story, and drama provide group activities with individual student responses. The actions stress rhythm, movement, perceptual development, basic locomotor activities, directionality, body control, and readiness. Action songs: "The Saints Go Marching In," "Tinker Tinker Doo," "Call It Macaroni."
Games: Statue Game, Mirror Game.
Chants: "Foot Stomping," "Digga-Do."
Dances: "Follow and Go Back," "La Raspa," and "The Bottle."
Story Drama: "Little Red Fox."

Kimbo Educational

P.O. Box 477
Long Branch, NJ 07740
800-631-2187

Readiness Skills

Toes Up, Toes Down (Pre K-2)
KIM 7041 or 7041C

Kids will love these activities set to upbeat music filled with lively sound effects. Activities will help children develop body identification, rhythm, listening skills, and more. Songs include "Toot," "Jollywonks," "Jumping Jacks," and others.

Expressive Skills

Animal Walks
KIM 9107 or 9107C

Every animal has its very own special walk that kids love to imitate. *Animal Walks* appeals to young imaginations and provides fun ways to exercise and stretch.

• • •

Make Believe in Movement, by Maya Doray
KIM 0500C

Stimulate imagination through creative expression, stories, and music. This recording encourages children to pantomime a bouncing ball, stretching pizza dough, an elevator, a cloud, and a ghost.

Rhythms

Rhythms for Basic Motor Skills
KIM 9074 or 9074C

This recording will help children learn basic rhythms and tempos as they practice seven motor skills: skip, hop, gallop, jump, tiptoe, waltz, and march.

Manipulatives

Bean Bags

Bean Bag Activities
KIM 7055 or 7055C
ACC 7055 Bean Bags

Join the bean bag activities in all these wonderful activities. Songs are "Bean Bag Parade," "How Many Ways Can You Carry a Bean Bag?," "Bean Bag Rock," and others. Join in the fun with these easy-to-do games and dances by Georgiana Stewart.

• • •

Bean Bag Fun
KIM 2018 or 2018C

A fun-filled series of games and activities that develop coordination, rhythm, and listening skills. Slower tempos make these activities ideal for preschool, K-3, and special students. Activities include Tom Tom Bean Bag, On the March, Bean Bag Carousel, Beanie's Song, and more.

• • •

Me and My Bean Bag
KIM 9111 or 9111C

Don't just pass that bean bag—balance it, juggle it, toss it, dance with it! Team up with your bean bag "friend" for fun and creative exercise. Do "The Mexican Hat Dance," "Bean Bag Hop," "Bean Bag Pretend," "Bean Bag Boogie," "Bean Bag Toss," and many more bean bag activities.

Rhythm and Lummi Sticks

Disco Lummi Stick Activities
KMS 2035
Side A English
Cara B Espanol Narracion
By Georgiana Liccione Stewart

Georgiana Stewart provides a fun variety of lummi stick activities accompanied by the sound of disco. Directions are in English and Spanish.

• • •

Disco Rhythm Stick Activities
KIM 2035 or 2035C

Popular rhythm stick activities for middle grades are provided on this recording. Songs include "The Hokey Pokey Disco," "Copacabana," "We Go Together," "Mr. Bojangles," and more.

• • •

Lively Music for Rhythm Stick Fun
KIM 2000 or 2000C

ACC 2000 (sticks)

Bright tempos and challenging rhythm stick patterns make this recording ideal for grades 4 through 6. Songs can be used individually or in groups, and include "12th Street Rag," "LeRoy Brown," "Alley Cat," and "I Believe in Music."

• • •

Multicultural Rhythm Stick Fun, by Georgiana Stewart
KIM 9128 or 9128C

Authentic folk tunes and popular songs from around the world provide the setting for easy, enjoyable rhythm stick activities. The activities help children develop their coordination and motor skills. The styles of music are as varied as the countries they come from. For ages 3 to 7, this recording offers routines set to music from Vietnam, Russia, Puerto Rico, Japan, Uganda, West Africa, China, Greece, Israel, and many other countries.

• • •

Puili-Hawaiian Rhythm Sticks
KIM 7046 or 7046C
ACC 7046 (sticks)

Unusual rhythm stick activities are combined with enchanting island music. Individual and partner routines are set to songs such as "Hukilau," "Enchanted Island," and "Lanakila."

Rhythm Sticks for Kids
KIM 2014 or 2014C

This is a collection of rhythm stick activities by Laura Johnson. Students in preschool through grade 3 tap out easy rhythm stick routines as they develop coordination and motor skills. Twelve exciting activities are provided with music from such shows as "Fame," "Electric Company," "The Flintstones," "Strawberry Shortcake," "The Smurfs," and more.

• • •

Simplified Rhythm Stick Activities
KIM 2015 or 2015C
ACC 2015 (sticks)

Ever-popular rhythm stick activities for preschool through grade 3 develop motor skills and coordination. Songs include "Sesame Street," "The Wizard of Oz," "It's a Small, Small World," "Mickey Mouse March," and "Chicken Fat."

Parachutes

Chute the Works
KEA 9095 or 9095C

Designed for students with previous parachute experience, these exercises progress from easy to more challenging skills. Activities such as the twist, the bump, the grapevine, call ball, chute soccer, and chute ball are played to songs that include "In the Mood," "I Can See Clearly Now," "Saint Louis Blues," and "Yesterday."

• • •

Parachute Activities With Folk Dance Music
KEA 9090 or 9090C

Parachute activities are intertwined with folk dance steps. Authentic folk dance music includes "Irish Washerwoman," "La Raspa," "Mayim Mayim," "Seljancica," and "Pop Goes the Weasel."

• • •

Parachute Roundup (3-6)
KIM 7044 or 7044C

Gallop, lasso, stomp, and swing to popular country tunes with simple steps. The upbeat routines are designed for use with a 12-foot or 24-foot parachute. Tunes include "Cotton-Eyed Joe," "Nine to Five," "Thank God I'm a Country Boy," "On the Road Again," and more.

• • •

Playtime Parachute Fun
KIM 7056 or 7056C

Children learn teamwork and develop their gross motor skills as they practice playing various parachute routines. Songs by Jill Gallina include "Parachute Rollerball," "Parachute Pow Wow," and "Floating Cloud."

• • •

Pop Rock Parachute (3-6)
KEA 6025 or 6025C

Parachute games include Circle Tug-O-War, Row the Boat, Bubble Squash, Bombs Away, Bubble House, and Disappear. Exciting routines develop strength, endurance, and flexibility.

• • •

Rhythmic Parachute Play
KEA 6020 or 6020C

Ideal for all ages, this is a favorite parachute play recording. Parachute activities such as umbrella, mountain, and mushroom are played to songs like "Windmills of Your Mind," "Pink Panther," "76 Trombones," "Fly Me to the Moon," and "What the World Needs Now."

Others

Ball, Hoop, and Ribbon Activities for Young Children
KIM 8016 or 8016C

Children ages 4 to 8 will enjoy these fun, easy routines using balls, hoops, and ribbons. The routines are set to popular movie themes and familiar classical music. Instructions for homemade equipment are included. Songs include the themes from *E.T.* and *Chariots of Fire*, "Ding Dong the Witch Is Dead," "Tomorrow," and more.

• • •

Have a Ball
KIM 0835 or 0835C

Original games and songs by Jill and Michael Gallina set the tone for exciting ball-playing activities. Ball-handling skills and motor coordination can be developed even in limited spaces. Hot Potato, Roly Poly, Loop Ball, Team Ball Pass, The Name Game, and Mash the Trash are a few of the ball activities included.

• • •

Stretch Loops for Sensory Learning
KIM 7057C
ACC 7057 (loops)

Stretch, jump, and exercise with easy-to-use stretch loops. Children develop coordination and motor skills while practicing routines to songs such as "Stretch Bounce," "High and Wide," and "Jump the Loop."

Action Games

Children's Games
KIM 9068 or 9068C

"Musical Chairs," "Statues," "Follow the Leader," "Through the Gates of Town," and other active songs comprise this wonderful recreational/party recording that children will love.

• • •

Homemade Games and Activities
KIM 9106 or 9106C

Children will learn not only to play games to music, but also to actually create their own fun items such as newspaper balls, cardboard flute tubes, juice can rattles, and bean bags. "The Alphabet Rag," "Puppet Pals," "Rooty-Toot-Toot," and "Peter Hammers" are a few of the many songs included.

Dance

All-Time Favorite Dances
KIM 9126 or 9126C
KMS 9126 or 9126C (Spanish)
Video KV 100V (English)
Video KVS 200V (Spanish)

This is a great collection of dynamic popular dances. The steps are easy and fun. Dances that do not involve partners are great for many settings, such as birthday parties, preschool, and adult gatherings. Included are the Bunny Hop, Alley Cat, Hokey Pokey, Virginia Reel, Hora, Conga, Chicken, Twist, Cotton Eyed Joe, the Mexican Hat Dance, and more!

• • •

Disco for Kids
KIM 7035 or 7035C

This is a sequenced approach to disco that presents easy rhythms to great disco sounds. Kids can't help dancing to ''Heel Twist Hustle,'' ''Knock Knee Bump,'' ''Slow Stomp,'' and more.

• • •

Get Ready to Square Dance (K-6)
EA 68 or EA 68C

Easy song and movement games teach square dance patterns to the beginning dancer. These songs are ''Honor Your Partner,'' ''On Belinda,'' ''Turkey in the Straw,'' ''Shoo Fly,'' ''Irish Washer Woman,'' ''Comin' Round the Mountain,'' ''Hinkey Dinkey, Parlez-Voux,'' and ''Tie a Yellow Ribbon.'' On these songs there is enough wait time for students to move and respond to the calls.

• • •

Heel, Toe, Away We Go (K-3)
KIM 7050 or 7050C

Students can improve coordination skills through familiar and easy folk dance patterns. Songs include ''Sailor's Hornpipe,'' ''Glow Worm,'' ''Little Brown Jug,'' ''Polly Wolly Doodle,'' ''Shortnin' Bread,'' and more.

• • •

Simple Folk Dances
KIM 07042 or 07042C

The slow-paced, motivational folk dances are fun and easy to learn, and are ideal for preschool and special learners. The Danish Dance of Greeting, Chimes of Dunkirk, Shoemakers Dance, Bleking, and Hansel and Gretel are just a few examples of the delightful dances included in this recording.

Fitness Activities

Aerobics

The Aerobic Express for Kids
KIM 9092C

All aboard! It's the Aerobic Express to fitness via music and rhythmic routines. Grades 2 to 5 will enjoy the easy-to-learn activities set in the classroom or gymnasium.

• • •

Aerobics for Kids
KIM 7043 or 7043C

Fitness made fun! A vigorous 18-minute program for children in the lower and middle elementary grades. This recording includes warm-ups, conditioning exercises, endurance activities, and cool-down. ''Slow Down Mama,'' ''Funky Fiesta,'' ''Flying Wedge,'' and ''Bouncing Back to You'' are a few of the songs on this recording.

• • •

Aerobics U.S.A. (Pre K-3)
KIM 8065 or 8065C

Warm up and work out to the music of Bruce Springsteen. These exciting sounds motivate one to jog, jump, stretch, and skip across the USA. Simple exercise patterns can be followed by all ages. ''Born in the USA,'' ''Glory Days,'' ''Born to Run,'' ''Be All That You Can Be,'' and ''Dancing in the Street'' are a few of the songs on this recording.

• • •

Jacki Sorensen's Aerobic Club for Kids
KIM 1230 or 1230C

Sorensen offers a fitness sport anyone can play! This recording includes warm-ups, strength exercises, aerobics, and stretching exercises. Follow Sorensen through ''Ghostbusters,'' ''Girls Just Want to Have Fun,'' ''Hands Up,'' ''Footloose,'' ''The A-Team,'' and many more high-spirited, motivational routines.

• • •

Jump Aerobics
KIM 2095 or 2095C

Exciting routines combine dance, aerobic exercise, and rope jumping. Improve skills such as balance, strength, coordination, and flexibility while moving to tunes such as ''Nine to Five,'' ''Thank God I'm a Country Boy,'' and ''Mr. Bojangles.''

• • •

Preschool Aerobic Fun (Pre K-3)
KIM 7052 or 7052C

Exciting musical activities encourage warm-ups, stretches, vigorous activities, and a cool-down. Typical easy-to-follow sing-along songs are ''Wake Up, Warm Up,'' ''Hot Diggity,'' ''Finger,'' and ''Poppin'.''

Exercise

Get a Good Start (Pre K-3)
KIM 7054 or 7054C

Start each day with aerobic activities ideal for very young children. Short, simple, fun activities include Warm-Up Time, Jumping Jack, Bendable, Stretchable, I Can Do More, and others.

• • •

Good Morning Exercises for Kids (Pre K-3) by Georgiana Stewart
KIM 9098 or 9098

Clap, stretch, skip, and move into a great morning. Every song has a morning theme to inspire children to exercise. Enjoy all-time favorites such as "Oh What a Beautiful Morning," "Carolina in the Morning," "Red, Red Robin," and "Oh How I Hate to Get Up in the Morning!" Exercises are short, simple, and fun.

• • •

Rock'n'roll Fitness Fun
KIM 9115 or 9115C

Georgiana Stewart entices children of all ages to exercise to the "oldies but goodies" of the 50s and 60s. "Rock Around the Clock," "Let the Good Times Roll," and "At the Hop" are a few of the songs included.

• • •

A Thriller for Kids: Dynamic Fitness Activities (K-6)
KIM 7065 or 7065C

This is a fun and complete 20-minute workout that includes a variety of easy-to-learn fitness exercises. Warm-ups, stretches, jogging, and cool-down feature the Michael Jackson hits including "Beat It," "Billie Jean," and "Thriller." Other known tunes are "Flashdance," "Footloose," "Dancin'," and others.

Combinations

Fun Activities for Perceptual Motor Skills
KIM 9071 or 9071C

This is a favorite recording that aids in motor skill development. Simple rhythm games, clapping, hand shakes, easy dance steps, and finger exercises are included in the songs such as "Sneaky Snake," "Ukulele Man," "Ease on Down the Road," and more.

• • •

Preschool Favorites, by Georgiana Stewart
KIM 9122 or 9122C

Fun-filled learning is packed into this collection of rhythmic activities taken from Stewart's most popular recordings. Kids will love these hits from *Bean Bag Activities*, *Children's Games*, *Shapes in Action*, *Folk Dance Fun*, and others.

Curriculum Material Producers and Equipment Suppliers

This chapter lists sources for curriculum materials and physical education equipment. It can serve as a resource for all your physical education class needs. Sources are grouped by the following 10 categories:

- Equipment
- Films and Videos
- Information Sources
- Music
- Publications
- Combination Publishers/Video or Equipment Suppliers
- Software
- Testing Programs
- Training and Certification
- Miscellaneous

Equipment

ABC School Supply, Inc.
3312 North Berkeley Lake Rd.
PO Box 100019
Duluth, GA 30136-9419
800-669-4ABC

Grades K-6. Various educational products, such as puzzles, games, music, playground equipment, etc.

• • •

Abilitations-Sportime
One Sportime Way
Atlanta, GA 30340-1402
800-283-5700

Equipment to encourage and improve motor movements

• • •

Accusplit, Inc.
Sports Timing Division
2990A Ringwood Ave.
San Jose, CA 95131
800-538-9750

Fitness equipment and testing

• • •

ADA Racquets
3904 Clark
Kansas City, MO 64111
800-234-0460

Rackets for various sports

• • •

Advance Athletic Equipment, Inc.
PO Box 3187
Central Point, OR 97502
503-777-6870

Sport flooring

• • •

All American Recreation
1290 73rd Ave. NE
Minneapolis, MN 55432
612-572-8000

Playground and park equipment

• • •

American Athletic, Inc.
200 American Ave.
Jefferson, IA 50129
800-247-3978

Youth fitness and recreation products

• • •

Aquatic Access, Inc.
417 Dorsey Way
Louisville, KY 40223
800-325-LIFT

Aquatic access lifts for pools and spas

• • •

AstroTurf Industries
727 Goddard Ave.
Chesterfield, MO 63005

800-358-8553

Turf for batting cages, golf mats, dugouts, etc.

● ● ●

Bill Fritz Sports Corp.
125 N. Salem St.
Apex, NC 27502
919-362-1748

Various physical education supplies

● ● ●

Brewer's Ledge
34 Brookley Road
Jamaica Plain, MA 02130
617-983-5244

Manufactures a rock climbing simulator

● ● ●

BUKA
20710 Manhattan Place, Suite 104
Torrance, CA 90501
800-683-4100

Grades K-12. Balls to increase eye-foot coordination

● ● ●

Chime Time Movement Products
2440-C Pleasantdale Road
Atlanta, GA 30340-1562
800-477-5075

Grades K-2. Products to develop movement

● ● ●

Concept II, Inc.
RR1, Box 1100
Morrisville, VT 05661
100-245-5676

Fitness equipment and testing

● ● ●

COSOM Sporting Goods
Mantua Industries, Inc.
Grandview Ave.
PO Box 10
Woodbury Heights, NJ 08097
609-853-0300

Family games and sporting equipment

● ● ●

Courtime U.S.A.
PO Box 1257
21 Denise St.
Sag Harbor, NY 11963
516-725-9049

Racquet sport court equipment and pro shop supplies

● ● ●

Cramer Products, Inc.
153 W. Warren St.
Gardner, KS 66030
913-884-7511

Physical education products

● ● ●

Creative Health Products
7621 E. Joy Rd.
Ann Arbor, MI 48105
313-996-5900

Exercise equipment and fitness and health testing products

● ● ●

Cybex
2100 Smithtown Ave.
PO Box 9003
Ronkonkoma, Long Island, NY 11779-9003
800-645-5392

Fitness products including strength training, cardiovascular, testing, and rehabilitation systems

● ● ●

Dayton Racquet Co., Inc.
302 S. Albright St.
PO Box 12
Arcanum, OH 45304
513-692-8556

Steel rackets

● ● ●

Delmer F. Harris Co., Inc.
517 Broadway
Concordia, KS 66901
913-243-3321

Exercise and playground equipment

● ● ●

Dinoflex Manufacturing Ltd.
PO Box 3309
Salmon Arm, British Columbia
CANADA V1E 4S1
604-832-7780

Athletic and playground surfaces

● ● ●

Douglas Sport Nets & Equipment Co.
3441 S. 11th Ave.
Eldridge, IA 52748
800-553-8907

Sport nets and equipment

• • •

Dudley/Spalding Sports
521 Meadow St.
Chicopee, MA 01021
800-523-5387

Softball equipment

• • •

Dynamic Fitness Equipment
PO Box 2866
Livonia, MI 48151
313-425-2862

Weight-lifting equipment

• • •

Edwards Sports Products
429 E. Haddam-Moodus Rd.
Moodus, CT 06469
800-243-2512

Tennis court equipment

• • •

Exercycle Corp.
667 Providence St.
Woonsocket, RI 02895
401-769-7160

Fitness equipment and testing

• • •

Ex-U-Rope, Inc./Funtastic Creations
73 Williamsville Road
Hubbardston, MA 01452
508-928-5388

Jump ropes and simple educational toys

• • •

Fisher Athletic
2060 Cauble Rd.
Salisbury, NC 28144
704-636-5713

Equipment for physical education and athletics

• • •

Fitness First
6045 Martway St., #110
Shawnee Mission, KS 66201
800-421-1791

Exercise equipment, music, and videos

• • •

Fitness Wholesale
895 Hampshire Road
Cuyahoga Falls, OH 44224
800-537-5512

Fitness equipment, charts, music, videos, etc.

• • •

Fit Nest
PO Box 2178
San Leandro, CA 94577
800-288-BFIT

Fitness equipment and testing

• • •

Fitter International, Inc.
PO Box 906
Osburn, ID 83849-0906
800-FITTER-1

Balance and coordination equipment

• • •

Flaghouse, Inc.
150 N. MacQueen Parkway
Mount Vernon, NY 10550
800-793-7900

Distributor of athletic and recreational products

• • •

Future Pro, Inc.
200 N. Main
Inman, KS 67546
316-585-2364

Basketball equipment

• • •

George Santelli, Inc.
465 South Dean St.
Englewood, NJ 07631
201-871-3105

Fencing equipment

• • •

Gerstung/Gym-Thing, Inc.
6308 Blair Hill Lane
Baltimore, MD 21209
800-922-3575

Grades K-12. Inventive equipment for skill building

• • •

Gibson, Inc.
2618 S. Raritan
Englewood, CO 80110
303-937-1012

Gymnastic products

• • •

Gopher Sport
120 Oakdale St.
Owatonna, MN 55060
507-451-3880

Various sport supplies and equipment

● ● ●

Great Lakes Sports
2921 13th St.
Menominee, MI 49858
906-863-5797

Sporting goods and playground/physical education equipment

● ● ●

Greg Larson Sports
PO Box 567
Brainerd, MN 56401
800-950-3320

Physical education equipment

● ● ●

GSC Sports
PO Box 7726
Dallas, TX 75209
800-527-7510

Grades K-12. Athletic and physical education supplies

● ● ●

Gym Closet
2511 Leach Road
Rochester Hills, MI 48309
800-445-8873

Athletic and physical education equipment

● ● ●

Gym Equipment Co., Inc.
198 PineLynn Drive
Ridgewood, NJ 07452
201-447-2884

Ivanko barbell free weight products and safety equipment for working out alone; muscle dynamic fitness equipment

● ● ●

HL Corporation
PO Box 3327
Manhattan Beach, CA 90266
800-HL-SPORT

Equipment for racquet sports

● ● ●

HydraFitness Industries
120 Industrial Blvd.
Sugar Land, TX 77478
800-433-3111

Fitness equipment and testing

● ● ●

Illinois Juggling Institute

143 N. Pershing
Bensenville, IL 60106
800-766-1437

Instructional juggling supplies

● ● ●

Iron Mountain Forge Corp.
One Iron Mountain Drive
PO Box 897
Farmington, MO 63640
800-325-8828

Commercial park and playground structures

● ● ●

Jayfro Corp.
976 Hartford Turnpike
Waterford, CT 06385
203-447-3001

Physical education and athletic field equipment

● ● ●

Jugglebug
7506J Olympic View Drive
Edmonds, WA 98026
206-774-2127

Juggling supplies

● ● ●

Jugs, Inc.
PO Drawer 365
Tualatin, OR 97062
800-547-6843

Pitching machines for various sports

● ● ●

Kast-A-Way Swimwear
9356 Cincinnati/Columbus Road, Rt. 42
Cincinnati, OH 45241
513-777-7967

Aquatic training aids, equipment, and books

● ● ●

Korney Board Aids, Inc.
312 Harrison Ave.
Roxton, TX 75477
800-842-7772

Coaching and training aids and equipment

● ● ●

Kwik Goal, Ltd.
140 Pacific Drive
Quakertown, PA 18951
215-536-2200

Equipment for various sports

● ● ●

Lafayette Instrument Company
PO Box 5729
3700 Sagamore Parkway North
Lafayette, IN 47903
317-423-1505

Performance and strength testing

● ● ●

Life Fitness, Inc.
9601 Jeronimo Rd.
Irvine, CA 92718
800-543-2925

Aerobic and strength training equipment

● ● ●

Louisville Badminton Supply
1313 Lyndon Lane
Suite 103
Louisville, KY 40222
502-426-3219

Badminton supplies

● ● ●

Mancino Manufacturing Co., Inc.
4732 Stenton Ave.
Philadelphia, PA 19144
215-842-0690

Wall padding and athletic mats

● ● ●

Mark One Distributors, Inc.
924 W. 17th St.
Bloomington, IN 47404
800-869-9058

Recreational equipment

● ● ●

Marty Gilman, Inc.
30 Gilman Road
Gilman, CT 06336
800-243-0398

Grades K-6. Balls used to teach a variety of skills

● ● ●

Mason Corporation
7104 Crossroads Blvd.
Suite 121
Brentwood, TN 37027
615-373-8787

Physical education scooters

● ● ●

Milton Bradley Company
443 Shaker Road

E. Longmeadow, MA 01028
413-525-6411

Dodge balls

● ● ●

Miracle Recreation Equipment Co.
PO Box 420
Monett, MO 65708
417-235-6917

Playground and recreation equipment

● ● ●

Nautilus Sports/Medical Industries
709 Powerhouse Rd.
PO Box 160
Independence, VA 24348
800-874-8941

Fitness equipment and testing

● ● ●

New England Camp & Recreation Supply
PO Box 7106
Dallas, TX 75209
800-343-0210

Various athletic supplies

● ● ●

Nordic Track
141 Jonathan Blvd. N.
Chaska, MN 55318
612-448-6987

Fitness equipment and testing

● ● ●

Novel Products, Inc.
PO Box 408
Rockton, IL 61072
800-323-5143

Fitness equipment and testing

● ● ●

Palos Sports, Inc.
12235 S. Harlem Ave.
Palos Heights, IL 60463
800-233-5484

Physical education, recreation, aquatic, and athletic equipment

● ● ●

Passon Sports
PO Box 7726
Dallas, TX 75209
800-527-7510

Grades K-12. Various types of physical education and athletic equipment

● ● ●

PCA Industries
5642 Natural Bridge Rd.
St. Louis, MO 63120
800-727-8180

Preschool and special education playground equipment

● ● ●

Peak Performance Technologies, Inc.
7388 South Revere Parkway
Suite 601
Englewood, CO 80112
303-799-8686

Sports motion measurement for video and computer

● ● ●

Penn Monto, Inc.
63 Middle St.
Hadley, MA 011035
413-585-4914

Equipment and supplies for field hockey and women's lacrosse

● ● ●

Physical Educators, Inc.
1041 E. 23rd St.
Brooklyn, NY 11210
718-258-7333

Fitness and movement educational equipment

● ● ●

Pick-A-Paddle, Inc.
PO Box 41
Wheaton, IL 60189
708-665-9813

Paddles and ball game sets

● ● ●

Porter Athletic Equipment Co.
2500 South 25th Ave.
Broadview, IL 60153-9006
708-338-2000

Equipment for various sports, including basketball, volleyball, and outdoor sports

● ● ●

Product Merchandising, Inc.
7226 John Silver Ln.
Sarasota, FL 34231
813-921-6343

Grades K-12. Physical education, athletic, and gymnastic equipment

● ● ●

Rip Flag

408 S. Federal Ave.
Mason City, IA 50401
515-423-0044

Gym floor covers and belts for flag football

● ● ●

George Santelli, Inc.
465 South Dean St.
Englewood, NJ 07631
201-871-3105

Fencing equipment and supplies

● ● ●

Saunders Archery Co.
PO Box 476
Columbus, NE 68601
402-564-7177

Archery supplies

● ● ●

Schwinn Cycling & Fitness
1451 W. Webster Ave.
Chicago, IL 60614
312-528-2700

Fitness equipment and testing

● ● ●

Sentinel Sports Products
70 Airport Road, Box S
Hyannis, MA 02601
508-775-5220

Sporting goods

● ● ●

Shield
425 Fillmore Ave.
Tonawanda, NY 14150
800-828-7669

Gym and street hockey products

● ● ●

Snitz Manufacturing Co.
PO Box 76
2096 S. Church St.
East Troy, WI 53120
414-642-5909

Various fitness and sport products

● ● ●

Sportime
One Sportime Way
Atlanta, GA 30340
800-845-1535

A wide variety of creative and standard physical education and sport equipment

● ● ●

Springer
148 Jarnagin Drive
Athens, GA 30605
706-548-9836

Vertical jump training and testing

● ● ●

Sprint/Rothhammer
PO Box 5579
Santa Maria, CA 93456-5579
800-235-2156

Aquatic exercise equipment

● ● ●

Stairmaster-Randal Sports
12421 Willows Rd. NE
Suite 100
Kirkland, WA 98034
800-635-2936

Fitness equipment and testing

● ● ●

Step Company
400 Interstate North Parkway
Suite 1500
Atlanta, GA 30339
800-SAY-STEP

Fitness equipment and testing

● ● ●

STX, Inc.
1500 Bush St.
Baltimore, MD 21230
410-837-2022

Lacrosse supplies and equipment

● ● ●

Tachikara, Ltd.
10300 W. 103rd St.
Suite 200
Overland Park, KS 66214
913-888-1550

Various balls for physical education and athletics

● ● ●

Toledo PE Supply
PO Box 5618
Toledo, OH 43613
800-225-7749

Physical education and gymnastic supplies and equipment

● ● ●

Total Gym Pull-up Machine

9225 Dowdy Drive
San Diego, CA 92126
619-586-6080

Grades K-12. Pull-up attachment

● ● ●

Tour True Turf Technologies
384 Oyster Point Blvd.
Suite 14
South San Francisco, CA 94080
415-244-0690

Synthetic turf for golf greens, hitting cages, etc.

● ● ●

Trackmaster Treadmills
4300 Bayou Blvd.
Suite 36
Pensacola, FL 32503
904-969-0633

Fitness equipment and testing

● ● ●

Tunturi, Inc.
8210 154th Ave. N.E.
Redmond, WA 98052
800-827-8717

Fitness equipment and testing

● ● ●

UCS, Inc.
One Olympic Drive
Orangeburg, NY 10962
914-365-2333

Soft play equipment, mats, and track and field equipment

● ● ●

Ultra Play Systems, Inc.
425 Sycamore St.
Anderson, IN 46016
317-643-5315

Playground equipment

● ● ●

United States Table Tennis Association
One Olympic Plaza
Colorado Springs, CO 80909
719-578-4583

Table tennis supplies and information

● ● ●

Universal Gym Equipment, Inc.
930 27th Ave., SW
Cedar Rapids, IA 52406
319-365-7561

Fitness equipment

● ● ●

Universal Sports
4414 Jarboe #11
Kansas City, MO 64111
800-553-8335

Various rackets for physical education

● ● ●

U.S. Games
1901 Diplomat Dr.
Farmers Branch, TX 75234
214-484-9484

Grades K-12. Physical education games and equipment

● ● ●

VersaClimber
3188 Airway Ave., #E
Costa Mesa, CA 92626-6601
800-237-2271

Fitness equipment and testing

● ● ●

West Coast Netting, Inc.
10576 Acacia St.
Unit C2
Rancho Cucamonga, CA 91730
800-854-5741

Athletic nets and equipment for volleyball and baseball

● ● ●

Westerbeke Sport Nets
Fish Pier Road
Boston, MA 02210
800-536-6387

Nets for a variety of sports

● ● ●

Wet Vest/Wet Belt/Bioenergetics
200 Industrial Drive
Birmingham, AL 35211
800-WET-VEST

Equipment for aquatic fitness and exercise

● ● ●

Wittek Golf Supply Company
3650 Avondale Ave.
Chicago, IL 60618
312-463-2636

Golf products

● ● ●

Wolverine Sports
745 State Circle
Box 1941

Ann Arbor, MI 48108
313-761-5690

Sport and gymnasium equipment

● ● ●

Worth, Inc.
PO Box 88104, 41A Hwy.
Tullahoma, TN 37388-8104
615-455-0691

Products for baseball and softball

Films and Videos

Agency for Instructional Technology
1111 W. 17th St.
Bloomington, IN 47404
812-339-2203

Grades K-6. Instructional videos and television programs

● ● ●

American Temperance Society
6830 Laurel
Washington, DC 20012

Grades K-12. Various educational films

● ● ●

Best Films
PO Box 692
Del Mar, CA 92014

Grades K-12. Fitness films

● ● ●

Cambridge PE and Health
PO Box 2153
Dept. PEB
Charleston, WV 25328-2153
800-468-4227

Grades K-12. Sport instructional videos

● ● ●

Christy Lane's Let's Do It! Productions
PO Box 5483
Cheney, WA 99004
509-235-6555

Dance and fitness videos, books, workshops, etc.

● ● ●

Churchill Films
12210 Nebraska Ave.
Los Angeles, CA 90025
310-207-6600

Grades K-12. Various films

• • •

Coast Community College
15744 Golden West St.
Huntington Beach, CA 92647

Grades K-12. Various educational/instructional films

• • •

CSPI Marketplace
1875 Connecticut Ave., NW
Suite 300
Washington, DC 20009
202-332-9110

Grades K-12. A/V materials

• • •

Document Associates
211 East 43rd St.
New York, NY 10017
212-682-0730

Grades K-12. Various educational/instructional films

• • •

Dynamix Music Service
711 W. 40th St. #428
Baltimore, MD 21211
800-843-6499

Motivational tapes and videos for aerobics and steps classes

• • •

Educational Telecommunications Network (ETN)
Los Angeles County Office of Education
9300 E. Imperial Hwy.
Downey, CA 90242
310-922-6307

Grades K-12. Videos of telecasts of physical education curriculum, instruction and assessment, and other subject areas

• • •

Fairview General Hospital
18101 Lorain Ave.
Cleveland, OH 44111
216-476-7000

Grades K-12. Various educational films

• • •

Games in Motion
PO Box 4434
Tulsa, OK 74159-0434
918-299-9134

Grades K-12. Physical education videos and workshops

• • •

Human Relations Media
175 Tompkins Ave.
Pleasantville, NY 10570
800-431-2050

Grades K-12. Various educational/instructional films

• • •

Let's Do It Productions
PO Box 5483
Cheney, WA 99004
509-235-6555

Grades K-12. Various films

• • •

Media Services
101 Fletcher Bldg.
Provo, UT 84602
801-378-2713

Grades K-12. Fitness films

• • •

Mini-Gym Co.
354 Halle Drive
Cleveland, OH 44132
216-261-7562

Grades K-12. A/V materials

• • •

National Geographic Society
Educational Services
PO Box 98019
Washington, DC 20090-8019
800-368-2728

Grades K-12. Fitness films

• • •

Polished Apple
1249 Harrison Ave.
Centralia, WA 98531
206-736-5694

Grades K-12. Films on nutrition, health, the environment, etc.

• • •

Pyramid Films
2801 Colorado Ave.
Santa Monica, CA 90404
310-828-7577

Grades K-12. Educational films on various topics

• • •

Science and Mankind, Inc.
Communications Park, Box 1000
Mount Kisco, NY 10549

914-666-4100

Grades K-12. Various educational/instructional films

• • •

Spenco Medical Corporation
6301 Imperial Drive
Waco, TX 76712
817-772-6000

Grades K-12. Various educational/instructional films

• • •

Sugar Associates
254 W. 31st
New York, NY 10001

Grades K-12. Various educational/instructional films

• • •

Sunburst Communications, Inc.
23 Washington Ave.
Pleasantville, NY 10570
800-431-1943

Grades 2-12. Fitness films and A/V materials

• • •

SyberVision
One Sansome St.
Suite 1610
San Francisco, CA 94104
415-677-8616

Grades 7-12. Instructional videos and audio cassettes for various sports

• • •

Walt Disney Educational Media Co.
ATT: Dept. 110 SP
500 S. Buena Vista St.
Burbank, CA 91521

Grades K-12. Fitness films

Information Sources

Amateur Athletic Union
AAU House, 3400 W. 86th St.
PO Box 68207
Indianapolis, IN 46268
317-872-2900

General fitness and athletic information

• • •

American Alliance for Health, Physical Education, Recreation and Dance (AAHPERD)
1900 Association Drive
Reston, VA 22091-1599
703-476-3400

Grades K-12. Professional association for individuals who work in the areas of health, physical education, athletics, recreation, and dance. Resources for a complete physical education program

• • •

American Association of Cardiovascular and Pulmonary Rehabilitation
7611 Elmwood Avenue #201
Middleton, WI 53562
(608) 831-6989

Organization for professionals in cardiac or pulmonary field

• • •

American Association of School Administrators
1801 N. Moore Street
Arlington, VA 22209
(703) 528-0700

A professional and advocacy organization for school leaders

• • •

American Cancer Society
1599 Clifton Rd., NE
Atlanta, GA 30329
800-ACS-2345

Grades K-12. Health and fitness information, particularly as these areas relate to cancer prevention

• • •

American College of Sports Medicine
401 W. Michigan Street
Indianapolis, IN 46202-3233
317-637-9200

Professional organization for persons who work in sports medicine

• • •

American Council on Exercise
5820 Oberlin Drive #102
San Diego, CA 92121
(619) 535-8227

Aerobic dance information and fitness certifications

• • •

American Dietetic Association
216 W. Jackson Blvd.
Suite 800
Chicago, IL 60606
312-899-0040

Grades K-12. Various types of fitness information

• • •

American Heart Association
122 E. 42nd Street

New York, NY 10168
214-373-6300

Grades K-12. Health and fitness information, particularly as these areas relate to the prevention of cardiovascular disease

● ● ●

American Medical Association
515 North Dearborn St.
Chicago, IL 60610
312-670-2550

Grades K-12. Various types of fitness information

● ● ●

American Nurses Association
Public Relations Dept.
600 Maryland Ave. SW
Suite 100W
Washington, DC 20024-2571
202-554-4444

Grades K-12. Various types of fitness information

● ● ●

American Public Health Association
1015 15th St. N.W.
Washington, DC 20005

Grades K-12. Various types of fitness information

● ● ●

American Running and Fitness Association
4405 East West Hwy.
Suite 405
Bethesda, MD 20814
301-913-9517

Grades K-12. Various types of fitness information

● ● ●

American School Health Association
7263 State Rte. 43
PO Box 708
Kent, OH 44240
(216) 678-1601

Promotes health instruction in schools

● ● ●

Association for Work Site Health Promotion
60 Revere Drive
Suite 500
Northbrook, IL 60062-1577
708-480-9574

Promotes health in the workplace

● ● ●

Badminton Canada
1600 James Naismith Drive

Suite 808
Gloucester, Ontario
CANADA K1B 5N4
613-748-5695

Badminton information

● ● ●

Boy Scouts of America
1325 Walnut Hill Avenue
Box 152079
Irving, TX 75015
(214) 580-2000

Educational programs for boys and young men

● ● ●

Canadian Association for Health, Physical Education, and Recreation
1600 James Naismith Dr.
Gloucester, Ontario
CANADA K1B 5N4
613-748-5622

Grades K-12. Information on health and fitness

● ● ●

Canadian Heart Association
129 Adelaide St., West
Toronto, Ontario
CANADA

Grades K-12. Various types of fitness information

● ● ●

ERIC Clearinghouse on Teacher Education
One DuPont Circle NW
Suite 610
Washington, DC 20036
202-293-2450

Grades K-12. Index of educational publications

● ● ●

International Dance Exercise Association
6190 Cornerstone Court E.
Suite 204
San Diego, CA 92121

Aerobic dance information

● ● ●

International Rope Skipping Organization
5721 Arapahoe Ave.
Boulder, CO 80303
303-444-6961

Various events and information on rope skipping

● ● ●

Krames Communications

1100 Grundy Lane
San Bruno, CA 94066-3030
415-742-0640

Grades K-12. Various types of fitness information

• • •

Metropolitan Life Insurance Co.
Health and Welfare Division
1 Madison Ave.
New York, NY 10010
212-578-2874

Fitness information for school-age children

• • •

Minnesota Association for the Education of
Young Children
1821 University Avenue
#273-5
St. Paul, MN 55104
(612) 646-8689

Training and information for early childhood professionals

• • •

National Academy of Sciences
Food and Nutrition Board
Office of Information
2101 Constitution Ave.
Washington, DC 20418

Grades K-12. Fitness information

• • •

National Archery Association
One Olympic Plaza
Colorado Springs, CO 80909
719-578-4576

Programs and educational information for archers

• • •

National Association for Girls and Women in
Sport (NAGWS)
1900 Association Drive
Reston, VA 22091
703-476-3452

Serves teachers and coaches

• • •

National Association for Physical Education in
Higher Education (NAPEHE)
Dept. of Human Performance
San Jose State University
San Jose, CA 95192-0054
408-924-3029

Organization for teachers supporting and using an interdisciplinary perspective of physical education

• • •

National Association for Sport and Physical
Education (NASPE)
1900 Association Drive
Reston, VA 22091
703-476-3410

Publications, apparel, brochures, and posters on sport
and physical education

• • •

National Association for the Education of Young
Children (NAEYC)
1509 16th St., NW
Washington, DC 20036
202-232-8777

Information for the teaching of young children

• • •

National Association of Governor's Councils on
Physical Fitness and Sports
201 S. Capital Avenue
Suite 560
Indianapolis, IN 46225
(317) 237-5630

Promotes physical fitness and healthy lifestyles; an association of the Governor's Council exists in every U.S.
state and territory.

• • •

National Association of Secondary School Principals
1904 Association Drive
Reston, VA 22091
(703) 860-0200

Provides support for secondary school principals

• • •

National Dairy Council
10255 W. Higgins Rd., #900
Des Plaines, IL 60018
708-696-1020

Grades K-12. Various types of fitness information

• • •

National Dance Association (NDA)
1900 Association Drive
Reston, VA 22091
703-476-3436

Dance resources and education

• • •

National Heart, Lung, and Blood Institute
National Institutes of Health
9600 Rockville Pike
Bldg. 31

Room 5A52
Bethesda, MD 208923
301-496-5166

Grades K-12. Various types of fitness information

• • •

National Intramural-Recreational Sports Association
805 SW 15th St.
Corvallis, OR 97333-4145
503-737-2088

Publications and materials dealing with recreational sports

• • •

National PTA
2000 L Street, N.W.
Washington, DC 20036
(202) 331-1380

Promotes children's education through parental involvement

• • •

National Recreation and Parks Association
2773 S. Quincy Street
Suite 300
Arlington, VA 22206
703-820-4940

Organization for those who lead leisure-time activities

• • •

National Strength and Conditioning Association
300 Old City Hall Landmark
920 O St.
Lincoln, NE 68508
402-472-3000

Promotes applied sport science research

• • •

Ohio State University
School of HPERD
215 Pomerene Hall, 1760 Neil Ave.
Columbus, OH 43210
614-292-0956

Physical education research

• • •

President's Council on Physical Fitness and Sports
701 Pennsylvania Avenue, N.W.
Suite 250
Washington, DC 20004
202-272-3421

Promotes physical fitness and sports programs

• • •

Road Runners Club of America
1150 E. Washington St.
Suite 230
Alexandria, VA 22314
703-836-0558

Promotes long-distance running

• • •

Special Olympics International
1325 G Street NW
Fifth Floor
Washington, DC 20005
202-628-3630

International sports program of training for people with mental retardation

• • •

Sport Information Resource Centre
1600 James Naismith Drive
Gloucester, Ontario
CANADA K1B 5N4
613-748-5701

Bibliographic database for all aspects of physical education, sport science, and recreation

• • •

Sporting Goods Manufacturers Association
200 Castlewood Drive
North Palm Beach, FL 33408
407-842-4100

Promotes the sale of sporting goods through various means

• • •

Superintendent of Documents
Government Printing Office
Washington, DC 20402

Books on various topics

• • •

United States Amateur Ballroom Dancers Association
8505 Timber Hill Ct.
Ellicott City, MD 21043
800-447-9047

Grades K-12. Instructional information for ballroom dancing

• • •

United States Consumer Product Safety Commission
Washington, DC 20207
800-638-2772

Grades K-12. Information on playground safety

• • •

United States Dept. of Agriculture
Human Nutrition Research Branch
14th St. and Independence Ave. SW
Washington, DC 20250

Grades K-12. Fitness information and publications

• • •

United States Department of Health and
Human Services
200 Independence Avenue SW
Washington, DC 20201
202-619-0257

Federal agency protecting citizens' health and providing
necessary services

• • •

United States Field Hockey Association
One Olympic Plaza
Colorado Springs, CO 80909-5773
719-578-4567

Information on field hockey

• • •

United States Handball Association
2333 N. Tucson Blvd.
Tucson, AZ 85716
602-795-0434

Grades K-12. Information for teaching handball

• • •

United States Physical Education Foundation
PO Box 5076
Champaign, IL 61825-5076

Non-profit organization that provides grants to community and state physical education groups

• • •

United States Public Health Service
Public Inquiries Branch
200 Independence Ave. SW
Washington, DC 20201

Grades K-12. Various types of fitness information

• • •

United States Swimming, Inc.
1 Olympic Plaza
Colorado Springs, CO 80909
719-578-4578

Swimming information

• • •

United States Table Tennis Association
One Olympic Plaza

Colorado Springs, CO 80909
800-326-8788

Table tennis products and information

• • •

United States Taekwondo Union
1750 E. Boulder St.
Suite 405
Colorado Springs, CO 80909
719-578-4632

Taekwondo information

• • •

United States Volleyball Association (USVBA)
3595 E. Fountain Blvd.
Suite I-2
Colorado Springs, CO 80910-1740
719-637-8300

Volleyball publications and videos

• • •

United States Weightlifting Federation (USWF)
One Olympic Plaza
Colorado Springs, CO 80909
719-578-4508

Weightlifting information

• • •

Women's Sports Foundation
Eisenhower Park
East Meadow, NY 11554
516-542-4700

Educational and motivational publications and videos
for women in sports

• • •

World Association of Girl Guides and Girl
Scouts
World Bur
Olave Center
12C Lyndhurst Road
London NW3 5PQ, ENGLAND
71 794 1181

Educational programs for girls and young women

• • •

YMCA of the USA
Associate Director for Health and Fitness
101 N. Wacker Drive
Suite 1400
Chicago, IL 60606

Information on the YMCA and its programs

Music

Aerobic Beat Music
7985 Santa Monica Blvd.
Suite 109
Los Angeles, CA 90046-5186
213-653-5040

Music for aerobics, step training, and dance and exercise classes

• • •

Dynamix Music Service
711 W 40th St. #428
Baltimore, MD 21211
800-843-6499

Motivational tapes and videos for aerobics and steps classes

• • •

Fitness Wholesale
895-A Hampshire Road
Cuyahoga Falls, OH 44224
800-537-5512

Fitness equipment, charts, music, videos, etc.

• • •

Folkraft Records and Tapes
PO Box 404 / Columbia Turnpike
Florham Park, NJ 07932
201-377-1885

Various types of records for movement education

• • •

Ken Alan Associates
7985 Santa Monica Blvd.
Suite 109
Los Angeles, CA 90046-5186
213-653-5040

Music and motivation for aerobic/fitness instructors

• • •

Kimbo Educational
PO Box 477
Long Branch, NJ 07740
800-631-2187

Grades K-12. Fitness and dance programs

• • •

Lloyd Shaw Foundation
Sales Division
PO Box 11
Macks Creek, MO 65786
314-363-5865

Grades K-12. Educational/recreational dance music

• • •

Physical Educators, Inc.
1041 E. 23rd St.
Brooklyn, NY 11210
718-258-7333

Various records for folk and square dancing

• • •

Rhythms Productions/Tom Thumb Music
8869 Venice Blvd.
Los Angeles, CA 90034-0485
310-836-4678

Grades K-12. Fitness records and cassettes

• • •

Square Dancetime Records
146 Clinton St.
Yuba City, CA 95991
916-673-1120

Grades K-12. Square dance records

• • •

SRP Productions
24-16 Steinway St.
Suite 664
Astoria, NY 11103
800-515-8986

Music, videos, and instructional materials for dance classes

• • •

SyberVision
One Sansome St.
Suite 1610
San Francisco, CA 94104
415-677-8616

Grades 7-12. Instructional videos and audio cassettes for various sports

• • •

Wagon Wheel Records
8459 Edmaru Ave.
Whittier, CA 90605
310-693-5976

Records for various activities, such as dancing and exercise

Publications

American Alliance for Health, Physical Education, Recreation and Dance (AAHPERD)
1900 Association Drive
Reston, VA 22091-1599

703-476-3400

Grades K-12. Complete physical education program, curriculum guides and lesson plans, textbooks, and computer software programs

● ● ●

American Education Publishing
150 East Wilson Bridge Rd.
Suite 145
Columbus, OH 43085
800-542-7833

Grades K-6. Materials on individual activities

● ● ●

Bellwether Press
Burgess International Group, Inc.
7110 Ohms Lane
Edina, MN 55435

Grades K-6. Information on health and physical fitness

● ● ●

Campbell Taggart, Inc.
6211 Lemmon Ave.
Dallas, TX 75209
214-358-9211

Grades 1-6. Kits for training for the triathlon

● ● ●

Challenge Masters, Inc.
821 Dock St., Box 1-16
Tacoma, WA 98402
206-279-0052

Reference books to games and initiatives

● ● ●

Council for Exceptional Children's Products
and Services
Dept. S9
1920 Association Dr.
Reston, VA 22091-1589
703-620-3660

Materials on products/services for exceptional children

● ● ●

D.C. Heath
125 Spring Street
Lexington, MA 02173
617-862-6650

Textbooks and other related materials

● ● ●

Education Company
3949 Linus Way
Carmichael, CA 95608
916-483-8846

Physical education books and equipment

● ● ●

Fitness Information Technology, Publishers
PO Box 4425T
University Ave.
Morgantown, WV 26504
800-477-4348

Publish *Sport Marketing Quarterly* and sport textbooks

● ● ●

Great Activities Publishing Co.
1809 Chapel Hill Rd.
Durham, NC 27707
919-493-6977

Grades K-12. Physical education information and materials

● ● ●

Houghton Mifflin Co.
101 Campus Dr.
Princeton, NJ 08540-6493
800-733-7075

Books on various topics

● ● ●

Hunter Textbooks, Inc.
823 Reynolda Road
Winston-Salem, NC 27104
919-725-0608

Grades 7-12. Physical education textbooks

● ● ●

John Wiley & Sons, Inc.
605 Third Ave.
New York, NY 10158-0012
212-850-6800

Books on various topics

● ● ●

Kendall/Hunt Publishing Co.
4050 Westmark Dr.
Dubuque, IA 52002
319-589-1000

Grades K-12. Curriculum development, textbooks, curriculum guides and lesson plans

● ● ●

Macmillan/McGraw-Hill
Merrill/Macmillan Publishing Co.
866 Third Ave.
New York, NY 10022
800-442-9685

Grades K-12. Instructional strategies and books on various concepts

● ● ●

Mayfield Publishing Co.
1240 Villa St.
Mountain View, CA 94041
415-960-3222

Grades K-12. Books on various topics, such as teaching philosophy, skills, curriculum development, and lesson plans

● ● ●

Mosby College Publishing
11830 Westline Industrial Drive
St. Louis, MO 63146
800-325-4177

Grades K-12. Instructional strategies

● ● ●

National Intramural-Recreational Sports Association
805 SW 15th St.
Corvallis, OR 97333-4145
503-737-2088

Publications and materials dealing with recreational sports

● ● ●

Phantastic Phinds for Physical Education
74923 Highway 111
Suite 205
Indian Wells, CA 92210
619-341-3438

Newsletter for teachers of secondary physical education

● ● ●

PRC Publishing Inc.
4418 Belden Village St., NW
Canton, OH 44718-2516
800-336-0083

Legal and professional aspects of exercise, fitness, sports, etc.

● ● ●

PRO-ED, Inc.
8700 Shoal Creek Blvd.
Austin, TX 78757
512-451-3246

Curricular materials

● ● ●

Scott Foresman
1900 East Lake Avenue
Glenview, IL 60025
800-554-4411

Grades K-12. Physical education textbooks

● ● ●

Shelter Publications, Inc.
Box 279
Bolinas, CA 94924
415-868-0280

Books on various topics

● ● ●

Sidall and Ray Research Foundation Publications for Dance
549 Walton Drive
Whitewater, WI 53190

Grades K-12. Publications on dance linked to physical fitness

● ● ●

Superintendent of Documents
Government Printing Office
Washington, DC 20402

Books on various topics

● ● ●

3S Group
Box 5520, Station B
Victoria, BC
CANADA V8R 6S4

Publications related to physical education, health, and fitness

● ● ●

Tobi, Catalog
PO Box 460055
Escondido, CA 92046
619-489-9405

Sport rules, tests, health and fitness topics, etc.

● ● ●

Times Mirror/Mosby College Publishing
11830 Westline Industrial Drive
St. Louis, MO 63146
800-325-4177

Texts related to health, physical education, sports medicine, etc.

Combination Publishers/Video or Equipment Suppliers

Can.-Ed. Media Ltd.
43 Moccasin Trail
Don Mills, Ontario
CANADA M3C 1Y5

416-445-3900

Music, movement games and sports, recordings, etc.

● ● ●

Creative Walking, Inc.
PO Box 50296
Clayton, MD 63105
800-762-9255

Grades K-12. Products on walking fitness

● ● ●

Educational Activities, Inc.
PO Box 392
Freeport, NY 11520
800-645-3739

Grades K-6. Educational materials for physical education, fitness, and curriculum programs

● ● ●

Front Row Experience
540 Discovery Bay Blvd.
Byron, CA 94514
800-524-9091

K-6. Movement, special education, and motor-development curriculum guidebooks and materials

● ● ●

Human Kinetics Publishers, Inc.
PO Box 5076
Champaign, IL 61825-5076
800-747-4457

Grades K-12. Instructional strategies, emphasis on kinetics, team sports, individual activities. Materials include texts, professional journals, and videos. Hold American Master Teacher Program courses and continuing education workshops.

● ● ●

Orange County Dept. of Education
Media Services Unit
200 Kalmus Dr.
PO Box 9050
Costa Mesa, CA 92628
714-966-4341

Grades K-12. Complete training and coaching programs

● ● ●

P.E.T.A., Inc.
(Physical Education Teaching Accessories)
1023 St. Paul St.
Baltimore, MD 21202
410-752-1060

Assist physical educators with various instructional materials

● ● ●

PGA Foundation/Golf in Schools Program
100 Ave. of the Champions
Palm Beach Gardens, FL 33410
407-624-8456

Instructional materials and schools

● ● ●

Prentice Hall
School Division of Simon & Schuster
4350 Equity Dr.
PO Box 2649
Columbus, OH 43272-4480
800-848-9500

Grades K-12. Books and films on various topics, wellness approach to physical fitness, and strategies for instruction

● ● ●

Princeton Book Company
PO Box 57
12 West Delaware Ave.
Pennington, NJ 08534
609-737-8177

Publications and videos on dance

● ● ●

Quintessential
8375 Leesburg Pike, Ste. 227
Vienna, VA 22180
703-893-4724

Printed and A/V instructional materials for archery

● ● ●

Research Press
Dept. B
2612 N. Mattis Ave.
Champaign, IL 61821
217-352-3273

Grades K-12. Books and video programs on school counseling, school psychology, developmental disabilities, parent training, etc.

● ● ●

SRP Productions
24-16 Steinway St.
Suite 664
Astoria, NY 11103
800-515-8986

Music, videos, and instructional materials for dance classes

● ● ●

Stretching, Inc.
120 Glenway

Palmer Lake, CO 80133
800-333-1307

Grades 6-12. Books, posters, charts, pads, software, etc. for stretching instruction

• • •

Wm. C. Brown Communications, Inc.
Brown and Benchmark Publishers
2460 Kerper Blvd.
Dubuque, IA 52001
800-338-5578

Grades K-12. Books and software covering curriculum development and teaching approaches for a variety of areas

Software

Aguzzi, Robert
32 Long Hill Rd.
Clinton, CT 06413
203-669-6944

Quiz software on sport proficiency for Apple

• • •

Arizona State University
HPE Department
Tempe, AZ 85282

DOS software for adult fitness programs

• • •

Atkins, V.
7019 N. Teilman #102
Fresno, CA 93711
209-435-4291

Software for testing motor proficiency

• • •

Bonnie's Fitware
18832 Stefani Ave.
Cerritos, CA 90701
310-924-0835

Grades K-12. Physical education software

• • •

CompTech Systems Design
44 W. 1st St.
Waconia, MN 55387
612-442-9776

Grades 6-12. Fitness assessment and physical fitness materials, including software

• • •

Comp-U-Sports
Box 1340

Frederick, MD 21702
301-663-3257

DOS software for the analysis of games and players

• • •

Computer Outfitters
4633 E. Broadway Blvd., #130
Tucson, AZ 85711
800-827-2567

Fitness and nutrition software

• • •

Couldry, W.
4525 Downs Dr.
St. Joseph, MO 64507
816-271-4488

Apple fitness testing programs

• • •

Cramer Software Group
153 W. Warren
Gardner, KS 66030
913-884-7511

Apple software for athletic conditioning and physical education

• • •

Dine Systems, Inc.
586 N. French Rd., #2
Amherst, NY 14228
716-688-2492

Fitness programs for computer

• • •

Eden Interactive
1022 Natoma St.
San Francisco, CA 94103

Grades 6-12. Instruction for biking and software dealing with playground safety

• • •

Educational Technology Consultants
8915 Kitmore
Houston, TX 77099

Individual fitness test software

• • •

ESHA Research-Nutrition Systems
PO Box 13028
Salem, OR 97309
503-585-6242

Educational fitness and nutrition software

• • •

Fitness Lifestyle Design, Inc.

2317 Eastgate Way
Tallahassee, FL 32308
800-353-4621

Grades 7-12. Educational interactive software for fitness

• • •

Georgia Southern University
Landrum Box 8076
Statesboro, GA 30460
912-681-0200

Grades K-12. Software to analyze AAHPERD Youth Fitness Test

• • •

Gunnels, J.
RR1, Box 120
Jefferson, SD 57038
605-232-4097

Athletic scheduling software

• • •

Hartley Courseware
3451 Dunckel Rd.
Suite 200
Lansing, MI 48911
800-247-1380

Grades K-6. Software on various topics, including those used to compute President's Challenge physical fitness program

• • •

Hubbard
Box 2121
Ft. Collins, CO 80522-2121
800-289-9299

Physical education program management

• • •

Hurwitz, D.
208 Water St.
Chardon, OH 44024
216-286-3036

Individual fitness evaluation and prescription software

• • •

Institute for Aerobic Research
12200 Preston Road
Dallas, TX 75230
214-239-7223

Various software programs

• • •

Intellimedia Sports, Inc.
Two Piedmont Center

Suite 300
Atlanta, GA 30305
800-269-2101

Grades 6-12. Interactive sports instruction

• • •

Keys, L. and Simons, M.
8637 Pebble Hills Dr.
Sandy, UT 84070
801-594-5881

Fitness analysis software

• • •

Milesis, C.A.
2228 Lee St.
Augusta, GA 30904
404-736-8640

DOS software for fitness training and inventory

• • •

Morton Publishing Co.
925 W. Kenyon Ave.
Englewood, CO 80110

Various software programs

• • •

Oregon State University
College of Health and Human Performance
Women's Building 120
Corvallis, OR 97331-6802
503-737-3257

Apple software related to physical education

• • •

Parsons Software
1920 Briar Meadow
Arlington, TX 76014

Runner's log for DOS

• • •

Peak Performance Technologies, Inc.
7388 South Revere Parkway
Suite 601
Englewood, CO 80112
303-799-8686

Sports motion measurement for video and computer

• • •

Softshare
CSU Fresno
PE Dept.
Fresno, CA 93740
209-294-2016

Grades 7-12. Physical education software

• • •

University of Georgia
School of Health and Human Performance
PE Building
Athens, GA 30602-3652
706-542-4422

Software for fitness evaluation, as well as degrees in human performance

• • •

Valdosta State College
Dept. HPEA
Valdosta, GA 31698
912-333-5800

Exercise prescriptions

• • •

Wellsource, Inc.
15431 SE 82 Dr.
Suite E
Clackamas, OR 97015
503-656-7446

Grades 7-12. High school fitness profiles

• • •

Wholebody Health Management
18653 Ventura Blvd., Suite 137
Tarzana, CA 91356

Fitness evaluation for DOS

• • •

Win Sports Software
15892 Redlands St.
Westminster, CA 92683-7612
714-894-8161

Sports programs for the computer

• • •

Youth Fitness, Inc.
PO Box 25081
Fort Wayne, IN 46825
800-868-0183

Various types of fitness software

Testing Programs

Chrysler Fund-AAU Physical Fitness Program
400 E. 7th St.
Poplars Room 708
Bloomington, IN 47405
812-855-2059

Physical fitness programs and testing materials

• • •

Fitness Finders, Inc./Feelin' Good
PO Box 160
Spring Arbor, MI 49283
800-789-9255

Various fitness products, including books, equipment, and computerized testing

• • •

President's Challenge Physical Fitness Program
400 E. 7th St.
Poplars Room 710
Bloomington, IN 47405
812-855-8969

Grades K-12. Programs of the President's Council on Physical Fitness and Sports to promote youth fitness

• • •

Prudential Fitnessgram
12330 Preston Rd.
Dallas, TX 75230
800-635-7050

Grades K-12. General information on youth fitness

• • •

Thought Technology, Ltd.
2180 Belgrave Ave.
Montreal, Quebec
CANADA H4A 2L8
800-361-3651

Health and fitness testing

Training and Certification

American Camping Association
5000 State Road 67 North
Martinsville, IN 46151-7902
371-342-8456

Certification for camp/recreation workers

• • •

American Master Teacher Program
PO Box 5076
Champaign, IL 61825-5076
217-351-5076

Grades K-6. Various courses and materials

• • •

American Sport Education Program (ASEP)
1607 N. Market St.
PO Box 5076
Champaign, IL 61825-5076
217-351-5076

Multi-level coaching education program, in-service training, self-study courses, continuing education programs

• • •

Coaching Association of Canada
1600 James Naismith Drive
Gloucester, Ontario
CANADA K1B 5N4
613-748-5624

Program for coaching at various levels in a number of sports

• • •

Coalition of Americans to Protect Sports
(CAPS)
200 Castlewood Drive
North Palm Beach, FL 33408
800-338-8678

Programs and information dealing with sport safety education

• • •

Games in Motion
PO Box 4434
Tulsa, OK 74159-0434
918-299-9134

Grades K-12. Physical education videos and workshops

Miscellaneous

Cradlerock Outdoor Network
Box 1431
Princeton, NJ 08540
609-924-2919

Consulting services for adventure-based programs

• • •

E.F.I., Inc./Total Gym
7766 Arjons Drive
Suite B
San Diego, CA 92126
800-541-4900

Grades K-12. Various conditioning exercises

• • •

Health Skills for Life, Inc.
PO Box 22936
Eugene, OR 97402
503-485-3708

Grades K-12. Skill-based program to promote community, physical, and mental health

• • •

Hershey's National Track and Field Youth Program
19 E. Chocolate Ave.
Hershey, PA 17033
717-534-4411

Grades 1-6. Program in track and field

• • •

Jump Against Drugs
PO Box 29654
Atlanta, GA 30359
800-368-JUMP

School assembly program and instructional video

• • •

Mark I of North America, Inc.
PO Box 978
304 Sibley Ave. S.
Litchfield, MN 55355
800-932-7235

Various coaching systems

• • •

NASCO
901 Janesville Ave.
Fort Atkinson, WI 53538
414-563-2446

Grades K-12. Educational aids

• • •

Olympic Recreation, Inc.
5811 E. Dunes Highway
Gary, IN 46403
800-255-0153

Grades K-12. Playground equipment and fitness courses

• • •

Pickle-Ball, Inc.
835 NW 45th St.
Seattle, WA 98107
106-784-4723

Paddle tennis sport

• • •

Project Adventure, Inc.
Grapevine Rd.
Wenham, MA 01984
508-468-7981

Experiential education workshops

• • •

Safety Play
2411 E. Diane St.
Tampa, FL 33610

813-237-4096

Audits for playground inspection

● ● ●

Sauk Valley Sports
Sauk Valley Sports Resort
Brooklyn, MI 49230
517-467-2061

Sports equipment and apparel, specializing in field hockey, lacrosse, soccer, and volleyball

● ● ●

Southwood Corp.
4700 Westinghouse Blvd.
Charlotte, NC 28273
704-588-5000

Exercise system

● ● ●

Sports for Understanding (SFU)
3501 Newark St., NW
Washington, DC 20016-3199
800-TEENAGE

Exchange program to teach youth about sport and culture internationally

● ● ●

SPRI Products
1554 Barclay Blvd.
Buffalo Grove, IL 60089
800-222-7774

Grades K-12. Resistance equipment for strength training

● ● ●

YABA/In-School Bowling Program
5301 South 76th St.
Greendale, WI 53129
414-421-4700

Bowling programs for physical education classes

Index

Other great PE Resources for children

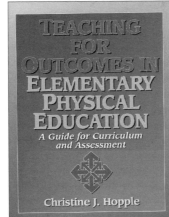

Christine J. Hopple, MS

1995 • Spiral • 232 pp
Item BHOP0712
ISBN 0-87322-712-3
$28.00 ($41.95 Canadian)

"A practitioner-friendly book dealing with the major concepts involved in the educational reform movement. It will be valuable to professionals interested in designing physical education programs that meet the needs of students in the 21st century."
  Suzann Schiemer
  Elementary Physical Education Specialist
  Bloomsburg Area School District, PA

Susan L. Kasser

1995 • Paper • 120 pp
Item BKAS0639
ISBN 0-87322-639-9
$15.00 ($22.50 Canadian)

"Kasser provides a variety of age and functionally appropriate activities and games designed to recognize individual differences among all children with and without disabilities, from preschool to elementary school-age and older. The busy teacher will especially find the "Game Finder" located at the beginning of the book helpful for identifying games quickly by the skills needed, the developmental level, and number of children who can participate."
  Barry Lavay, PhD
  Professor
  California State University, Long Beach

Don Hellison

1995 • Paper • 122 pp
Item BHEL0654
ISBN 0-87322-654-2
$17.00 ($25.50 Canadian)

"The groundswell of interest in at-risk youth has made Don Hellison's work a centerpiece for teacher education and school programs. **Teaching Responsibility Through Physical Activity** *provides an array of ideas and strategies for getting children to reestablish themselves as responsible and productive citizens. The text's uniqueness lies in the origins of its content; it comes from 'real' teachers who struggle daily to get oppositional children back on track."*
  Thomas J. Martinek
  Professor
  University of North Carolina-Greensboro

Prices subject to change.

Human Kinetics
The Information Leader in Physical Activity
2335

To request more information or to place your order, U.S. customers call **TOLL-FREE 1-800-747-4457**.
Customers outside the U.S. use appropriate telephone number/ address shown in the front of this book.

Human Kinetics Journals

Human Kinetics continues to provide elementary, middle school, and high school physical educators with practical news and information to keep them on top of their profession, but now it's in an all new format!

Our newsletter, *Teaching Elementary Physical Education,* has been redesigned and now comes in a journal format. Elementary physical educators will find the same quality information written in the same readable style.

Our other two newsletters, *Teaching Middle School Physical Education* and *Teaching High School Physical Education,* have been combined into one new journal called *Teaching Secondary Physical Education.* This journal will keep the same editorial focus as the two newsletters and will contain one distinct section for middle school physical educators and one for high school physical educators.

Each new journal will continue to focus on the topics that are important to today's physical educators:

- Advocacy activities
- Fitness and fitness testing
- Class management and discipline
- Developmentally appropriate activities
- Assessment
- Dance, gymnastics, and games
- Curriculum priorities
- Accountability
- Public relations
- Self-esteem and responsibility
- Inclusion of <u>all</u> students
- Special needs issues
- And much more!

Physical educators who want to get on the cutting edge of their profession will love these useful resources. They can take the practical information that comes in each journal issue and apply it immediately to their own classes.

Teaching Elementary Physical Education (TEPE)

Linda Morford, Editor

Frequency: Six times a year (January, March, May, September, October, December)
Current Volume: 7 (1995-96 school year)

	Individual	Institution	Student
U.S.	$18.00	$36.00	$12.00
International—surface	24.00	42.00	18.00
International—air	36.00	54.00	30.00
Canada—surface	33.00 Cdn	57.00 Cdn	24.00 Cdn
Canada—air	49.00 Cdn	73.00 Cdn	41.00 Cdn
Europe—surface	£15.00	£26.00	£11.00
Europe—surface	£23.00	£34.00	£19.00

All journals shipped from the U.S.A.
Back Issues Available: All but Volume 1(4), 1(5), 2(3), 2(6), 3(1), 3(2), 3(3), 3(4), 3(6), 4(3), and 4(4).
Back Issue Price: *Individuals*—$4/issue ($5 Canadian; £3 Europe—surface, £5 Europe—air); *Institutions*—$7/issue ($10 Canadian; £4 Europe—surface, £6 Europe—air). Complete volumes are available at the annual subscription rate.

ISSN: 1045-4853 • **Item:** JTEP

Teaching Secondary Physical Education (TSPE)

Linda Morford, Editor

Frequency: Six times a year (January, March, May, September, October, December)
Current Volume: 2 (1995-96 school year)
Prices: Same as for *TEPE.* See above.
Item: JTSPE

TSPE is the combination and continuation of *Teaching Middle School Physical Education* and *Teaching High School Physical Education.* Volume 1 of the original publications can be purchased at the volume price.

Human Kinetics
The Premier Publisher for Sports & Fitness
2335

Prices subject to change.
To request more information or to place your order, U.S. customers call **TOLL-FREE 1-800-747-4457**.
Customers outside the U.S. use appropriate telephone number/address shown in the front of this book.